MW01518549

The Processes of Defense

The Processes of Defense

Trauma, Drives, and Reality

A New Synthesis

Joseph Fernando, MDCM

JASON ARONSON
Lanham • Boulder • New York • Toronto • Plymouth, UK

Published by Jason Aronson
An imprint of Rowman & Littlefield Publishers, Inc.
A wholly owned subsidiary of The Rowman & Littlefield Publishing Group, Inc.
4501 Forbes Boulevard, Suite 200, Lanham, Maryland 20706
http://www.rowmanlittlefield.com

Estover Road, Plymouth PL6 7PY, United Kingdom

British Library Cataloguing in Publication Information Available

Library of Congress Cataloging-in-Publication Data

Fernando, Joseph, 1958-
   The processes of defense : trauma, drives, and reality : a new synthesis / Joseph
Fernando.
     p. ; cm.
   Includes bibliographical references and index.
   ISBN 978-0-7657-0729-1 (cloth : alk. paper)
   1. Defense mechanisms (Psychology) I. Title.
[DNLM: 1. Defense Mechanisms. 2. Psychoanalytic Theory. 3. Stress Disorders,
Post-Traumatic—psychology. WM 193 F363p 2009]
RC455.4.D43F47 2009
155.2—dc22

                                                                    2009044908

⊗ ™ The paper used in this publication meets the minimum requirements of
American National Standard for Information Sciences—Permanence of Paper
for Printed Library Materials, ANSI/NISO Z39.48-1992.

Printed in the United States of America

To Sue, Jonathan, Kiri, Nicky, and Rosie

With love

"All I was trying to do was to explain defence, but I found myself explaining something from the very heart of nature."

—Sigmund Freud, August 16, 1895,
letter to Wilhelm Fleiss (Freud 1954)

Contents

Acknowledgments

I would like to thank the patients who gave permission for their case material to be used in this book. I would also like to thank Cyril Levitt for all his help, which included reading every page of the manuscript at least twice, making many helpful suggestions, and keeping my spirits up with his encouragement and genuine belief in the value of what I was doing. My thanks go to Sarah Usher who read and gave valuable advice on portions of the manuscript, and to Elisabeth Young-Bruehl, for her support and help in finding a publisher. My mother, Mary Agnes Fernando, and my wife, Sue, both edited the entire book, and gave me valuable suggestions about making it more readable and reader friendly.

Introduction

The psychoanalytic ideas of defense and repression first appeared over 100 years ago in the work of Sigmund Freud (1894; Breuer and Freud, 1893) contemporaneously with the birth of psychoanalysis itself. In these early publications defense was seen as operating to keep ideas and feelings that were incompatible with the dominant ideas in the ego from entering conscious awareness. Freud said that "the patients can recollect as precisely as could be desired their efforts at defence, their intention of pushing the thing away, of not thinking of it, of suppressing it" (1894, p 47).

In the same paper, as part of his attempt to conceptualize defense, Freud introduced one of his most fundamental, and most controversial, postulates: the energic hypothesis. He said, "I should like, finally, to dwell for a moment on the working hypothesis which I have made use of in this exposition of the neuroses of defence. I refer to the concept that in mental functions something is to be distinguished—a quota of affect or sum of excitation—which possesses all the characteristics of quantity (though we have no means of measuring it), which is capable of increase, diminution, displacement and discharge, and which is spread over the memory-traces of ideas somewhat as an electric charge is spread over the surface of a body" (1894, p 60).

In the following years, as Freud went on to explore the nature of the unconscious, the primary process (1900), and infantile sexuality (1905), defenses came to be conceptualized as methods for blocking the discharge of the sexual drive and the conscious awareness of the feelings and ideas associated with it (Freud, 1915a, 1915b, 1915c). The energic hypothesis, of

1

a quantity of energy that spread over or was invested in an idea, came to be associated with defenses in two ways. Defenses could stop or retard the sexual drive (libido) from being invested in an idea by various means, and the defenses themselves used quantities of excitation, perhaps withdrawn from the drive they were battling, to set up counter-investments (counter-cathexes) to block the drive (Freud, 1915b).

In his later work Freud explored defenses, such as disavowal (1927) and splitting of the ego (1938b), that blocked the awareness of unpleasant realities. It was left to his daughter Anna Freud, however, in her classic book *The Ego and the Mechanisms of Defence* (1936), to more systematically explore the relationship between defenses against the drives and feelings versus defenses against unpleasant external realities. In summarizing her book, Anna Freud noted the parallels between these two forms of defense:

> *Repression* gets rid of instinctual derivatives, just as external stimuli are abolished by *denial*. *Reaction formation* secures the ego against the return of the repressed impulses from within, while by *fantasies in which the real situation is reversed* denial is sustained against overthrow from without. *Inhibition* of the instinctual impulses corresponds to the *restrictions* imposed on the ego to avoid unpleasure from external sources. *Intellectualization* of the instinctual processes as a precaution against danger from within is analogous to the constant *alertness* of the ego to dangers from without. (1936, p 174)

One would have thought that with such a clear statement of the parallels between these two basic forms of defense, along with the excellent beginning Anna Freud had made in exploring the detailed dynamics of various defenses against reality, psychoanalysis would have been well on its way to a new view of defense, one that saw the ego as defending itself on the two fronts of external reality and of inner pressures from wishes and affects.[1] In fact there did develop a growing literature on denial, splitting of the ego, and various other defenses against reality. Partial theories, which see one or another type of defense as primary, have been proposed by some. Others have tried to conceptualize two or more basic forms of defense, such as splitting and repression. It is a major contention of this book, however, that the actual integration of ideas related to defenses against reality with the older findings related to defenses against drives and affects, in order to form a comprehensive theory of defense, has not occurred.

The purpose of this book is to explore in detail the nature of a number of defensive processes in order to arrive at this comprehensive theory, and then to test its usefulness and to further develop it by looking at a few clinical entities from this new perspective.

This book is divided into three parts. The first contains chapters on a number of different defenses: repression, denial, externalizing and internalizing defenses, and the defenses particular to trauma. At first two basic forms of defense are described, conceptualized, and illustrated with clinical material: counterforce (repressive) defenses and attentional (denial) ones. In the chapter on trauma a third basic type of defense, dissociation, is presented, as well as a different form of mental functioning—which I have designated the zero process. While I illustrate the interactions between these different forms of defense, one of the key ideas of this book is that they cannot all be reduced to an even more basic mechanism. Neither is any one of them primary in importance.

Each chapter contains a discussion of a number of basic ideas, illustrated by extensive clinical material. This is followed by a section on therapeutic technique. While there is a review of some of the relevant literature related to each topic, the main thrust of the discussions is to develop certain new ideas, to make some important conceptual distinctions, and to show how these various ideas—new and old—relate to each other and help us to comprehend clinical data. In keeping with this basic aim, the sections on technique explore a few selected clinical issues upon which these ideas throw some new light.

This first part builds up, piece by piece, an integrated theory of defense. (In fact, while I have referred to my ideas as new, many can be found somewhere in the work of other authors, and it is especially the integration of the ideas and the deeper investigation of them, aided by this integration, that is new.) I have tried to develop the conceptual building blocks slowly and carefully so that the reasons for their adoption can be explained and made comprehensible, and so that the theory itself can properly be comprehended by the reader. I believe that concepts are tools that help us to perceive and to understand aspects of reality. In our endeavor of understanding the workings of the human mind, the importance of choosing the correct tools cannot be overestimated. Words are tools that allow us to talk about and to think about concepts. Issues about these words (terminology) can be crucial if clarifying the terminology is related to conceptual clarification or conceptual innovation. These issues are not "merely terminological," as is sometimes said. (Of course if the actual relations between terms, concepts, and reality are not kept in mind and if, for instance, one attempts to decide questions about an aspect of reality by arguing only about terms, then the discussion is unlikely to be productive.) In order to help the reader with the new terms introduced and with the usage in this book of old terms, I have listed these at the end of the chapter in which they first appear, along with short explanations. All of these terms and explanations are also gathered at the back of the book in a glossary. I would urge the reader to refer to the glossary when in doubt about the meaning of expressions that are used.

The second section of this book contains chapters on a few disorders: narcissism, masochism, and perversions. Each of these words can be said to designate a set of phenomena and dynamics that can appear as an aspect of a person's symptoms, behavior and personality and, if they come to dominate the clinical picture, the word can be said to designate a type of disorder. My original intent was to trace how the defenses described in part one manifested themselves in specific clinical conditions, but a funny thing happened on the way to the completion of each of these chapters: in looking at the disorders through the lens of the theoretical integration developed in the earlier part, I found myself formulating quite a number of additions to this theory, and to psychoanalytic theory in general—among them the formulation of specific types of compound defenses, of the idea of contrast defenses, and of the concepts of specific zero process defenses and zero process symptoms.

Skeptics may say that I have merely invented further additions to my theory as I looked at these disorders through the distorting and limiting lens of this theory. We live in an age of great skepticism toward larger scale theoretical endeavors, and the tendency is often to stress all the possible detriments of these endeavors, with Hartmann's ego psychology as the main exhibit. While these detriments certainly exist, I think that the ideas emerging out of the application of the theory from part one demonstrate its dynamic and productive potential. I hope the reader will see how these ideas are not forced upon the data but rather help us to understand many aspects of mental functioning better. Each of the chapters in the second section as well ends with a consideration of technique. I myself have found a number of the technical ideas that flow from the theoretical ones quite useful in my practice, and I would hope this will be the same for many readers who are involved in clinical practice. Trying out these technical ideas will also allow readers who are clinicians to make more informed judgments about the value and validity of the larger theoretical integration that I have attempted.

The third and last section is a single chapter, dealing with general theoretical issues such as the nature of reality and our knowledge of it, what kind of a science psychoanalysis is, with regard both to method and to theory construction, and the nature of the specific theory I have constructed during the course of this book.

This book has taken over seven years to write. The demands of a busy private practice, family time, and administrative responsibilities usually succeeded in keeping progress to a steady but slow pace. I would at times get frustrated by this. I came to realize, however, that the extra time given me to chew over the ideas I was developing, and to think about the thoughts of others that were related to them, was having a very beneficial effect. I ended up rejecting many of my initial ideas, while others were modified considerably as I discovered inconsistencies and logical errors and as I tested them against what I saw in working with my patients.

The result of all this I present now to the reader with perhaps more than the usual amount of trepidation that comes with such an undertaking, trepidation occasioned by the knowledge that I found useful—and have used in my theory building—some concepts which are at present judged by many analysts to be outmoded and superseded by other concepts. Prominent among these is the hypothesis of psychic drive energy which can be both displaced and neutralized to varying degrees, but even a detailed analysis of various ego functions and their interaction, or the focus on intrapsychic processes as often having a good deal of independence from the interpersonal world, are decidedly out of fashion. In fact in its theoretical outlook this work may to some appear old-fashioned. Fortunately fashion is not the final arbiter of truth, but it can certainly influence people's attitudes towards ideas and theories. Thus I would ask the reader to consider the ideas that follow on their own merits, with an open mind, and where possible to test them against their own experience, clinical and otherwise, rather than assessing them against the received wisdom of the age.

Of course there is self-interest in this plea, since I would want my ideas to gain a wide hearing and acceptance. But in this case I hope that my own interests and those of my readers may coincide, in that the ideas presented here are of value in allowing us to understand many psychological phenomena, and are also of great clinical utility. While I said that some aspects of the approach taken in this book may seem old-fashioned, I think that the totality of the theory presented is new and in some ways quite revolutionary. I say this not to support the truth or value of this theory, since being new or revolutionary is no guarantee of these things. Rather, I simply think that the particular integration of ideas about the importance of reality factors and defenses against reality, of trauma and dissociation, and of drives, drive derivatives, defenses against drives, and drive energy and its transformations, has not really been attempted, or certainly not thought through in the detail and depth that it has been in the pages that follow.

I have found that treating each of these factors as something that enters as an independent variable into symptoms, behavior, and mental functioning in general, as well as dealing with each of these factors on its own terms, leads to a much more robust explanatory theory. The particular types of dynamics seen in each of these areas (reality awareness and the defenses against this awareness, drives and their associated fantasies and defenses, and trauma and its aftermath, including the ensuing defenses) are quite distinct from each other, and each of these need their own concepts and explanatory ideas. This does not mean that there are not overlaps and interactions between these areas—after all they exist in the same individual—but I believe that their separate conceptualization allows a better understanding of these interactions, as well as clearing up many confusing aspects of psychoanalytic theory and practice.

To go any further in this discussion, and to move from these general comments to the particular issues, would be to move into the substance of the forthcoming chapters, so I will call a halt here to my introductory comments. I hope they have helped orient the reader to the basic underlying themes in what is certainly a long and at times demanding discussion. I have tried as best I can through summaries, glossaries, and repetition of the basic ideas to ease the reader's passage through this complex web of ideas, but I have also tried my best *not* to simplify the theory, attempting rather to fashion a theory that does at least a little justice to that most complex, most difficult, and yet most fascinating of phenomenon—the workings of the human mind.

Note

1. This view was implicit in Freud's writings, but was stated more explicitly in his later work, such as the *Outline of Psychoanalysis* (1938a). However, the most unequivocal presentation by Freud of this view is actually in the *Project for a Scientific Psychology* (1895), although in this work the idea is clothed in neurological language.

PART ONE

BASIC FORMS OF DEFENSE

CHAPTER ONE

~

Basic Concepts

The Basic Components of a Defense

A forty-year-old female patient, B, came into a psychotherapy session and began by talking rather vaguely about "feeling such familiar feelings." She said that she seemed to overreact to situations by feeling these feelings. She went on to describe an evening out with her boyfriend and a female friend of his. Both her boyfriend and his female friend were studying a foreign language that B did not speak well, and they spoke in this language to each other all night, not bothering even to translate for her. "But then I think to myself, maybe I'm making too much of it all."

"What was the familiar feeling?" I asked.

"Jealousy. Feeling left out. This woman has been interested in him for a long time. He barely paid any attention to me."

"So he treated you quite badly."

This comment opened up the floodgates. B told me all the details from the night before: how her boyfriend had asked the other woman quite politely (and this time in English) if she wanted a drink, and then turned to B and said curtly, "and you too?" B had tried to talk to her boyfriend about this at the end of the evening, and he had brushed her aside, saying he was tired. But of course he never did talk about anything with her, ever. She described how he would go out and not tell her where he was going or when he would be back.

"When you describe all of this," I said, "I feel like I'm hearing about a different person from the one you described last session. You were talking then about how your suspicions about Andy [B's boyfriend] were so unfounded, about how he always called you to reassure you and tell you where he was, how he always reassured you when you were out with others, by paying attention to you, to show that you were important to him."

"Well it's not as if he can't do those things once in a while. I guess I don't like to see how things really are. I want to preserve the relationship."

"I wonder what it is you want to preserve. You have talked of how you two hardly ever talk about anything, how he doesn't like to talk much or interact much with you, or pay much attention to you. Is he especially attractive physically to you, or do you have a particularly good sex life?"

"No," said B, who at this point looked both sheepish and sad. "But this is just like with Zack [her previous boyfriend]. We've looked at this already." As she began to talk of Zack, her sadness disappeared. I pointed out to her how she found it hard to continue talking about the hollowness of her present relationship. B began again to look very sad, with tears welling up in her eyes.

"But I want to stick with him because I'm always quitting and giving up on relationships. I don't want to just keep going from one relationship to another. I want to figure out what's wrong with me." By the end of this statement, B did not seem sad but, rather, worried and a bit guilty.

"I wonder where you get the idea that you give up on relationships too easily. It seems to me we've spent quite a bit of energy looking at how you work to stay in relationships that aren't working. I wonder if what you are saying applies more to Andy. You felt sad seeing what little effort he puts into your relationship, but felt better once you accused yourself of this failing."

B again looked sad, and talked of how she seemed to be doing the same thing here that she had done in the two other relationships we had looked at. I pointed out the connection of all this with the emotional coldness and hollowness of her family relations, and she talked of the details of this for a while, with obvious emotion.

Near the end of the session, B began talking of her present relationship again, backtracking on many of her accusations against Andy. After all, this was only one particular incident and perhaps she had to learn how to control her emotions and not blow things out of proportion. As she went on I felt a rising tide of anger and frustration at her lack of any real action to get out of the relationship and at her denial of just how bad things were. I felt pushed by these feelings to interpret to B, as I had done many times previously, her denial of just how badly she was treated in the relationship. Having been through this movement of B being upset and then my being upset a number of times already, I found myself taking a different tack. I said, "It seems to me we've been here before. You detail all of the terrible things that are done to you in a relationship, and once you've deposited your outrage with me or with a friend you feel relieved, and distance yourself from these feelings."

B laughed. "It's true. My friends complain about it. They're always telling me to break up with Andy, that he's treating me terribly, and I argue with them. But they are just repeating back what I say."

"I think as soon as they or I get indignant and express the wish that you should leave, you are relieved of that wish. It's as if you give it to us to keep for you, and then you can take the other side."

The interpretation of B's ascribing aspects of her wishes and feelings to others led to important shifts in her behavior, although the particular example described was of course only the beginning of prolonged work on this defense.

There is nothing remarkable about this example of defense analysis, but its very straightforwardness may help us in orienting ourselves conceptually in relation to the topic of defense. Anna Freud (1936) noted that we can ascertain the motive for a defense by the patient's state of mind when the defense is undone and the strength of the defense by the strength of the resistance we have to work through in order to undo it. It would seem, from the sadness and painful feelings that appeared each time I interpreted B's denial of her boyfriend's lack of caring, that these were the motives for the defense. It is worthwhile, in order to avoid confusion, to distinguish the thing that motivates a defense from the thing against which the defense is directed, which we could call the object of the defense. In order to reduce or eliminate her sadness, B attempted to defend against her awareness, which was really the outcome of a process of judgment, that her boyfriend cared very little for her, except to the extent that she could be of use to him. Thus B's defense was directed against an awareness of certain realities. This type of defense is usually designated as denial.

As we shall see through the course of this book, denial covers a number of quite varied defenses with certain basic commonalties. In her book on the mechanisms of defense, Anna Freud (1936) classified defenses based on their motives. For instance she distinguished defenses motivated by the strength of the instincts from defenses motivated by fears about reality. If one wishes to penetrate more deeply into the basic nature of the defensive processes, one needs to supplement this classification with one based on the thing against which a defense is directed, a classification that Hartmann, Kris, and Loewenstein (1947) designated as a functional one. It looks at what function (e.g., to keep a drive unconscious) a defense serves. Of course this is the immediate, or proximal, function. The ultimate function of any defense is the reduction of an unpleasant feeling. We usually refer to this unpleasant feeling as the motive for the defense. While the motive for a defense is important, it is the thing against which a defense is directed (the object of a defense) that usually determines the specific form of defense that is used. In the case of B, the motive was sadness or psychic pain, while the objects of her defenses were certain realities about her boyfriend.

To look now at Anna Freud's second methodological point, that one can estimate the strength of a defense by the amount of resistance one meets in attempting to undo it, in B's case, one would at first glance think that her defense of denial was not particularly strong, since I was able to undo it and bring her sadness to awareness easily by single interpretations. If one follows the workings of such a defense over time, however, it becomes clear that it is quite tenacious. Every analyst is well aware of this particular aspect of denial defenses: their slippery nature. One thinks again and again that one has them in one's grasp, that one has finally undone the denial and made the patient fully aware of a certain reality, only to see the defense slip out of one's hands and reinstate itself. I would suggest that this is not merely an example of the working through that has to be done to firmly establish any new insight, but is, rather, an expression also of something basic about the nature of denial. In seeing this one becomes aware of a further methodological point: that one learns not only about the strength of a defense but also about the basic nature of the defense (that is, its inner workings) through the nature of a patient's resistances and by his or her responses to interpretation.

Different Forms of Defense

Denial is essentially an attentional defense. It involves the shifting of the ego's attention from the reality that is defended against to another reality. For instance when I had drawn A's attention to her present boyfriend's lack of caring, she first tried to turn her attention to a former boyfriend and our previous discussion of this issue, which decreased her sadness. When I interpreted this defense she attempted a different shift. She turned her attention to herself, thinking of how uncaring *she* was, of how she had trouble keeping a consistent investment in a man (which was not in fact true).[1]

The difference between this type of attentional defense and one that uses a counterforce can be seen if we compare this example to the situation of attempting to unearth sadness in someone who has repressed it, along with anger and other feelings brought on by, as an example, the death of a parent in childhood. In this case there will be no quick recovery of the feeling of sadness, as there was with B. It may take years to analyze the repressive defense sufficiently for any feelings of sadness to appear. On the other hand, once it appears it will not keep slipping away so consistently and maddeningly as when denial is used. Of course there will still need to be a good deal of working through to consolidate the insight, but one gets a sense of chipping away at a stable counterforce that slowly weakens, with some amount of back and forth movement in the strength of the defense during its analysis. By contrast when analyzing denial one gets the sense of being able to relatively easily undo a shifting of attention, which then just as easily snaps back into place, giving one the feeling of having written on water. Obviously the stability of denial defenses depends on something other than a stable counterforce. We will explore this issue further in the chapter on denial.

If we now attempt to apply the conceptual distinctions made here to the last part of the session with B, it would seem plausible that her externalizing something of her perception of, or reaction to her treatment by, her boyfriend onto me was motivated by sadness and painful feelings. It may just as plausibly be maintained that she was motivated by an unbearable inner tension to externalize one side of an ambivalence (her wish to leave) onto me, by attempting to get me to feel these feelings for her. The only way to know for sure is to look at B's state of mind when the defense was undone. B laughed, which suggests some release of tension, but did not show signs of sadness. However, the defense was only in the first stages of being analyzed, so it is impossible to be sure on the basis of the session presented. In later sessions it became clear that here too sadness and acute inner pain were some of the motivators of the defense.

An interesting question arises when we look at another aspect of this defense: against what was it directed? Against B's awareness of her boyfriend's lack of caring, an awareness that was externalized onto me? Or against anger and a wish to leave, which were similarly externalized? And beyond this functional (object) aspect, what of the basic nature of this defense? Was it largely an attentional defense, a form of denial? Or did it involve a good deal of counterforce, as in other defenses such as isolation and repression? It would seem at this point that our simple example is not looking so simple, and a fuller discussion of these issues is better reserved for the chapter on externalizing defenses, after we have delved more deeply into the nature of repression and denial.

These questions, however, raise the possibility that there can be denial defenses against the awareness of inner reality, that these may operate by attentional processes similar to those of the denial defenses related to external reality, and that they are thus to be differentiated from counterforce defenses that block the forward movement into awareness and action of drives and affects. Some authors (Lewin, 1950; Hartmann, 1956) have pointed out that denial can work against the awareness of inner as well as outer reality, but the general lack of attention to this important fact has been the source of much confusion in analytic defense theory.

The neglect of denial of inner reality is only one part of a larger trend within Freudian analysis to downplay defenses against reality. Anna Freud herself, who did so much to bring these defenses to the attention of other analysts, called them preliminary stages of defense (1936), as if they were not quite full-fledged defenses. Many analysts, when discussing defenses, assume that they are directed only against the drives (Hoffer, 1968; Brenner, 1982; Gray, 1994; Inderbitzen and Levy, 1994). As Simon (1992) noted in discussing sexual abuse, psychoanalysts are uneasy theoretically with external reality. Expressing a common view, Blum (1983) and Abend (1981) both comment that Anna Freud's distinction between defenses against external reality versus the drives cannot be made too strictly because reality has subjective and intersubjective aspects and is pervasively influenced by unconscious fantasy.

The reader might wonder what all the fuss is about, though, since everyone knows there is such a thing as denial and since even those analysts who may conceptualize defenses as operating against drives at the theoretical level will, in their clinical work, routinely analyze defenses against reality. This may be one of those instances, however, where our theory has lagged well behind our clinical practice, to the detriment of both. Defenses against reality are discussed often enough, especially in the context of specific disorders such as perversions, but there is a certain ambivalence about how much importance to accord them and an uncertainty about how exactly they relate to other defenses.

Many newer theories have stepped into the breach. These theories, such as self psychology and various object relations theories, have over time contributed many valuable insights related to defenses against reality, such as ideas about splitting and projective defenses and the investigation of the reactions to deprivation and lack of maternal attunement shown by young children. Cooper (1989) talked of a bifurcation of theories of defense, some seeing defenses as directed against the drives and others seeing them as dealing with self-cohesion in relation to the external object. He suggests that "as the scope of psychoanalysis widens, there is an integrative benefit to a conceptualization of defense that takes as its core the instinctual underpinnings of defense while attempting, through detailed clinical observation, to understand and integrate the roles of the external world and experiential aspects of defense" (p 889). Even in this suggestion one can still see, in the phrase "instinctual underpinnings of defense," the reluctance to accord defenses against reality equal status. The question as to whether this reluctance is based on the facts or on an allegiance to an aspect of analytic theory that, for historical and clinical reasons, happened to be developed first is best explored concretely, in relation to clinical material, and through a detailed consideration of theoretical issues. Before undertaking this exploration, however, I would like to set the stage for the discussions on technique in the chapters that follow by looking at a few basic aspects of the psychotherapeutic situation and of the analysis of defense.

Therapeutic Technique

Analyzing a Defense

What do we mean when we talk of "analyzing a defense"? Most defenses operate unconsciously. Because they involve organized, structured processes we think of defenses as residing in the unconscious part of the ego. Almost all of the contents of the ego are unconscious at any one time, since we can only be consciously aware of very little at a time. Much of the unconscious content of the ego is able to be made conscious with little trouble if need be. Freud (1915c) referred to this as the descriptive unconscious. A few defenses, such as suppression, are only descriptively unconscious. An example of this would be suppressing the anger one feels at an acquaintance in order to be civil to them at a party. At any particular moment one may not be consciously aware of suppressing one's anger, but if one wanted to one could, simply by shifting one's attention, become aware of it.

Most defenses do not share this characteristic. They are not only descriptively unconscious but also dynamically so. What is meant by this is that there are forces opposing attempts to become aware of these defenses, forces that we refer to as resistances when they occur within analysis. From the presence of these resistances, Freud (1923) inferred that there were defenses protecting against the awareness of defenses. When we speak of analyzing a defense, we could actually be referring to an interpretation about the defense or about the defense against becoming aware of the defense. Things are rarely if ever so easily parsed out as this, though, and interpretations of defense can appeal in many directions. For instance an interpretation that I gave B at a time after the session detailed above was, "Do you notice that as you talked of your boyfriend's lack of caring, you became sad but then shifted to your own faults and became less sad?" This interpretation mentions the motive for the defense (sad feelings), the thing defended against (B's awareness of her boyfriend's lack of caring), and something of the inner workings (mechanism) of the defense (the shifting of attention).[2] This might seem like an ideal interpretation, but it is only ideal from an intellectual point of view, in touching on all the bases. Interpretation of defense is, however, not an intellectual exercise but a means to an end—the end of making a defense conscious.

What does it mean, though, to make a defense conscious? For one thing, keeping in mind the different meanings of the term unconscious, I would say it means taking a dynamically unconscious (i.e., defended against) defense and lessening the resistance against awareness of it. One moves it to the realm of something that is only descriptively unconscious, and that *could* be made conscious if the patient were to turn his or her attention to it. Why put it in this way, rather than simply say that the aim is to make an unconscious defense conscious? Certainly as we interpret, the hope is for at least a passing conscious awareness of the defense, but consciousness of something is by its nature fleeting. It would be impossible, and a ludicrous expectation, for the patient to remain continuously conscious of the defense. Saying "we try to make a defense conscious" is really a shorthand way of talking of moving the defense into the area of the preconscious that is not too defended against and that can easily be brought into conscious awareness. The shorthand version works fine for most clinical discussions, but to delve more deeply into the nature of defenses and the dynamics of their interpretation requires a more accurate way of saying things. Among the reasons for this I will only mention at this point that as analysis proceeds, one cannot become consciously aware of all that is freed from defense and becomes preconscious. Rather, as masses of material undergo this change, the patient only becomes aware of some of them, while new integrations take place in the preconscious, moving the analytic process along, only partly with the aid of conscious awareness.

Let us leave further consideration of these complications for later and look at the brief clinical example from the beginning of this chapter. In the examples given of my interactions with B, most of my interventions are not explicit interpretations of defense. Mainly I confront B with realities from which she seems to be running away. For example, in response to B saying that she wanted to preserve the relationship, I said, "I wonder what it is you want to preserve. You have talked of how you two hardly ever talk of anything, how he doesn't like to talk much or interact much with you or pay much attention to you. Is he especially attractive physically to you? Or do you have a particularly good sex life?" There are other confrontations and questions in the material presented. A purist regarding defense interpretation, such as Paul Gray, would probably find much to criticize in my bypassing the patient's defenses and making direct interpretations of the content (reality) that was defended against. I may be seen as partially redeeming myself by my one stab at interpreting a defense directly, at the end of the example, when I say, "I think as soon as they or I get indignant and express the wish that you should leave, you are relieved of that wish. It's as if you give it to us to keep for you, and then you can take the other side."

I myself would not praise the sequence of interactions with B as a stellar example of the analysis of defense, but neither would I condemn it for its conversational tone or its lack of adherence to certain technical rules. It is really this broader issue of technique and its limits that I would like to address now, since this discussion is needed in order to set the stage for, and to put in perspective, the detailed discussions of specific technical issues in later chapters.

The Limits of Technique

What do I mean by the limits of analytic technique? In this context what I *do not* mean is the *limitations* of the technique, in the sense of what sorts of problems it can be of help with or not, and to what extent it can help. This has been the subject of extensive study and debate, but what I want to discuss at this point is something quite different: how far within the psychoanalytic and psychotherapeutic situation are ideas and rules regarding technique valid, and how broadly and deeply should they be applied? Samuel D. Lipton (1977) addressed this issue many years ago in a well-known paper arguing for the superiority of Freud's technique over modern technique. One of Lipton's main points was that Freud had a *narrow* view of technique, as compared to the so-called "standard" technique of the 1970s, when the paper was written. Such ideas as transference, neutrality, and abstinence had for Freud a narrow area of application. Freud saw the personal relationship as existing outside of the area of technique and of the transference, although some aspects of it would enter the transference.

Lipton supported his view of Freud's ideas especially by looking at Freud's behavior in the "Rat Man" analysis, an analysis from which some of Freud's original case notes have survived (Freud, 1909c). For example Freud noted that in one session his patient was hungry when he arrived and that he was fed. No details were given, but various opinions have been offered about whether this was a good thing or not and about Freud's purpose in providing the food. Was he providing, intentionally or not, some sort of oral gratification related to the transference? Or was Freud just naive about the effects of breaking his own rules around neutrality and abstinence? Lipton argued that neither of these was true: Freud was not trying to achieve anything therapeutic by feeding the "Rat Man," but neither was he just naïvely acting in an anti-therapeutic manner. Rather, Freud saw these personal relations between therapist and patient, related to realistic aspects of the situation, as not within the area of technique. In other words the patient was fed for the relatively straightforward reason that he was hungry and that food was available. Freud was not naive about the possibility that his action of feeding his patient could possibly acquire unconscious transference meanings but was, in fact, sophisticated enough to realize that he could not predict beforehand *whether* this would happen, and if it did happen what *form* it would take. As it was, the "Rat Man" reacted with a strong feeling of disgust and derision to the herring he was served, which came to have an important transference meaning. This particular reaction could not have been predicted beforehand, and in fact attempts to predict the reaction (for instance looking for an oral reaction or something related to early mothering) may have interfered with recognition of what the patient's actual reaction was. One could also have not fed the patient, and perhaps asked him what came to his mind around the idea of being hungry. This would not be an unreasonable way to proceed, but it would be unreasonable, I think, to believe that this behavior would be more "neutral" than Freud's. The patient would no doubt have a reaction to this particular way of proceeding as well, but it would be naïve to think one could predict what it would be. On the other hand if the patient often felt hungry or needy at the beginning of sessions, the analyst may reasonably wonder about a transference reaction and an abstinent and neutral stand of not offering food and either waiting for the reaction to develop further or asking for associations or making an interpretation would seem reasonable.

One often becomes aware of transference in less straightforward or explicit ways. For instance the therapist might have noticed a general tendency to always need something from the therapist and/or a particular feeling of tension within themselves that would be a clue to some sort of transference enactment. One can never be sure. One might not notice any of these things and still the patient's reaction might have a transference aspect. One might think something is transferential when it is weighted much more towards present reality. There is no safe place in relation to these matters. I would suggest that the way out of this uncertainty, however, is not to assume transference everywhere and use the technique for dealing with transference in all interactions with the patient. At present many analysts see all of the patient's reactions as having a transference component. This may well be true, but the important issue is the size of this component, relative to reality-based aspects. This size varies considerably from one reaction to the next.

Because Freud was not very explicit on these matters, he can easily be misunderstood, and quotes about surgeons and mirrors can become part of this misunderstanding. I think Lipton was correct, however, that a careful reading of Freud's work demonstrates that he held to this narrow view of technique and that his ideas about such technical issues as transference, neutrality, and abstinence were bounded by this view. Other analysts from these early days generally shared these views, and some were more explicit than Freud. For instance in his short book on technique Fenichel (1941) defined abstinence as not offering the patient any transference gratifications, and described being a mirror (neutrality) as being careful not to play along with the transference, but rather to reflect back the meaning to the patient. If read from a modern perspective, which sees the entire relationship between the patient and analyst as transference or countertransference, this can be misunderstood, but this broadened view of transference only emerged later, and for Fenichel to say that abstinence and neutrality applied to the handling of the transference was to take a narrow view of technique. For the rest Fenichel stressed the importance of being natural and human with the patient. He noted that to do otherwise played into the patient's wish to separate analysis from their regular life, and especially with obsessional patients fostered the ascribing of magical powers to the analyst. Even at a somewhat later date, as a broader view of technique was starting to take hold, Loewald (1957) described neutrality as involving objectivity in relation to transference distortions, noting that the analyst is more than a transference object for the patient. Anna Freud (1954) noted that the almost total neglect of the real relationship by some analysts can lead to hostile reactions by patients that are then often mislabeled as negative transference.

A number of authors who looked more deeply into these issues conceptualized certain aspects of the therapeutic situation not so much as outside technique, but rather as involving a different aspect of technique than the handling of the transference. Elizabeth Zetzel (1965) conceptualized the therapeutic alliance as having at its base the mother's attunement to and adaptation to her young child's needs and communications. Ralph Greenson (1967) conceptualized the working alliance as a more rational alliance, with contributions from both the positive transference and the real relationship, as well as selective identifications with the analyst's work ego and analyzing function. Greenson (1969) felt it was the real relationship that was especially crucial to the working alliance, since the positive transference waxed and waned in ways that were impossible to control or predict. He felt it was important to note the combination of realism and distortion in any of the patient's responses. Acknowledging the reality of a perception as one analyzes it is one aspect of supporting the patient's ego strengths. Hausner (2000) has written a detailed and excellent discussion of the therapeutic alliance and

the working alliance. I have touched on them here because of their relationship to the issue of the limits of technique.

So far I have only presented one side of the argument around these issues—the side with which I agree. Beginning already in the 1950s and gathering steam beyond this time, there were many criticisms of Freud's idea of
an unobjectionable positive transference, of the idea of a real relationship,
and of the later ideas developed around these issues such as Zetzel's concept
of the therapeutic alliance and Greenson's of the working alliance. Stein
(1981), for instance, criticized the idea of the unobjectionable positive transference, noting how resistances could hide in this aspect of the relationship,
and that these might not be spotted if one considered this area free from
conflict. I myself fail to see how the fact that a concept or aspect of analysis
can be used for the purposes of resistance argues against its use or usefulness
since any aspect of analysis—intellectual understanding, feeling, empathy,
the analysis of defense—can be used at times by some patients or analysts
for the purposes of resistance. If one attempted to evade resistance by avoiding anything that may cause it one would have to stop performing analysis.
Clearly this is not the way to deal with resistance. I will return to this point
in the next paragraph, but would like first to present another example of the
attack on the narrow view of technique and on the idea of a real relationship. Charles Brenner (1980b) argued vigorously against Greenson's ideas
of a real relationship, of a working alliance, and of what I think seemed to
Brenner the naïve idea of being "human" in analysis. He gave the example of
a patient who comes in to a session and says that a loved one has died. The
"human" thing to do might be to express one's sympathy and condolences.
Brenner thought Greenson might recommend this also because it would
strengthen the working alliance. This all sounds very nice, noted Brenner,
but by expressing sympathy the analyst could very well make the patient
reluctant to express such feelings as, for instance, anger at the dead person or
glee at their death. He argued that it was more useful to analyze the patient's
responses than to attempt to support the alliance through "human" gestures.
But something that Brenner failed to mention is that in situations such as
this there is no neutral ground. The "neutral" response of not saying anything
and waiting for the patient's associations may lead to the patient feeling
that the analyst is uncomfortable with the topic of death, and he or she may
themselves then avoid the topic. If the analyst consistently avoided such
responses as giving his or her condolences, especially if no explanation were
given for these omissions, the patient may develop the sort of angry response
Anna Freud (1954) described as a product of the neglect of the real relationship. I am not saying that these responses would necessarily occur, any more

than Brenner could be sure that his predicted response, of the patient being inhibited by expressions of condolence on the analyst's part, would occur, but this again emphasizes my point that in relation to these sorts of situations it makes little sense to think of a "neutral" response, or an abstinent one that denies a wished-for gratification.

These issues are complex—so complex that, as I have already said, I can only touch on a few aspects of them. The point I am trying to emphasize is that while the narrow view of technique held by Freud and some of his followers has been seen by many as naïve, attempts to broaden it involve a kind of naïve one-sidedness as well, as shown by the assertions of Stein and Brenner. To my mind it only makes sense to talk of taking a neutral or abstinence stance in relation to a specific transference wish or action that the analyst recognizes as such. As the analysis progresses this area of the transference usually comes to involve not only specific single actions but whole patterns of interaction and relationship, but I think the example of a patient who has just suffered a loss demonstrates how impossible it is to talk of neutrality or abstinence outside of a transference that is recognized as such. However, by the 1950s and 1960s, the idea that silence was somehow more neutral than saying or doing something started gaining ground, and it was clearly present in Brenner's criticism of Greenson. A critique of the idea of silence as neutral was another key point in Lipton's paper. He noted that the sanctioning of silence could be seen as part of a trend to emphasize the analyst's actual behavior rather than understanding. Lipton saw modern technique as moving from retrospective understanding of what had been said and done to prospective prescription about what should be said and done. This applied, I think, to the analysis of resistance as well. For instance Stein described the dangers of conceptualizing and fostering a benign positive transference, because of its potential use as a resistance. Others warned about the dangers of feeding an intellectualizing defense if one engaged in theoretical or more general discussions with patients. Not to say that it is not worthwhile being aware of these potential dangers, but one should also be aware of the danger—one that I think is usually greater—of attempting to analyze resistance prospectively, by anticipating it and heading it off at the pass through avoiding saying and doing certain things. Lipton (1977) summed up this danger quite well: "Then, to the extent to which such avoidance is prospective, it tends to move technique from collaboration to unilaterality, since it is unlikely that the patient is both aware of and collaborates with the prospective exclusion of interventions" (p 262).

Is it worthwhile going into these debates from decades ago? I believe it is, for a number of reasons. First, a number of analysts still hold to positions similar to those of Stein and Brenner. Second, in reacting against the distant and rigid technique that analysts adopted based on what I have called the "broad" view of technique, many modern analysts have thrown out the baby with the bathwater, discarding completely ideas about neutrality, for instance, as a reaction against their overextension. Thirdly, and worse yet, I think many analysts have thrown out the baby and *kept* the bathwater—the bathwater, that is, of an overly broad view of technique. Thus self psychology and many relational analysts stress the importance of the real relationship but see it as an important technical and transference issue (although they might not use this terminology), for instance engaging in micro analyses of aspects of this interaction as part of their technique. While I also think this can be quite useful at times, if it invades the real relationship too much this technique can lead to the same problems Lipton pointed out as occurring in the technique of his day. He pointed out that "without the actuality of the non-technical personal relationship, irrational elements of the transference remain imaginary or intellectual" (1977, p 271). In this kind of situation, with no real relationship to both serve as a basis for a cooperative alliance and build an object related transference upon, the patient may appear more narcissistic than they actually are. While the content may differ from the older schools, many a modern analyst will also approach their patient with very powerful anticipatory ideas rather than conversing with the patient, and sharing with the patient what the analyst is thinking of. The modern analysts may also see all interactions with the patient as involving transference/countertransference elements and enactments that need to be analyzed, leaving little if any room for the real relationship. This is the most common modern version of the broadened view of technique Lipton described from his own day, and it has the same aura of being both comprehensive and sophisticated, while leading to the same problems of failing to truly engage the patient in his or her real life and deeper emotional reality.

All this paints things in rather too broad brush strokes, I realize, and may sound more accusatory or negative than it is meant to be, but there are important issues to be addressed here. I do not think one can discuss the specifics of analyzing certain defenses without clearing up these core issues first. The real relationship and the working alliance are important components of the analysis of defense, and serve as the substrate from which good analysis of defense grows.

Greenson (1967) noted the way in which abstinence could support the flowering of the transference, while humanness was important in supporting working alliance. He described in detail the ways in which maintaining the working alliance and analyzing the transference often demanded contradictory behaviors and how difficult, and yet how necessary, it was to balance the two needs. We shall also see in the pages that follow that counterforce (repressive) defenses, attentional (denial) defenses, and the defenses and memories related to trauma each need quite different and at times contradictory approaches to *their* analysis, and that a flexible technique is necessary in analyzing the complex defensive structures that hold symptoms and negative behaviors in place. By grounding technique in the real relationship and the alliance, neither of which is specific to the analysis of certain types of structures or defenses, one can maintain a solid but flexible base upon which to practice the various techniques needed in the analysis of these structures and defenses.

Summary

In this chapter I described the three basic components of a defensive process. First there is the motive, which is what sets the process in motion. It is always the avoidance of a very strong negative affect such as anxiety or psychic pain. The affect sets in motion the defensive process itself. This is the second component. I referred to this process as the "inner nature" of the defense. Others have called it the mechanism of the defense. While this is the second component, narrowly defined this is the defensive process proper. On the other hand, looked at more broadly, one could think of the motive and thing defended against as essential aspects of the process, since there is no defensive process without these two other components. This brings us to the third component: the thing defended against or object of the defense. This is what the defense attempts to block from conscious awareness and/or from behavioral expression. This "thing" could be a strong feeling, a drive derivative, a judgment about an aspect of reality, or some other aspect of the mind.

In terms of the inner workings (mechanisms) of defensive processes, I mentioned two: a strong counterforce that blocks something from consciousness and a shifting of attention from one thing to another. I noted that one infers the nature of a defense from the form of the resistance one meets in analyzing the defense. With attentional defenses one can often shift the patient's attention with relative ease back to the avoided reality, but this attention just as easily flits away again and the person loses awareness of this reality. In the case of counterforce defenses such as repression one meets a relatively solid resistance that gives way to interpretation with great difficulty, in a slow and steady manner (at least when compared to the resistances that are a product of attentional defenses).

In the section on technique I began to explore what we mean by "analyzing a defense" or "making a defense conscious." Moving beyond the specific topic of defense analysis I then argued, following Lipton, for a narrow view of the technical ideas of abstinence, neutrality, transference, and countertransference. By a narrow view, Lipton meant that these concepts and the technical maneuvers connected with them did not constitute the whole of the analytic situation or relationship. Rather they were bounded by the real relationship, which is necessary both for the patient to develop a deeper, non-narcissistic transference, and in order for the patient and analyst to converse with each other and clarify with each other what they are thinking about. Thus the real relationship is necessary for a deep, full alliance between patient and therapist. Ralph Greenson and others have tried to clarify the nature of the real relationship and the therapeutic and working alliances, which are built on both the real relationship and on aspects of the transference. These ideas not only contradicted those of such classical analysts as Martin Stein and Charles Brenner, but also those of many modern (and postmodern) analysts of today who see the entire analysis as a transference/countertransference field from which it is impossible to take an objective stance or claim that anything, including an aspect of the analytic relationship, is "real."

Terms

This section in each chapter contains descriptions of some of the new terms introduced in the chapter, as well as older, established analytic terms, such as defense or primal repression, if they are discussed in depth and/or given a more specific meaning for the purposes of conceptual clarification. The terms and their definitions from all the chapters are collected at the end of this book in a glossary. I would urge the reader to refer to the glossary whenever they are not clear about a term. Some of the theoretical discussions in the following chapters will be much easier to follow if the meaning of a few terms are clearly understood.

Attentional (Denial) Defense: A form of defense, usually directed against unpleasant realities (internal or external), which uses a shifting of the ego's attention as its basic mechanism.

Broad view of technique: A view that sees the technical aspects of the analytic relationship, and the technical aspects of patient/analyst interactions, as applying to the totality of these interactions and of the relationship.

Counterforce (Repressive) Defense: A form of defense, usually directed against a drive derivative or strong affect, which uses a strong counterforce to push its objects out of awareness and to keep them unconscious. The counterforce is formed from partially neutralized aggressive drive energy.

Defense: A psychical reaction or process that attempts to keep some mental content—a wish, feeling, judgment, etc.—from conscious awareness and/ or behavioral expression. The usual, narrow definition sees a defense as the mental process or mental mechanism—as an example a shifting of attention—that accomplishes this end. Looked at more broadly a defensive process involves a *motive* that sets in motion the mechanism that acts against a mental content (the *object* of the defense) to keep it from awareness.

Motive for defense: The motive for defense is what sets the defensive process in motion. The motive seems always to be an unpleasant affect (conscious or unconscious), such as anxiety or psychic pain.

Narrow view of technique: A view that sees the technical aspects of the analytic relationship as only one aspect of the interaction, existing within a matrix of the reality aspects of the situation and the real relationship.

Object of a defense: The thing (a mental content) against which a defense is directed, in order to keep the object from conscious awareness and/or behavioral expression. Wishes that are derived from basic drives, and judgments about reality are examples of objects of defenses. Not only mental contents but also mental functions such as specific cognitive functions or the integrative function can also become objects of a defense.

Therapeutic Alliance: The mutual adjustment and attunement of the analyst and patient to each other, most of which takes place unconsciously, based on preverbal and non-verbal aspects of the relationship. This was the original definition of the term when Elizabeth Zetzel introduced it, but at present therapeutic alliance is often used to refer to both the working and the therapeutic alliances together, while the term working alliance is less used. I have kept the distinction between these two terms in this book, because it helps us to think of these different aspects of the mutual work in analysis.

Working Alliance: A more rational alliance between patient and analyst, with contributions from both the positive transference and countertransference, the real relationship, and the patient's selective identification with aspects of the analyst's analyzing function.

Notes

1. There was also clearly splitting of the image of B's boyfriend in her mind, into a "good" and a "bad" boyfriend, between whom B oscillated when thinking of him. I

have not discussed the complex issue of different forms of splitting and their relation to denial at this point (see chapters 3, 5, and 8), in order to concentrate on elucidating the basic components of a defense.

2. There is no mention of the defense against becoming aware of the defense. This last type of defense will be discussed in chapter 3, in relation to denial defenses.

CHAPTER TWO

~

Repression

In this chapter we look at a number of topics related to repression. First I will distinguish repression from denial. Denial uses a shifting of attention, while repression uses a strong counterforce to push its objects into the unconscious. Excerpts from the analysis of two patients will be presented. I will use examples from these cases to elucidate a number of topics: different forms of primal repression, the relation of anxiety and traumatic anxiety to repression, and the differentiation of the different types of defenses (after defenses and secondary defenses) that help to buttress primal repression. I will then argue for the derivation of the counterforce of repression from aggressive drive energy, demonstrating the evidence for this in the clinical material, as well as discussing the more general issue of the characteristics of the sexual and aggressive drives. Finally, we will look at the sort of memory against which repression defends, and at some issues in the analysis of repression.

Of all the chapters in this book, this one is the most difficult. Partly this is due to a number of important new concepts being introduced and there having to be longer theoretical discussions in order to elucidate the concepts properly. Among these ideas are the differentiation between primal defenses, after defenses, and secondary defenses; the delinking of the traumatic and defensive processes through rejecting the idea of traumatic anxiety, and substituting for it pervasive anxiety; and the description of drive-based counterforce as an important mechanism of defense. Each of these ideas will be used many times in later discussions. They are the building blocks for the new theory of defense that I develop in this work.

I realize some readers will be more familiar with the theoretical background to these discussions than others. I would urge readers who are having problems to refer to the glossary, as well as to read the detailed summary at the end of this chapter. I would also like to assure readers that there will be rewards, both theoretical and clinical, for having mastered the ideas in this discussion of repression. I think the reader will come to appreciate in later chapters the clinical relevance and usefulness of the new theory that I am developing, as we delve into specific clinical issues.

The Nature of Repression

In the early years of psychoanalysis Freud used the term repression in two ways. He used it both to refer to a specific counterforce defense, and as a general term for all forms of defense. During these early years, however, Freud did mainly study the defense of repression more narrowly defined—that is, the counterforce defense that pushes drives, strong affects, and memories into the deeper unconscious. His classic first paper on motivated forgetting (1898) demonstrated very well the loss of a proper name that had become too closely linked to repressed thoughts. Repression is rarely airtight, however, and derivatives of these repressed thoughts around sex and death came to Freud's mind when he attempted to recall the name. It may be worthwhile to consider the question of how one would distinguish between what I called a shifting of attention in the case of B, and the emergence of derivatives in the case of a repression. Or, to ask the more basic question, is there any difference?

Theoretically, the difference is clear: in repression, a counterforce blocks the emergence into consciousness of a wish and the memories and feelings associated with it, and the repressed wish makes connections with more distant derivatives—compromises between the wish and the counterforce, which are allowed entry into awareness. In denial, attention is shifted from an unpleasant reality to either a reality that lies readily at hand or that is created for the purpose, and it is the thing upon which attention has been shifted that appears in consciousness. In repression, the counterforce is the main thing and the derivative that appears is a secondary phenomenon, while in denial the maintenance of something in consciousness (e.g., B's feeling that she never stuck with relationships) is the very core of the defense.

How can we tell these two processes apart clinically? In a relatively straightforward situation where repression is operative and the patient is free associating, the derivatives will at times come too close to the repressed, and the patient's mind will go blank. By contrast, when denial defenses are operative the patient seems to be able to associate quite freely, but these associations will be a product of the denial defenses and not at all as free as they may appear. Abraham (1919) pointed this phenomenon out long ago as characteristic of patients with narcissistic pathology.

We infer the nature of the defense from the nature of the resistance we meet when we try to analyze it. The shifting to other topics in the examples related to B mark them as attentional defenses, while her mind going blank when we touched on certain oedipal aspects more directly (I did not give examples of this) demonstrated the forceful exclusion from consciousness of unwanted thoughts that is the hallmark of repression.

Although one could be misled into thinking of repression as a defense that attacks reality as much as the drives, an unpleasant reality that has not been made unpleasant by its connection with a prohibited drive will usually be dealt with by other means than repression. A good example of this was B's denial of her boyfriend's lack of caring, which can be contrasted with her repression of any connection of the masochistic sexual feelings for her boyfriend with similar feelings for her narcissistic father. It would seem that in order to master the powerful force of the drives, one needs an equally powerful counterforce that effectively buries both the force of the drive and the memories, ideas, and feelings associated with it. In denial defenses there is not the same energetic burial of memories.

There is quite a spectrum of repressions, from the relatively easily reversible forgetting of a name to some that are a good deal more forceful. Let us look at some clinical material in order to tease out the differences between these different forms of repression.

Clinical Example: C

C, a woman in her early thirties, came for help with depressive feelings that she was experiencing following her father's death, and with marital problems that had come to a head recently. She was a friendly, intelligent, and cooperative woman with a certain matter of fact way of dismissing or minimizing problems, giving the impression that except for a few minor ones, things were under control. She was in fact a very capable person who had managed quite well under, at times, very trying circumstances.

In telling me her history, C told me that her mother, with whom she had been very close, had died when she was twelve, after an illness of two years. "Of course I grieved, and was upset," she said. "But maybe because I was a teenager, I moved on with my life. I was very close with my father. We were like the best of friends."

After giving me an outline of her history, C talked mainly of her present-day problems, especially those related to her husband. At one point, when she said that she may not have mourned properly for her father (who had died when she was an adult), I wondered if her difficulty mourning fully and deeply may have been related to her reactions to her mother's death. She said she had never thought of this, but it was possible. "It didn't really affect me that badly, you know. Of course I was very sad, but really I was all right. It's interesting what you say. You know I haven't really thought about it much at all." C then went back to talking of her marriage, wanting advice from me about what to do with her husband, who was quite distant.

C was very late for the next session. She was rarely this late for something, she told me. She had in fact been late by a few minutes for her therapy appointments previous to this. Later in the therapy we learned that she had somewhat exaggerated her lack of lateness, that she was always late for meetings and social occasions, and that the lateness was unconsciously related to a fear of death as symbolized by arriving at the end of one's journey.

She recounted a dream that involved complex machinations on her part as she attempted to get to the house of an aunt of hers who lived in another country. C related the dream to a letter that she had written recently to her aunt. She said that her aunt had been like a surrogate mother to her while she was growing up.

"So I wonder if the dream relates to your mother," I said. "I brought her up yesterday, and perhaps your thoughts related to her were stirred up."

"I hadn't thought of that," said C. She was silent for a bit, then said she did not really know what to say about it. She then went on to talk about her relatives, and how there had been a lot of closeness and love surrounding her as she grew up. She then described in detail some of the circumstances surrounding her mother's illness and death. She had been extremely sad at her death, thinking quite a bit about her and the many happy times they had had together. "And then one day—I remember it quite well—I just decided that was enough. I wasn't going to think about it any more, and I didn't. It's not that I completely forgot about her but in a way I did. It was time to move on."

At this point I wondered whether, by talking of her mother the session before I had also stirred up this decision to just not think about all of this any more, and that was why she had forgotten about today's session until it was almost too late to come.

"It may be," she said, not sounding very convinced. "I certainly didn't try not to come. I had every intention of coming, but somehow around the time I should have left, I was involved with something and didn't check the time."

C did not show up for her next session at all. She phoned an hour or two later, leaving a message in which she apologized over and over and over again for forgetting. She would of course bring the money for the missed session to the next one, she said, and then proceeded to apologize some more. The apologizing continued immediately as she came into the next session. I pointed out the connection with her having talked of her mother in the last session, and that her decision to avoid her feelings around her mother's death seemed to be very powerfully active, although at this point quite outside of her awareness. She now seemed much more convinced that this was the case, but this conviction did not make the defense itself in the least conscious.

In the sessions that followed, C continued with her difficulties remembering our appointments following any instance when we talked of her mother. Despite our work on the issue, any real feelings related to her mother's death remained stubbornly buried. Over time the transference meaning of C's forgetting was elucidated, as well as the profuse apologizing which followed. They had to do with her pleasure at her mother's death, which for her at the time represented the fulfillment of long repressed but powerful oedipal wishes. She remembered a fantasy that quickly passed through her mind soon after her mother's death, in which she was getting a lot of attention from everyone because of her tragic circumstances. There was a fleeting conscious feeling of pleasure in this. This fantasy was a derivative of fantasies of triumph over her mother, and it was as these fantasies, derivatives themselves of aggressive drives related to her mother, became connected to her mother's death that C was led to repress many of the memories and feelings connected with it. As is typical of the adolescent period, the repression attacked the feelings to a much greater extent than the memories (Blos, 1962).

Clearly C's repression of feelings related to her mother's death was much more energetic and stable than the forgetting of a name. At the same time we can draw a line connecting C's oedipal repressions, her later repressions at age 12, and the forgetting of her appointments after I had brought up the issue of her mother's death. The last of these is reminiscent of the various slips, forgettings, and errors that Freud (1901) described in detail in his book on the psychopathology of everyday life. The key in deciding the nature of these last defenses, of forgetting appointments, is not, to my mind, their reversibility. In the case of other defenses as well, such as denial, later versions of the defenses are usually far more reversible than some of the early ones.

C's repressions in early adolescence were certainly much more stable than the forgetting of a name. They affected her character decisively. C became in some ways quite a different person following this repression: more proud and controlled, with a much greater intolerance for strong emotions, and with a predilection for coming late to any appointment. Later repressions are not only influenced by earlier ones, but operate within a structure that the strongest of these early ones helped to create. It would seem that the ability to form strong and stable new repressions is gradually lost through development, as can be seen by the differences between C's oedipal repressions, her later adolescent repressions, and her forgetting of the appointment. If we trace this line back, we come to the decisive primal repressions of the oedipal period, which are in certain respects more powerful than anything coming before or after, and which also have the most profound effect on psychic structure.

Having described this developmental series, it should be emphasized that there is no absolute correlation between earlier age and stronger repressions. The ability to repress does not appear until the latter half of the second year of life. As soon as this ability appears the tendency to slips, forgettings, etc., conditioned by these repressions, also appears. Repressions of many grades exist in early childhood, with the ability to form massive, far-reaching ones increasing in the phallic-narcissistic and oedipal stages, and then waning through latency and beyond, although the example of C shows this is still possible in adolescence. By adulthood, this ability is generally lost except in exceptional circumstances. New conflicts are not dealt with by repression unless they make an important connection with the repressions of childhood or adolescence (Sandler and Anna Freud, 1985). It is to an enquiry into these first repressions, which Freud (1915b) called primal repressions, that I would now like to turn.

Passive Primal Repression

The concept of primal repression was defined in two different ways by Freud. As Frank and Muslin (1967) detail, in Freud's earlier writings primal repression was seen as a passive lagging behind leading to a fixation on developmental grounds. That is, as the secondary processes developed out of the primary processes, certain wishes and memories were simply not taken up into the preconscious and thus remained under the influence of the primary processes, inaccessible to conscious awareness or control. This form of repression Frank and Muslin (1967, see also Frank, 1969) designated as passive primal repression. This term, and Freud's early ideas about primal repression, actually cover a number of different processes. The use of the term "primal repression" by Freud to describe these processes in his early writings has contributed to the conflation of certain processes and certain types of memories with the process of repression. As I have said, in his early work Freud used the term repression to refer to many different types of defensive processes, at the same time as he used it to designate a specific one. Among these different processes were psychotic de-investment in the world and various obsessional defenses. It is in this context that Freud used the term primal repression to designate the way in which certain early memories were never given verbal form nor taken into the secondary process (the more organized part of the mind). This was strictly speaking not a defensive process, but rather a particular outcome of development. Freud's use of the term primal repression to describe this process was probably partly related to the broad and rather loose way he used the term repression in his early writings, but he also clearly felt that later repressions were conditioned by these processes. Was he right? There is no easy answer to this question because of the complexity of the intertwined processes, but looking at things carefully, I would have to say no, Freud was not right. These early processes interact with and intertwine with later repressions, but they do not determine or condition them—not in the way that C's oedipal repressions conditioned her later repression of her feelings and conflicts after her mother's death, nor in the way that both these repressions conditioned and determined C's repression of her knowledge of her analytic appointments, leading to her being late for and missing sessions.

What makes the situation even more confusing is that other processes have also been conflated with the developmental process of passive primal repression. Among these are the unprocessed memories left after a trauma (see chapter 5) and the defense of primal denial that I will describe in the next chapter. It is worthwhile expending the effort to clarify this confusing tangle of phenomena and concepts because doing so is one of the keys to developing a more coherent and much more clinically powerful theory of defense. As a first step towards this end, I would suggest not connecting the term repression at all with the outcome of the maturational processes that lead to most very early memories not being connected with language and not being integrated with other declarative and autobiographical memories. The difficulty accessing these memories in later life has nothing to do with active defensive processes, and yet many analysts to the present day connect these phenomena with primal repression. This connection has perhaps paved the way for other analysts to equate repression with forms of memory—such as procedural memory—that do not normally, and do not easily, become conscious, again for reasons related to forms of storage and processing rather than active defense.

I will take up this discussion, especially with regard to ideas about different forms of memory, at the end of this chapter. This will allow us to compare these newer ideas about what constitutes repression with the active counterforce that I will now try to describe further and illustrate with a clinical example.

Active Primal Repression

In his later writings Freud (1915b, 1926) defined primal repression as the barring of the ideational representative of the instinct from consciousness, by means of a counterforce. He said in his paper on the unconscious (1915c) that "anticathexis is the sole mechanism of primal repression: in the case of repression proper (after-pressure), there is in addition withdrawal of *pcs.* cathexis" (p 181). Frank and Muslin (1967) designated this process active primal repression. I would prefer to refer to it simply as primal repression. As I said previously, I think the concept and term "passive primal repression," and the idea it represents, even for those who do not use the term, is very confusing, and should be dropped. I think the essence of repression is an active counterforce that bars the forward movement of a drive and the feelings and ideas to which it is attached, so that designating a repression as active is redundant, and designating it as passive is contradictory.

To give a proper example of a primal repression would involve describing in detail the development and analysis of a transference neurosis. Freud's descriptions of the "Rat Man's" death wishes towards his father, which he re-experienced in his analysis towards Freud (Freud, 1909c), is a good clinical description of primal repression and of one manner in which it can emerge in the transference. There are of course many other detailed case descriptions that illustrate the analysis of primal repressions, the most famous of which are probably those of Ernest Kris (1956a, 1956b). I will present a short clinical example to serve as a basis for further discussion.

Clinical Example: D

D was a man in his early forties who came seeking help with tendencies to act out that had gotten him into serious trouble. He had a need to see himself as an exception, as well as difficulty accepting responsibility and a tendency to externalize guilt onto others. I will discuss these characteristics of D in later chapters. In the time leading up to the present example, his tendency to externalize and not accept responsibility had been worked on extensively, along with many other aspects of his use of denial. It was a number of years into the analysis, and D had clearly developed a father transference.

D and his father had had quite a warm relationship. There had been a certain reversal of generations, as his father looked up to him in some ways, as well as looking to him to fulfill his frustrated ambitions by proxy. D had sought from the start of therapy to explain his problems by pointing to his mother's self-centeredness, but had seemed to me to avoid delving into his relationship with his father. It became clear as the analysis progressed that a breakdown that D had suffered in his late twenties was related to his father's death shortly before. A number of times when he came upon thoughts about his father's death while analyzing a dream or in the course of a train of thought, D had burst into uncontrolled sobs, which led him to realize how he had not fully mourned for his father. In a way that was absolutely typical of him, he had avoided facing, and minimized the importance of, the conflicted feelings brought on by his father's death. At the same time D acted out in some very self-destructive ways as an expression of these feelings.

D's father's death seemed to have set him an insoluble problem. No doubt this was partly related to his strong tendency to deny unpleasant realities, but there were other factors at work in this instance. By his transference reactions, it could be seen that D was involved in a struggle to drag his father down. He did it in his own quite charming and friendly way and, as he often insisted, he did not want to destroy me or other father surrogates, merely to bring us down to his level so we could be equals. As analysis of these transference reactions showed, "equal" did not mean equal in the present as two adult men—a perfectly reasonable expectation—but rather that he would have been the equal of his father when he was a little boy. Aspects of the way he was treated by both his mother and father had fostered—even inflamed—this expectation. I will be exploring these parts of D's history, which related to his wish to be special, in later chapters. At this point I would like to describe certain reactions related to our analysis of one of D's major primal repressions.

Sometimes in a session as he associated D would stop short and say something like, "I have a thought about this but I'm sure it's just because I'm in analysis and you're a Freudian." He might then describe the thought, such as that his intrusive idea of putting his fist through the glass of my window related to his penis being injured. If I had said something just before he would usually get angry, feeling that what I had said was meant to lead him to the thought he had had. Even if I had not said anything immediately before, D might still get angry that I was somehow suggesting these ideas to him. As we looked at these responses, D saw that he did not like the ideas that were coming up, and attributed them to me, usually on very slender evidence. Even with this awareness his anger would still appear, although at times he would have enough distance from it to laugh at the anger, even as it continued to bubble up.

D had these responses when associations came up relating to phallic symbolism, castration, anal symbolism or impulses, and oedipal wishes: that is to say, anything related to childhood sexuality. This had not been the main interpretive thrust of our early work together, which had centered on D's reluctance to face unpleasant realities, based on his fixation to certain narcissistic overgratifications of his childhood, as well as his denial of his mother's self-centeredness, because of the pain it had caused him. When I did venture to interpret something related to childhood sexuality, D would have the same angry response as when he came upon these ideas on his own, although he also demonstrated the same ability to gain enough observing distance to continue reporting his associations and to listen to what I had to say, despite his anger.

Certain of D's sexual conflicts began to come into focus. I interpreted the resistance embodied in D's acting out by going to massage parlors a number of times just as we were getting to the core of these conflicts. I said the acting out seemed to rob our analysis of these issues of a sense of immediacy, and things would cool down and become more intellectual for a while. D immediately took this comment as a strong injunction against acting out. (I would not deny that he perceived a sense of anger and frustration that was in my voice, but at this time I would like to concentrate on what D made of the perception.) After this D did not stop the acting out, but became worried that I might kick him out if he continued it, which we analyzed as related to fears of, and traumas related to, emotional abandonment by his mother. D also began forgetting to tell me when he had acted out. He said he was not really lying since it never came to mind during the session, but had to admit as we discussed it that he decided after acting out and also before sessions to try very hard to think of other things and not let it come to mind. The relation of all this to his father transference became quite transparent on more than one occasion.

In a session, D began by talking quite openly about acting out. The words "he showed no remorse" came to mind. It led him to think of psychopathic mass murderers, who showed no remorse. But of course he was not talking about murder, he said, so this did not apply to him at all. He felt no guilt at all, only maybe a bit ashamed. D seemed in a triumphant mood. The oedipal situation, and telling his father to get out of the way and let him at his mother, came to mind. "It seems trite, though," he said in a dismissive tone. "Here I am in an analyst's office talking about the whole oedipal thing."

"You had a strong feeling of wanting to dismiss your father, and now you are dismissing and minimizing the significance of what just came up."

"Now I'm thinking of wanting to kill my father and it scares me. Why would I want to kill him? I love him. Oh yeah, there's my mother. I really can feel some kind of feeling towards her. But I can feel how I really love my dad. It's like the two feelings are right there—loving him and wanting to just do away with him. It's a problem that can't be solved. That's enough. A lot of stuff has come up. It seems like enough for one session. Oh, I don't know! I just want to curl up here. I want you to take control. Can't you just do some nice interpretations now? Tie the whole thing together?

"I really feel like a very small child," said D as he started to cry. "Why can't you take care of me? Just tell me what to do. You do the work."

"Your conflicted feelings about your father seemed insoluble, and you regressed, from a big boy to a small helpless child."

"So what's wrong with that?" said D. But he then began to link the regression with particular aspects of his acting out. D then had intrusive thoughts of putting his hand through the glass of the French doors separating two parts of my office, with lots of blood being spilt. His associations led to other thoughts of injury he had had in the sessions, then to various images of red paintings, and then to an incident of anxiety in his adolescence, throwing a brilliant shaft of light on a detail of the incident that had been particularly obscure. He then had very anxious, scary images of his mother's genitals associated with blood. I did not have to interpret the connection of these castration fears with what had come previously in the session to D's mind. He did it himself, and this time showed no inclination to blame the idea on me.

To begin the next session D recounted a long and involved dream with some very interesting imagery. He proceeded to analyze the dream. It struck me that D's associations kept going off into remote areas and that there was something missing. At a certain point his thoughts went to acting out and he abruptly blurted out that he had gone to a massage parlor again. He burst into sobs, expressing alternately how sorry he was for himself and how scared he was that I would be angry at him and throw him out of analysis. He calmed down quickly and then realized on his own that feeling sorry for himself was a way of protecting himself from what he realized was, at least for a few seconds when he had first told me, a genuine physical fear of me.

D said he had woken up with an image of his mother naked, and strong sexual feelings. He had been driven by a compulsion stronger than anything before to act out in a manner quite different than previously, by not just being masturbated at the massage parlor but also having sex with the woman. As we were talking about this I noted how a particular detail of his sexual feelings toward his mother was represented by what he had done.

"But how do you know I had sexual feelings towards my mother? I saw her in quite a non-sexual pose, with her legs crossed and sitting down."

"But she was naked and you were sexually turned on."

"But I was thinking of the woman I'd seen at the party. It's not like I wanted to sleep with my mother."

"I thought you had said you only thought about the other woman a little while after having the image and being so turned on."

D laughed and admitted this was quite true. "But I don't want to think about my mother sexually. It just feels wrong."

In this last interchange one can see denial in operation. D attempted to shift attention to aspects related to the image of his mother that distorted the actual meaning of what had happened. This shifting of attention and meaning was relatively easily undone but, as is generally the case with denial, it quite persistently returned. For many months afterwards, as we worked on the sexual feelings, wish to kill his father, and castration fears that had begun to emerge from primal repression, D would resort to denial. For instance in one session he argued quite forcefully, using a rather tortured logic, that he really just wanted to move his father out of the way to get at his mother. He really meant him no harm. After all he loved the guy. Why would he want to hurt him? D would also project the responsibility for what he had discovered onto me, saying that I had led him to discover these things because I considered that one had to do that to have a good analysis. The projection was about as easily undone, and about as persistent in returning, as the denial.

Central to the resolution of D's primally repressed oedipal wishes and castration fears was our analysis of their appearance in the transference. In the session described, when D broke into sobs after telling me about his acting out and his image of his mother naked, it seemed he was afraid that I, as the transference father, would castrate him for his wishes. Behind this fear lay his own wishes to harm or do away with his father. In the following months and years of analysis, these issues became a central focus of the transference and of the analysis. D tended to act out the conflicts by trying not to tell me about some activity that usually had the meaning, when we analyzed it, of masturbation, related to the childhood masturbation which he had performed while being sexually excited about his mother. At times the activity was masturbation itself in the present day, at other times other activities that had the meaning of being "bad."

Traumatic Anxiety versus Pervasive Anxiety

I have presented a few details of D's analysis in order to demonstrate some aspects of primal repression. To begin with motive, it would seem, from this example at least, that the motive for primal repression is intense anxiety. This was certainly Freud's (1926) view. He felt that a traumatic state or traumatic situation, in which the ego was overwhelmed by anxiety, was what initiated primal repression. The overwhelming anxiety set the unpleasure principle (the avoidance of pain or unpleasure) in motion and led to primal repression, which was thus an automatic process brought about by quantitative factors. Freud (1926) distinguished the traumatic situation from what he called a danger situation, in which the ego gave a signal of anxiety based on an expectation of being overwhelmed, in order to set the unpleasure principle in motion, leading to defense. Signal anxiety was the motive for *after repression*, while traumatic anxiety called *primal repression* into play. In signal anxiety the ego used the previously experienced traumatic anxiety, but gave itself only a little taste (signal) of how bad it could get if the repression is undone. This led to the after repression of whatever it was (something connected to what was primally repressed) that caused the signal anxiety.

Looking at the example of D, one can see the intense anxiety that shows itself as thoughts and wishes emerge from primal repression. As he became aware of his wish to fight and kill his father, he regressed to a passive wish to be taken care of, and when the defensive meaning of this was interpreted, ideas related to anxieties about bodily injury began to bubble up. This anxiety reached a much greater intensity when D admitted he had lied to me, and he felt for a few seconds mortally threatened. Intense anxiety such as this, which feels so threatening because it is outside of the ego's control and feels like it will go on forever and engulf the ego, in my experience inevitably accompanies the weakening or lifting of a primal repression. It was data such as this, for instance from the analyses of "Wolf Man" (Freud, 1918) and "Little Hans" (Freud, 1909b), that led Freud to link traumatic anxiety with primal repression.

Unfortunately for the future course of psychoanalytic theorizing, Freud (1926) equated anxiety that escapes the ego's control and leads to primal repression with trauma caused by an overwhelming of the barrier against external stimuli. Certainly it is an easy enough connection to make, since in both situations the ego feels overwhelmed and appears not to be in control. However, in terms of feeling state, effect on ego functions, defenses that are brought into operation, and outcome the two are very different. Traumatic overwhelming of the ego from external sources leads to a feeling of numbness, non-registration (as opposed to repression or denial) of incoming stimuli, a shutting down of many other ego functions as well (most notably the synthetic function), the use of dissociation resulting in splitting defenses, and a very strong tendency to both repetition of aspects of the trauma and phobic avoidances. The strong anxiety that motivates repression, on the other hand, feels like it will never stop, which is the key experiential aspect of the unpleasant feelings that drive primal defenses. While this experience is intensely unpleasant, it involves a functioning ego that is still having feelings, a situation quite different from that in trauma. The most important reason for making the differentiation between trauma and the intense feelings that lead to primal defenses is that doing so greatly clarifies the theory of defense and in the end promises to have a similar clarifying, and also invigorating, effect on clinical understanding and practice.

All this is not to say that all analysts have followed Freud's distinction between traumatic and signal anxiety, and between primal and after repression. There has been a significant movement in American Freudian analysis, following the lead of Charles Brenner (1966, 1982), to collapse these distinctions into simply differences of degree of anxiety and of repression. While this view has some similarities with my own, I feel it goes too far in neglecting crucial differences in modulation between pervasive versus signal affects, differences which are reflected in the different defenses to which they lead. I think it is reasonable to designate the much more powerful anxiety by another term, but "traumatic anxiety" is an inaccurate and confusing one. "Pervasive anxiety," a term suggested by Yorke, Wiseberg, and Freeman (1989), seems much more appropriate. I will discuss this issue in more detail in the chapter on trauma, but I introduced the term here to facilitate our discussion of primal defenses in the next few chapters. Pervasive anxiety (or any other pervasive affect, such as pervasive psychic pain) is an affect of such strength and intensity that the ego's usual methods of dealing with affect (including expression in bodily processes, action, and words, containment by symbolic processing, and suppression) are not sufficient, and powerful defensive processes such as primal repression are put into action to manage the affect. They often do not manage the affect directly—for instance primal repression does not usually repress the anxiety, or at least that is not all it does. Rather the cause of the affect—for instance in the case of D his sexual and aggressive oedipal wishes—is attacked by the defense.

After Defenses and Secondary Defenses

To return now to the case of D, from these more general considerations, we can see that a good deal of analysis of other defenses had to be done before we could mobilize the primal oedipal repressions. There is nothing new in this observation, but it would perhaps be worthwhile to dwell a little on the connections between primal repression and other defenses.

One particular connection that is worth emphasizing from the point of view of technique is that between primal repression and some later, relatively energetic after repressions. These after repressions are not likely to be missed when they relate to the immediate precipitating causes that brought the patient to analysis, nor if they relate to easily identifiable periods of difficulty in the patient's past, such as the time around D's father's death. However, after repressions are many and often interrelate with each other and with primal repressions in complex ways.

It is quite possible for a number of significant after repressions to remain hidden and to thus impede the analysis of primal repressions. This can be facilitated by a technique that too quickly attempts to analyze early childhood, skipping any intermediate steps, and by one that emphasizes analysis of the transference to the exclusion of non-transference interpretations of the present and past. In the case of D there were significant after repressions from the period around his father's illness and death and from adolescence, that were crucial in analyzing his primal oedipal repressions.

One of the best known examples of this issue in the literature is contained in Ernst Kris's (1956b) paper on the personal myth. He described three patients who had developed a seamless story of a period of their lives, in latency or adolescence—a story that in one case had withstood a lengthy previous analysis. Certain conflicts had been stirred up in these patients by the situation they had found themselves in in these later periods of life, conflicts that related back to traumas and primal repressions from earlier childhood. The repressions, screen memories, and denials from these later times had to be analyzed before aspects of the earlier primal repressions of these patients could be meaningfully engaged.

Even after the primal repressions have been engaged in the analysis, the use of other defenses continues. For instance when D first clearly recovered a memory of a wish to kill his father, he regressed to a passive position, asking me to help him, and saying he had done enough. When I interpreted this regression, associations and powerful feelings related to castration anxiety appeared. In the next session, when D admitted he had lied to me, and was in fear of me, he thought of a sexual image of, and sexual feelings towards, his mother. Clearly these feelings were emerging from repression, but now D tried a different tack. He denied that what he had described were really sexual feelings about his mother. He also tried to deny that he wanted to kill his father. On top of this he attempted to project the responsibility for the awareness of these wishes onto me.

These defenses of regression to passivity and self-pity, denial, and externalization of responsibility had occupied our interest for a good part of our time together in the first years of D's analysis. We analyzed their use largely in relation to narcissistic conflicts, as will be detailed in chapter 6. At the later point in the analysis described above they were used as a second line of defense once wishes, memories, and feelings had emerged from primal repression. One can see from the sessions described how D's denial of these things differed from his repression of them. For all of his life after he had established his primal oedipal repressions, except for fleeting moments during adolescence, D had been completely unaware of his sexual love for his mother and his wish to kill his father. Once these wishes had emerged from repression, he attempted through shifting attention to deny the true meaning of what he was feeling, and as these attentional shifts were interpreted his true wishes emerged again, only to sink back down into the preconscious as D established a new denial.

Ernst Kris (1956c) pointed out that this use of secondary defenses, as repressions are weakened, is universal. He noted that hysterics usually use denial, as did D, while obsessionals will use especially isolation of feelings to fight this rearguard action. The analysis of these secondary isolations is far more difficult than the analysis of the denials of patients with a hysterical propensity, and this is one reason why the analysis of obsessional patients is so laborious. The place where one can most easily observe the use of secondary defenses consequent to a weakening of repressions is in borderline patients, who suffer terribly through having to struggle continuously to shore up their inadequate repressions with various other defenses.

It is worthwhile distinguishing two types of defenses that help a primal defense: after defenses and secondary defenses. The first type (an after defense) is a less energetic version of the original primal defense—in fact it is an offshoot of it. Freud's (1915b, 1926) description of after repression is a model for these defenses. There are also other forms of primal defenses with their corresponding after defenses, such as primal denial and after denial. One gets a glimpse of the nature of the primal defense through these after defenses. Once D's primal repression had been weakened, however, what he especially brought in to attempt to hold the fort were defenses such as denial, regression, and externalization. These were not at all direct offshoots of the primal repression, but were brought in from other areas to do the job. If we retain Freud's term of after repression (after defense) for the direct offshoots, these other defenses are probably best referred to as secondary defenses. Secondary defenses are much less powerful and stable than a primal defense. *A secondary defense is any defense, other than an after defense, that helps to buttress a primal defense.*

Repression and the Aggressive Drive

D's reactions, when he thought of certain things related especially to childhood sexuality, of getting angry at me and saying that I had put these ideas into his head, could be conceptualized as examples of a secondary defense (externalization of responsibility) used to shore up a primal repression. These instances occurred quite often prior to the sessions where oedipal wishes actually emerged into consciousness. Leaving on one side the externalization, however, what are we to make of D's anger, evidenced also when I actually interpreted such things as anal wishes and oedipal conflicts?

At one time in the history of analysis the answer to this question would have been quite clear. D's reaction was a negative transference reaction, brought forward because it would serve well as a resistance to the further uncovering of repressed wishes. Today many analysts would see these reactions as related to the narcissistic injury engendered by my interpretations. This emphasis began especially with Kohut's (1971) work with narcissistic disorders, which was quickly expanded by him and others to include all patients. The explanation given today not just by self psychologists but by analysts from many persuasions influenced by these views, might be that there was some kind of transference/countertransference interaction going on, where I might have been subtly and not so subtly influencing D to have the kind of associations he did, perhaps as a reenactment of an early coercive or molding relationship. D's anger could then be seen as a legitimate response to this kind of coercion by me, as well as a response related to interactions from early childhood.

Of course the negative, angry responses by patients during treatment do not all have a single cause, but I am trying to narrow the focus here to angry responses engendered either by the interpretation of defense or simply by the emergence of defended against material into consciousness as the patient associates. Even with this limitation, various instances will have different causes. For instance the appearance of an old angry rebellion by D against his father that was transferred onto me, and which increased as his oedipal wishes threatened to break through his defenses, may be a better example of a transference resistance than the flashes of anger D felt as ideas related to infantile sexuality came to mind. Thus I would like to narrow the focus even more, to the particular anger D felt as ideas related to childhood sexuality were either interpreted or came to mind spontaneously.

In relation to this particular reaction, I think the evidence favors an explanation given by Heinz Hartmann, an explanation that is decidedly out of favor at present. Hartmann (1950b, 1953) thought that evidence such as

D's reactions as repression was breaking down pointed to a derivation of the counterforce in defenses such as repression from partially neutralized aggression. As a portion of this counterforce is rendered unnecessary or unusable by the analytic process or by a specific interpretation, and as portions of the repressed became conscious, some of the partially neutralized aggression that formed the counterforce assumes its old form of relatively unneutralized aggression, and leads to (or at least adds its strength to) an angry feeling towards the analyst.

I have no illusions as to the extent of the negative reaction I will draw upon myself by avowing my support for such a theory. I am assuming that with many readers it will at least equal the negative reaction D displayed as repressed material emerged. However, rather than engaging in a theoretical polemic on the issue, which in my experience convinces no one but those who are already convinced (which in this case is almost no one), I would propose to do something different. If the reader will attempt to keep an open mind on the issue I will, at appropriate times through this book, point to specific clinical phenomena that are quite puzzling, that are not easily explained by theories such as narcissistic wounding, and which I think at least raise the possibility that the counterforce used in repression is derived from aggression.

In the case of D, the phenomena I would like to point to are the rather surprising (to D as well as myself) flashes of anger that he would feel as repressed psychosexual material emerged. It is interesting that when I had, earlier in the analysis, interpreted various aspects of D's narcissism and of his clinging to the feeling that he was special, there were not the same flashes of anger. Nor were they evident as we talked about a number of incidents from his past and present, to think of which caused him deep shame and humiliation. I am not saying that D did not become irritated at times or show displeasure when I brought up these things, but these reactions were muted, were more commensurate with the unpleasant nature of what I was asking him to talk of, and also did not appear with the regularity with which the flashes of anger did when oedipal and anal material emerged from repression. This is not what one would expect if the angry responses were correlated with the level of narcissistic injury.

One counterargument to this would be to say that D's oedipal loss of his mother to his father, and the passive anal wishes to which he regressed to defend against phallic anxieties, were perhaps the most humiliating and narcissistically wounding aspects of his childhood. I would certainly agree with this idea. One might think that this would explain the anger that appeared as these aspects of his childhood became conscious. Another possible counterargument, which does not contradict the one above, could be that anger was mobilized as a resistance, and that it appeared especially in relation to psychosexual issues because the resistance, due to overwhelming anxiety, was greatest there.

In answer to these arguments I would point out that it is interesting that the anger only appeared as the repression broke down and the material began to emerge. When D was completely in the thrall of these feelings, for instance feeling very vividly the love and hatred for his father existing strongly and simultaneously in his mind, his anger and irritability vanished. There could appear at these times very strong resistances to going any further, even an anger at me for not making things easier on him, but again the anger did not burst forth as was characteristic when the repression barrier was first breached, but was more modulated and more understandable given the unpleasantness of what he was feeling. Similarly, in the months after these feelings had emerged, as I vigorously interpreted D's attempts to secondarily deny or minimize them, the flashes of anger did not appear unless the repression was reinstated and then interpreted. D might be peeved at me for bursting the bubble of his denial, or at other times laugh out loud as he recognized the tortured logic he was using to prove he had no ill wishes toward his father or sexual love for his mother, but the characteristic burst of anger that appeared when these wishes first came out of repression was not present. Here again, if it were a question of narcissistic injury, perhaps caused by the reenactment of an early unempathic relationship, and/or a product of resistance, why was this response only evident when the repression of these conflicts was being undone, and not with the analysis of other defenses that were directed against exactly the same conflicts? In relation to another possibility, that D's anger at me was a transferred derivative of his anger at his father, one could wonder if this were so, why it would flash forth as we undid the repression of this anger, but not its denial.

Patients such as D, who have no borderline features leading to a serious weakness of repression, are the best examples with which to begin our investigation of this issue, since with them the situation is relatively uncomplicated.[1] In these cases, I would suggest that the characteristic burst of anger as repression is undone is a product of aggression that had formerly been used to fend off a drive becoming freed from that utilization. I am certainly not suggesting that all anger around interpretation of counterforce defenses has this source, only that some of it does. There are many other causes of anger, and on top of this the anger that has its source in the aggression used as a defensive counterforce can be put to other uses once it has been freed from its defensive use—in the long run it serves admirably to shore up resistance in other ways, by powering a negative transference or other forms of transference resistance. Further, this is only one of the uses to which it can be put, and this intermingling of the many sources of and uses for anger complicates the picture quite a bit. But I do not think that it obscures it so much that one cannot make sense of it.

If the sense I have tried to make of these phenomena have any validity, it leads to an insight into the basic nature of counterforce defenses and denial defenses. Since the specific type of anger that I think indicates that aggression is utilized to form the counterforce defense appeared in D only with the undoing of repressions, not denials or externalizations, it would seem that only repression is formed by the partial neutralization and redirection of aggression. Denial must use some other kind of energy to achieve its ends. Of course one case such as D's cannot prove the truth of the particular explanations I am putting forward. Rather, I am using the example in order to point to the sort of concrete phenomena that lend them support, and hope that readers who have the opportunity to make similar observations will look closely and with an open mind at their own data.

In the example with D, we see the transformation of the partially neutralized aggression used in repression back into aggression in a more raw form when the repression is partially undone. We can also often enough observe the transformation of aggression in the opposite direction, although here too there are many factors interacting and making it hard to see things clearly. In these situations, when raw aggression that has been repressed or otherwise kept from being available is freed up through analysis and (at least in non-borderline, neurotic patients) becomes available, one can observe a number of uses to which it is put. As an example D's death wishes towards both his parents and his sister were defended against by a combination of repression, denial, externalization, and splitting of the ego. Once these death wishes were brought into conscious awareness and worked through, D became more able to be assertive in many situations, as well as finding more energy to move forward in projects and to persist in the face of obstacles. These changes are relatively obvious and straightforward sublimations of aggression. He also developed a better ability to selectively repress certain perverse sexual wishes, as part of a general strengthening of his counterforce defenses, which is a sublimation that is also quite common, but that often passes unnoticed in these sorts of situations.

The Drives

Having asserted the derivation of repression from aggressive drive energy, and having noted how unpopular this way of thinking about things has become, it may be worthwhile to say a few words about the drives.

Often the biological aspects of the drives are stressed: how they arise from the body and represent powerful bodily needs to the mind. Freud often spoke in these terms, but to do so can, I think, obscure what are some of the most important characteristics of the drives, and what were some of Freud's most important discoveries about them. No doubt the drives have important connections to the body both with regard to source and aim, but a number of the ego functions, notably perception and motility, are just as closely tied to the body. Similarly even "higher" ego functions such as rational thought and objective judgments are just as much a product of our biology as are sexuality and aggression, not only in the sense of being tied to brain functioning, but also in the sense that they are products of evolutionary processes and of our evolutionary history, and are just as closely tied to adaptation and survival as are the drives.[2]

Another idea that I think often obscures some fundamentally important characteristics of the sexual and aggressive drives is reducing the drives to their motivational aspect and/or seeing them as the only important motivators. This is done by some supporters of Freudian theory who overextend the drive concept, as well as by critics and those who look to revise the theory. I myself think there are quite a number of motivations that are not derived from the drives. Hunger and thirst come immediately to mind, as do physical pain and psychic pain. Hunger and thirst were grouped under the ego instincts in Freud's (1915a) first drive theory.

Psychic pain brings up that whole class of motivators: the affects. Some of these, such as anger, rage, and sexual excitement, are often derivatives of drives. However I do not think affects are all drive derivatives, and even those that often are, such as anger, can have other sources. Affects, especially those *not* derived from the drives, such as anxiety and psychic pain, are the basic motivators of defenses.

So if drives cannot be reduced to their motivational aspect and if they cannot be demarcated from ego functioning by their ties to the body, what is it that distinguishes them from other motivators and what is it that marks them as specifically psychoanalytic ideas? I believe the answer to these questions is the very great capacity for displacement and extraordinary malleability of the sexual and aggressive drives. These characteristics were in the first instance not theoretical ideas but clinical discoveries. These discoveries were made along with Freud's great discoveries of infantile sexuality (1905) and of the primary process (1900). What Freud and those who came after him discovered clinically through such phenomena as therapeutic regression, which led to the drive roots of various interests and behaviors emerging, was the enormous plasticity of the drives. A little boy's love of carrying a stick and hitting everything in sight, his later adolescent interest in pocket knives and in using his arms and legs as weapons in learning the martial arts, and his interest in certain types of machinery may all (depending on the individual case) be traced back to a strong sexual interest in, and sexual pleasure he got from, his penis from a young age. Not that any of these interests would *only* be derived from this original source, but a number of the other sources (of course not all of them) would also involve transformations of other drive aims, including aggressive ones.

This malleability of the sexual and aggressive drives is well enough known but is surprisingly often lost sight of when the issue of motivation is discussed, at which time drives are often grouped with other motivations as if they were on equal footing. The actual inequality stems not from strength or importance, but from malleability. This plasticity is the reason these drives in the end have such a wide-ranging influence. It is, I believe, as a tool to help us conceptualize and think about this plasticity and transformative ability of the sexual drive that Freud developed the libido theory.

Libido was seen as a quantity of sexual energy that could spread over and invest (*besetzung*) ideas to varying degrees, transferring both its force and quality to these ideas, and also being able to detach or de-invest from them. Freud referred to these ideas as the economic point of view (having to do with quantities of energy and their movement) and lamented even during his time that analysts seemed disinclined to use this conceptual tool. Hartmann (1948, 1953) and Hartmann, Kris, and Loewenstein (1947) developed these concepts, applying them to the aggressive drive and developing the ideas of neutralization and degrees of neutralization of the aggressive drive and of libido. There are few ideas that have been attacked as vehemently by other analysts as these of Hartmann around transformations of drive energy. To my mind these ideas, like Freud's libido theory, are useful tools that help us to think about certain types of transformations that drives go through.

Neutralization is to be distinguished from displacement. In displacement drive investment is moved from one idea—a penis let's say—to another, such as a stick. In neutralization, which often combines with displacement, there is a distancing of the drive from its original aims. If the stick that is a displacement is used for poking (sexual) and hitting (aggressive), the aims are relatively unneutralized, despite the displacement. One can imagine from here all sorts of gradations where the displacement remains the same but the neutralization increases. The child may not hit or poke anything and anyone in sight, but rather hold the stick as a defensive weapon, or use it in imaginative play, or for structured games where the stick becomes a hockey stick or a baseball bat. A further displacement onto a pen, and further neutralization, may be used in writing, as I am doing here, with the phallic sexuality used in probing into the dark secrets of the mind and the aggression used in arguing against opposing views. Displacement does not have to stop at pens, as concepts and ideas can be used for these purposes even if not written down with a pen. On the other hand the displacement can go far, for instance onto concepts, while there may be less neutralization and the sexual and aggressive roots may be more obvious and interfere with the more rational use of the concepts. (The concept of sublimation is very closely linked to neutralization and displacement, although I think it is often used to refer to alterations in specific wishes that are multiply determined, by neutralization, displacement, and other processes.)

In relation specifically to the counterforce of repression, the destructive aims of raw aggression are somewhat tamed, although some amount of the "fight" aspect of the aggression is used in the pushing of drives and feelings into the unconscious, and in keeping a strong barrier to their entry into conscious awareness. Thus we could say that the counterforce is formed from partially, but not wholly, neutralized aggressive drive energy. Another very similar use of partially neutralized aggressive drive energy is in erecting and maintaining self-other boundaries. In this case the use of aggression is more evident. The two stages when self-other boundaries are especially erected are in the toddler stage and during adolescence. During both these stages one can observe the use first of interpersonal aggression to push the other person away and say "no" as an assertion of personal will and identity, and then the gradual internal use of this aggression in a more neutralized form, but with still some characteristics of aggression, to erect and maintain a boundary between the self and other in the mind.

The arguments used against these sorts of examples are that the energic hypothesis is a relic, borrowed by Freud from the physics of his day in an attempt to make psychoanalysis seem scientific, and also that energic ideas are really only descriptive—that is that they look like they explain something, but really just re-describe certain observations in the pseudoscientific language of energy transformation. It is certainly true that Freud borrowed the idea of energy from other sciences, but I am not convinced that he did it mainly for the reasons often cited. I think Freud developed the libido theory and the economic point of view to help him comprehend and further explore the quite striking properties of displaceability and malleability that he discovered in the sexual drive. When these concepts are discarded, the phenomena and observations remain. I do not think analysts have been as successful in dealing with these phenomena using only ideas related to meaning, affect, etc., and leaving out energic ideas. In conceptualizing new findings every scientist brings in ideas from the intellectual climate around him or her, from everyday life, and from other fields. After all physicists originally took the idea of energy for human experiences with their own bodies and minds, and more specifically from psychology, but we would not on that account declare the concept of energy in physics invalid because it is anthropomorphic. What matters is not from where you get your concepts, but the use to which you put them, the manner in which you modify and develop them, and their suitability for the phenomena to which they are applied. Of course if one naïvely assumed that drive energy in psychoanalysis is equivalent to physical energy, or that it had to follow the same laws as energy in physics, this borrowing could be problematic. Freud was guilty of this to some extent, but I do not think this should be allowed to obscure the tremendous usefulness of the drive energy idea as an autonomous psychoanalytic concept, with properties that are established through psychoanalytic observations and theory development. As for the issue of explanation versus description, I think there are varying amounts of both in most psychoanalytic theories. It is by looking at the use of the concepts more broadly that their explanatory value can be seen. While I have argued for the value of energic ideas in helping us to preserve our knowledge of, and to think about, certain key properties of the drives, their explanatory value can especially be seen by how they help us to further develop aspects of analytic theory and practice.

I see that despite my earlier promise not to do so I have engaged in a certain amount polemical argumentation about energic concepts—necessarily so, I think, given the present climate of accepted "truths" about the invalidity of these ideas. In relation to their value in further developing psychoanalytic theory I can again go back to saying that I will try to demonstrate this at a number of points through this book in relation to clinical material, rather than merely argue the point.

Repression is a many faceted topic. At this point I will just touch briefly on a few more issues (the superego, selective repression, screen memories, and memory more generally) before looking at some clinical aspects of repression.

The Superego

The superego plays a crucial role in repressions after the early childhood phase. Just how important this role is is usually not appreciated because much of the work that the superego does is unconscious. It is when the superego's power is reduced that its role in repression becomes clear. The most common instance of this is the adolescent's estrangement from his or her superego, secondary to the general estrangement from the parents, which extends to anything connected with them. As Anna Freud (1936) pointed out, because of this estrangement the adolescent loses a powerful ally in establishing selective repressions, and in dealing with the drives he or she is thrown back on more global mechanisms such as blocking of drives (asceticism) and intellectualization. Both the intellectualization and blocking are less selective than the common circumscribed intellectualizations or repressions we see in most younger children and adults. These attack a particular sexual or aggressive wish, rather than all sexual and aggressive wishes, as is the case in these adolescent defenses.

Selective Repression

The mention of the non-selective blocking that takes place during adolescence points out that what we usually refer to as repression is a more selective process. The more general blocking, which can also be seen in borderline patients with weak repressions, seems not to be nearly as stable as selective repression, since both adolescents and borderlines will at times be flooded by the drive they are repressing, and act out quite strongly, while at other times they will repress anything to do with it. I think that one aspect of the selectivity of mature repression is probably related to the higher degree of neutralization of the aggression used in the defense. There is evidence of a more general difficulty with neutralization in both adolescents and borderlines. What I mean by a decreased level of neutralization is that in blocking there is a quite general attack on whatever is considered dangerous (for instance anything connected with sexuality) which retains much more of the character of raw aggression. The increase in neutralization in selective repression allows a more differentiated response. The accent falls less on an aggressive attack on a whole class of drives or affects, and the defense can be more adaptive. It is not held as much a hostage, so to speak, to the aims of the raw drive, while it can use the drive energy and its characteristic of opposition for adaptive purposes.

All this is more profitably discussed in the context of clinical material. If we think of D's repression of his sexual love for his mother and death wishes towards his father, or of C's repression of her memories and feelings related to her mother's death when she was 12, we see a relatively stable and selective force standing in the way of these things coming into conscious awareness. As we analyze the resistances we meet after repressions including the forgetting of sessions, forgetting what we talked of in the previous sessions, as well as various secondary defenses such as denial and externalization. There are at times bursts of anger as the repression is challenged and undone and this can develop into a more sustained aggressive (negative) transference, which is itself hard to deal with, but which is also stable, sustained, and contained, with some room left over for the working alliance and the real relationship. This can be compared to the situation when analyzing repressions in a borderline patient, where the aggression is much closer to the surface and much more raw and destructive, and much less stable. When we interpret a repression there will be an aggressive, rageful rejection of what is repressed and is now emerging. Often the wishes and feelings emerging from repression are projected onto the analyst, who is then attacked vehemently, all of which attests to the lack of stable and adequate neutralization of the aggression used in the defense. In fact what is then formed is a different, much less adaptive, interpersonal counterforce defense, usually referred to as projective identification, where the defended against derivatives of a drive (for instance sadistic wishes) are violently injected into the therapist. The therapist is both bullied into accepting the drive derivatives, and then angrily attacked and rejected, just as in repression a much more modulated aggression forcefully pushes the drive wishes into the unconscious and keeps them there, apart from the person's conscious perception of the self.

Screen Memories

An important aspect of selective repression which gives it stability and flexibility, as compared to blocking, is the setting up of screen memories. Ernst Kris (1956c) felt that the screen memories in repression were cathected (invested) with libido, while aggression provided the countercathexis (counterforce) of repression. Kris's three papers published in 1956 (a, b, c) presented detailed clinical material where the interplay of counterforce and of the creation of libidinally invested screen memories—really entire stories or myths—is beautifully described. The screen memory or screen myth provides a partial expression of what is repressed, but in a distorted manner. As an example D, whose emergence of oedipal conflicts from repression I described, had a story of his childhood that centered around his mother as uncaring, and a specific memory of being in his crib crying, with his mother not coming to him. He also had memories of being a very young infant and of being left terrified on the toilet seat, too small to get down, as his mother left for what seemed like hours.

D's mother had been in fact quite a self-centered, narcissistic woman, who often (but not always) had trouble empathizing with her son. However, as I will detail in the chapter on narcissism, D's focusing on the deficiencies of his mother was part of an attentional defense, in which this story screened the fixation that he had on the intense pleasure of the many ways in which his mother and father had overgratified him, especially in the realm of narcissism. I bring up this particular aspect of D's story and dynamics here, prior to the more detailed description of them in later chapters, for the purpose of making a point: along with the many determinants that influence the choice of a screen memory or a screen story that helps with a primal repression, an important one is often that the memory or story is part of a complex of denial defenses. In the case of D emphasis on his mother's lack of warmth and on his anger at her helped with the repression of his oedipal sexual love for her, and of his death wishes towards his father, even as it served as a denial of the reality of the narcissistic gratifications gained from his mother.

There were in fact many complications and twists and turns to this intertwining of D's denial and repressive defenses. D had a primal denial of his mother's narcissism, which defended against its full acknowledgment, but a more superficial acknowledgment of this narcissism and anger at her self-centeredness[3] served to defend against awareness of his mother's overgratification of him. At the same time D's complaints about his mother's mistreatment of him had a libidinal side, being unconsciously linked to anal and phallic passive/masochistic wishes directed at both his mother and father. These complications should not obscure a very simple conclusion, and in fact they help to demonstrate it even more clearly: the shifting of the ego attention in denial defenses and of libidinal investment in the formation of screen memories in repression cooperate and find common ground in certain memories and stories that serve the purposes of both the denial and the repression. This is one of the major ways in which denial defenses and repression intersect and interact, and in so doing form a good part of what people consider to be their early memories and the story of their lives.

I mentioned D's traumatic memory of being left alone on the toilet seat. It turned out that this was a set of memories about an actual trauma, and their use as screens for some of D's repressions is a very instructive example of the interaction of trauma, traumatic memories and defenses, and repression. I will go into this aspect of D's case in detail in chapter 8, on perversions. I will anticipate what will be demonstrated in that chapter with much clinical material, by saying that some of the unprocessed memories that are a consequence of trauma are used as screen memories in much the same way that the memories and ideas that are formed through denial defenses are used as screen memories in relation to repression. This is one way in which trauma and its defenses intersect and find common cause with the process of repression.

Memory

One of the hallmarks of repression is its ability to block memories. Ernst Kris (1956c) called the form of memory affected by repression autobiographical memory. He pointed out that while the infantile amnesia effectively barred large chunks of autobiographical memory from consciousness, the skills that had been learned during this same time survived the primal oedipal repressions intact. Using modern terminology, we would say that repression blocks the retrieval of declarative memories, but not of procedural memories. In saying that repression blocks retrieval of memories, I am also indicating the point in the processing of memory (perception—short term memory processing—consolidation into long-term memory—retrieval) at which it exerts its effect.

There has been a lot of interest within psychoanalysis lately in different forms of memory and how they relate to psychological disorders, repetition of the past, and change brought about by psychotherapy. Certain authors have championed the cause of implicit memories as major causative factors in neurosis and more severe disorders, as well as being the main site of therapeutic action. Many analysts of various theoretical persuasions seem to have been strongly influenced by these ideas, and from my experience often accept the ideas of the proponents of these views as being well proven without delving further into the matter. I myself feel that the reach of these important processes has been overextended to explain phenomena related to repression, denial, trauma, and the aftermath of neglect that are better explained by dynamics related to declarative memories.

The ideas about memory have been developed by cognitive psychologists and by neuroscientists who have discovered that there are different areas of the brain involved in these different forms of memory. The basic division is between implicit and explicit memories. Implicit memories are divided into skills and habits (procedural memories) and emotional memories. Both of these generally do not become conscious, not because of repression, but because of their form of registration. An important point to keep in mind is that these concepts refer to specific types of memory processes, and that it would be a mistake to assume that any action that is habitual or any seemingly automatic emotional reaction is mediated wholly by procedural or emotional memory systems.

The terms "implicit" and "explicit" can also be a source of confusion, and I think they have been so in some analytic writings on the subject. In these writings all unconscious memories are equated with implicit memories and only conscious memories (or those easily capable of becoming conscious) are considered explicit or declarative. In fact the terms explicit and declarative refer to forms of memory processing that are connected especially with the hippocampus and adjacent structures in the brain in terms of formation, and the cerebral cortex in terms of storage, and which Kris referred to as auto-biographical memories. They are not necessarily "explicit" in the sense of being conscious or easily capable of becoming conscious. To clarify these at times confusing terms: there are two basic types of memory processing: *explicit* and *implicit*. *Explicit* memories can be subdivided into *episodic* (also called *declarative* or *autobiographical*) memories, which are the sort of re-creation of past perceptions that we usually think of as memory, and *semantic* memory, which involves knowledge abstracted from specific situations: for instance our knowledge of our birth date or other facts or ideas. *Implicit* memory can be subdivided into *procedural* memory, involving knowledge about how to do things, such as ride a bike or type on a computer, and *emotional* memory, involving the connection of certain situations with the emotions felt at the time, not in an explicit manner, but through non-conscious conditioning.

I think Kris's (1956c) observation, enunciated over half a century ago, still holds true: repression works against explicit (declarative, autobiographi-cal) memories and does not generally bar procedural or other forms of im-plicit memory from expression. For instance C's repression occasioned by her mother's death when she was 12 attacked a surprisingly large part of her childhood memories, so that she had only a few islands of memories remain-ing, but of course her procedural memories related to such things as riding a bike or writing were untouched. Even in the realm of declarative memories repression is selective and even a massive, far-reaching one such as C's spares some declarative memories, although in primal repressions many of them are woven into a web of screen memories and screen stories.

A number of influential authors, such as Daniel Stern (Stern et al., 1998) and Peter Fonagy (1999), have largely rejected these findings related to repression and the connection of repression with later repetition, as well as the relation of all this to therapeutic technique. For instance Fonagy (1999) notes that the declarative memory system matures later than the implicit memory systems, and that therefore early pathogenic relationships are stored in implicit memory. Thus in therapy it is intensive work on the transference that leads to change by altering these implicit memories. Fonagy sees the changes in autobiographical memory that occur during therapy as relatively superficial byproducts of the deeper and more important changes in implicit memories. Referring to the idea of memory recovery being therapeutically important Fonagy (1999) asserts that "there is no evidence for this and in my view to cling to this idea is damaging to the field" (p 215).

As so often happens in psychoanalysis, Fonagy has taken an important idea and vastly overextended it. He himself notes that his ideas about therapeutic change are speculative, and yet he uses them to denounce ideas with far more evidential backing. In discussing Fonagy's ideas Blum (2003) asks what the evidence is that emotional reliving with the analyst is what leads to change. Often the evidence seems to consist of summaries of neuroscientific and cognitive research findings and concepts combined with relatively superficial clinical examples. The clearest evidence that Fonagy's ideas about implicit memory are not up to the explanatory task that he asks them to perform is that he is led to bring dynamic concepts related to declarative memories into his explanations even as he more generally asserts their irrelevance. For instance in talking of early implicit memories Fonagy asserts that "the models are not replicas of actual experience but are undoubtedly defensively distorted by wishes and fantasies current at the time of the experience" (1999, p 217). If fantasies are active at the time of the experience, then clearly the declarative memory systems are up and running at that time, which is not what Fonagy asserts elsewhere. Fonagy nevertheless uses ideas about the dynamics related to declarative memories to make sense of how these other, implicit, memories enter clinical work.

At this point our discussion of memory processes leads to ideas related to modes of therapeutic action and the importance of autobiographical memory and its analysis in the unraveling of repressions, and it is to a brief consideration of these ideas that we now turn.

Therapeutic Technique

Memory Recovery and Reconstruction

Recovery of childhood memories was always an important part of analytic therapy for Freud, although from relatively early on it was regarded as only one aspect of analytic technique. Very early on in his development of psychoanalysis Freud realized the extent to which childhood memories were distorted and falsified through the process of repression, the formation of screen memories, and retranscription later in life (Freud, 1899). These ideas of Freud and their expansion and deepening in Ernst Kris's classic papers on memory and repression (1956a, b, c) are often used as a starting point for analysts to assert that after all we cannot know what really happened given these distortions, and that all we can know is what happens in the here and now and in the transference, and that therefore work at the level of the transference/countertransference is the main—perhaps the only—therapeutically effective work. The extreme proponents of this viewpoint assert that it is impossible to know anything about reality so that the search for what "really" happened in the past is meaningless.

This more extreme subjectivist position (which is perhaps now on the point of becoming mainstream rather than extreme) has many difficulties from a logical and philosophical point of view, difficulties that I will discuss in detail in the chapter on general theoretical issues (chapter 9). In relation to the topic at hand, if we take a statement such as "we know from the findings of Freud down to the present that memories of childhood are distorted both at their first registration, and then further distorted and retranscribed all through development, so that we have no true memories of our past, and from this we can see that we really cannot trust our memory in the least and therefore we can never really know what happened"—we can see that it contains a contradiction. If it is impossible to know what happened, then how can we know that our memories are distorted rather than truthful, much less know to what extent they are distorted and in what manner they are distorted? The findings and ideas of Freud and Kris only make sense within a framework of critical realism (Hanly and Fitzpatrick-Hanly, 2001), where the existence of a reality separate from our perception of it is assumed, but our ability to properly comprehend this reality is seen to be often flawed and subject to all sorts of error—but error that is at least potentially correctable.

Even leaving aside issues of reality and truthful memories, many psychoanalysts have attacked the idea of the recovery of repressed memories as a therapeutically useful technique. I have already quoted Fonagy, whose basic idea is that it is by improving a patient's mentalization (their ability to conceptualize and be aware of their own and others' mental processes) that patients are helped, and that memory recovery is only a byproduct of this process. Sugarman (2006) echoes these ideas, noting that even when we uncover content it is as a means to an end—the final aim being to make patients aware of their own functioning. Quite unfairly—but again echoing Fonagy—Sugarman describes earlier analysts as largely analyzing content. He notes that at times this may be necessary, "but even then, the point of this exploration is not to make the unconscious conscious or to promote ego ascendancy over the id. It is to promote our patient's mentalization" (2006, p 971). The views of others with different theoretical outlooks in other respects—such as Paul Gray (1994), or many modern adherents of object relations theory—converge on this idea of concentrating on the processes going on in the patient at the moment and downplaying memory and reconstruction of the past.

My own view is that this is another example of valuable ideas in analysis being overextended and overgeneralized. My reason for discussing these ideas at this point is that they represent one of a number of trends in modern analytic technique that work against the analysis of repressions. With some luck, but mainly through trial and error and clinical intuition, Freud developed a technique that was very well designed for the analysis of repressions, including primal repressions. As we shall see in the chapters that follow, this technique has certain limitations when it comes to analyzing denial defenses and traumas. Even with these it did not do too badly in its original form, which was quite flexible and which had a narrow definition of technique. In the 1950s and 1960s the broadening of this technique for analyzing repressions to include the entire therapeutic situation and relationship, which I described in the previous chapter, had a number of deleterious effects. Many analysts who were trained and analyzed with this technique rebelled against its coldness and actual lack of therapeutic efficacy and, as I also mentioned in the last chapter, ended up throwing out the baby (the techniques needed to analyze primal repressions) and keeping the bathwater (of an overly broad view of technique, which makes all aspects of analysis matters of technique).

So what is this baby? What are the techniques that aid us in analyzing repressions, and can we understand how and why they work based on our understanding of repression? And how do some newer ideas blunt these techniques, and thus our ability to analyze primal repressions?

Repression works against a drive by using its counterforce against the memories, fantasies, and feelings which the drive has spread over and into. These are pushed into the id, where the primary process reigns.[4] This mode of functioning involves condensations of a number of ideas into one, displacements along lines based on what to logical thought seem like superficial similarities, and a special type of symbolization. These characteristics reflect some of the malleability and connection with non-verbal, archaic thinking of the drives themselves. Through these processes of displacement and condensation the wishes and energy of the drives transfer onto more distant derivatives which can give some distorted and concealed expression to the repressed drive.

It has often been described how aspects of the analytic situation make use of these characteristics of the repressed. The recumbent position, the fundamental rule that asks the patient to say whatever comes to his or her mind no matter how unimportant or embarrassing it may be, and the analyst's listening silently, all aid both in a relaxing of defenses and in the transference of drive derivatives onto the analyst and the analytic situation. I gave a dramatic example of this in the case of my patient D, when he felt physically terrified of me as an attacking, castrating oedipal father. I noted how this intense reaction arose from a more general, subdued, and seemingly friendly father transference. I described the intense eruption of an oedipal conflict following the partial breakdown of a primal repression because it showed clearly a number of things: the use of secondary defenses to shore up repression, the burst of raw aggression consequent on the weakening of a primal repression, and the proper (i.e.—narrow) use of abstinence and neutrality.

In relation to the last issue, the reader may remember that D was thinking about wanting to kill his father and the wish was bubbling up. He finally said, "Oh, I don't know! I just want to curl up here. I want you to take control. Can't you just do some nice interpretation now? I really feel like a very small child." At this point he started to cry. "Why can't you take care of me? Just tell me what to do. You do the work." D was by this time very upset, crying, and pleading for help. In answer to all this I said, "Your conflicted feelings about your father seemed insoluble, and you regressed from a big boy to a small helpless child." In this response I could be seen to be acting like Freud's mirror or a blank screen and perhaps also with the coldness of a surgeon, given D's pleadings. I am not suggesting that it is necessary to make transference interpretations in as formal and mirroring a way as I made this particular one. My point is only that it is when faced with this sort of situation (an intense transference paired with reasonable therapeutic and working alliances) that various degrees of abstinence and neutrality are helpful in analyzing the transference and the patient's repressions.

Essentially abstinence and neutrality are helpful in both enhancing the flowering of the transference and in allying with the objective part of the patient in analyzing it once it has come to full flower. Most of the work with D—as with any patient—was not as dramatic as the sessions described. A combination of a friendly interest, neutrality and abstinence in relation to transferences that were arising, and interpretation of defenses and transference resistances led to a deepening of D's father transference.

The present-day tendency to look upon all aspects of the relationship as transference—to essentially flatten out the transference—acts against the interpretation of repression. The primal preoedipal, oedipal, and adolescent repressions are the core of the organized, powerful transferences referred to as the transference neurosis (Reed, 1994). It is the fostering, recognition, and interpretation of these that is the basis for the undoing of primal repressions. For instance, D began to wonder about what car I drove, noticed some small wooden model cars in my office, and a few times when I had taken phone calls (I usually do not answer the phone during sessions, but for various reasons did so a few times during our sessions) he was certain I was getting a call about my car getting repaired. All of these reactions related to specific aspects of his relationship with his father, to specific memories of being with his father, to certain fantasies related to his father, and had symbolic phallic sexual meanings. It would take up a good deal of space to demonstrate this in detail, but I would like to emphasize the key importance, in analyzing his repressions, of recovering the specific memories and fantasies that D's aggressive and sexual drives had spread over and invested. As Ernest Kris (1956a, c) so well described it, at a certain point in the analysis of these sorts of reactions a need for reconstructive interpretation is felt by both analyst and patient, and this self-propelled nature of good reconstructions goes beyond mere intellectualization.

Kris felt that memory recovery was especially important in analyzing repression. It helped to undo the repression through a process of the memory recovery leading to the loosening of repressive anticathexis (counterforce), the energies of this counterforce then being used to improve integration and the integrative function, this improved integration then aiding in further loosening the repression and further memory recovery, in a circular process. This is what happened in the case of D. I will give a detailed description of some of this analysis in chapter 8, on perversions. Kris's (1956a, b, c) case presentations are beautiful, and beautifully described, examples of this process, while Gail Reed (1993) has also given a detailed example of the value of explicit interpretation and reconstruction. The most detailed case presentations in this vein, as well as the most comprehensive discussion of the basic aspects of technique that help in the analysis of repressions, are contained in Greenson's (1967) classic book on analytic technique.

Interpreting the Mechanism of Repression

The interpretation of every defense requires the interpretation of the content defended against (the object of the defense), as well as interpretation of the nature of the defense (its mechanism), and its motive. These three basic aspects of any defense need each to be addressed in turn and, as time goes on, together, to show their interconnection. In the preceding section I discussed memory recovery and reconstruction, which is the interpretation of the object of the defense of repression. Interpretation of "content" (what I have referred to as the object of a defense) is no more inherently intellectualizing or speculative than the interpretation of the actual mechanism of the defense. In this section I discuss the interpretation of the mechanism of repression, which takes place concurrently, of course, with content analysis.

I described in chapter 1 how, in analyzing B's denial of her boyfriend's lack of caring, I pointed out to her that she herself had just described his lack of attention to her, and how he did not talk or interact much with her, but she still wanted to preserve the relationship. The patient turned the conversation to her previous boyfriend and her sadness, which was brought on by my mentioning her boyfriend's lack of caring, disappeared. I then interpreted her shift of attention, and B again became sad. Here, by confronting B with the object of her defense (her knowledge of her boyfriend's lack of caring), I fostered the emergence of the motive for the defense (sadness), and when this motive led to the shift of attention, this mechanism (an attentional shift) could be interpreted.

One can see relatively easily in this interpretation of a denial defense how confrontation of the patient with the content of the defense made the defense itself visible. How does this happen in the case of repression? The whole thing plays out quite differently in this case because both the object of the defense and the repression itself are partially formed by the drives and share their characteristics, and the characteristics of the primary process. When content interpretations such as reconstructions related to associations and transferences stir up the repressive defenses, they appear in the analysis in a manner in keeping with the malleable, displaceable aggressive drive from which they were formed. They do not appear, as do defenses based on ego functions such as attention and thinking, relatively straightforwardly as an ego maneuver to which the patient's attention can be drawn. Rather, with repression the partially neutralized aggression used as a counterforce is partially deneutralized, is captured by the transference, and is directed at the analyst.

Let us look at an example of this. I described the burst of anger D had when I interpreted his oedipal wishes. The rather sudden emergence and ego alien nature of this burst (at least many neurotic patients such as D will find it ego alien) mark it as a product of the breakdown of repression. I have found that with a little practice and attention paid to this manifestation, one can learn to distinguish it from the many other causes of anger. This is helpful in getting a sense of where the patient's repressions lie and, at times at least, it is helpful to point out this connection to the patient, as I did a number of times to D.

During the course of an analysis or analytic psychotherapy, however, it is especially as a transference resistance and negative transference that the defense of primal repression is transformed into an analyzable resistance. As one analyzes the objects of repression, they often appear as a transference. Resistance can appear in many ways in relation to the transference. There can be resistance to becoming aware of the transference, as well as displacement of the transference onto someone else. These resistances are, I would suggest, the product of the secondary defenses that, as described earlier, help to shore up primal repressions. The primal repression itself appears in the strengthening of the aggressive transference and in the use of other aspects of the transference for the purposes of resistance.

To continue with our example: D told me early on that he had, with two previous male therapists, become quite friendly and had ended up discussing movies and chatting about other things as a way of avoiding more painful issues. While even telling me about this may be seen as part of the resistance, I felt that D was also expressing a genuine concern and a piece of insight about how he might derail the therapy. We did in fact develop a quite friendly, warm relationship, much like the one D had had with his father. There was a hidden aggression in this transference, in that it expressed the wish to drag me down, as he had felt the wish to have his father at the same level as him—a friendly enough wish on the surface but with the wish to get rid of his father hidden within. We saw this more aggressive but deeply repressed aspect of the relationship come out in the sessions described previously. When D had begun to wonder about my car, and then had said that it was surely the car repair garage phoning when I took a phone call, I wondered out loud what this meant for him. D produced, with some slight resistance, a number of connections to times when he had felt close to his father. When we probed more deeply and found a childhood wish to have a penis as big as his father's, he then had the thought of me putting my penis in his anus. "But I'm only thinking that because I'm here. It's really your idea."

"But I never mentioned anything of the sort."

"Oh, you know what I mean. It's the sort of thing you *would* think about and you led me there."

"Maybe you are trying to throw it on me to disavow it and not look at the idea."

"Now I'm getting angry. You may actually be right but I don't like it. I'm angry you're pushing me and probing me. It's all your doing."

This is the sort of burst of anger I would associate with the partial undoing of a repression, but I bring up the example also to demonstrate what happens after this. D woke up the next day somewhat irritated at me and this lasted for a while. At the same time he became much more insistent on our friendly relationship. He regaled me with stories both comic and interesting, and when I interpreted either the story's content or its defensive use he insisted that he really just had to finish this one story, but then would go off on another interesting tangent that he "just had to finish" telling me about.

I would get lost in all this, not quite remembering where we had started and whether perhaps I was being pushy or too single-minded. Then at times

I would come out of it enough to realize what was going on and interpret that D's interaction with me was serving the function of resistance, specifically resistance to the sexual ideas that were emerging. This line of interpretation was not a matter of a few weeks or months, but rather continued throughout D's long analysis. Again and again, in different ways, I would be led to point out the resistance function of aspects of the transference, although at different times the particular aspect of the transference used as a resistance differed, as did the things each particular transference resistance protected. I would argue that it is this analysis of the transference resistance—taking place over the course of therapy and moving between content analysis, reconstruction, and the analysis of the resistance, including the transference resistance—that constitutes the analysis of the mechanism of primal repression.

It is from the nature of the resistance that we infer the nature of the defense, and I would argue that from the long drawn out process of analysis and working through required to analyze the transference resistance, we infer the strength and wide reach of a primal repression, and from the way the resistance takes the form of direct anger at the therapist and aggression that infiltrates existing transference reactions and gives them the character of resistance—from these we infer the nature of the counterforce in repression as being formed from partially neutralized aggressive drive energy. We also get a sense of the drive origins of the mechanism of repression by its very great malleability—by the way in which the counterforce of repression can metamorphose into an angry rebellion against the analyst, or into a much more subtle use of a warm relationship to avoid certain feelings and memories. The ability to transform the counterforce is much reduced in borderline patients, where it generally manifests in a powerful angry negative transference and in projective identifications. (This lack of malleability of the counterforce in borderlines is a clue to their major deficit, which relates to drive neutralization.)

In relation to the changes in analytic technique that work against the analysis of primal repression, I have already mentioned the new ideas about different forms of memory, which downplay the importance of declarative memories and their retrieval, a retrieval that is crucial in the analysis of the drives that have invested these memories and the fantasies built upon them. Because of the depth and wide extent of major primal repressions, reconstruction of not only autobiographical memories, but also of an autobiography that ties all of these together and integrates them, is important. A tendency to stress the transference-countertransference, "here-and-now" as being what is significant, and a postmodernist distrust of nailing down what "really happened," leads many therapists to de-emphasize or even completely abandon this crucially important work. (An exception, interestingly, is often made for the reconstruction of what went on in very early infancy.) There has also been a change in the way that many analysts view resistance, and especially transference resistance. It is said that what were seen as transference resistances and enactments are actually communications and are informative of the past and present, and that they should be treated as such. This is often not incorrect, but it is now used to argue against the interpretation of the resistive aspects of the transference. The idea of interpreting to a patient that they are resisting is now in many quarters seen as a negative comment—a condemnation of the patient rather than part of a collaborative effort to understand the patient's defenses.

Leaving aside for now the more general issue of resistance analysis and looking at the analysis of primal repression, one particular development is particularly relevant: the idea, proposed by Heinz Kohut and others, that the patient's anger at the therapist is always or almost always a product of empathic failure and a misattuned response on the part of the therapist. The idea that this may sometimes be the case and that there are in fact quite a number of possible causes for a patient being angry at the therapist, is surely not open to question. But in his book *The Restoration of the Self*, Kohut (1977) states emphatically that *whenever* a patient becomes angry at the analyst, the therapist should pull back from the particular line of interpretation that he or she was following and look into the specific empathic ruptures that led to the angry response. This, he proposes, is the method of cure. Through the transmuting internalizations that follow from the working through of these empathic failures, defects and a lack of cohesion in the patient's self are ameliorated. My argument is not so much with Kohut's ideas of cure as such but with their overextension and with the jettisoning of the analysis of the transference resistance. If this overextension is carried through to the extent that Kohut proposed, the resulting technique can be guaranteed to never undo a primal repression. It may be argued that after all many self psychologists, and many other therapists who use Kohut's ideas, do so in a more circumscribed manner than Kohut himself. This may be so, but I do think that the ideas of Kohut and others with regard to the aggressive reactions of patients and the transference resistance have led to a decline in the analysis of primal repressions.

In saying this I am not suggesting that every angry response should be interpreted in relation to repressive defenses. These responses can have many other sources. However, when one can clearly see the relation of these responses to a repression—as in the case of D—it is imperative to bring the response to the patient's attention. I think the technique should certainly not be admonishing or accusatory, but should consist of pointing out to the patient the surprising extent of the anger, and linking it to a possible repressive defense. One attempts to get the patient to look at this reaction and wonder about its origins. I have also found it helpful to point out to patients the striking difference between this explosive anger—which often then settles into a transference resistance of one sort or another—and their reactions when even very strong denials or dissociative defenses are confronted. Many patients become quite good at spotting this particular reaction when they have it, and in differentiating it from other angry responses and from the responses when other types of defenses are confronted. They thus get to know and feel and see close up the nature of their strongest repressions, which is of great help in weakening these repressions, as well as being a wonderful piece of self-knowledge in its own right.

Some sort of confrontation of the patient with the content of the repressed is necessary in order to mobilize, and allow the analysis of, these responses, but as they are analyzed and weakened, one gets access to more and more repressed material, the analysis of which strengthens integrative capacities and further weakens the repression, leading to a virtuous circle of defense and content analysis reinforcing each other's effect. Maintaining a friendly, respectful attitude towards the patient, giving the real relationship its full due, and working to foster and maintain a reasonable alliance, are all crucial in analyzing primal repressions. These both foster the object related transferences that bring the repressed to light, and allow the neutral, abstinent stance needed in the analysis of these transferences and transference resistances to be understood and appreciated by the patient as helpful techniques, rather than as painful attacks or deprivations.

Summary

The idea of repression as involving a counterforce, introduced in the last chapter, was further investigated. In order to aid in this investigation, two conceptual clarifications were presented. First, Freud's early conceptualization of primal repression was discussed. During this early phase Freud saw primal repression as a passive lagging behind of certain mental contents during early development, so that they were never taken into the secondary processes and connected with language. Frank and Muslin (1967) called this passive primal repression. I argued that this outcome of developmental processes involves no active defensive processes and does not condition later repressions, so that calling it primal repression is inaccurate and confusing.

I argued for not designating this process as primal repression, but rather reserving the term, as Freud did in his later writings, for the powerful, active counterforce defense that pushes drive derivatives and associated feelings and memories into the deeper unconscious, and uses a constant counterforce to keep them there. Freud called the motive for primal repression traumatic anxiety, and my second conceptual clarification was to argue for the replacement of this term by "pervasive anxiety" (Yorke, Wiseberg, and Freeman, 1989). In true trauma there is a massive shutdown of many ego functions, including those that process affect and integrate experience, leading to a numb feeling. In this state, defenses such as repression are not brought into play. I think there is ample clinical evidence that it is pervasive anxiety, rather than a traumatic state, that is the motor that drives primal repression, just as other pervasive affects can motivate other primal defenses.

Armed with these conceptual clarifications, we looked at the nature of repression. We saw that the basic counterforce of repression was supported by other defenses. These included after repressions that built directly upon the primal repression, were motivated by a signal of anxiety rather than pervasive anxiety that flooded the mind, and involved a smaller counterforce plus ego de-investment. These after repressions were distinguished from secondary defenses, which can be any sort of defense, such as denial or externalization, which assist in keeping derivatives that escape primal repression from becoming conscious.

In terms of the actual mechanism of primal repression, I tried to demonstrate that the clinical data pointed to a derivation of the counterforce from partially neutralized aggressive drive energy. This led to a discussion of the psychoanalytic conceptualization of the drives. I argued that the drives are not the only motivators of behavior, but that they are distinguished from other motivators, such as hunger, thirst, and affects, by their immense malleability, their displaceability, and their susceptibility to being neutralized to varying degrees by the ego: that is, to having their energy left largely intact but their aims and nature distanced from their original state.

In looking more closely at the mechanism of repressions we were led to distinguish the blocking seen commonly in adolescence, in which a rather indiscriminate counterforce is the main mechanism, from selective repression. In selective repression a greater drive neutralization leads to the drive being used in a more differentiated, selective way in barring certain drive derivatives and the feelings and memories/fantasies associated with them from conscious awareness.

In looking at the object of repression, we saw that repression is directed generally at drives and the wishes and feelings that derive from them. Given the way in which sexual and aggressive drive energy spreads over and invests certain declarative memories, these also become an important object of repression. Implicit (procedural and emotional) memories are generally spared by repression. For this reason, analysis of repression necessarily involves interpretation of declarative (autobiographical) memories.

In the technique section I emphasized the importance of content analysis (reconstruction). By interpreting these declarative memories (which, with their drive investment, are the main objects of repression) one rouses the resistance derived from repression. When one does this something that is problematic for the therapist, but quite fascinating theoretically, takes place: the patient develops an aggressive response to the therapist, in a direct outburst of anger and/or in an increased aggressive use of already existing transferences. I argued that the differences in these angry responses and transference resistances when repression is challenged as compared to challenging even very strong denials or dissociative defenses demonstrates the derivation of repression from partially neutralized aggression. To put it another way: the resistance produced by the defense of repression is some form of negative transference and/or transference resistance, and the way in which the mechanism of repression is malleable and displaceable enough to form into a transference betrays its derivation from the drives. This can be contrasted to the way in which defenses based on ego mechanisms form resistances, such as the shifting of attention in denial, which do not display the same malleability, displaceability, and capability of neutralization and deneutralization that we see in the drives.

Terms

Active Primal Repression: See *primal repression.*

After Defense: After defenses are milder versions of a primal defense that build upon the primal defense and buttress it. They are motivated by milder versions of the pervasive affect that motivates the original primal defense. These milder versions are referred to as signal affect. As an example, after repression helps by repressing drive derivatives (for instance derivatives of a murderous impulse) that manage to get by a primal repression, and is motivated by a signal of anxiety that the ego puts out as it senses the danger associated with these derivatives.

Neutralization: In neutralization of a drive, the energy of the drive is left largely intact but its aims and nature are distanced from their original state. As an example, partially neutralized aggressive drive energy is used to form the counterforce of selective repression. In this defense the raw destructive aims of the drive are tamed and put to use to push other drives and strong feelings into the unconscious, and hold them there through a continuous application of force. This counterforce has some of the aims of the drive, but tamed and stabilized. A very similar partially neutralized aggressive drive energy is used in erecting and maintaining stable boundaries between the self and others.

Passive Primal Repression: An outcome of development, in which as the mind matures and language and symbolic processing is acquired, some of the mind's contents (affects, memories) are not taken up into the more mature, secondary process functioning, and remain behind in the id, subject to the primary process. This was Freud's original idea of primal repression, which he later abandoned.

Pervasive Affect: An affect of such strength and intensity that the ego's usual methods of dealing with affect (including expression in bodily processes, action, and words, containment by symbolic processing, and suppression) are not sufficient, and powerful defensive processes called primal defenses are used to manage the affect. They often do not manage the affect directly—for instance primal repression does not usually repress pervasive anxiety, or at least that is not all it does. Rather the cause of the affect—for instance sexual wishes that lead to the pervasive castration anxiety—is attacked by the defense.

Primal Repression: A defense in which partially neutralized aggressive drive energy is used in forming a powerful counterforce that bars drive derivatives (wishes) and the affects and explicit (declarative and semantic) memories associated with them from conscious awareness. These are the *objects* of primal repression. The motive for this defense is usually pervasive anxiety.

Primary Process: A form of mental functioning, closely related to the drives, in which energies are easily displaceable, along lines of superficial similarity, and in which one element can come to stand for many (condensation). The primary process is geared towards immediate gratification and discharge of drive energies. There is a disregard for logical consistency. Contradictory ideas and impulses coexist side by side without conflict. There is no time sense nor are elements of the primary process affected by the passage of time.

Secondary Defense: A secondary defense is any defense, other than an after defense, that helps to buttress a primal defense. These may be any sort of defense that the ego finds at hand and finds useful in secondarily defending against contents that escape the original primal defense. For instance it is common for various forms of denial to be used against some of the derivatives that escape primal repression.

Secondary Process: A basic form of mental functioning, the secondary process works with tightly bound, stable energies. It uses verbal symbols and logical, rational thought. It is ruled by the reality principle, compared to the primary process, which is ruled by the pleasure principle.

Traumatic Anxiety: Freud gave this name to the overwhelming anxiety that motivates primal repression. It is a misleading term, however, and I have suggested that it should be dropped in favor of the term pervasive anxiety. In true trauma many ego functions, including processing of affects and the defensive processes, are temporarily put out of commission. This does not lead directly to repression.

Notes

1. In psychoanalysis, nothing is ever uncomplicated. In chapter 6 I will describe certain narcissistic aspects of D's character that did weaken his repressions, although not to the extent found in borderline disorders. This weakness is evident in the example of work I have described, where the oedipal conflicts appear more easily than one might expect.

2. In chapter 9, as part of a broader discussion of psychoanalytic theory, I will present some more detailed ideas about the drives, ego functions, and evolution.

3. The anger also helped to defend against the sadness and intense psychic pain that were the true motives for the primal denial of the knowledge of his mother's lack of deeper love for him.

4. This spatial metaphor is really just a shorthand way of talking and thinking of these very complex processes involving changes of functioning.

CHAPTER THREE

~

Denial

In this chapter we probe more deeply into the basic mechanism of denial, comparing it with, and differentiating it from, that of repression. I will first describe this basic mechanism and then look at some of the ways in which denial and repression interact. Next, I will discuss the nature of our reality awareness that allows the attentional shift of denial to be used so effectively to defend against it. We will see that there are aspects of inner reality that can also be defended against using denial. Defenses are also part of inner reality, and the defenses that defend against a conscious awareness of defenses are also denial defenses. These first set of discussions continue some of the more detailed theoretical work of the last chapter, and lay the groundwork for what is to come. After describing these, I will present a clinical example of a primal denial. Primal denial is the analogue of primal repression. It is a stable, powerful defense motivated by pervasive affects. I will also describe universal primal denials that we all share, such as our denial of our own fragility and death. Finally, I will discuss how denial is analyzed, arguing for the importance of the therapist actively speaking for the denied reality. This need for a greater degree of activity in the analysis of denial versus the analysis of repression can be understood based on both the nature of the defense, and especially based on the nature of what is defended against. Reality, unlike the drives or strong feelings, does not have a very strong push towards awareness, and our greater activity when analyzing denial substitutes for this push.

While denial is usually used to defend against the awareness of unpleasant realities, it is important to define it based on its mechanism (use of attentional and other processes of the ego), rather than its usual object (reality). Doing so allows a deeper understanding of the nature of denial. Denial does not always present in as straightforward a manner as B's denial of her boyfriend's lack of caring. In her paper on denial and repression, Edith Jacobson (1957) presents examples of the use that psychotic patients make of denial processes when their repression barrier and the rigid reaction formations with which they attempt to shore it up break down. For instance, a male patient may explicitly express his sexual love for his mother. On first inspection this may be taken as an example of pure id wishes flooding into consciousness. Jacobson, however, points out that with closer scrutiny one will find a more feared wish against which the expression of the positive oedipal one defends: the wish for a passive homosexual surrender. Jacobson describes this as one id fragment being used to defend against another. She points out that something similar may be taking place in the ultra-clear memories such patients will have for whole periods of their early childhood, which seem to defend against other periods for which there may be a suspicious absence of any memory.

Basic Nature of Denial

Jacobson's examples highlight some interesting aspects of denial. To begin with, we may ask why we would consider them as instances of denial. It is clearly not because they involve a defense against the awareness of external reality. In fact, I would think Jacobson chose these examples specifically because they show that there is something important about the process of denial that does not depend on the defense being used against reality. This something is the shifting of attention, in this case from one id fragment to another. In the classic denial defenses described by Anna Freud (1936)—denial in word, in act, and in fantasy—the shifting of attention from an unpleasant reality to a pleasant one, real or imagined, is obvious. In the case of B, the woman with the uncaring boyfriend whom I described in chapter 1, it was easy to see the various places to which she shifted her attention each time her awareness of her boyfriend's lack of caring began to make her sad.

Unfortunately, the *word* denial does not suggest the attentional shift that is at the heart of the *process* of denial, but rather suggests only the purpose of the defense—to say "no" to something, or to negate a reality. This purpose is the purpose of every defense so that in this colloquial sense, as Brenner (1982) pointed out, every defense involves a denial. But in the more specific sense, in which the word denotes a process, this is not the case. Jacobson (1957) and Fine et al. (1969) note that in this sense denial involves a hypercathexis of an alternate percept or fantasy, in contrast to repression, which involves a countercathexis (what I have called a counterforce). Stewart (1970) said that repression takes place between the ego and the id, while denial is intrasystemic—that is, it takes place within one system: the ego. He continued, "This would also imply in economic terms that drive cathexis is removed in repression, whereas in denial or disavowal, the energy withdrawn is primarily attention cathexis" (p 11). Here Stewart is making two points: a structural/topographic one (about where in the mind these defenses work) and one about forms of energy and investment (cathexis). I would like to take each of these points up in turn.

From a structural point of view, is it true that repression only takes place between the ego and the id? In the previous chapter I gave examples of after repression such as the forgetting of a name. If one looks closely at such mild instances of unconsciously motivated forgetting (after repression), one can see that even in these cases, the forgotten word or other material has become subject to the methods of working of the primary process. Freud (1901) showed this with numerous examples long ago, and it can easily be confirmed if one looks at the associations that enter one's mind in such instances. It is obvious that the forgotten material has come under the sway of the familiar primary process mechanisms of condensation and easy displacement along lines of superficial association. Thus it would seem to be true that repression, even if it is a relatively transient one, is something that takes place between the ego and the id or, to put it another way, involves the replacement of secondary process, reality oriented functioning with primary process functioning.

And what of denial? Is it true that it takes place completely within the ego? A quick inspection of our example, of B's denying her boyfriend's lack of caring, shows that this must be true, for this instance at least. What came to B's mind when her denial was in operation were not ideas derived from the thought of her boyfriend being uncaring being subject to condensation and displacement (i.e., the primary process). Rather, she thought of ideas, for instance that she was narcissistic and uncaring or that her boyfriend could on occasion be quite nice, which were the opposite of the idea with which she was uncomfortable.

How can we know, however, that B's thinking that she, rather than her boyfriend, was self-centered, was not a product of primary process displacement? I think the answer is that each of the things that came to B's mind, even those that involved displacing her awareness of self-centeredness from her boyfriend onto others, followed logically from her wish to not be aware of a painful reality. They were not a product merely of displacement along lines of superficial similarity, as happens for instance in the case of a word that has been forgotten. To look at an example of this given earlier: D, the patient whose primal repression was described in the last chapter, came up with a long series of associations relating to blood and bodily injury after I had interpreted his defense of regression to passivity. It became clear during the course of the session, and the rest of the analysis, that these ideas were derivatives of D's terrible fear that his penis would be cut off, as well as of certain incidents where he had been shocked at the sight of blood in his very early childhood. The associations that flowed from these repressed memories and fantasies involved paintings he had seen that had red in them, intrusive thoughts of injuring other parts of his body, and an incident in adolescence the details of which I have withheld. It is clear that D's associations were often connected to the repressed material by the most superficial and irrational of displacements, and involved similarly non-rational condensations of many memories and fantasies from the past.

Having pointed to the sort of evidence supporting the truth of Stewart's statements regarding the structural differences between denial and repression, I think it can be seen that these structural differences are related to the energic ones. If repression involves a mental content coming under the sway of the primary process, then it is clear that its investment by the secondary processes would have to be given up. Up to this point we have looked at the counterforce aspect of repression, but it is most likely that both counterforce and de-investment are involved. Freud (1915b) felt that primal repression involved only a counterforce, while after repression consisted of a counterforce plus a preconscious de-investment. The way to ascertain this is to observe the form of resistance one meets as these defenses are analyzed. We have looked at this in detail in relation to primal repression in the last chapter. The level of counterforce is quite different in after repression than in primal repression. After repression is more easily reversed, without the emergence of the same level of angry responses that are evident upon the reversal of a primal repression. I would take this particular occurrence as evidence for the relatively smaller contribution of counterforce in after repression, while the fact that the mental content still becomes subject to the primary process indicates that a preconscious de-investment takes place.

To turn now to denial: Stewart suggests, as have other authors, that it involves a withdrawal of attention. But we could wonder, given what we have been discussing just now, how the withdrawal of attention in denial relates to the withdrawal of preconscious investment in after repression. We know there is a difference by the different outcome. In after repression the content becomes subject to the primary process, while in denial it does not.

This is why I prefer to describe the process in denial as a shifting, rather than a withdrawal, of attention. The mental content is kept within the sphere of the secondary processes, and in this sense it is still invested in by the ego.

It seems to me misleading to refer to a "hypercathexis" in denial, since the term suggests drive investment. When Jacobson (1957) uses it she is probably referring to attentional processes, but other authors explicitly state the similarity between the forces used in repression and denial. Altshul (1968), for instance, considered the hypercathexis of an opposing reality in denial to be analogous to the countercathexis used in repression. While few analysts today would use this terminology, many would agree with the idea that repression and denial use similar forces.

I think, on the contrary, that a number of lines of evidence point to quite different origins for these two forces. I have already described one: the angry outburst that occurs when primal repression is weakened, which points to the counterforce being derived from partially neutralized aggression. This consistent response is not seen with the undoing of denial. Of course for some people, in relation to certain denials, there is no better way to elicit an angry response than to challenge the denial. But in many of these cases there are other factors involved, such as that the denial has been shoring up weakening primary repressions in patients with structural weaknesses (borderline disorders), or that the denial has been helping to keep a superego attack at bay by denying responsibility, and when the denial is challenged the superego aggression is directed at whomever challenged the denial. The case of D is a very apt one in showing the difference between repression and denial, since he had some very striking narcissistic features, and used denial a great deal. As I pointed out in the previous chapter, in the early part of the analysis, as we dealt especially with these narcissistic issues and denials, the characteristic burst of anger that followed on the undoing of his primal repressions was not present.

Another line of evidence comes from borderline and psychotic disorders. In borderline conditions, where the repression barrier is, to a varying extent, weak, denial defenses are resorted to in order to shore up this weakness. Similarly, but much more dramatically, in psychosis, as shown by Jacobson's example from the beginning of this chapter, as the counterforce mechanisms of primal repression and reaction formation break down completely, denial processes involving attention are still much more functional and are enlisted to defend against one id wish by emphasizing another. Clearly the weakening or loss of the ability to develop counterforce defenses does not lead to a similar weakening of the functioning of denial, which certainly suggests that different processes using different energies are at work.

I would suggest that denial uses the neutral energy that is available to the ego, and that is used in such ego functions as attention, while repression uses partially neutralized aggressive drive energy. If one looks more closely, this generalization breaks down, since repression can certainly use ego energies as well, while a more careful look at the development of the ego would demon-strate that some of the energies that it has at its disposal are derived from the drives. Still, the statement about the different energies used in attentional and counterforce defenses captures the major trends, and is adequate for most purposes.

Interaction of Denial and Repression

Repression and denial interact with each other in interesting and important ways. So far, we have seen how the shifting of attention in denial makes common cause with the libidinal investment involved in screen memories, and at examples of denial being used as a secondary line of defense when primal repression is weakened. The opposite sequence, in which denial is used to deal with a conflict that is subsequently mastered using repression, is also common. Jacobson (1957) said that oedipal wishes and fears are prob-ably first held in check using denial prior to their repression. As the oedipal conflict increases in intensity, repression is brought into play to deal with the powerful sexual and aggressive wishes that are leading to intense conflict, as it was in the case of D.

Why does denial work so well against a feeling (such as B's sadness at her boyfriend's lack of caring) and so badly against a drive (such as in Jacobson's example of a psychotic man described at the beginning of this chapter)? The answer lies, I think, in some basic differences between drives and affects. A drive exerts a continuous (although variable in intensity) pressure, with its origins in the interior of the mind. This pressure pushes a person toward some behavior, a behavior that leads to the lowering of the drive tension. While the massive counterforce of primal repression is capable of blocking the forward movement of a drive, the attentional shift of denial is helpless against it. When we say that someone is using denial against a drive, we usually mean that he or she is using it against the perception that they have certain wishes (a denial of inner reality), perhaps to help out a weakening repression that is trying to hold the fort against the force of the drive. This is what I described happening in the case of D, as he denied he had any aggres-sive wishes toward his father or sexual ones toward his mother, just as they were threatening to overwhelm his repression.

Affects, on the other hand, may either be an expression of a drive or a reaction to external happenings. In fact, in many situations where a feeling may be thought to be simply the derivative of a drive, things are more complex. Take D's anger at his father during the oedipal phase, for instance. Is this simply a manifestation of D's aggressive drive? Initially, as with most young boys in this situation, his anger, as part of a strong feeling of jealousy, was stirred by seeing his mother and father together. At this point, denial of the parents' emotional and sexual involvement with each other worked to keep his jealousy from developing. This suggests that the feelings of jealousy and anger were largely a reaction to this reality, and not to as great an extent a direct manifestation of the aggressive drive. Later, as the intensity of D's sexual love for his mother and his corresponding jealousy and anger grew, the fear of retaliation from his father also grew, motivating repression of the whole complex of wishes and memories.

In this sequence it is only in the later stages, as D's jealousy of his father grew to a burning hatred that included death wishes, that the full force of the aggressive drive was turned against his father. Earlier, since it was a reaction to an external perception, his denial of this reality effectively cut short the development of the feeling of anger, just as B cut short her feelings of sadness and anger at her boyfriend by denying his lack of caring.

In general, if an unpleasant feeling is a reaction to an aspect of reality denial can be, and often is, used to defend against it. To be more precise, we should say that the unpleasant feeling motivates the use of denial against that portion of reality that caused the feeling. The efficacy of denial has its limits, however, and I think we can see, in the example of D's oedipal conflicts, when these limits were reached. At a certain point D's feelings about his parents became fully embroiled in sexual and aggressive conflicts, and it was at this point that some version of repression was called in. The previous use of denial in relation to events going on between his parents was not adequate to handle the powerful drive conflicts involved.

A sequence of defenses such as that demonstrated by D is actually quite common. Two well-known examples are the family romance fantasy (Freud, 1909a) and the beating fantasy (Freud, 1919). In the family romance fantasy, young children develop an elaborate story in which they are actually adopted, and in which their "true" parents are much finer in many ways than their "adoptive" parents. This is a reaction to painful feelings engendered by the child's growing awareness of the various failings of their actual parents. It is essentially an exercise in denial in fantasy, although the idea of distancing oneself from one's true parents obviously also aids in the repression of oedipal wishes. At the same time, after the fantasy is formed it can attract, and be influenced by, various sexual and ambitious wishes. It is its connection with these wishes that leads to the fantasy being, in many cases, repressed. Similarly the beating fantasy begins, at least according to Freud (1919), with something that looks very much like a denial in fantasy: "My father doesn't love that new baby because look at how he hates it and is beating it," seems to be the meaning of the first version. Although this first version certainly gives expression to strong aggressive wishes against the young rival, it is only as the fantasy becomes embroiled in, and is reworked to become an expression of, the masochistic aims of the oedipal phase, that it is forcefully repressed.

What we have in these instances, however, is not a simple two step process of denial followed by repression. Even as the repression attacks certain fantasies and memories because they have become connected to anxiety producing wishes, the reality that led to the original denial usually continues, requiring the continued use of denial defenses. To put all of this in different terms, we could say that even as certain judgments about reality and the fantasies used to deny them are put under the power of the primary processes by primal or after repression, denial defenses continue to operate against these realities, and produce fantasies. The awareness of the realities that are denied remains within the secondary processes; however, because there now exists repressed content related to aspects of what is denied, they are much more likely to again be drawn into the primary processes by after repression. This can work in the opposite direction as well, in which a fantasy that is a compromise formed secondary to repression is taken up and used for the purposes of denial. Some parts of the family romance fantasy are born in this way as products of the primal oedipal repression, and are then reworked in early latency into a fantasy which denies the failings of the child's parents. This second fantasy then becomes caught up in later sexual and aggressive conflicts and is for this reason repressed. That denial and repression, along with other defenses, can form complex chains of this sort has been noted by many authors (e.g., Linn, 1953; Wurmser, 2000).

Reality

Having looked at the basic nature (in terms of mechanism, topographic location and energy used) of denial, as well as its motives and its interactions with repression, we are now in a position to consider what denial is usually directed against—reality. It makes sense that a defense that involves a shifting of attention works so well against reality, or at least against the memories of reality. These memories do not push for satisfaction or expression as do drives and affects. In fact, they require that attention be turned towards them in order to become conscious. Even perception itself, as shown by decades of research (Fisher, 1954, 1956; LeDoux, 1996), is at first an unconscious process, and a further act of attention is needed to make it conscious.

Thus, a shifting of attention is often sufficient in itself to keep an aspect of reality out of consciousness. From this fact is derived one of the most interesting and most frustrating things about denial: its amazingly stubborn persistence despite a surface appearance of being relatively easily undone. Since the defense involves, at least in the most straightforward cases, a shifting of attention, it is often sufficient to merely shift the person's attention back in order to undo it temporarily. (I am leaving aside issues of splitting of the ego for now, although in many instances of denial, this splitting adds to the underlying persistence.) For instance, I could point out to B various aspects of her boyfriend's narcissism or meanness, qualities she herself had described or that were relatively easy to deduce from her descriptions, and she would begin to become aware of these denied aspects of what he was really like. The resulting feelings of sadness and pain would then lead her to turn her attention away again from these realities. Unlike a wish or a fantasy that is an expression of a drive, the reality of her boyfriend's extreme narcissism and lack of caring did not press forward on its own account towards consciousness. Of course as long as she was around him, B saw things that again and again showed this side of him, but even here the pressure towards awareness was of a different order than that of a drive. Also, various secondary maneuvers, such as acting in such a way as to keep her boyfriend in a good mood, could be brought in by B to help bolster her denial.

I would not want to give the impression that defending against the awareness of an unpleasant reality is a relatively easy matter. It is, rather, that what opposes a defense against reality is quite different from that which opposes a defense against a drive derivative. In the latter case, it is the pressure that the drive itself exerts towards awareness and action that opposes a defense, while in the former case it is the ego's attachment to, and investment in, reality, and in an objective judgment of it.

A person's ability to test reality, in the narrow sense of being able to distinguish a wish or a fantasy from reality, is present from a very young age. However, in the early years this ability is vulnerable on two fronts. On the one hand, as a newly acquired and immature function, it is easily lost under any situation of stress that leads to regression. On top of this a young child simply does not care as much about the differentiation between reality and fantasy as does an older child or an adult. As the ego grows so does its allegiance to a clearer delineation of what is real and what is not. (It is easy to overlook this allegiance in these so-called postmodern times, but even the most ardent postmodernist adherent to ideas of a constructed reality will demonstrate this allegiance continually in their day-to-day life, despite their theoretical ideas.)

Thus a young child is able to deny many unpleasant realities of his or her life. While these early denials are generally adaptive, and to some extent give way to an acceptance of reality as the child matures, certain of them, which I propose to call primal denials, provide the template for the denials of later childhood and adulthood. These later denials (after denials) have to take account of a greater allegiance on the person's part to reality, and thus often (though certainly not always) operate by subtler means than primal denials. For instance, a reality might be intellectually accepted even as its deeper significance is denied. Basch (1983) suggested that the term disavowal be used to describe this process of not acknowledging the full meaning of a percept, while denial should be used to designate a defense against the perceptual process itself (a radical de-investment in reality), such as occurs in psychosis. He argues, using a careful reading of the texts, that Freud also had two concepts in mind and gave them two different names (*verneinung, verleugnung*).

To the extent that this is merely a terminological issue there is nothing at stake, and one could just as well refer to the process I have described either as denial or disavowal. What I would like to stress is not so much the actual word but something else: the process of an attentional shift can be used to defend directly against the awareness of an aspect of reality; it can be used to defend against a subtle aspect of the meaning of a reality that is seemingly acknowledged; and it can be used to defend against many realities that lie in between these two extremes. In all these cases what is interfered with is neither the perception, nor the registration into short-term memory, nor the consolidation into long-term memory, of a reality, but rather the retrieval of the memory from short- or long-term memory storage and/or the integration of sets of memories and the subsequent formation of judgments about their meaning.

To look at the example of B in relation to these ideas: she would often describe a particular behavior of her boyfriend, but then by making excuses for him ("he was quite tired, really") or changing the topic to describe other times when he was not mean, or instances when she or someone else had been nasty, B would manage to avoid drawing the obvious conclusions from the behavior she was describing: that her boyfriend treated her quite badly and that the implication of the totality of his behavior toward her was that he cared very little for her and was using her for his own ends. Basch would call this disavowal, since it was especially the broader implications of what was perceived that were kept from awareness. A young child faced with a

similar situation—for instance with a self-centered and unloving parent—
would most likely attack the distressing reality more directly, with a fantasy
of the parent being loving, or of having a different parent who was loving. In
fact B was one such child, with an extremely narcissistic and nasty mother
and a father who was not much better. Her later denials of her boyfriend's
lack of caring were based on primal denials of similar characteristics in her
parents. The differences in the earlier and the later denials were of degree,
not kind. The earlier denials tended towards more wholesale defenses against
the reality that confronted her. As B grew a little older they began to involve
more subtle mechanisms such as making excuses for her parents. The adult
versions of these defenses could themselves at times descend to bald statements, such as that her boyfriend was always very loving and caring with her,
even as they often involved less blatant distortions of reality. Both versions
were directed, using the attentional processes of the ego, against the conscious awareness of memories and judgments.

The crucial differentiation is not between an attentional shift that defends against the awareness of a reality and one that defends against the
awareness of the significance of a reality (both of which I have chosen to
call denial, but which could also be called disavowal), but rather between
these maneuvers and others that also affect the retrieval of memories through
different processes (repression), as well as still others that affect the percep-
tion/memory processes at different stages, such as reception or consolidation.
These latter processes include the massive drive de-investment of reality and
breakdown of the ego function of reality testing that occurs in the psychoses,
as well as the overwhelming and temporary paralysis of ego functions that
occurs in trauma. In both cases denial may, and usually does, operate as well,
but it should be distinguished from other processes that have a quite different
mechanism.

Inner Reality

Hartmann (1956) noted that beyond the narrow aspect of reality testing—
to know what is real versus what is imagined—there are more interpretive
aspects that can be impaired by defense (as we discussed above), as well as
conventional realities and social norms. Hartmann noted that social reality
and norms work to block knowledge of inner reality. He also made the important point that inner reality should not be equated with psychic reality
(which, in the terminology of the time, meant fantasies, wishes, and other
drive derivatives), and that inner reality can be tested, and defended against
by denial, in much the same manner as external reality.

Examples of aspects of inner reality that are not direct derivatives of the drives include a knowledge of one's feelings and moods, a knowledge of the existence and meaning of the intuitive "gut feelings" one gets upon meeting someone new, a knowledge of one's thoughts in general, and a knowledge of the existence and manner of working of one's defenses. Awareness of each of these inner realities can be interfered with by denial. Knowledge about feelings and moods can be denied. For instance, a person quite prone to depressive moods may declare with full conviction that they are rarely depressed. The denial of this inner reality does not by itself affect the actual development of the mood.

A gut feeling is actually the conscious perception of the outcome of a complex preconscious assessment of another person, unconstrained by verbal and other superficial aspects of their presentation. This has some of the characteristics of a feeling because it is connected to the early intuitive awareness of others, from a time when thoughts and physical feelings were not separated off, and when thoughts generally led to body feelings. However, a gut feeling does not have the same strong push toward awareness that affects do, and in this sense it resembles a thought. Because of this lack of push, gut feelings, just like thoughts, can be kept out of awareness by denial processes. The denial of gut feelings (or "intuitions") plays an especially important part in moral masochism—for instance in patients such as B, for whom a denial of inner reality ("I feel quite comfortable around him") complemented denials of outer reality ("he's really quite a nice man"). Denial of thoughts is very common, and in fact denial of external reality is almost always supplemented by a denial of the outcome of various judgments about reality, which are in fact thought processes. As one gets older the focus of denial shifts, from being largely directed toward external reality to being more and more directed against inner reality, which is the type of denial Basch (1983) designated as disavowal. I do think, however, that any adult, no matter what their state of mental health, is perfectly capable of denying portions of external reality as well, and in fact I think all of us do this relatively often.

The denial of most aspects of inner reality is facilitated by the fact that conscious awareness is intimately tied to perceptual qualities. Much of inner reality does not have these qualities. Thought is, to begin with, unconscious, and in fact much of it remains so, not because of any defense directed against it, but because it is at first not linked with perceptual qualities (Freud, 1911b). Only when thoughts are attached to either words or images can they become conscious, and thus defenses against this aspect of inner reality can work by blocking the attachment of words and images to thoughts (what Altshul [1968] referred to as ego arrest). Also the defense can work by using a shifting of attention once the thought has acquired some perceptual qualities, or there can be a combination of these two methods.

The defenses themselves are an important aspect of inner reality. Like thoughts, defenses are at first without perceptual qualities, and do not have any intrinsic push towards awareness. Anna Freud (1936) pointed out long ago that this lack of push meant that any attempt to make a defense conscious meets with no aid from the defense itself, in contrast with an attempt to bring drive derivatives or affects into awareness. In the latter case the push of the drives and affects meets the interpretation half way. This difference necessitates more activity on the therapist's part in analyzing denial, including in analyzing those denial defenses used to defend against the awareness of defenses.

Defenses against the Awareness of Defenses

I find it surprising, given the importance, both practically and theoretically, of defenses against defenses, how little attention has been paid to their basic characteristics. An exception is Gill's (1963) monograph, which deals at length with the topic. He sees the fact that defenses do not become conscious as a great puzzle, and proposes a layering of defenses as a solution. In this conception, each drive/defense conflict leads to a compromise formation that at the next level (with more binding of energy and closer to consciousness) acts as an impulse in the next impulse/defense configuration, and so on up toward consciousness. Gill saw the same defense—such as reaction formation or repression—operating at each level of one of these chains, so that repression would in the end defend against the awareness of repression, reaction formation against reaction formation, etc. In his monograph Gill saw defenses as exclusively directed against the drives, and I think this is why the whole issue of defenses against defenses seemed to him to be such a complex problem.

Let us now look at these defenses against defenses from the perspective of the basic categories described in chapter 1: what motivates them, what they are directed against, and their basic nature. I think the motive for a defense against the awareness of a defense is reasonably clear: it is the same motive that led to the original defense. If one attempts to undo a defense against the awareness of a defense, the particular unpleasant feeling (anxiety, painful longing) that motivated the original defense begins to reappear, motivating the strengthening of the defense against the defense. In terms of what defenses against the awareness of defenses are directed against, this, too, is clear. They are directed against an inner reality that has no propulsive force toward action or awareness. Just from this fact we would expect such defenses to be denial (attentional) defenses. If we look at the nature of the resistance to bringing defenses into awareness, we are not disappointed in this expectation. As we attempt to make a patient aware of a defense, and if there is enough resistance that they do not become aware of it easily, they will generally shift their attention to various other aspects of the situation, to something else they had been talking about, or even to other defenses or to other conflicts that may have been discussed previously.

The difficulty in seeing the mechanism of defenses against the awareness of defenses clearly is that it operates at the same time as the defense that it hides, so that one is generally analyzing the two defenses at the same time, and their mechanisms appear together as the analysis is carried out. Thus as one analyzes a defense, it will often be repeated. This may have been one reason that Gill felt that a defense is kept from awareness by the use of the very same defense. However, if one watches carefully as one attempts to bring a defense into awareness, one can sometimes see the attentional shift to another aspect of reality. At other times it is hidden by the operation of the primary defense.

As an example, I will briefly mention a patient who had been in analysis with me for several years. I had been attempting, with some success, to unearth the sadness that he rather conspicuously never felt, despite having some very good reasons for feeling it. We had been looking at how he firmly rejected any tendency to feel sad about himself, but seemed to always have at least one person, or sometimes a number, who was constantly on his mind. He felt sorry for these people's plight and would from time to time visit them and play the benefactor. I had pointed out how it was interesting that he could be so intensely interested in the particular person at the time, but would later move on to feeling sad for another person, and then not give a second thought to the first one. "It seems I don't really care for them at all," he said.

"Well, it may look like callousness, but I wonder if what it really means is that they are just stand-ins for you, just covers for your sadness about yourself, so they are easily interchanged."

The patient was quite struck by this observation, although he did not seem in any rush to actually relinquish his defense. He came into the next session and announced that I had been quite right. He had gone on a walk with the express purpose of feeling sad, by leaving all distractions behind. He noticed a lady with a baby and began to feel that she may need some help crossing the street. Unfortunately she crossed quite easily, at which point he became agitated, looking around for someone to help. He eventually passed a homeless person on the street, and gave him some money. He immediately felt relieved and went home.

I said that he had managed to show the maneuver very well. He must have been just on the point of feeling sad and in need of help or sympathy when he started looking around for someone else to help. "On the other hand," he said, "maybe it makes sense to just put sadness aside. It must be built into us by evolution. You might not survive too long and pass on your genes if you're walking around feeling sad all of the time."

"Well maybe that makes some sense, but really you've shifted the ground. You're talking in general terms, but in your specific case it obviously has not served you very well, and in fact you come here partly because of all of the troubles these defenses to avoid sadness have caused you."

It is evident that as the patient told the story of his looking for someone to help and feel sorry for, he was becoming more aware of his defense of externalization. When I specifically pointed to the sadness that I considered to be the motivation for the defense, he began to rationalize, finding reasons why what he was doing was actually the best thing to do. This rationalization was motivated by the wish to hang on to his defense. He argued that it was biologically programmed and important for survival. The very imagery of not being able to reproduce if you do not have the defense gives a hint of the deeper motivations for the defense. There were two layers to this defense: the idea of castration that would make him unable to reproduce, and below this, the idea of his father's spectacular lack of concern for and neglect of him, which had left him with overwhelming longing and sadness, and an inhibition against being a father. At the same time the patient, by shifting the ground and talking of other sorts of defenses that are necessary for survival, derailed the progression of his awareness of his defense of externalization. Thus, this shifting was also a defense against awareness of a defense.

This example shows very clearly how difficult it is to get a clear view of defenses against the awareness of defenses, because their operation is so intertwined with the continued operation of the primary defense. One of the best ways to see the operation of these secondary defenses clearly is to perform some self-observation. If one watches carefully what happens as one attempts to become concretely aware of the operation of a defense that one is intellectually aware of, one can often see clearly the attentional shifts that block this awareness and that mark this type of defense as a denial.

In this discussion I have dealt only with the defensive (dynamic) ways in which defenses are kept out of awareness. These dynamic means are supplemented by others: the aforementioned lack of perceptual qualities of defenses, as well as the automatization (Hartmann, 1939) of the defensive processes that occurs over time. This process of automatization involves the defensive maneuvers becoming part of procedural memory systems, which are not capable of becoming conscious in the same manner as are declarative (explicit) memories. These aspects of defenses partly account for the greater need for activity on the analyst's part when trying to make them conscious, but they do not account for the specific resistance we meet when we attempt to do so. This, I contend, is a denial defense directed against the awareness of an inner reality.

Primal Denial

E, an artist in her late thirties, came for help with recurring severe depressions and with what she described as a pattern of staying in relationships that were psychologically abusive. It quickly became evident during her four times weekly psychoanalysis that at least one major contributor to E's present-day difficulties was a childhood dominated by a severely disturbed mother who was verbally and physically abusive. Her mother saturated even the most day-to-day, seemingly innocuous interchanges with aggression and sexuality, suggesting that she had difficulties with using repression that were in the borderline to psychotic range. E herself was friendly, had a sharp, quick mind and an ability to be perceptive that led to relatively rapid progress at first. There was a tendency, however, to follow any session where we had gotten along particularly well by a few days of long silences and seeming distrust. By her third year of analysis, it was becoming clear that my interpretations of repressions of sexual wishes and conflicts led to a severe worsening of her mental state, a worsening that was not a prelude to a subsequent improvement. I will discuss one aspect of what this meant in the chapter on trauma, where E's sexual abuse by her father will be described, while E's difficulties with self-abuse and allowing others to abuse her will be explored in the chapter on masochism (chapter 7). In this section I would like to describe some work we did on one of her primal denials.

At a point in her fourth year of analysis E had been overwhelmed by anxiety and depression as we had explored her repression of passive sexual wishes toward, and what we reconstructed as episodes of actual genital stimulation by, her mother. We agreed it might be helpful if she sat up. In this position we worked especially on her difficulty in stopping strong feelings from running away on her, and in structuring her life and her house. A number of things that had been touched on here and there and given a variety of interpretations earlier in the analysis came into sharper focus. E could not sit down to eat at home. She would make a quick meal and stand or walk around while eating, never really relaxing. She was quite capable of enjoying a meal while sitting down outside her house, at a friend's or at a restaurant. E was also engaged in an endless struggle to make her house livable. She would arrange the furniture this way and that, but she could never be comfortable.

Upon my inquiring further about the details of these difficulties, E described how she found it hard to let herself curl up on the couch and watch television. When she had been cold the other day, she had not thought to get a blanket. Often she would forget to eat and in an intellectual way would figure out that she should probably eat something because it had been so long since her last meal. As she talked of these things she seemed somewhat embarrassed, giggling as if it were all very silly, and then saying that these seemed like such unimportant details to bring into an analysis. I wondered whether she had taken over this feeling from her mother, given her mother's attitude toward attending to such basic aspects of her children's care as comfort and food, compared to her fanatical and eccentric decorating and arranging of the house.[1]

"My mom really had trouble showing me affection," said E. "I think it was because of her anger at my closeness to my father."

"But I wonder whether you've shifted ground here, from your mother's more basic difficulty giving you physical and emotional warmth, and being interested in taking care of you. After all fighting with you over your father was a form of interaction at least."

"Well, I think she was better able to show affection for my sister."

"Can you remember an instance of it?"

E thought for a minute, and then said, "Once she told me that she much preferred dealing with my sister because I was so difficult."

"But that's not an instance of her treating your sister affectionately, but of her using her to make you feel bad. Can you actually remember an instance of her treating your sister with affection or warmth?"

E began to cry quietly. "No," she said. "She really couldn't be warm. But I don't want to see it. I really don't want to look at it."

"I know it's very painful. I think what has been coming up about your difficulties with self-care are related to the type of care you received from her from very early on."

"I used to lie on rocks to warm up when I was small, so that the heat would soak into me."

"I wonder about her ability to provide bodily and emotional warmth by holding you close and cuddling."

E laughed. "I can't even begin to imagine my mother cuddling a child. I don't like her even touching me." E again began to cry. She said it was so unpleasant to feel these feelings that she simply was not going to do it. She was upset at me for bringing this all up and pushing her, she said. The rest of the session continued in this vein, with E using a denial defense against the very distressing reality that was emerging and then, if I interpreted the defense, feeling sad and feeling that she simply did not want to go any further with the recognition of these realities.

Despite the strength of E's painful feelings as we discussed her mother's basic inability to show warmth or take care of her physical needs, she did not deteriorate, but instead felt much better, after the session. She continued to improve as we dealt with bodily feelings and difficulties in self-care that seemed to relate to early and later experiences with her mother, and with E's attempt to defend against the painful feelings attached to these experiences by the use of denial.

What is the rationale for referring to the defense demonstrated by E as primal denial rather than, for instance, passive primal repression (Frank, 1969) or splitting? To begin with, the resistances demonstrated by E showed the use of attentional processes that characterize denial. What we see, even in this short interchange, is the intermingling of denials related to many stages of development, from the denial related to the cold, negligent handling of E in infancy and as a toddler to later denials of her mother's inability to show warmth and affection. The earliest denials were aided by the fact that many of these experiences had never been put into words, and so the blocking of their translation into words helped in keeping them from consciousness. Frank (1969) proposed that we call such early defenses developmental primal repression or passive primal repression.

In this instance I think the question is not merely a terminological one, but involves matters of substance. Even though these early defenses use a certain amount of counterforce, this is clearly distinct from that of primal repression since in the example of E, and in all of the examples presented by Frank in his paper, the defense was quite easily undone and the defended against realities brought into awareness. Of course in the case of the very early experiences against which this defense works, being brought into awareness does not involve the recovery of biographical memories, but rather the connection of various bodily and mental reactions with a plausible construction which is believable and believed (Freud, 1937).

While in the case of the very early experiences of deprivation there are no biographical (declarative, episodic) memories that can be accessed, I think it is important to recognize that what is being defended against are not drive derivatives but rather early inner and outer perceptual experiences, which are not processed in the same way as they are in later life. This is so in the case of E, in all of Frank's (1969) cases, and in all of the other instances of this type of defense I have seen. The way in which the defense works is also very characteristic of denial—the memories of the perceptual experience are defended against so that the unpleasant feelings that they evoke do not develop. This is in contrast to repression, in which drives are defended against so that the specific feeling of overwhelming anxiety does not develop.

However, the most basic reason for calling these early defenses denial, rather than repression, is a more controversial one, but one that I believe is of great theoretical and practical importance. These early defenses work, as do all denials, with the neutral attentional energy of the ego, while repression works largely with the partially neutralized energy of the aggressive drive. In fact, I believe that it is more accurate to rephrase this to stress the energic aspect: the use of the neutral and well-neutralized energy of the attentional processes of the ego for defensive purposes is what characterizes denial, while the use of partially neutralized aggressive drive energy for defense is what is called repression. If we look at the reaction of patients to the partial undoing of a primal denial—and E's response is typical—there may be anger, but it is quite commensurate with the fact that the analyst is pushing the patient in the direction of feeling some extremely unpleasant feelings. There is not the outburst of unexplained aggression that one sees, for instance with D, upon the undoing of primal repression. In fact, this contrast was even more marked with E than with D. As is the case in patients with relatively unstable or porous primal repressions, E was flooded with an almost pure hatred of me as we undid her primal repressions—for instance of her sexual feelings for her father.

What is quite striking as one undoes a primal denial is the amount of new energy that is available to the person, a point that was emphasized by Frank (1969). Here, too, E's case was typical. She not only felt better as we more fully analyzed the connection of her difficulties in making herself warm and comfortable and well fed with the early treatment she had received from her mother. E also noticeably perked up. Over a number of months she looked brighter, shed some of her chronic tiredness, and seemed to carry herself more erect and move with more energy.

Pervasive Affect and Primal Defenses

Having given some reasons for considering E's defense a denial, the next question to consider is why I would choose to call it a *primal* denial. I think the reason for doing this should not be based merely on the denial being a very early one. Many denials in early childhood, just as many repressions, are not primal defenses. They are relatively easily reversed and do not serve as templates for a whole line of later defenses. What marks a defense as a primal one is not, I believe, its time of occurrence, but rather its intensity, immense strength, and stability, all of which are related to its motivation. A primal defense is instituted in response to a feeling that seems to the person as if it will never stop, which thus seems uncontrollable and overwhelming, and which is sometimes referred to as a traumatic feeling. I think there are good reasons, as I explained in the last chapter, for not referring to overwhelming anxiety as traumatic anxiety. Doing so hinders our thinking on these issues, and I think it has done this for over three-quarters of a century now, by leading us to confuse traumatic overwhelming of the stimulus barrier with the overwhelming anxiety that motivates primal repression. Whatever terminology one chooses, whether to keep calling this feeling traumatic anxiety or, as I prefer, to refer to it as pervasive anxiety, what is most important is that we make the conceptual distinction.

Making this conceptual distinction, which I think is aided by making a terminological one, has an enormously clarifying effect on both our understanding of trauma and of defense. If one accepts the definition of primal defense as a response to a feeling that overruns the ego's control and thus feels as if it will never stop, then it becomes clear that there are actually quite a number of primal defenses. The reason I would refer to E's denial of her treatment by her mother as a primal one is because it was motivated by pervasive sadness at her mother's inability to love and nurture her, as well as pervasive anxiety that her physical well being was in danger because of her mother's sadism and neglect of her basic physical needs and safety. The strength of these motivating feelings may not be clearly demonstrated in the excerpt from E's analysis that I presented above. It became more and more clear as we analyzed her primal denial further, and she said quite explicitly that she did not want to go any further because it felt that the sadness would just engulf her or go on forever. These are words that patients will often use when the analysis of a primal defense has reached past the secondary defenses that buttress it. As we analyzed her defense, E did feel extreme sadness and psychical pain from unrequited longing, and although they did not engulf her, these feelings did threaten to overwhelm her and did leave her feeling helpless. This threat of being overwhelmed by a feeling is how D felt as we penetrated his primal repression of his oedipal wishes.

In E's case denial was used in response to her overwhelming sadness and anxiety because it could be. The feelings were the result of the difficult reality of a severely disturbed mother, and of E's growing awareness about the significance of this. Thus a primal denial of the reality (a massive shifting of the ego's attention to other things) worked to block the development of these feelings. The strength of the feelings that motivated the defense was one reason for its stability and endurance, since any tendency to reverse this shift of attention threatened to bring the feelings back.

Universal Primal Denials

I would not want to leave the reader with the impression that primal denial takes place only in extreme circumstances such as those suffered by E. In fact, as with primal repressions, a store of primal denials is part of the human condition. These primal denials determine the sort of experiences to which each of us will react in later life with after denials. As well, there are a number of primal denials that are universal, although their extent and specific content vary. These include the denial of our own death and the denial of the extent of other people's self-interest and thus the relatively small extent of their investment in us.[2] These two denials converge in the denial of the lack of interest of the powers of fate and nature in what might happen to us. While this primal denial is one of the bases of religion, even the non-religious are incapable of doing without a good dose of it, if not at the intellectual level, then at least at the level of feeling and action. Geelard (1965) described this as denial related to the wish to live, and said that it is similar to the instinctive behavior of animals. She traced it back to the young child's need for human relationships.

How the denial of death can be related to the need for human contact can be seen if we consider its developmental roots. A very young child is not afraid of death as an adult would conceive it, but rather of being abandoned and of being overwhelmed by his or her own needs such as hunger, and by external stimuli such as cold and pain. Protection from these threats is provided by an adult or adults, but is far from complete even in the best of circumstances. An attachment to the caring adult develops, which has instinctive roots, but is powerfully reinforced by the protection that the adult provides. Along with this early attachment comes a belief in the omnipotence of the caregiver. This belief is very soon threatened by various perceptions and experiences and by the child's growing understanding. As a counter to these threats the basic primal denials are instituted. These include denial of the lack of complete investment, and lack of omnipotence, of the caregiver, as well as denial of the child's own smallness and fragility. The adult's denial of death and of the indifference of the forces of nature to his or her wishes grow from these basic primal denials. The child's fear of being overwhelmed to the point of ego dissolution is replaced by fear of death in the adult version, while the forces of nature and fate, or God, replace our parents.

It is a striking thing to witness the partial dissolution of this most basic of primal denials. A male patient of mine who had been in analysis with me for a number of years, during which time we had made very significant progress in analyzing his tendencies to use denial, had a number of medical investigations related to a pain he was having. A tumor was discovered, although ascertaining its extent and nature required further investigations. He remained optimistic and in a surprisingly good mood, but was quite aware of what he was doing. He said that he was keeping his worst fears and feelings at bay, saving them for the bad news, if he got it. I was not sure of this, but treated this maneuver as an adaptive denial and rather than analyze it, merely discussed its existence intellectually with the patient.

Not long afterwards the bad news was delivered. The tumor was malignant, large, maybe inoperable, and there was the possibility of metastases. It turned out my patient had been quite right about the adaptive, flexible nature of his previous optimism. After hearing the bad news he was capable of feeling the full extent of the sadness and upset one would expect. He could cry and feel alternately sad and angry about his situation. He could allow himself to be comforted by his girlfriend and alternately could pull himself together and comfort her as she became distressed.

In the sessions after he heard the news the patient demonstrated the same flexible ability to access a whole range of feelings related to the diagnosis. With a little help from me, but largely on his own, he connected these reactions to issues in his family about death, as well as to traumatic fears of abandonment from very early childhood. He was quite concerned for his friends and family, and wondered about the best way to inform them honestly about the reality. In the midst of this swirl of thoughts and feelings the patient, in looking for a word to describe his state of mind, came up with "exuberant," but rejected it laughingly as out of place. In trying to come up with a better word, he thought of "wonderful adventure," but felt he had to reject this for similar reasons. Still, he could think of no better descriptions.

"It's not that I'm not sad and upset," he said. "I'd much rather not be in this situation, but here I am. Somehow facing it head on—there's something invigorating about that."

"So perhaps these words aren't so out of place," I commented. "Maybe they describe the increasing energy you have, energy that you used in your denials of unpleasant reality, and these denials have been so thoroughly given up."

The patient said this made absolute sense to him and went on to describe his increased energy lately, especially since hearing the news. Such increased energy certainly brings up the possibility of a manic defense against sadness, but the ready availability and expression of this emotion spoke against such an interpretation, as did the patient's actions. Actions are the last refuge of denial, and actions that deny a reality are usually kept going even as a person seems to have accepted the reality intellectually. In contrast to this, the patient conscientiously made all the arrangements he needed to with respect to his death, often over the objections of others who found it too upsetting and wanted to avoid these details. At the same time he looked into getting other medical opinions, researched his particular cancer, sought out acquaintances who worked in the field, and kept up an attitude of optimism tempered by a feeling that there was a good chance he would die in the near future. (In emphasizing the adaptive and realistic aspects of my patient's responses, I do not want to overstate the case. There were, no doubt, other dynamics at play, as there always are, and various connections to unconscious fantasies. One dynamic that we analyzed, for instance, was my patient's externalization of his fear of death onto others, so that they could be the scared ones and he the comforting, powerful parental figure. None of this, however, contradicts my point that what was also going on was the *partial* relinquishment of a universal primal denial.)

In another session the word "enjoyable" came to my patient's mind to describe what he was going through, even though he was again tempted to reject it as out of place. He commented on the many manifestations of his increased energy. He was better organized, tended not to put things off or be indecisive any longer, got more things done in a day, slept better than he ever had, experienced a full range of strong feelings, and thoroughly enjoyed his friends. And so it was that in facing fully and unflinchingly the possibility—in fact the high probability—of dying, he came to be more fully alive than he had ever been before.

This observation of increased energy and aliveness upon facing death is one that has often been made (e.g., Feinsilver, 1998). I have described an example of it here because it allows us a view into a basic primal denial that, as much as the primal repressions of the oedipus complex, we all share. Such an example also gives an idea of just how much energy each of us uses to maintain this primal denial.

Repression and Denial

In order to round out our discussion of denial, it may be worthwhile to compare it briefly with repression. Primal denial works mainly with the attentional energies of the ego to strongly block certain realities in order that distressing feelings related to these realities do not develop. Primal repression uses partially neutralized aggressive drive energy to set up a stable and strong counterforce against a drive. The motivation for primal repression is narrow, involving only pervasive anxiety, versus a broad range of overwhelming feelings, including anxiety and painful longing, that can motivate primal denial. Both of these defenses are selective in opposing particular drive derivatives or aspects of reality, as opposed to certain non-selective defenses such as asceticism (A. Freud, 1936) or various forms of blocking.

Both after denial and after repression continue the work of the primal defenses, in selectively keeping certain realities or drive derivatives out of awareness. After denial works through a shifting of attention, after repression through a withdrawal of preconscious investment. In the case of after repression, this leads to the mental content so treated becoming subject to the primary processes; this does not occur with after denial. There are also various secondary defenses that aid the primal defenses. I gave examples of denials used to shore up D's crumbling primal repression in the last chapter. Conversely, repression is often used as a secondary defense when primal denials are on the point of crumbling. I will discuss this below, in the section on therapeutic technique.

Splitting

In considering examples of primal denial I have left aside the fact that a number of them related to traumatic experiences. The experiences of E, in not having her basic physical needs attended to as a young child, were no doubt traumatic at times. Despite the often close connection between denial and trauma, I have treated them separately because I think that the basic defense related to trauma—dissociation—is distinct from denial, although the motivation to deny something often makes secondary use of the split in the ego brought about by dissociation. To put this another way, I do not think that the defense of denial causes, or comes about due to, a splitting of the ego. Rather I think that splitting of the ego is related to the primary dissociation that follows upon trauma. Of course denial, as with any other defense, leads to a "split" in the general sense of the term, in that one view of things is allowed into awareness while another is barred from it, but in the more specific sense of the term, denial does not necessarily entail a splitting of the ego. While making these conceptual distinctions can be clarifying, patients and their dynamics are rarely, if ever, pure expressions of our concepts.

A number of readers may have wondered about the issue of splitting as I was giving examples of denial. For instance, my very first example, of B's denial of her boyfriend's lack of caring, may have led to questions about B's split image of her boyfriend, which could have been the basis for her denial. There was no doubt splitting of object images in this example. I left this aside when I presented B, in order not to complicate the discussion. In relation to this issue, however, I think one can find examples of simple denial (i.e., attentional shifts plus some other ego maneuvers) that do not ride on the back of splitting defenses. Some of E's denials related to her mother were of this type, but the picture is complicated by the high level of trauma that she had suffered. More clear cut cases of "pure" denial are D's secondary uses of denial when his oedipal wishes were emerging, and the denial that is used as a defense against becoming aware of defenses. I have simplified things at this point in the discussion, and have not considered the splitting defenses that often are found entwined with denial, in order to present a clearer picture of the basic mechanisms of denial. In chapters 5 (trauma) and 8 (perversions) we will consider splitting defenses that are a product of trauma, and their interactions with denial and repression.

There are also other forms of splitting, the most important being that which is based on a more general weakness in the ego's synthetic function that is seen in borderline disorders. In this case as well, the very frequent intertwining of this splitting with post-traumatic splitting has impeded a clearer conceptualization and deeper understanding of both defenses. This is especially so because borderline patients have often experienced a good deal of trauma, and also because their ego weaknesses make them much more prone to being traumatized by events and by developmental progressions that are not traumatizing to more resilient individuals.

The larger issue that these considerations point to is that we are often presented with defenses that are a combination of two or more basic defensive processes. We have usually conceptualized these compound defenses, such as splitting of the ego, as single entities. This way of going about things will only get us so far in our investigation not only of defenses, but also of various other phenomena, such as trauma and borderline personality disorder, as well as impeding improvements in psychotherapeutic technique. I state this in general terms here, but in some of the chapters that follow I will attempt to demonstrate it in more detail both conceptually and in relation to clinical material. In chapter 8 especially, as part of a discussion of trauma and perversions, I will describe two compound defenses: splitting of the ego (traumatic splitting plus attentional defenses) and splitting of the identity (traumatic splitting plus counterforce defenses).

Therapeutic Technique

The Analysis of Denial and Repression Compared

There are certain respects in which the interpretation of denial is more straightforward than the interpretation of repression. Unlike repression, which uses transformed drive energy as the heart of its mechanism, denial involves the use of certain ego functions, especially that of attention. Even though our mind is not well suited to the perception of its own workings, since our perceptual system is largely adapted to sensing the outside world, it is still easy enough to make patients aware of their use of shifting attention. I have already given examples of this in the cases of E and of B. It was not too difficult to make them aware of the motive, mechanism, and object of their defenses.

This can be contrasted to the analysis of D's repression of his oedipal conflict described in the last chapter. As was the case with E and with B, it was a relatively straightforward matter to make D aware of the denial and externalization that helped to shore up his repressions, but the actual analysis of the repressions was more complicated. Similarly to the analysis of denial, it involved interpreting the objects of the repression, such as D's wishes to harm his father, which could be inferred from some of his associations and transference reactions, and from my counter-reactions of feeling controlled even as he was being very friendly. Interpretation of the objects of the repression helped to stir up both the repressed material and the repressive defense, again similarly to when I pointed out to E and B the objects of their denials (the lack of caring of their mother and boyfriend, respectively). This is where the similarity ended, however. The repression entered the analysis as a transference resistance. I went into this point in detail in the last chapter, so I will only restate the findings described there: because primal repressions are fashioned from drive energy, they enter the analysis in an analyzable form through the processes of displacement, condensation, and deneutralization that characterize the drives, by forming a transference resistance.

Thus analyzing and undoing primal repressions involves a long and difficult process of stirring up transferences and transference resistances, recognizing their nature and tracing them back to their roots, and an even longer and more arduous process of working through these insights once they have been achieved. Because the objects of repressions are at base drive wishes and investments, this working through is necessary to loosen the attachment (investment, *besetzung*) of these drives to their aims and objects.

If we look at the analysis of E's primal denial of her mother's lack of caring and love, we can see that, from beginning to end, it involved a straightforward confrontation of E with the avoided realities, the interpretation of the further attempts to avoid these realities, and the interpretation of the avoided affects (motives). At the point where the avoidances had been repeatedly interpreted and, in a sense, there was nowhere left to hide, E simply stated that she did not want to believe that her mother was the way she was.

At this point in the analysis of a primal denial it is quite usual for the person to say, "I know what you say is true, but I just don't want to believe it and I won't! I just won't!" Here the original energetic rejection of the distressing reality is quite plainly brought into view for both analyst and patient to see. Often, and this happened with E as well, I have found that secondary repression is used to shore up the primal denial as it is analyzed. That is, a much weaker counterforce than primal repression, but one still capable of blocking certain memories and feelings from consciousness, is used to help out, but this repression is not based on a previous primal repression. It is analogous to the secondary denials that D used to shore up his faltering primal repression. This secondary repression leads to transferences that give way to interpretation relatively easily. I will discuss this aspect of the analysis of primal denial in the section after the next one.

To compare the analysis of E's primal denial to the analysis of D's primal repression: we can see in D's case that from the beginning to the end the actual nature of the defense was obscure, hard to get a handle on, and only at times easily evident to either analyst or patient. This did not mean that D could not be made aware of his repressions or the nature of their operation, but this knowledge involved more inference from D's immediate experience, compared to E's knowledge of her primal denial. I pointed out in the last chapter that a number of trends in modern-day analytic theory and practice work against the analysis of primal repressions, among them the reluctance to make, and the distrust of, explicit reconstructions of the past, and the tendency to view all angry outbursts and negative transferences of the patient as related to narcissistic injury. To this list we should add, in relation to the preceding discussion, the present-day allergy to so-called "experience distant" knowledge that rests on many inferential steps. The knowledge not only of the objects of repression but also of the process of repression is a product of a number of these steps. I believe it is actually quite useful to help patients gain this knowledge, but there is certainly a bias against this in many analytic circles.

So far the comparison of the analysis of the two defenses would seem to have been to the detriment of repression. However, while discovering repression, the primary process, and the nature of the drives, Freud fashioned a therapeutic instrument that was remarkably effective in analyzing primal repressions. I described in the previous chapter how primal repression was made analyzable. The fostering of the transference through the interpretation of drive derivatives, the frequency of sessions, and the recumbent position all help to capture and make analyzable primal repression, through its expression in the transference resistance. Once the counterforce of primal repression has been transmuted into the transference resistance, the use of abstinence, neutrality, and the working alliance as tools to analyze the transference and transference resistance, and the use of reconstruction to bring into focus the objects of repression, all help to make repression an analyzable defense. Looked at from this angle, we might wonder if it is perhaps denial that is at a disadvantage compared to repression, since we seem not to have analogous tools that would allow us to bring primal denials so completely into the transference and under our power. Is this perhaps the reason for the slipperiness of denial that becomes evident as we attempt to analyze it? It often seems relatively easy to bring the denied reality into the patient's awareness, but even after years of doing this, it will just as easily slip out of awareness through various shifts of attention and other ego maneuvers. Even taking into consideration that splitting of the ego often plays a part in anchoring a denial, is this tenacious slipperiness partly a product of our inability to fully engage primal denial by siphoning it into the analysis and the transference, as happens in the best of cases with primal repression? It may be that our primal denials are never as fully undone or relinquished as some of our primal repressions can be.

On the other hand, the slippery nature of the resistance that is a product of denial is also a reflection of the nature of attentional defenses, and these defenses require somewhat different methods for their analysis. We will now consider these methods.

The Analysis of Denial

In analyzing the denials of both E and B, I was relatively active both in bringing the denied reality into the analytic conversation and in interpreting the various shifts of attention that attempted to defend against a full awareness of this reality. Compared to drive derivatives and affects, these realities do not have much of an inherent push towards awareness. A quiet, expectant attitude of friendly, interested listening and clarifying will usually elicit the affects and derivatives related to drive-based conflicts, as well as fostering transferences, since drives and affects will come half way to meet the analyst, and in a certain sense make common cause with the analyst against the patient's resistances. This not being so with denied realities, the analyst has to do more of the work and be more active in championing the cause of the denied reality.

It is important to remember that we are interpreting the patient's avoidance of something that they themselves know to be true (which, of course, does not mean this knowledge may not be inaccurate to a greater or lesser extent). To interpret denial is to interpret an intrapsychic dynamic, not to argue for one's view of reality in opposition to the patient's view. While in the examples given of my interactions with B and E, it may seem that I am pursuing arguments about what is real, I am in fact giving voice to the patient's own denied knowledge. It would be naïve to think that the therapist makes no judgments at all on the subject of the probable reality of what the patient is denying. However, when I talk of being forceful in speaking for the denied reality, it is largely the patient's own inner sense of what really happened, and their judgments about it (for instance E's knowledge about her mother's very disturbed personality), now denied, for which we speak. We speak up for these things more forcefully than for a repressed wish, because these realities tend not to speak very loudly for themselves.

This is not to say that realistic, objective perceptions and judgments have no push towards awareness. Through development, as the ego's attachment to reality and to objective judgments about reality grows, this push becomes stronger. This push towards awareness is, however, different from that of the drives—different, I would say, not only in quantity but also in quality. An ego interest is quite a different thing from a drive derivative.

Thus in the analysis of denial the analyst's relatively forceful introduction of the denied realities substitutes for the upward push of drives and affects in the analysis of repression, and in this we have an ally in that portion of the ego that remains attached both to reality and to its objective evaluation. It may seem to some that this active introduction of the denied realities offends against the analytic stance, with its abstinence and neutrality on the part of the analyst. Much ink has been spilt in the analytic literature on the issue of whether, when, and how to introduce avoided realities into the analysis. I think that if one views neutrality and abstinence as tools for fostering and handling specific transferences, rather than as all-pervasive aspects of the analytic interaction, then many of the perceived difficulties surrounding this issue disappear.

This is where what I described in chapter 1 as a narrow view of technique shows its usefulness. The base of the analytic relationship, and of analysis, is provided by the therapeutic alliance, the real relationship, and the working alliance that is built on the former two. Just as there are certain tools (neutrality, abstinence, use of the analyst's counterresponses to guide interpretation) that we use, starting from this base, in analyzing repressions, so there are other tools that we can use at other times to analyze denials. Some of these technical tools, such as interpretation of the defense mechanism, its motive, and the defenses against becoming aware of defenses, are similar to those used in analyzing repression. Others, such as more actively bringing forward denied realities, interpreting often outside of the transference, and asking more questions, differ at least in emphasis from drive/defense analysis. A narrow view of technique allows each of these interventions, interactions, and ways of listening a place, since none is overgeneralized to become the whole of analytic technique.

This is not to say that approaching things in this manner clears up all problems related to the different demands of analyzing repression and denial. To begin with, these defenses are not analyzed sequentially. Rather, their analysis often takes place all in a jumble. As we saw in the last chapter, one often has to analyze denial defenses that shore up repressions, and this is only one, and actually one of the simpler, interactions between these defenses. Added to this jumble are the defenses related to trauma and the particular methods needed to analyze them (chapters 5 and 8). However it is especially because of the already complicated situation that confronts us, and the at times contradictory interventions needed to analyze different forms of defenses, that we should avoid making our task even harder by an attitude that overgeneralizes one aspect of technique.

The basic tools for analyzing denial are simple: bring the denied reality to the patient's attention patiently but persistently; interpret the painful emotions that arise as the motive for the shifts of attention; and interpret the mechanism of the shifting of attention itself. A good alliance is a key for this, but explaining what one thinks and is hoping to achieve, and in general being natural and straightforward at all times, is helpful. Primal denials work against declarative memories as well as judgments that are made about the meaning of these memories. It is common for there to be some amount of intellectual affirmation of the denied reality, but various maneuvers are put in place, sometimes quite ingeniously, to blunt the full emotional impact. For instance, E would talk quite a lot about her mother's bad behavior and aggression, but would leave some of the worst bits out. She also would minimize things right after she had said them, as well as combining this with telling me some shocking thing and getting me angry and all riled up and then, once this attitude had been safely deposited in me, not having to own it to the same extent.

I would like at this point to mention one form of denial defense that is often not analyzed, but the analysis of which is quite effective—the defense of denial in action, described by Anna Freud (1936). In this defense, the person will be able to talk about the denied reality and avow it, but will act as if it were not true. For instance E would visit her mother and go shopping with her, even though she knew from experience that this would always end disastrously. Despite her intellectual knowledge, she would go full of hope, or at least without what should realistically have been distaste and dread. Here denial in feeling and in action were combined. Often in these situations the analyst will analyze various other aspects of this repetitive behavior from the past and present, but not the denial in action. In the case of E, I wondered aloud why she went back with such seeming naive hope, and when she began to see the mismatch between this and the knowledge that she actually had about her mother, I went on to say that I thought her going shopping with her mother, and then being caught off guard by her attacks was a form of denial. "If you truly believe something, then you act as if it's true," I said. "Action is probably the last refuge of your denial of what your mom is really like, remaining long after you've become aware of these things intellectually. We could also turn it around, and wonder what would happen if you *acted* as if she were the sort of person she is. I think then you might have some very strong feelings." I said this at the point where E had been talking again of going on one of her horrendous shopping trips with her mother. My saying this led her actually to feel very pained, sad, and horrified at the sort of woman her mother was. I have found again and again that analyzing denial in action gives much better access to these sorts of feelings, and much more quickly, than other approaches. As with other denial defenses, one has to be relatively forceful and active in bringing the denied reality and the actions, or omission of actions, to the patient's attention.

Another aspect of the analysis of denial demonstrated by a number of the examples is the significance of intellectual understanding. This is important in the analysis of any type of defense. It has always been understood that there is the danger of the patient using this intellectual understanding as a resistance, but the way to deal with this resistance, as with any other, is not by actions to avoid it, but by interpretation. I have already mentioned this issue in the first chapter, in discussing the broad view of technique, which often leans on adjusting behavior to deal with resistances. This view may make some analysts reluctant to engage in longer intellectual explanations with patients, but I have found that these explanations are at times helpful in analyzing denials. I am not suggesting this as a general way to conduct the analysis of these defenses, but only that at times—and the only way to know these times is intuitively—it is not only useful but quite necessary to engage in some kind of explanation of the defense. I have found that these explanations, when timed well and judiciously mixed with more pithy or evocative interpretations, have been quite effective. There may be many reasons for this, but one related to the present discussion is that these interventions are helpful in bringing one part of the patient's ego, the one invested in an objective view of reality, onside, and rousing its interest. This is much more necessary in the analysis of denial. This sort of explanation can be added to the greater activity on the part of the analyst as another way in which we compensate for the lack of push from the objects of the defense when we analyze denials of reality.

Transference

So far I have said very little about the issue of transference in denial defenses. In fact, to the extent that the whole process of denial, including what it defends against (its objects), remains within the secondary process, the tendency towards displacement characteristic of the primary process is not as evident. Often enough denial dynamics get caught up in repressions, and then are transferred, along with the whole repressed memory/fantasy complex, into the analysis. A common example of this is the family romance fantasy, that generally becomes embroiled in repressed oedipal dynamics, but that began as a denial in fantasy of the flaws seen in the child's parents.

On the other hand there are primal denials—such as E's about her mother's psychological disorder and lack of caring—that do remain within the more organized part of the ego. This is not to say that the denied reality, for instance E's mother's aggression against her, will not get caught up in drive/defense conflicts and become part of a transference resistance based on repression. However, even as this happens, the primal denial continues within the ego. The analysis of these primal denials requires more work outside of the transference, as compared to the analysis of repressed conflicts. It is not a question of either/or but of emphasis. However, this emphasis is important. One should follow the patient's lead, and interpret what is most active at the time. Of course, one can always find at least vague hints of a transference and of countertransference responses, and if one is of the opinion that everything is best analyzed through the transference, or through the relationship, one can try to blow on these small embers and get a roaring fire going. In my experience to do so is a mistake, since it is forced and does not address the patient's emotional life and conflicts at their point of maximal intensity.

There is one particular transference response that I have noticed in these sorts of situations that is worth commenting on. As one approaches the memories and feelings defended against by a primal denial, transient transferences of the denied situation emerge, such as E feeling distrust of me and that I was pushing her or aggressing against her. In any analysis there are many things going on at the same time. In E's case there was the issue of the dissociated memories of the sexual abuse by her father that could be triggered. However, in certain instances it became evident that what was being transferred were experiences with her mother. In other patients, without quite as complicated a history of past traumas as E, this dynamic is easier to see clearly. What happens is that as the denied past realities are approached, not only will this transference emerge but the patient will say that their mind goes blank and that they do not remember what happened in the past. In fact, they find that they cannot remember things that they had previously remembered. For instance, E could not remember any instances of her mother being mean to her at these times.

All indications are that there is a repression at a point where previously we were dealing with a powerful denial. I would suggest it is this repression that leads to the transference, as some of the material defended against comes under the sway of the primary process and is displaced onto the analyst. This is, I think, actually a good example of the connection of repression and classic displacement transferences. These transferences are transient and do not develop into more powerful transference neuroses and from this, as well as from the way in which they give way relatively easily under interpretation, it is clear that we are dealing with a secondary repression—one that is being used as an aid to the primal denial. Were these repressions always there, merely having to be analyzed as part of the analysis of the whole complex of defenses around an unpleasant reality such as E's mother's lack of love? Or is secondary repression brought in as the primal denial is breaking down, just as D brought secondary denials forward to help as his primal repression crumbled? It is hard to decide between these options when these responses first arise, although further reconstruction will often show that some people have all along relied to a greater extent on secondary repression—that is, they will remember that even at a young age they would have no awareness of some of these realities, and have forgotten much of their earlier childhood. Others were generally using denial to a greater extent all along. In any case, the question cannot be answered one way or the other not only because the case is different for different people, but even more so because the whole defensive complex is in a dynamic state of flux, with at times more secondary repression called into play, because of external stresses (for instance E going to meet her mother as an adult would put more pressure on her primal denials about her) and for internal reasons (for instance as E matured cognitively, previously well-established denials were harder to maintain against a growing ability to think these things through and see through earlier excuses she had made for her mother).

Whatever their previous history, it is important to interpret these transferences as they come up. The nature of the transferences gives a vivid picture of what the emotional situation was like in the past. I would stress again, however, that as the main dynamic shifts back to denials of memories and judgments of the past, with less of a tendency for transference, then so should the main focus of the work also shift. Often even at the height of analyzing a primal denial, as well as often along the way, one works outside of the trans- ference. In later chapters (for instance in the next one on externalizing and internalizing defenses, and in the chapters on narcissism and masochism) I will be describing ways in which denial dynamics enter the analysis and get embroiled in the relationship with the analyst, but here I would like to stress that these dynamics often are analyzed outside of the transference when they appear in the relatively straightforward form of a primal denial involving mainly attentional shifts.

Summary

In this chapter a description of attentional (denial) defenses is presented. The idea that these defenses involve especially the use of the ego function of attention, introduced in chapter 1, is reinforced and amplified. It is ar- gued that these attentional defenses work with ego energies, as compared to repression, which uses partially neutralized aggressive drive energy. Denial can be used to defend against anything, and in situations where repressions are failing, such as psychosis, it is used against the drives. However it works best, and is used most, against awareness of, and judgments about, reality, both inner and outer. These realities do not have the inherent push towards conscious awareness and behavioral expression that the drives and strong feelings do, and so it is possible to defend against them with the attentional shifts of denial. It was proposed that defenses themselves are a part of internal reality without this inherent push, and thus that defenses against the aware- ness of defenses are denial (attentional) defenses.

The concept of primal denial was introduced. This type of defense is an extremely energetic and stable use of attentional shifts, that is motivated by a pervasive affect. Unlike repression, the range of pervasive affects that motivate primal denials is quite broad, including pervasive anxiety, pervasive psychic pain, and pervasive sadness. The defense is directed generally against the reality that caused the affect, rather than the affect itself. Thus denial can be used when an affect is largely caused by an awareness of a reality, such as anger caused by the awareness of one parent's love for the other parent, but it does not work well against affects that are derived from drives, such as when this same awareness starts to mobilize the aggressive drive and the rage becomes to a much greater extent a drive derivative. The concept of universal primal denials was also introduced and illustrated. These are the primal denials that we all share, because we all share certain realities, such as our own death and a world over which we have little control, that lead to pervasive affects, such as anxiety and psychic pain, and that thus lead to denials of these realities, usually not at the intellectual level, but at the level of full awareness and belief.

Because the objects that denial defends against have no very strong push towards awareness, and because the defense itself is formed from ego functions without the primary process properties of repression, some of the techniques for analyzing denial differ, at least in emphasis, from those used to analyze repression. The lack of a strong push of reality awareness towards consciousness is compensated for by greater activity on the part of the therapist, who becomes a spokesperson for a reality that has a hard time speaking up for itself. The fact that denial is not formed from drive energy and the fact that its objects usually remain within the secondary process mean that there is not as great a tendency to displacement transferences. In the next and some following chapters we will investigate ways in which denial defenses do lead to situations that look like those of displacement transferences, and we will use the ideas developed so far to try to differentiate these situations from transferences that are the outcome of repression.

Terms

Primal Denial: A process whereby a powerful and very stable attentional defense is used to defend against an unpleasant reality that evokes a pervasive affect. The pervasive affects that motivate primal denials include pervasive anxiety, pervasive psychic pain, and pervasive sadness.

Universal Primal Denials: These are primal denials that we all share because the realities that they defend against, such as the reality that we will cease to exist one day, are a part of the human condition and give rise in each of us to pervasive affects that necessitate these defenses. Universal primal denials are complex structures that usually include defensive guilt and contrast defenses, along with other defenses.

Notes

1. As we shall see in the section on trauma, E's difficulties in eating were not based solely to her mother's treatment of her. The other main causation was from her father's oral sexual abuse of her, but this does not invalidate the points I am making about primal denial.

2. This latter primal denial is perfectly capable of surviving alongside the opposite denial, seen in moral masochism, of the fact that many people are capable of being warmly interested and invested in us (see chapter 7).

CHAPTER FOUR

~

Externalizing and Internalizing Defenses

This chapter is relatively short not because the topic is of minor importance or small in extent, but for exactly the opposite reason. The topic is so large that only a brief overview and clarification of basic concepts and processes will be possible at this point. Externalizing and internalizing defenses are not only common, but the terms cover a variety of defenses, involving attentional (denial) processes, counterforce forms (including projective identification), and forms secondary to trauma that rely on characteristics of the zero process. These different forms of externalizing and internalizing defenses intertwine one with the other, so that it is often difficult to differentiate the underlying processes involved.

Using the concepts developed up to this point, I will in this chapter describe forms of externalizing and internalizing defenses based on attentional processes. These defenses (which I have designated defensive externalization and defensive internalization) will be the main focus. I will also briefly present a theory of the nature of projective identification. I will argue that it involves a combination of defensive externalization and a counterforce based on aggression similar to that used in repression, only this time deployed interpersonally. Projective identification is such a large, important, and complex topic that a full treatment of it will have to await a much more in-depth exploration of the nature of the zero process and trauma, and their relation to borderline functioning and borderline ego deficits. I hope to undertake this exploration in a future volume.

We begin with some clinical material.

Clinical Vignette: D

This vignette concerns D, the man in his early forties a small piece of whose analysis I presented in the section on primal repression. In that section I described some sessions a few years into his analysis, at the point where his sexual love for his mother and death wishes toward his father were emerging from primal repression and being lived out in the transference. The reader may remember that I said then that the early part of D's analysis had centered around his narcissistic conflicts, conflicts partly caused by the fact that a certain reversal of generations had taken place in his family, with D being admired and looked up to by his father.

The sessions I will describe at this point took place during the two times weekly face to face psychotherapy that we conducted for a year before conversion to five times a week analysis.

In one session we discussed, as we had many times previously, D's difficulty accepting responsibility. On this occasion, however, certain details had emerged that made a strong impression on him. Objecting to my observation that he had difficulty facing reality, he brought up the fact that he was straightforwardly responsible about such things as doing the dishes and driving. I asked him what he made of this, and he remembered how his mother would usually set up a chair beside her when he was small, so that he could help her do dishes, and had taught him how to go about washing them. Similarly his father had taken a great interest in teaching him how to drive properly. I pointed out that these were then both instances where his parents had not followed their usual policy of helping him avoid responsibility. He thought of the good feelings these activities gave him. It was a pleasure in the process of the activity, that was relatively muted compared to his usual swings from elation to depression, and that depended on an inner feeling of pride and not on other people's approval.

D reported in the next session that our discussion seemed to have helped him. Certain fantasies of hurting people who were close to a woman who had rejected him had disappeared, although they had reappeared as he was lying in bed at night. These fantasies had become so strong of late that he had become worried that he might carry them out, although he had no history at all of violence. I said, "Maybe our discussion last session of responsibility, and of how you were helped or not helped to assume it, helped you put the violent fantasies aside, but maybe they came back when you lay down and relaxed, physically and mentally."

D responded by giving details of how he had expanded a lie he had told some friends in order to gain their sympathy. He wondered if maybe he really wanted to be caught in the lie. "No, that can't be," he said. "It would be too painful and embarrassing to actually be caught. On the other hand I remember hoping I would be caught and punished in my childhood. But I rarely was. I remember one time, I was smoking as a teenager, and my mom just happened to drive by the street I was walking down. She stopped and she started screaming at me. I guess that was one time someone said something. But you know even then, after she'd stopped screaming she asked me to get into the car, and then she asked me to give her a cigarette. She lit up and was completely calm. It was strange—as if the whole thing had never happened."

At this point D looked at me with a sly smile and said, "I was just thinking how guilty you'd feel if you'd heard I'd actually committed the murders."

I felt a chill go through me, and a signal of mingled guilt and anxiousness. I regained my balance quickly, by a process that must have been largely preconscious, since I was aware of very little except that I found myself saying, "But why should I feel guilty if you kill someone?"

D looked puzzled and then said, "Well, you know the case in the States. You might be found guilty of negligence for not informing the police."

"But why would I be negligent? You've had violent fantasies but have no history of carrying them out. Under the circumstances, or for that matter under any circumstances, shouldn't *you* be the guilty one if you commit murder."

D again looked surprised and puzzled. "But it's normal to have violent fantasies. Everyone does. Why should I feel guilty about them?"

"We weren't talking about your violent fantasies, but about whether you should feel guilty if you commit murder."

D was struck by how he had not understood this. I said, "Do you see what's been happening? Your were talking about how you had wanted to be disciplined but your parents had let you off the hook, and then you tried two maneuvers to let yourself off the hook. First you tried to push off your guilt onto me, and when I pointed out that maneuver, you minimized the issue we were talking about."

D was again struck by how he had tried to get around guilt. He talked of how confused he got when we discussed these issues, but then would feel genuinely helped by the process. I pointed out that by not helping him through reasonable discipline and guidance, his parents had left him exposed to the fear of being overwhelmed by his impulses. He now did not trust his fickle and easily avoided conscience to help him control his impulses any more than he could trust his parents to help him control them in his childhood. This led to a fear of acting out his murderous fantasies. A few more times during the session D attempted to externalize or dodge his guilty feelings, and I attempted each time to demonstrate to him how he did this.

"That was a good session yesterday," said D to begin the next session. He talked of how he now saw how he had tried to convince himself certain immoral things he had done in the past were all right, when they really were not. A bit later in the session, he knocked a cover off the arm of the chair that he was sitting in, and noticed that a worn patch was now exposed. The cover was easy to knock off. He had done it many times previously, and could easily have noticed the worn spot, so his action was most likely unconsciously motivated.

"The worn chair makes me think that maybe you're in bad financial shape too. How do I know? For all I know *you* could have a problem with handling money and be quite hard up because of it." He said this with a somewhat superior smile, and I felt myself squirming as if I had been caught, even though his speculation was off the mark. "I saw you coming out of one of the buildings down the street a few times," he continued. "Maybe you're going to a therapist. I know analysts have to go as part of their training. Maybe you have as many problems as me. There was the therapist I was seeing who had to be hospitalized." D went on like this for quite a while, listing other times he had seen me and cutting me down a notch each time with speculations about my various possible failings and weaknesses.

"Does all this make you think of anything?" I asked.

"Well, it does make me think of trying to drag all my therapists and you down to my level. But why shouldn't you be at my level? Is there something so wrong with our having an equal relationship?"

"I'm not so sure this is about equality in our relationship," I said. "I think it's about your difficulty in having anyone in authority above you. We've been looking at how you can't have your conscience above you either, as a guiding and prohibiting force. It was in the middle of talking about accepting and being guided by some of the dictates of your conscience that you began to drag me down. I think it's about dragging your conscience down, so again it will lose its power over you."

D went on to talk about how difficult it was not to be special, to become one of the common run of humanity. If he was to accept the dictates of his conscience, he would be just like everyone else, "and that would be a terrible thing," he said. "I'd hate to give up that feeling of being special."

Forms of Externalization

There are interesting questions related to narcissism raised by these sessions that I will leave aside for the time being, in order to discuss forms of externalization.[1] The first projection by D was his attempt to pawn off his feelings of guilt related to his aggressive fantasies onto me. While the content may be different, the mechanism is the same as externalization of other aspects of the self. As an example, let's look at D's externalization in the next session, when he took the worn armrest of my chair as evidence that I was bad at handling money and was in financial trouble. Both these things were true at the time with regard to D. He had been talking about accepting the dictates of his conscience and of not doing certain immoral things. I would imagine that he began preconsciously to think of his lack of responsibility with money, and as these facts caused D to feel bad about himself, this unpleasant feeling motivated a denial defense. He preconsciously scanned his perceptions and shifted his attention from himself to an appropriate external perception—my worn armchair and my presumed lack of responsibility concerning money—that allowed him to avoid perceiving these things about himself. As he went on, he kept speculating about me in ways that allowed him to attribute to me certain of his failings, such as psychological instability, that caused him a good deal of shame. Here too there was a shifting of attention and manipulation of reality in order to block awareness of characteristics that belonged to him.

I would argue that D's attribution of guilt to me in the first projection had exactly the same dynamic. He felt a signal of guilt about having aggressive fantasies, and then shifted his attention from him as murderer to me as responsible for murder. With this shift his guilt feelings disappeared. Thus I think the basic process is the same but the motivation differs: in attribution of responsibility the motivation is avoidance of guilt while externalization of aspects of the self is usually motivated by an attempt to avoid feelings of shame. In many instances shame and guilt are quite intertwined, while in others they are more clearly differentiated. In fact attribution of responsibility is generally, as with D, an externalization of that portion of the self that is seen as responsible or guilty.

Perhaps at this point some readers may feel that I have left out of my description the most important aspect of externalization. It is not just that D shifted his attention from himself to me, but that he attributed to me aspects that actually belonged to him. Is this self/other confusion not, after all, the defining characteristic of projective processes? Jacobson (1957) talked of a regressive concretization of inner reality in denial defenses in general, while Sandler (1987, Sandler and Sandler, 1998) felt transient primary identifications that are operative even in normal adults allow the shifting of characteristics from self to object or vice versa. My own feeling is that externalization, and defensive internalization as well, do not depend to as great an extent as is sometimes thought on regressive processes, although more deeply regressive processes may be involved in specific instances of the use of these defenses, especially in young children and adults with ego disturbances. I would agree with Sandler and with Hanly (1992), however, that our normal, always present ability to regressively merge with others and with the world around us is used at least to some extent to facilitate projective mechanisms. One of the problems with this issue, not just in relation to externalization but to denial defenses in general, is that these defenses have been studied especially in relation to ego disturbances, and findings from more disturbed patients have then been generalized. In this way the regressive concretizations and fluidity of self-object boundaries that occur in borderline cases, and in very young children, have been conflated with the defensive processes themselves. Let us look at some more clinical material to see if we can further our understanding of this issue.

I would ask the reader to think back to chapter 1 and my patient B, the woman who had some strong denials of the meanness, self-centeredness, and lack of caring displayed by her boyfriend. As B became sad, thinking of her boyfriend's lack of true caring, she began to talk of a former boyfriend with similar characteristics, and she felt less sad. When I pointed out to B the maneuver that she had used she again felt sad, and this time she shifted the attention to herself, saying she did not stick with relationships, something that was more true of her boyfriend. This defense is the reverse of externalization. B looked away from a characteristic of her boyfriend's that it pained her to see, and looked at herself. In the first instance B shifted attention from the present to the past, in the second from her boyfriend to herself. In this second instance she at the same time gave herself one of his characteristics, and no doubt this was achieved partly by a transient blurring of the boundaries between her and her boyfriend. It was also achieved through a process of her simply distorting an aspect of her history just enough that she could imply that she had some difficulty with investment in others, just as her boyfriend did.

We do not have to choose between these two possibilities, of blurring of self/object boundaries and attentional shifts, as they occur in varying combinations at the same time in each individual instance. What is clear is that what we are dealing with is a denial defense, working in combination with other maneuvers which may be different in each specific instance. From a theoretical perspective this is what we would expect, since what is defended against is a perception of aspects of reality, and since the attentional processes of the ego are what are generally used to defend against perceptions of, and judgments about, reality. When D said that I would be guilty if he committed a murder, he also was shifting his attention to certain responsibilities that he knew therapists do in fact have, and then by exaggeration and selective attention he distorted the realities of the situation into one where I would be responsible. He then went one step further. In this now distorted situation he imagined—even identified for a moment with—how guilty I would feel if he committed a murder, and then conveyed all of this to me both directly and subliminally, leading to my discomfort. This whole process was motivated by, and effective in negating, a perception of his responsibility for harmful wishes.

In the next session, as he was facing up to the sort of things he had done in his life, I think the feeling of narcissistic mortification became too much for D, and again he turned his attention to me. In order to block out his unpleasant perceptions regarding himself he knocked off the armrest cover and made inferences from the worn patch about me that made *me* the troubled one. He then, keeping his attention firmly fixed on me, flipped through his memories of things he had noticed about me that would allow him to keep inferring, if he stretched things a bit, that I had a troubled life. We can see the same things being done by B when she felt sad upon seeing just how uncaring her boyfriend was. She turned her attention either to other boyfriends or to herself, in each case supplementing this by rationalizations and distortions of the thing to which she had turned her attention. In both B's case and in the case of D's externalization, what we are dealing with is an attentional defense.

Having established that externalization is an attentional defense, we can use what we have discussed previously about the nature of attentional defenses to understand the differences between the projection of a drive and externalization of aspects of the self. An example of drive projection would be a borderline patient who, as their negative feelings towards the analyst mounts, accuses the analyst of being sadistic and wanting to hurt them, and distorts everything the analyst says to give it this meaning. This can be contrasted to D's externalizing onto me aspects of himself that caused him shame, such as his money difficulties.

Novick and Novick (1970) link drive projection with the anal stage (as do Meltzer [1966] and Juni [1979]), while they see extensive use of externalization as betraying problems from an even earlier age, which impair the integrative functions of the ego. They see drive projection, on the other hand, as linked to a weakness in the defensive system that holds the drives in check. They point out that drive projection is rarely adaptive (as opposed to externalization of aspects of the self in the young child) and that it is quite inefficient at allaying the anxiety that motivates its use. This is also in contrast to externalization of aspects of the self, which is remarkably efficient in quelling the painful feelings that motivate it, as shown by the examples I have just given of D and B. The Novicks also point out that drive projection is one in a long series of defenses, and is often followed by other defenses, while externalization is a single mechanism that stands alone.

A number of these characteristics of projection of drives and external-ization of inner realities become comprehensible in the light of the basic characteristics of both as attentional defenses. As we saw in the last chapter, attentional or denial defenses simply cannot deal very well with the propul-sive force of a drive, which would explain the fact that drive projection is called in as a secondary defense as repression fails, and also the observation that it is so ineffective in stopping the development of anxiety in such situa-tions. The fact that drive projection works so poorly also explains why other defenses are often called in to supplement it. Externalization of aspects of the self works so well because here a denial defense is doing what a denial defense does best—defend against the conscious awareness of an unpleasant reality. Externalization is thus a normal, adaptive defense, at least in early childhood, while drive projection is rarely adaptive, although in the face of a crumbling repression it may be the best a person can do.

The form of drive projection varies greatly, depending on the state of the primal repressions. In psychosis, where these are either very weak or nonex-istent, at least in certain sectors of the personality, drive projection can be asked to take on the entire burden of defense usually carried out by repres-sion. This leads to situations such as the delusions of paranoia. Freud (1911a) traced the various displacements, reversals, and turning against the self in the projections of this disorder, characteristics which betray very well the functioning of the primary process. This makes perfect sense if we consider that primal repression has failed completely in such cases. In borderline cases primal repressions exist but are porous, leading to extensive use of drive pro-jection, but here the attentional defense is really at the service of a very char-acteristic counterforce defense that partially replaces repression—projective identification. These shade into cases with more and more secure repression barriers, where drive projection comes to resemble externalization, since what is involved is the externalization of the internal perception and the idea that one is sexual or aggressive, while repression does the actual work of defending against the propulsive force of the drive. A very common example of this is seen in the reaction of patients in therapy who blame the therapist for having made them think of a drive related fantasy or image. I gave an example of this in the case of D in chapter 2. I would expect, on theoreti-cal grounds, that if externalization were to truly defend against a drive or powerful affect, it would need to be paired with a drive-based counterforce. I believe that this is what happens in certain forms of the defense referred to as projective identification, in which there is an aggressive rejection of the person into whom the drive derivatives are projected.

Projective identification involves a much more extensive distortion of reality as compared with externalization, which again makes sense if we think of projective identification as replacing repression of primary process conflicts by their projection onto the external world, which comes to take on some of the characteristics of the primary process, such as condensation and displacement from one thing onto another. As well, in projective identification you see the lack of synthesis of different trends such as love and hate, sexuality and aggression, just as with the primary process. In this form of counterforce defense, characteristic of borderline disorders, the partially neutralized aggression used as a counterforce in repression, which I described and illustrated in chapter 2, is replaced by a much less neutralized form of drive-based counterforce: the rageful rejection of, and attacks upon, the person or persons who have become carriers of the drive conflict. As an example a borderline patient of mine became angry at me when I made an interpretation about her sexual conflicts. There were clearly masochistic and sadistic fantasies involved, although my interpretation was quite general, merely pointing out that her anxieties may relate to sexual issues. Her attitude towards me, which had been for a few weeks quite friendly, changed abruptly. She not only became angry but accused me of being sadistic and cruel. For a few weeks after this she kept up her angry rejection of me, now seen as a sadistic, uncaring therapist who in fact was enjoying his cruel treatment of his poor patient. I was quite shaken by my patient's responses, and felt invaded by a feeling that I really was this terrible person that she was describing. This feeling was much more persistent than the transient feeling of discomfort that I had when D accused me of being guilty for a murder he might commit. It could last well into the evening, long after I had seen my patient. These are the sorts of counter-reactions brought on by projective identification.

It may be clarifying at this point, given that I have made the conceptual differentiation between two forms of defense, to introduce terminology that reflects this conceptual distinction. I would suggest the term "defensive externalization" for the basic attentional (denial) defense that I have described, and suggest reserving the term "projective identification" for the defense that, while it uses this attentional shift, also uses a drive-based counterforce, deployed at the interpersonal level. We would expect from our previous considerations regarding counterforce defenses, that projective identification would especially be used against drives and the ideas and strong affects directly linked with them, and I think this expectation is largely born out by clinical experience.

There is no sharp demarcation between these two defenses. There are transitional cases where some amount of counterforce, in pushing away the externalized aspect of the self, is added to the attentional defense. This was the case with D, and is the case with other non-borderline narcissistic patients as well. In these patients there are weakened repressions due to adolescent fixations and a not very strong or useful superego (these aspects can be seen in D's material, including in the descriptions to come in chapter 6). In borderline patients, with more severe deficiencies in stable, selective intrapsychic repressions, we see purer forms of projective identification as an interpersonal counterforce defense. There is thus a series that goes from neurotic personalities who rely largely on the intrapsychic counterforce of selective repression, through narcissistic characters with somewhat weakened repressions and a greater use of the interpersonal counterforce of projective identification, to borderline characters with much weakened intrapsychic counterforce defenses and much stronger interpersonal counterforce defenses. What this series shows is that a counterforce of some sort is needed to protect the ego from being completely swamped by the drives and by primary process functioning, as happens in the psychoses. This counterforce consists of some combination of intrapsychic and interpersonal counterforce. It is important to remember, also, that in each individual there are usually specific conflicts where projective identification is used to a greater extent, and others where selective repression is relied upon more, so that there might be a dynamic in response to which a specific person with a neurotic personality may use a greater amount of projective identification, because of weakened repressions in that area, as compared to another person with a not too severe borderline personality, who with regard to those particular conflicts may be capable of using selective repression.

At this point, I would like to continue our discussion of attentional defenses related to externalizing/internalizing processes, by looking at different forms of internalization.

Internalization

While externalization has a part to play in normal development, in protecting the young child from overly strong narcissistic injury, the adaptive uses of internalization are far more extensive. In fact one of the defining characteristics of normal adaptive development from infancy till at least early adulthood, if not well beyond, is the progressive internalization of functions previously performed by others, from the feeding and cleaning of oneself to moral and ethical guidance and the setting of long-term goals. The importance of frustration in fostering these internalizations, and the tendency of those who, at least in certain respects, have been overgratified (such as D) to resist internalization, are observations that will help us to understand narcissistic disorders in which internalization is resisted, as well as the contrary tendency to overinternalize in those who have been severely deprived (see chapters 6 and 7).

Defensive internalizations are almost as ubiquitous as adaptive ones, and of course there is no sharp demarcation between the two. One type of defensive internalization is very much the obverse of defensive externalization, in that it involves an attentional shift, this time from object to self. An example of this was provided by B, in the session described in chapter 1. As her denial of her boyfriend's lack of caring broke down, and she became sad, she said that she did not stick with relationships, and she did not want to give up on this one. "I don't want to just keep going from one relationship to another. I want to figure out what's wrong with me," she said. As she said this her sad feelings disappeared.

I think that B was becoming more aware of her boyfriend's lack of investment in her—I had brought it to her attention by talking of the hollowness of the relationship—and as this brought on painful feelings, she shifted her attention to her own behavior in relationships. She in fact did not have her boyfriend's narcissistic inability to truly care for someone. But she exaggerated one thing—the number of relationships she had had—and put a different interpretation on another. It was true that she had problems in relationships, but this was actually because of her unerring ability to choose narcissists. By distorting these realities about herself, B implied that she had problems with sustained investment in another.

As with externalization, this form of internalization is very effective in curbing awareness of an unpleasant reality, and thus of stopping the development of unpleasant feelings engendered by this awareness. This effectiveness accounts for the persistence of these defenses, although it is bought at the price of full awareness of, and long-term adaptation to, reality.

The process of defensive internalization should be distinguished from both introjection and identification. Psychoanalysts have generally distinguished two broad categories of identification: primary, global identification and secondary, selective identification. Classical analysts such as Jacobson (1964) conceptualized primary identification as involving the merger of the person's self representation and an object representation. This takes place especially in early childhood, and in serious borderline and psychotic disorders. There is also a form of immediate perception of what the other is feeling and doing that lies at the base of empathy, and involves a kind of immediate primary mirroring identification that does not rely on regression or the blurring of self-object boundaries. I think this is what Freud (1921) was referring to when he talked of a primary identification that was the first form of relationship to objects. Joseph Sandler (1976) also referred often to this type of immediate imitation which he suggested was the basis for the analyst's role responsiveness. He described this as the unconscious, automatic pull towards playing certain roles unconsciously assigned by the patient, as a player in their internal drama. It is possible that a part of this form of identification is a more mature and modulated form of the psychotic and early infantile primary identification, but I think it is also a primary inborn ability that can be differentiated from these other processes. What is involved in such phenomena as role responsiveness is a combination of automatic, inborn mirroring and a modulated, temporary self/object fusion.

Secondary identification involves the selective, stable taking in of traits of someone else. These may be mannerisms, specific interests of the person, or characteristics such as honesty. One of the foundations of the working alliance in therapy is the patient's selective identification with those aspects of the analyst's activity related to analyzing. We could contrast this with the therapeutic alliance, as described by Elizabeth Zetzel (1965), which relies especially on different forms of primary identifications on the part of both the patient and therapist as they mutually adjust to each other in ways that allow a basic comfort, trust, and bonding to occur. Secondary identification is derived, through modulation and ego control, from the two types of primary identification—both the immediate, inborn mirroring function and the merging of self and object images.

Introjection is a very special process, in which an object, something like an inner presence, is set up inside a person's mind. This inner object, called an introject, behaves in many ways like a person in the outside world. Introjects become comprehensible if we conceptualize them as partaking of characteristics of the zero process. I will mention them later, once I have introduced the idea of the zero process. I would only like at this point to emphasize that defensive internalization, such as B taking on the badness of her parents, is a different process than the setting up of an introject as an internal object inside a person's mind.

I realize these very brief comments on different types of internalization do little justice to their complexity and to many of the controversies and unanswered questions surrounding them. I will be describing certain specific dynamics related to internalization in following chapters. My main concern has been to situate the new processes I have been describing, such as the attentional defenses of defensive internalization and defensive externalization, in relation to other processes and dynamics.

Psychotherapeutic Technique

Transference and Countertransference

Freud understood transference as largely a displacement, across the repression barrier, of memories, feelings, and drives from a past relationship onto the analyst. This displacement was aided by the nature of the primary process into which these memories, fantasies, and drives had been repressed (where displacements along lines of superficial similarity, primitive symbolization, and condensation reigned). The powerful push of the drives for expression also aided in the formation of the transference, which was a compromise between this and the equally powerful counterforce of the repression that forced this expression into alternate paths. For Freud the analyst's countertransference was either a similar process taking place in the analyst, directed towards the patient, or this process called up in the analyst by the transference of the patient. Freud differentiated this countertransference from the unconscious communication that allowed the analyst to pick up some of what was active in the patient's unconscious.

Since Freud's original formulations, many other forms of transference, countertransference, and mutual influence between patient and analyst have been described, including various forms of externalization of parts of the self, of the superego, and of introjects, as well as processes of turning passive into active, enactment of traumatic past events, and others. The idea of an inner object world and of projective identification as the main mechanism leading to the mutual interaction of the patient's and the analyst's inner object worlds and to enactments is now one of the dominant ways of conceptualizing patient/analyst interactions. One trend has been to blur the boundaries between, or to not differentiate at all between, the analyst's use of the unconscious communications from the patient in understanding him, and countertransference. This trend began with certain key papers on countertransference in the 1950s, for instance the very influential one by Racker (1957), which argued for the analyst's use of his or her countertransference feelings in comprehending the patient. While these two areas of the patient's influence on the analyst form a continuum, I think it is useful to differentiate them at times, as Freud did, while of course at others the difference between one and the other is more difficult to see. One reason for the difficulties in this area is that the specific interpersonal counterforce defense of projective identification creates a situation where the analyst's responses are often much more directly a reflection of the patient's impulses, fantasies, and experiences. It was as an attempt to comprehend this sort of situation that many of the newer ideas (for instance Kleinian ones) about transference and countertransference were developed. There is little doubt that the classical conceptualizations, and the classic analytic techniques related to displacement transferences, have difficulty with this dynamic, but they actually work very well in other situations. I believe that what is needed is a more integrated set of conceptualizations that retain the useful aspects of the older technique (as I tried to explicate it in the chapter on repression), but that expand the conceptualizations and technical ideas with respect to other forms of defense and other dynamics.

I think it is useful to distinguish between different types of transference based on different defenses and different modes of psychic functioning. A reasonable way to proceed may be to use transference (and countertransference) as the more general term for a dynamic process entering into the relationship between patient and therapist. We could use this term without qualifiers when the context makes it clear which type of transference we are referring to, or if we are simply talking more loosely and are not so concerned about conceptual accuracy.

Displacement transference is a term already in use to describe Freud's classical transference, based on repression and the primary process. I have suggested the terms defensive externalization and defensive internalization for two forms of attentional defenses that enter the transference and countertransference. Here an attentional defense is involved, and most of the action takes place within the secondary process. Both the different type of defense and of processing between a displacement transference and these attentional ones affect their way of manifesting, their effect on the therapist, how he or she can best gain information about them, and how they can best analyze them. I discussed some of the differences in the last two chapters. One topic I did not discuss in detail was how we gain information about these two transferences. The free association, evenly hovering attention, and unconscious intuition and empathy used with the displacement transference is well known and has often been described. One is aided in understanding what is going on by tuning into the patient's primary process functioning with one's own, although secondary process reasoning and understanding also play their part. In the case of transferences based on attentional defenses acting on largely secondary process material, there is also a kind of listening intuitively, but this is a different kind of intuition, involving an intuitive grasp of certain secondary process maneuvers. I had to use this kind of intuition, for instance, in understanding what D was doing to me when he said I would be guilty if he killed someone, in the earlier example in this chapter.

To get our bearings, before jumping into all of the complexities of these different reactions and their analysis, which will be presented in the next chapter and in part 2, we can note that there are three basic types of defense that have different transference and countertransference correlates: counterforce defenses, attentional defenses, and zero process defenses. There are also three basic forms of mental processing: the secondary process, the primary process, and the zero process. Each of these three has one type of defense with which it is predominantly associated. The primary process is predominantly associated with repression and other counterforce defenses, the secondary process with various attentional defenses, and the zero process with zero process defenses. (The zero process will be described in the next chapter, and zero process defenses in chapter 8, on perversions.) The two together (form of processing and of defense) determine the form that the transference takes. Using this basic scheme, we can comprehend the differences between a displacement transference seen with repressed conflicts, which displays many of the characteristics of the primary process, and the externalizing transference that D exhibited in the example that began this chapter.

In chapter 2, on repression, I gave the example of D's primal repression partially breaking down and how other defenses—denials and externalizations—helped to shore it up. Based on this example, I delineated the concepts of primal defense, after defense, and secondary defense. If we think of transferences as being based on defenses, then we may be able to use these ideas about defenses to help us untangle the intertwining of different forms of transferences and repetition in an analysis. Various transient transferences appear fleetingly in an analysis, and are usually a product of secondary or after defenses, while more powerful, deeper going transferences that develop as time goes by are usually the product of primal defenses. The classic transference neurosis is the best known of these, and can be seen from this perspective as a primal transference based on primal repression. This primal transference is supported by various transitory secondary transferences. For instance D's externalization of his responsibility and guilt for his murderous thoughts onto me, as well as his further externalization of his sense of himself as irresponsible and poor onto me, described at the beginning of this chapter, can both be seen as secondary transferences, in that they were related to his primal transference in which I was his oedipal father who threatened him with castration. This oedipal position was defended against by emphasizing his positive, nurturing relationship with his father, and with me, and generally regressing to a narcissistic position, in which he did not accept

responsibility for his impulses or actions. Even as these were secondary transference positions in relation to D's primal oedipal transference, they were
also related to certain primal denial defenses that D maintained in relation
to life's various limitations. Thus in relation to this issue, the externalizing
transferences were not secondary, but led right to the heart of D's narcissistic
fixations and narcissistic defenses, which I will describe in detail in chapter
6, on narcissism.

To give another example of primal and secondary transferences: B's internalizing transference, a transference of defense described earlier, acted along
with identifications, externalizations, and other transferences as secondary
resistances and adjuncts to her primal oedipal displacement transference
(transference neurosis). At the same time this internalizing transference was
the leading edge of a primal defensive internalization, in which she defended
against awareness of the narcissism of both of her parents by feeling she
was at fault. This primal defensive internalization (motivated by pervasive,
overwhelming painful feelings that this reality engendered) led to a primal
transference and, in relation to this primal transference of internalizing my
failures and mistakes, both the milder internalizing transference and other
transferences, including oedipal ones, acted as secondary transferences.
(This type of internalizing transference—the defensive use of guilt—will be
described in chapter 7, in its relation to masochism.)

Summary

Externalization and internalization are not basic forms of defense, as are
counterforce and attentional defenses. Rather, these terms are descriptive,
and cover a number of distinct processes.

I described two attentional defenses, defensive internalization and defensive externalization. These defenses use the attentional processes of the ego.
In the case of defensive externalization, an unwelcome internal reality (for
instance the realization that one has made a mistake or committed a moral
wrong) is defended against by shifting attention to something similar in the
outside world, for instance that someone else may have committed a mistake
or wrong. Defensive internalization involves the same mechanism going
the other way. These attentional defenses have at times been confused with
other processes. For instance, defensive externalization has been confused
with turning passive into active, with projective identification, and with role
reversal, while defensive internalization has been equated with identification
and introjection. Quite often externalization and defensive internalization are
used together with these other processes to form complex defensive conglom-

erates, all of which are often subsumed under the term projective identification. I described projective identification as a specific counterforce defense, which uses defensive externalization along with aggressive drive energy to put an unwanted feeling or impulse into the other, and then forcefully reject them.

In discussing the relevance of all this to psychotherapeutic technique, I argued for a multidimensional view of transference, with a number of basic transference and countertransference dynamics related to counterforce, attentional, and zero process defenses and the primary, secondary, and zero processes.

Next, in order to round out our survey of basic forms of defense, we turn to a consideration of the sequelae, defensive and otherwise, of trauma.

Terms

Defensive Externalization: An attentional defense in which, in order to avoid awareness of an unpleasant internal reality, such as an aspect of the self or a moral failing, the person shifts their attention to some similar aspect of external reality.

Defensive Internalization: An attentional defense in which, in order to avoid awareness of a distressing external reality, such as the lack of caring of a parent, the person shifts their attention to an aspect of themselves.

Identification: A process in which a person shapes an aspect of themselves on the model of someone else. Identifications can be more global, or involve partial characteristics of the person identified with.

Internalization: A general term that covers many processes in which some aspect of external reality or external relationship shapes an internal process or structure of a person's mind. Identification, introjection, and defensive internalization are all types of internalization.

Note

1. See chapter 6 for a discussion of narcissism along with a more detailed presentation of D's case. In chapter 8, more material from D will be presented as part of a discussion of his sexual dynamics and acting out.

~

CHAPTER FIVE

Trauma

Trauma is a complex and multifaceted phenomenon that relates to the processes of defense in a number of interesting ways. This chapter explores a few of these. We will first investigate the basic nature of the traumatic process and look at how it comes about through the breakdown of basic defenses, as well as of certain functions that support them. Next we will explore the anxiety response, the motivation for defense, and how these relate to the processes in trauma. I will then describe the form of functioning that is left in the wake of trauma. I will argue that it is distinct from both the primary and the secondary processes, and thus deserves a separate term: the zero process. The section on therapeutic technique will develop some of these theoretical ideas further, looking at the forms of transference and countertransference seen in relation to trauma, at the nature of the defenses that protect the zero process areas left over from trauma, and at the methods for analyzing trauma and reducing its push for repetition.

The Traumatic Process

Psychoanalysis began with a traumatogenic theory of the neuroses. Breuer and Freud (1893) noted that their observations "seem to us to establish an analogy between the pathogenesis of common hysteria and that of traumatic neuroses, and to justify an extension of the concept of traumatic hysteria" (p 15). They felt that fright led to memories of the incident not being worked over and the affects not being abreacted, and therapy was thus directed towards bringing this abreaction about. At the time of Breuer and Freud's publication there was quite a lot of interest in the topic of trauma (and the associated one of dissociation) on the part of other investigators as well, such as Pierre Janet and Alfred Binet. As Freud went on to study the conflicts related to childhood sexuality, and further developed his ideas of fixation and regression, his opinion about neurosogenesis changed. He asserted in the Introductory Lectures (1916—1917) that trauma was not equivalent to neurosis. He defined trauma at that time as "an experience which within a short period of time presents the mind with an increase of stimulus too powerful to be dealt with or worked off in the normal way, and this must result in permanent disturbances of the manner in which energy operates" (p 275). Such a definition brings up many questions. What is the "normal way" of working over a stimulus? How can the ability to do this be overwhelmed? And why would this then lead to "permanent disturbances of the manner in which energy operates"?

In order to begin our exploration of these questions, I would like briefly to describe an experience of mine that certainly led to no permanent changes, and thus could not be called a trauma in the strict sense, but which demonstrates some aspects of the traumatic process.

I was drying myself off after a rather long, hot, and quite relaxing shower. I remember being very little aware of my surroundings. I was thinking about something for which I now have no memory when the bathroom door suddenly opened and my son jumped towards me with a hissing sound. For a moment I had no idea what was happening. Quite a large number of thoughts and feelings passed through my mind in that moment, as I had the distinct feeling that time was standing still. I thought of a robber or some other type of attacker but then, rather implausibly, it seemed to me that our cat, which we had given away that week because of my worsening allergies, had come back with the size and ferocity of a lion to revenge herself on me.

I became aware, within a second or two, of what had actually happened. Attempting to surprise each other and the grownups had become quite a sport among the children in our family. Sometimes it was funny; sometimes I found it mildly annoying. I was shocked as I heard the tone of almost vicious anger in my voice as I scolded my son. It didn't take me very long to regain control of my behavior enough to apologize to him, which seemed to only partially mollify his own surprised upset at my reaction. Within a few minutes I felt completely back to normal, the whole thing having passed away almost as suddenly as it had started.

Two days later I was separating out a sheet of stamps when they tore unexpectedly along the perforations, and I had a very strong startle response, as I jumped up and my heart rate increased. I was surprised at my response, but as I thought about it I realized that the sound of the ripping perforations reminded me of my son's hissing sound as he jumped at me. This was the only subsequent reaction that I could link with my scare in the washroom. In fact, when I sat down to write the details of the incident two days afterwards, spurred on by my startle reaction with the stamps, I found that the memory had already faded, and I had a sense of doubt whether I really had had such a strong reaction. This fading seemed peculiar to me, given how strange and striking my reaction had seemed to me at the time. I am not sure if my description has conveyed this strangeness strongly enough. It felt quite outside my normal range of experience, and my feeling about the cat revenging herself on me felt uncannily like a dream.

The first thing I would emphasize about what happened is the element of surprise. It had occurred previously that in my children's efforts to startle me they had managed to catch me unawares, but in each of these instances I was paying at least some attention to the outside world. I am convinced that this is why my reactions at these other times never went beyond a slight fright with an increased heart rate. Lack of preparedness is well known as a key factor in trauma. Even having a second or two to assess and prepare for an event will often turn it from a traumatic into a merely upsetting one. It seems this preparedness allows the stimulus to be "worked off in the normal way," which is actually a complex process of barriers being raised to excessive stimulation, the stimuli being given meaning, categorized, and connected to memories, and affects evoked by the stimuli being expressed but modulated.

Another way of conceptualizing preparedness, or the lack of it, is in terms of the raising or lowering of a stimulus barrier. For Freud this concept was a key to the understanding of trauma. He (1920) felt that there was no shield against internal stimuli, but that it was the breaching of the barrier against external stimulation that began the traumatic process. This breach led to a large influx of stimulation, which now behaved like a drive in terms of the pressure it exerted on the mind, requiring a large amount of energy to hold it at bay and shore up the rent in the stimulus barrier. This lessens the energy available for other ego functions, leading to a final ego collapse. Freud also thought this breaching of the stimulus barrier put the pleasure principle out of commission. He saw the later sequelae of trauma, especially the repetition of the trauma in dreams and action, as being attempts to reinstate the pleasure principle. All of this no doubt sounds quite abstract, and difficult to connect to the actual experience of trauma, but as I explicate these points I will make these connections. I will begin with the idea of the stimulus barrier.

At its most basic the stimulus barrier could be identified with the ego's function of filtering stimuli and instituting various thresholds below which they are not perceived. These thresholds are quite fluid, and adaptable within certain limits. Coming back to a busy city from a visit to the countryside can be quite overstimulating, especially if the stay in the country was long enough for one's stimulus thresholds to adapt to the quieter environment. If one lives in the city and is used to the bustle, the adaptation in the opposite direction—a raising of the stimulus thresholds so city life again becomes bearable—will take place quite rapidly after the initial period of overstimulation.

A little consideration makes it clear, however, that trauma does not depend purely on levels of stimulation. Some would say that it depends not at all on such levels. Charles Brenner (1986), for instance, stated that it was not the level of the stimulus but rather its meaning that made it traumatic. I think this is too extreme a view, which is not born out by experience. Many events with an extremely distressing meaning do not give rise to the characteristic traumatic reactions of a shutdown of ego functions (felt as a numb state in which one is not taking things in), but rather lead to specific defenses being deployed, or to various other adaptive measures. On the other hand sudden shocks, such as my son leaping through the bathroom door, do lead to a breakdown of the normal processing of reality. Still, meaning does play an important role, which can be more clearly seen, for instance, when a child is told of the unexpected death of their parent. While such a situation is not always traumatic, and whether it is or not is partially determined by the element of surprise and the state of the child's ego (Furman, 1986), meaning is more important than stimulus level in such cases.

How are we to understand these contradictory aspects of trauma? Some would suggest that these difficulties demonstrate the lack of usefulness of the stimulus barrier concept. Others have attempted a broader definition of it. Erna Furman (1986) equated it with the entire defensive functioning of the ego. Furst (1978) thought it may be a correlate of the desomatization mechanism seen in R.E.M. sleep. He saw this passive stimulus barrier as being supplemented by the mother's care of the infant and eventually by active ego measures, including the defense mechanisms. Krystal (1978a) thought of the stimulus barrier as a complex of many ego functions, such as selective screening and attention. I agree with these views, but feel that it is possible to be more specific about the defenses involved in the stimulus barrier.

There is a hierarchy of ego functions that filter and process stimuli. What Furst called the passive stimulus barrier is present from birth but undergoes a progressive development in which it becomes a quite active complex of processes that dampen and select stimuli. Added to this barrier are the at-tentional processes of the ego as well as the use of these processes for defen-sive purposes—what I have called the denial defenses, which include primal denials. When an event impinges too suddenly and/or too forcefully upon a person, the adaptive capacities of these processes, which are quite good given enough time, are exceeded and they may begin to shut down. Why these processes, which together constitute the stimulus barrier broadly conceived, should shut down like this is an interesting question, but one that is probably outside of the ability of psychoanalysis alone, without the help of neurosci-entific and probably evolutionary ideas and data, to explain. However, given the fact of this shutting down, a cascade of reactions is set in motion that, if it goes far enough, leads to a trauma.

Furst (1978) felt that the defenses are the first ego functions to fail, and that once this happens one gets non-acute signal anxiety. If this level of reaction is overwhelmed, more primitive methods such as withdrawal are resorted to, and once these fail, the stimulus barrier has truly been breached, and the traumatic process ensues. A regression takes place along the line of development of how affects are dealt with, leading to dedifferentiation, re-somatization, and deverbalization of affect (Krystal, 1978a). In the example of my fright in the washroom, things did not go so far. It would seem that my reaction largely remained at the level of signal anxiety, which occurred once my primal denial of the possibility of serious injury or death had been suddenly breached. Even at this level, energies were quickly withdrawn from other ego functions to shore up the breach, and as my primal repressions were weakened by this, the whole situation took on the character of a dream. This allowed the image of a large cat attacking me to come up, and to be used by me as a way of putting a kind of psychic Band-Aid (that is, to give meaning, irrational as it was) over a rent in my processing of reality.

If I had not been able to quickly right myself psychically by seeing that nothing dangerous was actually occurring, if for instance a psychopathic murderer was actually lunging at me with a knife, then my way of under-standing the attack as a revenge for my having sent away our cat could have ended up (assuming that I survived the attack) being imprinted powerfully on my mind. Such understandings of a trauma, arrived at under the sway of the primary process during or immediately after the event, usually have a far-reaching and persistent effect on the traumatized person's life. If I had actually been subject to the knife attack, there would have been a regres-sion in affect modulation and desomatization, as well as a shutdown in the basic integrating function of my ego, leading to unsynthesized perceptual fragments being stored in my memory. These would serve as the basis for a

dissociation of the trauma. My primal denials related to the safety and pre-
dictability of the world and others, and the primal denial of my own death,
would have been much more deeply shaken—even shattered—compared to
what actually took place.

It is worthwhile to pause for a moment to consider the issue of the primal
denial of death. The sudden shattering of this denial in certain traumas has
a profoundly disturbing effect on the future course of a person's functioning,
and yet I have given an example of a not uncommon situation, in the chapter on denial, of the profoundly enhancing and positive effect of the gradual
partial relinquishing of this same denial. In this second situation the ego has
time to adjust itself and its functioning, demonstrating very well that it is not
only the meaning of an event—a meaning that is quite similar in the two
examples—but also and especially the suddenness with which the ego has to
confront the meaning, that leads to the traumatic process.

To give another example of this, an event having the meaning of helplessness has been proposed as a crucial aspect of what makes something traumatic,
for instance by Dowling (1986). But many events and situations in a person's
life may carry a powerful meaning of helplessness without leading to a trauma.
In fact here too there are many instances—for instance being able to face
and feel the sadness about the fact that one cannot make an unloving parent
love one—where accepting the fact of one's helplessness can be liberating. It
is other factors, such as a depleted or immature ego, or the suddenness of the
confrontation with the meaning of helplessness, that then shatters the primal
denial of the complete indifference of the world to our wishes, and that leads
to trauma. (Although I have been emphasizing the suddenness of the event in
trauma, here may be the point to note that surprise or suddenness is only one,
although a very common, means to get to the final end point of the collapse
of certain ego functions that modulate and process incoming stimuli. A slow
weakening of the ego to the point of this collapse, as occurs in certain types of
confinement or emotional abuse, is also a means to this endpoint.)

It should be clear from what has been said so far that the defensive breakdown that initiates the traumatic process takes place in the denial defenses.
Only secondarily does it involve the counterforce defenses, as ego energies
are called upon to shore up the failing stimulus barrier and as ego regression
takes place.[1] These events lead to the weakening of the counterforce defenses
and the invasion of the ego by primary process functioning. An example of
this was my sense of time standing still when my son leaped at me. Such time
distortions are common during trauma (Terr, 1984). Another example of my
ego functioning being closer to the primary process level was my fantasy of a
revenge attack from my cat, now returning as a huge beast of prey.

Actually, many analysts would see the relationship between this fantasy and the traumatic process differently from my description. They would see the fantasy, no doubt a derivative of aggressive, murderous ones from my childhood, as bubbling up for one reason or another around the time of my son's entry, and being the motive force for my reactions to it. In fact I can reveal that at around this time in my self-analysis certain angry feelings and a trauma from my early childhood that I could connect to my son's entry were emerging. Proponents of the primacy of unconscious fantasy and conflict in the causation of trauma will see this as clinching the argument in their favor. (I realize that what actually happened was not traumatic, but we could do the thought experiment of a murderous attack by a psychopath that I survived and would thus understand in terms of these fantasies.)

In supporting this view of trauma Abend (1986) argued that in the psychoanalysis of trauma, "it is the elements of unconscious conflict, and the patterns of compromise formation which these take in the psychic lives of our patients, to which therapeutic attention should always and unfailingly be directed" (p 103). In fact Abend's views are probably not as one-sided as this quote, since he does admit the importance of the actual events of the trauma, and in fact gives some very good examples of how analysis of memories of specific aspects of a trauma led to an understanding of certain symptoms. Still, he and Charles Brenner are both forceful proponents of a view that I think overextends extremely valuable analytic discoveries regarding the importance of unconscious conflict related to the drives.

As Phillips (1991) has remarked, merely because unconscious fantasies attach themselves to a trauma does not prove that they are causative. In fact it is the details of the actual trauma that occur in the flashbacks and other symptoms. (My jumping when the ripping stamps sounded like my son was a minor but striking example of this.) These phenomena are one piece of evidence for the importance of the actual events of the trauma. Another is the common clinical finding that it is only once the defenses against the traumatic event have been analyzed sufficiently and the split off feelings and memories have been recovered, that the connections with unconscious fantasies and drives come to the fore, opening up avenues for the analysis of childhood repressions. Detailed examples of this process have been given by Phillips (1991), Gaensbauer (1994), and Ira Brenner (2001). Abend's recommendations on technique, if fully put into practice, would not facilitate this kind of work and could lead (often do lead, I believe) to denying patients the full depth of analysis that is possible for them.

I would not want these comments to be taken as a complete denial of the importance of drive/defense conflicts and the unconscious fantasies based on them in trauma. Quite apart from the fact that once they have attached to trauma their analysis is crucial to resolving it, it is also true that there are various areas of sensitivity based on these conflicts—as an example the sensitivity to trauma in the phallic phase. However, I think it is a mistake to understand the sensitivity to traumatization in terms of a conflict being so active that it seeks out a point of attachment in reality and creates the trauma. The actual process is usually quite different from this. I would like now to delve further into this process, by looking first at anxiety and trauma, and then at the nature of the unique form of mental functioning that is a consequence of intense trauma.

Anxiety and Trauma

In the chapter on repression I criticized Freud's concept of traumatic anxiety as the motive for repression, proposing instead to follow Yorke, Wiseberg, and Freeman in calling this type of anxiety pervasive anxiety. These authors (1989) have presented a very useful set of conceptual distinctions regarding anxiety. They describe a developmental line beginning with vegetative excitation, which they say is reverted to in trauma. True affect begins with the mentalization of this excitation, leading to overwhelming anxiety (psychic panic), a complete helplessness that can only be relieved from outside. The next stage is that of pervasive anxiety, the motivation for crude defenses (primal defenses in my terminology), which is eventually tamed enough to lead to the beginnings of signal anxiety in latency. Adolescence leads to a major restructuring of ego responses and eventually to the development of mature signal anxiety. This scheme of Yorke, Wiseberg, and Freeman can also be used, I believe, with regard to other affects. Thus we could say more generally that pervasive affects are the motives for primal defenses. When these defenses are loosened, we can catch a glimpse of this pervasive affect—for instance D's fear of me as his oedipal repression was analyzed, or E's sadness that seemed as if it would never end when her primal denial of her mother's lack of caring was pierced.

Overwhelming anxiety is also seen in borderline conditions. Yorke and Wiseberg (1976) discuss the case of Norma, a young borderline child who became panicky when the ambulance that brought her to sessions missed its turn on the roundabout and went around again. "Norma at once thought they would go round and round the roundabout forever and never get off, so that they would never get to the clinic" (pp 116–117). This fear, a form of abandonment anxiety, then began to generalize to all round objects, which inspired the same terror. Norma then tried, with partial success, to contain the anxiety by using the word "round"—that is, to contain it by using secondary process symbolization.

Norma's deficiency in the ability to limit anxiety to a signal is the hallmark of a borderline condition. While she had difficulty developing signal anxiety, her anxiety state did not develop into the diffuse vegetative excitation seen in trauma. Clinically, however, because of their tendency to be swamped by anxiety, at least in relation to certain issues, patients with severe post-traumatic neuroses can be misdiagnosed as suffering from borderline conditions. In the psychiatric literature on trauma Herman and Van der Kolk (1987, also Herman, 1992) suggest that in fact borderline personality disorder is a form of post-traumatic disorder. Although of course they are often seen together, these two entities cannot be equated with each other, and in fact making the distinction between them can greatly clarify our understanding of both. Ira Brenner (2001) points out that post-traumatic patients have tremendous difficulties with trust in the treatment, while those suffering from borderline conditions have a more immature, ambivalently clinging attitude. The ego deficiencies in the latter are more global, relating especially to synthesis and the ability to modulate affects and not have them run away and become overwhelming. Patients with post-traumatic neurosis also have this problem, but in more circumscribed areas, relating to the trauma.

Through all this we have not really approached any closer to answering another question—why is trauma beyond the pleasure principle? Why does the avoidance of psychic, and often even physical, pain cease during the traumatic process? There is probably no way to answer such a question on purely psychoanalytic grounds. Most mammals have reactions to being overwhelmed by external stimuli that have many similarities with the human trauma response. Perhaps a beginning in answering the question posed could be made through combining ideas and findings from the experimental and naturalistic study of animal behavior with those of evolutionary biology, psychoanalysis, and the neurosciences.

Once the stimulus barrier has been breached and the reaction of avoidance of pain collapses, it is striking with what rapidity the traumatic process unfolds, and how little it is under the traumatized person's control. As Furst (1978) pointed out, the problem with trauma is that the ego is faced with a *fait accompli*. Its resources are directed largely at diminishing and then encapsulating and keeping at bay the area of disarray and severely regressed functioning within itself that trauma leaves in its wake. We will now turn to look at the sorts of defenses that the ego uses for this task, and at the type of functioning that is left after trauma. We begin with some clinical material that will give some concrete examples of the issues to be discussed.

Clinical Example: E

I will continue here with the history of my patient E, whom I presented in the section on primal denial. There I described our analysis of her denial of her mother's lack of loving investment in her. She had talked at times about the possibility that she had been sexually abused by her father. She always approached the topic in a very roundabout way, through veiled comments and innuendo. We came to call her way of doing this "hovering." Her hovering style seemed similar to what she described as her mother's way of making accusations about sexual abuse towards E's father, brother, and others. I wondered whether, as is common in a child onto whom a parent projects their drives (Novick and Novick, 1970), E's ability to securely repress her drives had been interfered with. Perhaps instead of a strong repression, she was relying on projection of her sexual wishes onto her father to keep them from awareness.

E talked much more about her mother than her father. Her mother had been at times quite physically brutal with E—for instance subjecting her to painful enemas in early latency. She had also consistently practiced a form of psychological brutality in which she was quite charming and then, just when E let down her guard, would blurt out vicious comments. Much of the first few years of the analysis were spent exploring this relationship as well as the way in which E reenacted it with other disturbed or narcissistic individuals.

Whenever we had had a session where we had been a bit more familiar—perhaps sharing a joke—I noticed that the next day E would look at me rather warily when she came into the office, and have a rather silent session. I pointed this out to her, making the interpretation that her reaction might be related to her mother's way of getting her to relax before making a cutting comment. This made sense to E, who also brought up the way in which she would find herself saying some quite vicious things to herself, and having some bizarrely sadistic images of what she would do to herself. I interpreted that she was beating her mother to the punch by these comments and images, and perhaps the bizarreness was an identification with her mother's bizarre ideas. She said she could certainly identify the way she attacked herself with her mother's style, and referred to the part of her that did this as her "inner mother."

Through these first years of the analysis E's hovering comments related to sexual abuse by her father appeared on and off. I found myself hovering as well, between thinking that E had been sexually abused, and thinking that she was identifying with her mother's way of hovering and accusing her father, perhaps as a defense against recognizing both her own sexual wishes and her mother's abuse of her. I somehow could not get a clear picture of things. Many indicators, such as E's naiveté about her anatomy and about sexuality even in her early twenties, seemed as attributable to her mother's sexualized abuse of her as to sexual abuse by her father. E enjoyed sex, and was orgasmic with vaginal intercourse, but did not like to have her clitoris touched or to engage in oral sex.

E talked about her closeness with her father. He was capable of giving her a kind of mothering warmth that she could not possibly get from her mother. She would go with him on whatever errands he would run on the weekend—for instance shopping at the hardware store—in order to get away from her mother. She felt she was her father's favorite. There were, however, some disturbing signs. He had a superficial but powerful ability to make almost anyone feel that he was very close to them. He mishandled the family finances with no sign of guilt. He also made certain off-hand comments, such as that he was perfectly glad that his younger brother had died in infancy since he afterwards had more of his parent's attention. All of this seemed to point to a relatively psychopathic personality. It was also clear her father did not go out of his way to protect E from her mother's attacks. He would let her come with him when he went places, but at other times seemed content to let E's mother act out towards her and leave him alone.

At a point about four years into the analysis, as we were dealing with her mother's abusive behavior toward her, especially the enemas carried out in a quite painful and sadistic manner, certain associations and feelings of E's led me to suggest that perhaps her mother had stimulated her clitoris. From this point E found it almost intolerable to come to the analysis, and her functioning outside of it deteriorated markedly. It seemed there was little I could do to stem the overwhelming anxiety and strong compulsion to harm herself. E seemed on the point of stopping analysis. I suggested she might try sitting up, while she insisted on cutting down her frequency of sessions to three times weekly from four. She was also started on an antidepressant (an SSRI), which was of some help in controlling her overwhelming depression.

As I described in the section on primal denial, we concentrated at this time especially on E's denial of just how disturbed and unable to give emotional or even physical care her mother was. We were led to this by looking concretely at the details of E's self-care, which concerned me given the depth of her regression. It became clear that to take care of herself—for instance to get a warm blanket to cover herself when she felt cold—threatened to make her feel sad and pained, and at times panicky, about the lack of care provided by her mother. The reason for this was that the contrast between her mother's attitude and E having enough investment in herself to attend to her sense of discomfort, brought the reality of her mother's lack of investment sharply into focus—in fact it made it real. This was one of the reasons she avoided taking actions that led her to feel that she had a strong investment in herself. The avoidance protected her against the sad feelings that followed such actions. I have come to refer to this use of a restriction of the ego (Anna Freud, 1936) to shore up a denial, by avoiding an experience sharply different from the denied one, as a contrast defense. I do not think my observation of this dynamic is necessarily original, but I do feel that the frequency of contrast defenses, and their importance in shaping attitudes and behaviors in all of us, has been under-recognized. Contrast defenses play an especially large part in post-traumatic reactions and in self-destructive and self-neglectful behavior (see chapter 7).

As E faced the extent of her mother's neglect and allowed herself to feel deep sadness about it, she became somewhat better able to invest in and take care of herself. She also began a relationship with a man who was quite attentive and kind towards her. As the relationship began E found various reasons to retreat from it—citing areas of incompatibility, and arguing that perhaps he was not as nice as he seemed. From our previous work, however, she was able to see that she might be having the same difficulty accepting this man's attention as she had had showing attention towards herself, and for the same reason—because his attentiveness contrasted with her treatment by her mother and led to sadness. That this was actually the case was demonstrated by how overwhelmingly sad she did become if she accepted his kindness. By linking this sadness to its roots in her mother's neglect of her (at this point I overemphasized the maternal aspect of this), I was able to help her to remain in the relationship and to allow it to deepen, although the wish to run kept reappearing.

E became better able to differentiate the actual difficulties in the relationship and shortcomings of her boyfriend from her defensive use of them. She began to talk more about her father and his glib, superficial niceness. We realized that her difficulty in acknowledging her boyfriend's emotional investment in her was also a contrast defense against seeing clearly her father's lack of this sort of investment. The more she was able to feel her sad, painful, and angry feelings about this reality, the less she had to resort to these contrast defenses. She found herself better able to recognize abusive situations and to stand up for herself.

At this point, E began to experience intrusive feelings of a penis in her mouth, and images of her father saying "thata girl" as he forced oral sex on her. It took her a few days to report these images when they first occurred, and she even then, as I learned later, downplayed their frequency. Her way of mentioning these images was much more straightforward than her former hovering. I tried to be just as straightforward in talking of what may have happened, while respecting her extreme distress when thinking of it, and her need to go slowly in uncovering the details.

E came into a session at this time and said that she had walked out of a potentially exploitive situation, related to employment. The thing that struck her was that it was relatively easy to walk away—she had not had to fight herself. "I've had things come into my mind which I don't like," she then said. "It's of something in my mouth and it not tasting good, and I don't like it and try to push it aside." After the image had come up, she said that she had actually found herself feeling much better. "But I don't want to talk about it here. Do I have to talk about it?" she asked in a rather pleading voice.

I interpreted that she seemed to be asking me if she really had to do something unpleasant with her mouth, and that perhaps in this pleading I was being seen by her as her father. E began to feel very sad. She said that when the memory had come she had found herself saying, "We can't think of that," in the way her father had of saying these words. She wondered if her feelings about getting fat had something to do with the oral sex.

"Again I'm thinking, 'That's enough now.' That's something my dad would say. I think of my sister and I feel sad for her. When my mother was in the hospital [for a physical illness] and had gone into a psychotic state, she said that my father did it for three to four hours with my sister."

"It's interesting how you go to these statements of your mother. Your have no way of knowing if they are true, and she certainly makes all sorts of accusations you know not to be true. I wonder if we see here something that's been going on all along, where you take on your mother's accusations, knowing many of them to be outlandish, as a way of defending against your own memories."

We had some discussion back and forth about this, with E agreeing with my idea of how she used her mother's accusations, and beginning to see concretely how it worked.

"It's no wonder my mother had trouble being a mother with me and my sister, with all this going on with my father," she said.

"But that suggests she could have been motherly if all this wasn't going on. Do you really think that's true?"

E looked very sad, with tears in her eyes. "I had no one. Not my father. Not my mother. I just wanted a mother. That's all I ever wanted," she sobbed.

Over the next few weeks, as she talked of really always knowing the oral sex had gone on with her father, E became alternately sad and quite angry.

At one point, after reading an article about evil, she had felt seriously suicidal. She talked of how badly she was feeling and how she was trying despite this not to run away, and not to give in to the internal pressure she felt to adopt a different persona. E had gone through periods in her life when she had dressed quite differently, and to a certain extent behaved and felt quite differently. One of these had involved a period of lesbian activity where she had had a feminine identity but had felt more active and able to face the world more easily.

We had analyzed her wish to cut her hair or in some other way assume this or other images as largely a defensive attempt to escape from emerging feelings. But thinking now of the intrusive images, I had a different idea about them. I wondered aloud whether I had played into her need to keep aspects of herself out of the analysis by the way that I had interpreted her compulsion to assume a different persona. "They may have something important to tell us," I said. E began to cry in a deep way I had not seen before, although she stopped herself after a few minutes. She began to talk of a "happy" part that dressed in an Elizabethan manner. She had the thought, "Oh, I can come too!" This was a little girl, weak and pathetic. She said that sometimes when she wakes up and looks into the mirror she thinks "Oh no, not you again!" "It's very hard," she said, "to maintain the persona, and I get tired of people not recognizing me when they see me. Maybe that's why I keep changing jobs. A friend didn't recognize me in a video from the past. I walked totally differently."

One of the interesting aspects of the personas to emerge was their different levels of doubt about her father having sexually abused her and her sister. She had very little doubt about this during the times she had her lesbian persona. The aspect of herself that actually carried the feelings of the abuse was like a little girl. This aspect initially appeared quite hesitantly. She thought of this persona as pathetic and weak at first. This was her way of distancing from the abuse, and she eventually came to see it quite differently. Once we got to the place where there were no words any more, where fragments of memory and feeling seemed to float around with little connection to each other, putting words to this experience and connecting them was enormously helpful. According to Ira Brenner's classification, presented in his book on dissociation and trauma (2001), E would be seen as an upper level dissociative character. We could contrast her with lower level dissociative character or true multiple personality (now referred to as dissociative identity disorder [DID]) where the various personas are amnesic for what happens when another persona has been operative. For descriptions of these more severe disorders, I would refer readers to Brenner's excellent books (2001, 2004), which are rich in clinical detail.

To give a sense of the analysis of E's abuse, I will mention two sessions that took place about two months after the session described above. I will only give a few details, not an exhaustive description.

E came in for her first session of the week saying that she had gone through a brief episode of feeling suicidal. She said she had thought of her father saying "thata girl." When I repeated what she had said she started crying. "Please don't say that," she said. She sobbed for a number of minutes. She said she had heard from her mother at a later age that her father was not circumcised, but she knew already by the feel of his penis. It had been dark, but she remembered what it felt like. I asked her what else she remembered, and she said it was mainly the feel, and feeling like throwing up.

"My brother was in the bedroom with me," she said, looking horrified. "He was really a bad man, wasn't he? A really bad man." She said this in a voice and manner that were like those of a little girl. Then in a more adult way, almost in answer to herself, she talked of how he really didn't care for anyone.

She went on to talk about the fact that she had an amazing ability to draw the outline of someone with just a few lines and make it recognizable. "Not the face," she said, "just the outline, like my father at the door with the light behind him."

"So that's the one visual picture you have of him," I said.

"I don't really want to think of it," she said. She went on to talk of her work, and of how she was arranging her place.

I noted how difficult it was to stick with the traumatic memories. She said it had been dark, and she had not seen much. Once it had begun, she had no memory because she was somewhere else. She had the thought that she had been arranging her place like she does when she is about to move, and wondered if she was preparing it for people to find after her death. "It's not that I'm thinking that at all consciously, but for some reason that idea just popped into my head. It's like the idea of my mother killing me if she finds out." I told her that this suicidal intention, if it existed in a split off form like this, might be a good deal more dangerous than her more conscious feelings of hopelessness and wanting to end it, since she had no opportunity to discuss it or struggle with it. She seemed relieved to talk about it openly.

She then commented on how she felt empty. "Not tired, but empty. Like I'm just a thin outer layer with nothing inside and I could just be blown away." She seemed quite distressed and anxious. She commented on how hard this was. I pointed out that she seemed to feel worse now that she was warding off the memories of the abuse and that, unless I was mistaken, she actually felt more integrated and solid when she was remembering these memories directly earlier in the session. She said I was not mistaken, but that it took a lot out of her. She just felt like curling up. "I wonder if that's how you felt after the abuse," I asked. E said it probably was. She could imagine just lying there in bed.

I wondered if perhaps in the session we had seen a muted reenactment of her feelings during an episode of abuse. She first brought in the memories of what her dad had said, and was quite upset, thinking what a bad man he was. She had then gone somewhere else, talking of other things, just as she had in the abuse, and then had felt hollow and fragile, perhaps as she had when she was lying on the bed curled up after it was over. E said this made sense to her, and then went on to talk about how ashamed she felt about all this.

"It's not the way I would want it. It's not a very nice picture," she said. As she talked of her shame I interpreted that while I could understand how she might have these feelings as she fully faced the details of what had happened, it may also be that she was experiencing a borrowed sense of shame. I said that this could serve as a way of not putting the shame where it really belonged, which was part of the ugly picture she did not like. She responded to this by feeling very sad but also saying how she had actually done not too badly given what she had had to deal with.

In the next session, E began by saying that she was thinking of running, of moving to the city where she had lived the lesbian lifestyle and cutting her hair. She also said that when her boyfriend had admired the way she had arranged her jewelry, she said wouldn't it be funny if after she left someone found them so beautifully arranged. "I didn't mean to say it. It just came out like that."

"Were you thinking of leaving or of dying?" I asked.

"Of dying. But I wasn't thinking of it consciously. But after I said it I wondered if I've been arranging my place like this for a while because I knew that some things were going to come out in the analysis."

We talked of this and I pointed out how she had trouble referring to the sexual abuse directly. She physically cringed when I said this and said, "Don't say that please," in a soft voice. We did talk about the abuse but a number of times she said she was feeling very sleepy or that she was seeing herself as under the chair. "You're relentless," she said when I mentioned an aspect of the abuse again. And a little later in the session she said, "It's like the same thing coming at me again and again. So repetitive. Exactly the same thing!" She seemed quite distressed as she said this, and I wondered if this was a sort of memory of the repetition of the abuse, or perhaps the rhythmical thrusting of her father. This particular interpretation seemed to make sense to her, but she began to get sleepier and sleepier as the session wore on. I said that while

I knew this was hard for her, her responses in the sessions were actually quite valuable to us, a form of memory that might tell us more of what she had actually experienced. She said she was fighting to stay awake and I asked her why she would not let herself fall asleep for a minute.

"I might not wake up," she laughed.

"I'd wake you," I said, also with a laugh.

"But I can't. It just wouldn't feel safe."

"So it doesn't feel safe with me here."

"No," she said in a quiet voice. She kept running away psychologically throughout the session, and presented quite a vivid picture of how she had lived her entire life, and of how she had felt during and after the abuse: she was running—running from a picture too ugly for words, but with nowhere to hide.

Dissociation

To begin with we could ask—what causes dissociation? Similarly to many other clinicians, my experience has been that every case of dissociation or splitting of the ego that I have been able to analyze to any depth has shown quite clearly the connection of the patient's tendency to compartmentalize with one or more traumas. This does not mean that there are not other factors. The fact that there is no tight correlation between the severity of the dissociation and the severity of the traumas would argue for the presence of these other factors, including no doubt constitutional ones.

The connection between dissociation and trauma was described by Breuer and Freud (1893–1896) over one hundred years ago. Ferenczi reiterated this connection when he said that "there is neither shock nor fright without some trace of splitting of the personality" (1933, p 60). Freud (1938b) noted that splitting of the ego was a reaction to trauma and involved a disturbance in the ego's synthetic function.

But what is dissociation? A broad definition often links it to changes in levels of consciousness as well as to a lack of integration of certain memories and feelings with the rest of the personality. Changes in level of consciousness are always associated with trauma because of the shutting down of many ego functions such as those that process sensory data. Changes in level of consciousness, however, are non-specific and can be found in many situations affecting sensory processing and other ego functions—situations such as intoxication, defensive maneuvers such as derealization, and others. If we use the term dissociation for all changes of consciousness it would have a confusingly wide range of application. It is probably less confusing to reserve the term dissociation for the specific splitting off of a portion of the psyche that happens as a consequence of trauma, as well as the ego's active imitation of this situation for defensive purposes.

There is good evidence that this original split is not a defensive maneuver, but rather an outcome of the particular mental (and neurophysiological) state that characterizes true trauma. The temporary shutting down of the ego's coordinating and integrative functions is probably especially respon-sible for the lack of cohesion and integration of the memories of a trauma. These memories, along with their strong affective load, seem cut off from the normal connection with other memories, with the person's self-image, and with his or her life narrative. As Person and Klar (1994) point out this lack of connection only applies in one direction. The split off traumatic memories continue to affect other mental products, and thus behavior, but they are walled off from the revision, retranscription, and melding with other memories that is the fate of non-traumatic memories.

Van der Kolk, Van der Hart and Marmar (1996) refer to this original lay-ing down of unintegrated memories as primary dissociation. While they do not propose it for this reason, I find their terminology congenial because it differentiates *primary* dissociation from what I have called *primal* defenses. This is an important distinction, since primary dissociation is not an ego response to pervasive affect, as are primal defenses, but is rather a product of ego breakdown to the point that such responses as primal defenses are impos-sible. Van der Kolk (1996) describes how functional neuroimaging studies (PET scans) done at his lab show that the left hemisphere in general and Broca's area (which subserves language production) in particular, are non-functional during traumatic memory recall, in contrast to their normal active role in the recall of other memories. Van der Kolk (1996) also hypothesizes a shutdown of the hippocampal area (which subserves the laying down of long-term, integrated memories) during trauma, while areas of the thalamus, the major relay and integrative station for incoming stimuli, also appear not to be fully functional during trauma. Thus traumatic memories are cut off from integration with each other and with other memories, as well as from verbal processing, both during the time of the trauma and afterwards.

This primary dissociation is the substrate, I believe, for both splitting of the ego and secondary (active) dissociation. The presence of unintegrated and often (except through special techniques) unintegratable memories and feelings is a true split in the ego. This original split has a tendency to influ-ence more and more of the person's past and ongoing present experience, with particular experiences being allocated to one side or the other of the split (Freud, 1938a). This leads to what Yorke (1986) has called the organizing effect of trauma, as it sucks into its structure many of the person's issues and conflicts. An important question is the extent to which this organizing effect is reciprocal. In other words, to what extent does the presence of powerful conflicts which structure themselves in relation to the trauma serve to fix and even magnify the original primary dissociation, and to what extent does this process work the other way around? I think we are faced here by a complemental series. At one end of this series the trauma and the primary dissociation are so severe that they structure and often make insoluble all sorts of conflicts which otherwise would have been dealt with easily, while at the other end a relatively mild primary dissociation which may have been itself resolvable is perpetuated by its entanglement in one of the person's major conflicts. As in most such complemental series, there are a large number of instances that fall into the middle ground, where there is a complex mutual influencing and fixating between inner conflicts and dissociated traumatic memories.

In a case such as that of E, where there are multiple traumas along with severe deprivations and developmental interferences, the situation becomes quite complex. I will just mention here that E's oedipal conflicts had been, as one might expect, refracted through the trauma, leading to a terrified certainty that her mother would kill her if she ever found out about the sexual abuse by her father. Later in her life E's awareness of the emotional difficulties and sexual coldness of her husband were split off into the compartment of her mind that contained the sexual abuse.

Whatever the complexities of the situation, it is usually the case that once in place primary dissociation offers itself as a ready made split, easing the way for other defenses to use the split for their own purposes. In fact so tempting and powerfully efficient is this solution that a person may become quite addicted to it, and not develop a healthy tolerance for facing unpleasant realities or distressing emotions. There are in fact quite a number of other factors that influence how strong this tendency will become, but the presence of the a primary dissociation is certainly one of them.

When analyzing trauma it becomes evident that there is a secondary dissociation that develops as a layer on top of the primary dissociation. This secondary dissociation is an active ego process that uses the split of the primary ego dissociation, and fights helplessness and further traumatization by actively bringing about a psychic situation in which the experiencing person separates him or herself from events of the present. Usually, if the child is old enough and the abuse is ongoing, they will dissociate (secondary dissociation) in some manner as they see the abuse coming. They will either go completely into an internal fantasy world or they will concentrate on a "neutral" distant physical feature such as a window, the ceiling, etc., and feel that they are out there, separate from themselves, perhaps watching. One patient retreated into an elaborate and constantly expanding fantasy of being on a tropical beach as she saw another vicious beating from her father about to begin. E did both of these things, concentrating on certain single sights or thoughts, or going somewhere else in her mind, as she saw her father at her door and knew the abuse would begin once more.

When splitting of self and object representations and of identity is interwoven with the primary dissociation, we usually talk of dissociation of the personality or identity. This is why E's case, with the assuming of different personas with quite different ways of feeling, dressing, and behaving, strikes us as an example of dissociation. Such a situation betrays a greater damage to the integrative function, and if this goes far enough we get the situation of multiple personality. E's case had not gone so far, but the different personas were to a certain extent cut off from each other. We can see this for instance when she talked with the little girl voice as she began to truly re-experience the sexual abuse. The personas act as if they were cut off from each other by repression, especially in the severer cases of dissociative identity disorder. The presence of repression could be partly explained by its very close connection with sexuality, since cases of DID are largely associated with sexual abuse. However, the way in which personas and their memories can come and go with relative rapidity is not the way repression usually behaves. Ira Brenner (2001) sees this disorder as the product of a complex set of interacting defenses. In a later chapter (8, on perversions), after having developed the idea of the zero process, I will describe splitting of the identity, the key defense in DID, as a specific zero process counterforce defense.

Splitting of the self and object representations is an important topic in its own right. In early infancy it is not defensive but is due to a lack of maturation of the ego's integrative function, and certain cognitive functions, such as memory and differentiation. With the maturation of these functions, the separate self and object images and identifications are integrated to a greater and greater extent. From this point on splitting of self and object is resorted to defensively to keep apart aspects that are felt to be troubling. For instance splitting may be used to avoid the pain of seeing the goodness of the mother being sullied by the times when she is angry or frustrated. It is in complex cases such as E's where very early traumas, deprivations, and other pathological influences interfere with development of the integrative function (and thus the ability to maintain reliable selective repressions) that the splitting of the self, primary dissociation based on trauma, and splitting of the identity come together to give the picture of dissociative identity disorder. Constitutional and/or early-acquired differences in the rate of maturation and the strength of the integrative function also influence the outcome, as shown by cases of early deprivation and trauma, including sexual abuse, in which self constancy and selective repression are relatively intact. In such cases the person will say that the trauma seemed to have happened to someone else, betraying the existence of a primary dissociation and an attempt to distance from the trauma, but there are no indications of actual different personas in day-to-day functioning. I myself have seen more than one case such as this, where the sexual abuse has been quite severe and prolonged but the individual's basic identity was largely intact. In these cases it is only as one penetrates to the core of the trauma that a separate aspect of the person becomes evident—for instance a "little girl" who always knew about the abuse and is rejected by the rest of the personality. In these cases as well, the specific zero process defense of splitting of the identity is present, but it is operative within a much more integrated basic personality.

E's early abuse at the hands of her mother involved deprivation of proper physical care, a cold, unempathic emotional atmosphere saturated with raw sexuality and aggression, reality distortions, and externalizations. These taken together interfered with her ability to set up secure selective repressions and to achieve a stable sense of self. She said she often felt she needed her clothes in a very concrete way to hold herself together. She at times became, as she described it, "fragile," feeling that she would literally fall into many little pieces if she did not keep herself very still and block distressing emotions from developing.

Each concrete clinical situation involves quite a tangle of factors, but the basic ideas about dissociation presented so far are relatively simple: primary dissociation is a passively suffered split in the psyche, brought on by a traumatic process. Secondary dissociation is the attempt to deliberately bring about certain aspects of this primary dissociation, especially the breakdown in integration, in order to protect against further traumatization.

In order to reach a deeper understanding of the nature of trauma, and especially post-traumatic repetition and defenses, I have found it necessary to formulate certain ideas about the form of mental functioning that comes about as a result of trauma, which I will present at this point.

The Zero Process

One of Freud's most important discoveries, his most fundamental in some respects, was that of the primary process. From the evidence provided by the analysis of dreams and neurotic symptoms he inferred the existence of a form of mental functioning quite different from that of which we are usually aware. This form of functioning took no cognizance of contradictions, logical consistency, or the relations between elements of thought. The passage of time had no meaning for it and thus memories and wishes did not fade or dim with time, and were not ordered in any way in relation to time. Freud (1900) called this mode of functioning the primary process, emphasizing that it preceded the secondary process chronologically and, since the secondary process grew out of it, that it was in certain respects the more fundamental mode of mental functioning. Two main characteristics of the functioning of the primary process that were discovered by Freud were condensation (in which many elements combined to form a new one with some features of each) and displacement (where the energy attaching to a content would be displaced to other elements quite easily based on very superficial similarities). Both of these processes led to the seemingly nonsensical nature of dreams and neurotic symptoms. At the energic level Freud described the energy of the primary process as unbound and mobile, in contrast to that of the secondary process, which was bound. Essentially this was a way of attempting to explain condensation, displacement, and the tendency to move toward hallucinatory wish fulfillment of the primary process. All of these characteristics suggested to Freud that the psychic energy invested in the contents of the primary process was highly mobile, displacing easily onto other contents.

I would propose that there is a form of mental functioning that differs from both the primary and secondary processes. Since Freud's original formulations there has been much discussion of these issues, a full description of which is beyond the scope of this section. As representatives of the ongoing work in this area I will mention two authors.

The ideas of Wilfred Bion, who worked within the Kleinian tradition, are of increasing interest to many analysts of other theoretical orientations, partly because he offered compelling conceptualizations of different forms of mental functioning. Bion (1962) described what he called the alpha-function of the mind, which he related to attention. Bion was leery of direct definitions of his terms, and he defined the alpha-function especially by what happened if it was disturbed. He felt if this happened, perception and feelings remained unchanged from their original state. (This suggests that the alpha-function involves the processing of raw experience into symbolized and symbolizable form.) These unchanged contents Bion call beta-elements. Essentially beta-elements are unprocessed bits of perception that have entered into memory. Bion felt beta-elements could not be used in dreams or thought, or be subject to repression. Beta-elements could be part of projective identification and acting out. These characteristics are the same as those that I have suggested belong to traumatic memories in areas of primary dissociation, and in fact Bion suggested trauma as the origin of beta-elements.

In the end, however, Bion (1962) considered beta-elements to be present as a primary factor at the beginning of development. He felt that the mother contained the infant's beta-elements, and through her reverie—a factor of the mother's alpha-function—processed them for the infant. Bion saw persisting beta-elements as caused by the infant's attacks on the breast and on the mother's alpha-function. These persisting beta-elements Bion linked to psychotic functioning and to full-blown psychosis. Here he followed Klein's ideas of the importance of very early aggression, and infantile fantasy related to the mother's body, in development and psychopathology. I would suggest that this conceptualization of beta-elements conflates developmental processes related to ego growth with the traumatic process.

Another author who has presented compelling conceptualizations of these issues is De M'Uzan. He (2003) distinguished repetition of the same, which is seen in neurotics, from repetition of the identical, seen in other states such as psychosomatic disorders and perversions. This latter form of repetition resulted from a rejection or non-functioning of symbolization. De M'Uzan coined the phrase "quantity is destiny" (2003, p 716) to describe this mental state, constituted in actual trauma. By "quantity" he was referring to the compelling nature of the push toward repetition, because of the lack of symbolization. As Simpson (2003) noted in his introduction to De M'Uzan's classic paper, De M'Uzan delinks anxiety from the traumatic state. To do this he introduced the concepts of disarray and turmoil. He said that he meant "by turmoil something that allows for memory to by reworked, that can enter as a pattern into a history and provides the nucleus of fantasy activity in the future" (2003, p 724). De M'Uzan's description of turmoil squares well with the idea of pervasive anxiety that I have taken from Yorke, Wiseberg, and Freeman (1989). He contrasted this state with that of disarray, which sounds similar to the basic traumatic state and what I have described as primary dissociation: "It is itself a consequence of a catastrophic traumatic situation, initially responsible for an evolution in which the state of disarray is ready to be reproduced at any time" (2003, p 719). He said that disarray stands in the way of the development of anxiety.

De M'Uzan's concept of disarray is in a number of ways analogous to Bion's idea of beta-elements, and like him De M'Uzan connects disarray to very early occurrences. He asserts that a state like disarray must have its foundation in very early functioning, and links it with the trauma of birth. I myself would not disagree that very early insults, and very early interactions between mother and child, could lead to areas of primary dissociation and to the sort of functioning—or actually breakdown of functioning—referred to by De M'Uzan as disarray and that Bion saw as causing the formation of beta-elements. I merely think that they both saw the causation of this type of functioning both too narrowly and at times too broadly. There are many paths that can lead to the final traumatic state, and on the other hand at times the paths described by these authors—such as a disturbed mother-child relationship and lack of a maternal containing function—can lead to things other than (or along with) the traumatic state (such as interference in various areas of development, primal denials, and defensive internalizations, as seen for instance in the case of E). The traumatic state is often the product of the confluence of many factors. I would also emphasize that this state can be produced at any time of life, and that adult traumas create their own areas of primary dissociation that are not mere derivatives of earlier ones, although they form points of contact with these earlier ones, as they do with many other aspects of a person's psyche. My main disagreement with both Bion and De M'Uzan is with their conflation of developmental processes with the traumatic process, a conflation which is also present in many other analytic authors who conceptualize trauma. In such a short discussion of their work it is, however, impossible to do it justice. As an example, Bion also talks of bizarre objects, which could be seen as describing the contents of the zero process as more separate from the developmental process.

I struggled to find a reasonable term for the type of functioning found in areas of primary dissociation. I had to exclude "primal process" because it could lead to confusion, since I have been using the adjective "primal" with quite a different meaning to describe certain defenses. The term zero process was suggested to me by Dr. William Shantz at a meeting of the Toronto Chapter of the International Neuro-Psychoanalytic Association, where I presented my ideas about trauma (Matthis and Deutsch, 2005). I like this term because it captures an aspect of this form of mental functioning that distinguishes it from both the primary and secondary processes: its frozen quality, with no movement such as the displacements seen in these other forms of functioning. There is no displacement of affect or energy as happens so easily in the primary process, and under more control in the secondary process. There is also no synthesis of elements, as seen in the condensations of the primary process and again in the more controlled and extensive synthetic function of the ego in the secondary process.

Thus I propose to designate the form of functioning left over after trauma and primary dissociation the zero process, and to call the areas where this type of functioning reigns *areas of primary dissociation* or, alternatively, *areas of zero process functioning*. Inventing and clarifying terminology is one thing, but the key question is as follows: does post-traumatic mental functioning deserve to be put on an equal footing with the primary process and the secondary process? And should the structures where it exists be added as independent structural elements on par with the id, ego, and superego?

Bohleber (2007), in an excellent paper on trauma, argues against a separate form of traumatic processing, and I think a consideration of his reasons for rejecting this throws some light on the nature of the zero process. He notes that most of the memories during trauma seem to be coherent and generally reliable, as long as the observing ego is present, though once this goes the memories are not coherently organized. In either case encoding, consolidation, and retrieval are similar to other memories, although they are not subject to retranscription or retranslation, as are other memories. Thus the memory processes during trauma and following are the same form of episodic memory found in the secondary processes, "but nevertheless some deviations in the registration must be expected, as well as an obstruction of the normal course of psychic processes" (Bohleber, 2007, p 338). There is also evidence for these memories not being excluded from the transformations of conscious and unconscious fantasies.

I agree with all of these points that Bohleber makes, and yet I think they do not make an argument against a separate trauma-related form of processing. To deal with the central issue first: it is true that what one sees in trauma is the same episodic memory that operates at other times, but I do not think any of the forms of processing—primary, secondary, or zero—is characterized by a completely different form of memory or perceptual processing. Freud's (1923) original description of the ego as controlling perception and motility, and Hartmann's (1950b) description of it as a structure, defined by its functions (such as perception, motility, and memory) can both be confusing in this respect, and need emendation. Almost a century of research on subliminal perception has shown that the primary process has direct access to perception. Shur (1966) described how, as the memory functions matured in early childhood, the nature of the id wish, and of the primary process itself, changed. Each major form of processing—primary, secondary, and zero—has at its disposal the perceptual and memory functions, as well as other functions normally ascribed to the ego and the secondary processes. Another way of putting it would be to say that perception and memory can be subject to either of these three forms of processing. In the case of memory this may happen at its inception (registration, consolidation) or affect its later processing (retrieval, retranscription).

We generally take for granted the really quite extensive processing of sensory data (which will of course affect the sorts of episodic memories that are formed) as well as the integration, differentiation, categorization, and other things done to memories after they are formed, when they are subject to the secondary process. At the core of the zero process, there is precious little processing of the raw bits of sensory data, which are then encoded into memory in a similarly raw, unprocessed form. The outcome is a set of bits of memory with little relation to each other, with little categorization with regard to content, time, theme, etc., and with no verbal or other symbolic processing. Thus the term zero process, while it overstates things a bit, does describe what traumatic and post-traumatic functioning in areas of primary dissociation looks like when compared to all the activity in the primary and secondary processes.

I said that this is what things are like at the core of the zero process because as one moves out from this core there are memories with a bit more processing and integration, slowly merging with regular primary and secondary process functioning. Thus, as Bohleber (2007) noted, memories further from the traumatic core look and behave more like regular memories, but this continuum from one type of processing to the other does not argue against the zero process as a separate form of mental processing. It has long been known in analysis, although at times forgotten, that there is a similar continuum between primary and secondary process functioning (so also between the ego and the id), with sharper, but by no means completely discontinuous, borders in areas where primal repressions separate the two types of functioning (Freud, 1923). One way to think about this aspect of mental functioning is to picture the zero, primary, and secondary processes as having core areas where one of these modes of functioning is in pure culture, and see these core areas as extending their influence in an ever-waning manner to areas further removed from the core. These areas of influence overlap, with there thus being areas with evidence of two or three types of processing.

Bohleber also argued against a separate traumatic and post-traumatic form of processing by noting the evidence for the transformation of traumatic memories in conscious and unconscious fantasies. However, that the contents of the zero process can affect and shape those of the primary and secondary processes is no more an argument against its existence as a separate form of functioning than the fact that the primary and secondary process contents influence each other is an argument against their conceptualization as separate forms of processing. Just as analysts have conceptualized symptoms as resulting from the interaction of these last two forms of processing, so of course there are situations that involve to a greater or lesser extent the influence of the zero process. Symptoms that I think have an especially important contribution from this form of mental functioning are conversion symptoms, phobias, and perversions. I will discuss perversions in chapter 8, and will there have an opportunity to go into the concrete details of an instance of the zero process and dissociation interacting with other processes to produce specific clinical manifestations.

To return to the characteristics of the zero process from these considerations of its interactions: one important difference between this form of functioning and the primary and secondary processes is that the zero process is a product of environmental impacts, rather than of development from birth on, as is the case with the other two major forms of processing. This is a major difference between my conception of the zero process and a number of other ideas, such as beta-elements, archaic functioning, and others. I do not think of zero process functioning as an aspect of normal mental functioning in very early infancy, that is contained and processed through infant-caregiver interactions. I do not think there is much evidence, either through psychoanalytic reconstruction or from infant observation, of a normal state of non-processing, such as occurs in trauma. This is not to say that possession of areas of primary dissociation with zero processing is not common—we all have a store of these from early childhood and often from later times as well. It is just that we each acquire these through environmental impingements, not through a developmental process based on the epigenetic unfolding of an inherited maturational trajectory that interacts with environmental influences, which is how the primary and secondary processes come into being.

The extent and depth of the zero process depends on the extent and depth of the traumatic processes that produced it. Unless certain secondary defenses (secondary dissociation, denials, and repressions) stabilize them and/or they become embroiled with fixations and conflicts related to the drives or reality, areas of primary dissociation tend to shrink as their affects get worked off. A large enough ongoing trauma such as a period of sexual abuse can lead to the zero process being stabilized largely through the use of secondary dissociation, as the victim actively separates everyday life from the trauma, and separates themselves from the trauma even as it is happening. In the case of E, her oedipal conflicts were very much entwined with the trauma of her father's sexual abuse of her. Thus the stabilization of E's zero process was achieved through her repression of her oedipal conflicts and through secondary dissociations, as well as being a product of a set of denial defenses that are very characteristic of trauma. A discussion of these aspects of trauma leads quite naturally into a discussion of the methods of analyzing trauma, and so I will now turn to this topic, in the context of which we will encounter some further characteristics of the zero process.

Psychotherapeutic Technique

The technique of analyzing trauma involves analyzing the various defenses that fix the areas of primary dissociation in place, as well as analyzing the core of the zero process in order to return as much of it as possible to secondary process functioning. I will describe the types of defenses that help to fixate trauma, as well as talking some more about the nature of the zero process. This section on technique contains quite a lot of theoretical discussion, but there is no way around this, since before we can usefully discuss the analysis of trauma, we have to come to a deeper understanding of its nature.

At the clinical level, trauma enters a therapy in varied ways. In E's case it was the analysis of her contrast defenses against the reality of her mother's lack of caring, and her subsequent entry into a loving sexual relationship, that led to the emergence of intrusive images and to the depictions of the trauma in dreams and physical reactions such as nausea. Phillips (1991) points out that such phenomena are a sign that the traumatic material has entered the preconscious.

Person and Klar (1994) argue that merely working diligently on analyzing the patient's transferences and resistances does not at all guarantee such an emergence of dissociated and repressed traumatic material. They give an example of a quite chance occurrence inducing a reaction that led to memories of a trauma. The emergence of E's intrusive images and other derivatives of her trauma followed on her becoming sexually involved with a kind man. This was certainly not a chance occurrence, but what subsequently emerged had not done so through four years of analytic work on her unconscious conflicts, resistances, and transference. It is occurrences such as this that lead me to strongly disagree with Abend's (1986) statement, quoted earlier, that an analyst should invariably direct his or her attention to unconscious conflict and compromise formation. There is no way to guarantee analysis of, or even awareness of the existence of, all of the important traumas in a person's life. In fact many analyses either have trouble reaching past a certain depth or founder completely due to significant unrecognized trauma. It is only when these are analyzed (i.e., the primary dissociation is at least partially undone) that entrance is gained to the deepest layers of a person's internal conflicts, which have been organized by the trauma.

Access to the trauma can depend on occurrences the significance of which it is impossible to grasp until after the emergence of the traumatic memories. The inability to completely control our success in such matters is no excuse, however, for falling back on one-sided attention to things with which we feel more comfortable, such as drive/defense issues or narcissistic deprivations from early childhood. Openness to the possibility of trauma greatly increases our chances of recognizing it. Person and Klar (1994), among many others, have pointed out that areas of functioning, reactions, or transferences that do not fit with the patient's more general characteristics often turn out to be related to trauma. In this vein I am reminded of E's rather strange suspicious look as she entered my office for a session following one where I had been relatively warm or friendly with her, a look that did not fit at all with her generally straightforward and friendly manner. I noticed how common this look became when dissociated memories of the sexual abuse were emerging. Person and Klar refer to such reactions as dissociated transferences.

Transference and Countertransference

Are there special types of transference and countertransference associated with trauma? I think there are specific characteristics of the zero process that can color a transference to a lesser or a greater extent. When they dominate a transference, we get what Person and Klar call a dissociated transference. What are its characteristics?

First there is the on/off quality of the transference. When triggered, the reliving of the traumatic incident is immediate and intense. For instance as we were talking of the abuse, E began to feel, in a way that quickly became overwhelming, that I was repeating the same thing over and over, so relentlessly and unfeelingly that it was all she could do not to run out. In fact once or twice when this "relentless" transference popped up, E did have to leave early, to overcome the overwhelming feeling of being helpless and trapped. This all turned out to be a transference of the core of one of E's traumas: her father relentlessly, and against her protests and choking, forcing his penis into her mouth and relentlessly thrusting till he ejaculated. What I want to emphasize is that it was especially this aspect of the trauma that came forward in this on/off manner into the transference.

My countertransference was at first to be confused about what was happening but as the accusations against me mounted, to feel the "reality" of my sadism quite strongly. In what I think was a reflection of the on/off quality of the transference, my countertransference was either to know nothing about what was going on, and then at times to know all of a sudden what it was—to get an image of her father orally abusing E, at times with details that she had not mentioned. Of course intuitions that feel similar to this occur when analyzing non-traumatic dynamics, in which case they represent a product of both unconscious communication and the outcome of preconscious thinking emerging into conscious awareness. This is also what happened in the situation described with E, but the nature of the unconscious communication, of the preconscious thinking, and of the emergence into the analyst's awareness were all colored by the nature of the zero process. They were quite concretely perceptual and immediately apprehended, as well as having the on/off quality already mentioned.

A second characteristic of a zero process transference is that once the switch has been turned on, the unfolding of the traumatic incident in its displaced form in the transference runs its course in a set way. As one of my patients who had been sexually abused over her whole childhood put it, "It's like a videotape with no reverse button. It just starts and runs its course." She said this about an episode of reliving similar to E's, relating to one of the core areas of her trauma. She could have added that there are no fast forward, stop, or pause buttons either. There is no ability to control the memory or the related transference in the usual ways. This characteristic is there both in transference/countertransference reliving, such as that between myself and E, as well as reliving of trauma that does not pull the analyst in to the same extent. The countertransference correlate to this is also to be pulled into the feelings and enactment not only with less control than usual but also with less symbolic processing and in the same inexorable playing out of a scenario from the beginning to the end. For instance when E had the "relentless" transference, I actually found myself repeating my interpretation and insisting on it more than I normally would, rather than giving it time to sink in and watching to see the effects that it had. On other occasions I was quite silent, in a manner uncharacteristic for me, and that felt cruel but that I at first felt helpless to challenge.

The Zero Process, Repetition, and Memory

What can these characteristics of traumatic transference tell us about the zero process and primary dissociation? There are particular characteristics that increase in intensity as we approach the core of a trauma, and it is especially from these that we infer the nature of the zero process. Both the on/off switching and rigid replaying of the trauma point to the lack of any processing beyond a very rudimentary stage of registration of bits of memory and some rudimentary sequencing of these bits. It would probably be more accurate to call these bits proto-memories, since they appear to have been halted at an early stage of processing, before their integration with each other and with other memories, before abstraction of aspects of the memories lead to classification, before collapsing of many memories into each other, before linking with verbal and other symbols, and before other forms of processing as well take place. It is this processing that gives us a regular episodic memory, and it seems that only with this further processing can the memory become psychically a memory, in the sense of something from the past that can be brought to mind under the control of the person. In trauma not only the processing of memory, but also the processing of the perceptions, feelings, etc., that are eventually laid down as memories are deficient.

The peculiar characteristics of dissociative (or traumatic) transferences can be explained if we conceptualize the contents of areas of primary dissociation as having characteristics of both a memory and a perception. The manner in which zero process contents are either present or not (their on/off characteristic), and when present the way in which they play out in a sequence not under the person's control, is usually a characteristic of perception, not regular memories. Non-traumatic memories can be voluntarily evoked in a stronger or weaker manner and scanned back and forth. The semi-hallucinatory qualities of the "memories" from the core of a trauma link them with perception. When one penetrates to this level the patient experiences the feelings and memories as a completely present experience. E experienced me as relentlessly and coldly pushing her and pushing at her again and again. When we had analyzed some of the secondary defenses and this experience came out in full force, it had many of the characteristics of an immediate perceptual, lived experience. There is one characteristic of memory that these experiences of E, and all the contents of areas of primary dissociation, have, and that is of course that they are retained through time in the mind and can be reproduced. But they are resistant to the normal condensation with other memories, retranscription, and distortion that normal memories undergo.

The nature of the first active defenses against zero process memories—secondary dissociation—are no doubt also related to the quasi-perceptual nature of these strange entities. As with an actually perceived situation, one turns away or walks away when it becomes overwhelming. In the case of secondary dissociation, this is what the person does mentally—escapes into a fantasy or memory or thoughts. In the case of ongoing trauma the person uses secondary dissociation to defend against an actual ongoing perceived reality situation, as they go somewhere else in their minds when a trauma, usually an abuse situation, is about to begin. When she saw her father's outline at her bedroom door at night E would start this process, going to different places such as pleasant memories, feelings, or fantasies. This maneuver was also used by E when the zero process memories of the trauma were evoked. In the analysis E at times pictured herself curled up beside or even under the couch or the chair. Another patient counted the noises of cars as they passed outside the office, thought of things she had to do at work, and worked on certain intellectual puzzles. She did this all not only during silences but, as came out fully only late in her analysis, much of the time during which we were talking and analyzing as well. As we talked of this issue she said, "Twenty-three. That's how many cars have passed since the start of the appointment. I haven't been counting them consciously, but I must have been counting them somewhere because I know that's the right number."

In relation to the quasi-perceptual nature of zero process contents, it is important to remember that the perceptual process during trauma is itself disturbed—stripped of many of its integrative processes, and the perceptions thus reduced to a more raw state. Thus the perception that is reproduced during reliving via the zero process is more intrusive and rigidly fixed than normal perception. This may be part of the explanation of the necessity for using secondary dissociation, where one actually goes somewhere else psychically, versus the milder shifts of attention seen in attentional defenses such minimization or intellectualization. These latter are used to defend against a reality that is not as intrusive because both the stimulus barrier and various other ego functions such as the integrative and organizing functions have already brought the raw perceptions much more under control, and in a sense have already tamed them. Everything looks different in the realm of the zero process. At the core of the zero process secondary dissociation—escaping through a psychic portal into another existence—is probably what an attentional defense looks like.

There is much more that could be said about the nature of the zero process, and much work remains to be done in exploring this strange world. Enough has been said at this point, however, for us to suggest a source of the repetition of trauma. This source is the nature of the zero process itself, that leads its contents to be retained over time as memories are, and yet to appear as an immediate perceptual experience that intrudes into the person's present life. The contents of the zero process are not yet in the past in the psychical sense. They are always about to happen or just happening, and thus belong more to the present and the future than the past.

In this explanation I have dealt only with episodic memory, which is also referred to as explicit or autobiographical memory. There is no doubt that trauma also leads to forms of classical conditioning, emotional memories, and procedural memories. These are often together referred to as implicit memories. It is worthwhile repeating that this designation often leads to the misleading conclusion that all unconscious memories are implicit ones, and that explicit (episodic and semantic) memories are explicit in the sense of being conscious. It is also thought that implicit memories are formed outside of conscious awareness, are in fact incapable of being made conscious, and are only changeable through different experiences, and especially relationships. I would like here to clear up a few points regarding these different memory systems and their relation to trauma.

Firstly, it is a mistake to think that episodic memory needs conscious awareness either for its formation or its recall. Using evoked potentials and subliminal presentation of stimuli, Shevrin and his associates have shown in different experimental setups (described in Shevrin, 2002) that episodic memories can be formed outside of awareness and also that they can elicit unconscious defensive behavior. This latter is something that can also be inferred from everyday clinical psychoanalytic experience. For instance when E (see chapter 3, primal denial section) was talking about her mother's lack of love and then shifted her attention by saying that after all she could be loving sometimes, it was the two forms of what are called explicit or declarative memory—episodic and semantic memory—that were at work unconsciously as part of the sequence of reactions that led to the defense. This sequence could be reconstructed as we unearthed the dynamics of E's primal denial and what it defended against. As we talked of her mother's lack of caring, memories of actual episodes of cruel and cold treatment (episodic memories) as well as the more general knowledge that her mother was cruel and uncaring (semantic memory) were both stirred up, but rather than becoming conscious, these memories evoked psychic pain that acted as a signal for secondary defenses, mainly after denials, that worked to keep these memories from conscious awareness. Here we see an everyday example of the unconscious effects of these two forms of so-called explicit or declarative memories. It is important not to let the names mislead us: many of the effects of these memories are neither explicit nor declarative if we take these words as synonyms for "available to conscious awareness."

As ideas about the different forms of memory and the importance of implicit memory have spread in psychoanalysis, many have argued for the importance of implicit memories in the tendency to repeat traumas. However, what I have proposed is that the specific form of episodic memory found in the zero process is actually one of the main culprits in this tendency. These zero process episodic memories can almost certainly be formed unconsciously, although there is often conscious awareness at the time of their formation. They also generally exert their influence unconsciously (as do primary process and secondary process episodic and semantic memories), pushing the patient into reliving the experience even as they are unaware of the pieces of zero process episodic memories that are influencing them. These memories are at such times implicit in the non-technical sense of something that is outside of explicit conscious awareness, but they are not implicit in the technical sense of a form of memory that has no declarative content and relates to different brain systems that store emotional reactions and procedures.

All this is not to say that the nature of the zero process episodic memories are the only thing behind repetitions of trauma. In the section after the next one I will describe certain attentional defenses that also play a part. However, even after the attentional defenses and repressions related to trauma are analyzed, the contents of the zero process will still lead to further mischief unless they themselves are analyzed. How is this achieved?

Analyzing the Core of a Trauma

The earliest ideas about analyzing trauma were presented over 100 years ago by Pierre Janet and Breuer and Freud. Many present-day non-analytic workers in the area of trauma have championed Janet's ideas. A recent book by Van der Hart, Nijenhuis, and Steele (2006) is a good example of this. It stays away almost completely from dynamic ideas or any mention of specific defenses, replacing their analysis by educational and supportive measures. In their examples of analyzing the core traumatic memories these authors combine supportive measures with direct evocation of the traumatic memories, moving eventually to the core traumatic memories—what I would call the core of the person's zero process functioning. They at times use a quasi-hypnotic technique, relying on a kind of benevolent authority to help patients in remembering and facing the core of the trauma. There is little or no dynamic work on other defenses related to this core. Other therapists use specialized hypnotic or related techniques, such as EMDR (Brenner, 2004). These techniques hark back not only to Janet but to Freud's pre-analytic and early analytic techniques. These were variously revised or rejected by Freud and most later analysts because of the instability of the cure, relying as it did on transference and the analyst's authority, and they were replaced by a technique that sought to analyze resistances and the unconscious roots of the transference, with the patient's reasonable ego as an ally.

In analyzing the core zero process memories of a trauma I have found the analytic stance I outlined earlier—of a narrow view of technique—to be useful. In this view the basis for the analytic conversation and relationship are the real relationship and the therapeutic and working alliances, while various technical maneuvers are seen as tools to be used at the appropriate time, rather than as determinants of the entire relationship or patient/ analyst interaction. Within this context, and after preliminary work, one needs to be quite active in asking questions and pushing to further the work on the core zero process memories. Given the on/off tendencies of the zero process and the zero process based transferences (dissociative transferences), it is often necessary for the analyst to bring the specific traumatic incidents back into the conversation, after they have been discussed and then, as usual, have disappeared. There is a contradictory technical demand in analyzing trauma, however. Because of the intrusive and sudden manner in which the zero process contents emerge, whether as quasi-perceptual memories or separate identities, it is also necessary to slow things down, to be the brake as the emerging traumatic memories threaten to flood the person. If one does not do this, the person will feel unsafe, resort to stronger defensive activity, and the work will slow down. How the contradictory demands, for activity and for slowing things down, are managed in the analysis of trauma, is an important part of the clinical art of work with traumatized patients.

Once a trauma begins to emerge in dreams, physical reactions, dissociated transferences, and intrusive memories and thoughts, its analysis often will require careful attention to the need at different times for activity and for braking on the part of the analyst. Analyzing trauma involves the need to undo the primary dissociation, necessitating taking the patient through a reliving of the trauma, which at first exists only in unintegrated bits, then providing verbal narrative and working towards an understanding of the trauma that allows an integrated memory to emerge. For instance, as we reconstructed the sexual abuse, E came to distinguish the memory fragments which we recovered from present-day reactions to the past abuse. These later reactions related to the trauma but were formed afterwards and included anger and sadness and a more complicated understanding of what had happened. (To avoid misunderstanding, I should say that E also recovered repressed feelings from the past.) A number of these reactions were not merely observations on the events from afar, but rather brought to completion emotional and intellectual processes that had been stopped dead in their tracks by the traumatic reaction. Some of these aborted processes had begun just before the traumatic process intervened, but others were reconsiderations and more mature understandings of what had happened, which also were aborted by the fact that the trauma was split off from everyday experience.

In the analysis of primary dissociation and the zero process, interpretation of resistance and transference plays a major part. We can see this in the sessions with E where she began to act out some of the feelings of her abuse in the analysis. For instance she felt I was relentlessly repeating the same thing over and over, reliving the rhythmic thrusting of her father's penis in her mouth. The analysis of this transference repetition was crucial in reconnecting E with what had happened with her father.

While this relatively straightforward interpretation of transference and other resistances can take one some way in the analysis of a primal dissociation, it cannot take one all the way. In my experience the analyst needs at the appropriate time to induce the patient more directly through questioning, combined with supportive measures and slowing down when necessary, to remember aspects of the trauma. This way of going about things may make some analysts uncomfortable for a number of reasons, among them the danger of suggestion and the contamination of the transference that makes it harder to analyze. I am convinced, however, as are many others who work with trauma, that such a method is of great usefulness in analyzing the primary dissociation. If it is not resorted to, one may end up analyzing myriad connections that the trauma has made to the person's life and conflicts, but leave the patient with a continuing area of vulnerability. The core of the primary dissociation will remain, ever ready to draw new issues into its orbit and make them insoluble.

A related issue is the therapeutic benefit patients derive from knowledge about the reality of what happened, whether gained through this sort of active remembering in therapy or through outside sources. Many psychoanalysts are suspicious of such measures, seeing them as mere intellectualizations and as resistances against the true work of analysis. Perhaps now, however, having seen how trauma involves the loss of the person's ability to properly process reality, how this is the basis for primary dissociation, and how the traumatized individual applies incorrect theories to the trauma like bandages to cover over the rent in their relation to reality, we may be better able to appreciate at a theoretical level how knowledge of reality can be of such therapeutic benefit.

This is something that has been recognized at the clinical level by many analysts working with trauma. For instance De Wind (1968) talked of the importance of confronting holocaust survivors with the reality of what went on in the camps. Eissler (1966) gave the example of a man who realized decades after a trauma that he was not actually in as dangerous a situation during the trauma as he had thought, and was immediately relieved of certain symptoms related to the trauma. Good (1994) described how a female patient learned that she had not had a clitoredectomy as she had previously thought. This realization led to quick and far-reaching changes in the patient. Frank (1969) presented the analysis of a boy of five whose transference behavior and obsessive interest in being tied up led his analyst to question the boy's mother. She confessed with shame that for one month when he was eight months old she had been severely depressed. During this time she had strapped her son into his high chair and left him like this for the entire day. Upon being informed of this by his analyst the boy immediately demanded to talk to his mother. He confronted her and got her to tell him what had happened. Though he recovered no memory of that time, this interchange was followed by rapid changes. He showed an increased ability to distinguish wishful fantasy from reality and he was able to work through the theme of being tied up, which was interwoven with fantasies from each psychosexual stage, but which had stubbornly persisted through earlier attempts to analyze it.

For E the eventual ability to clarify, with regard to the sexual abuse, what had and what had not happened was an enormous help to her. The world lost its vague and hard to pin down quality, a feeling that had generalized as a defense against acknowledging the reality of what she had lived through. Even as memories of the abuse were first emerging, and she was quite distressed, E would at times feel a spurt of energy and elation, a reaction that had a number of causes, but one of which was the relief of finally knowing what had happened.

From the point of view of the zero process, what the therapist is doing is finishing a process that was halted during the trauma—the process of forming a coherent and integrated set of perceptions and then having these serve as the basis for a similarly integrated set of memories. It is a process not of reconstruction but of a new construction. These memories never existed as proper memories previously. Together with the patient we construct them not from speculation or fantasy or theory, but from the pieces of quasi-perceptual proto-memories of the zero process. We use these as the raw material from which we fashion the new memory. By completing the formerly uncompleted task, we bring a portion of the zero process at least to some extent under the dominion of the secondary process.

This particular work of construction related to the analysis of the zero process is only part of the larger task of reconstruction that takes place in analysis in relation to the analysis of what has been denied and repressed. Or at least many think this reconstruction should take place, but more recently the importance of reconstruction in general has been questioned. I tackled this issue in earlier chapters, and will not argue again for the importance of this broader reconstruction at this point, except to state that I think it *is* important. Blum (1994, 2005) has presented the best and most complete discussion of this topic and, using detailed clinical material, has put forward persuasive and well-supported arguments in favor of the continued importance of reconstruction, both of traumas and of the person's life history more generally.

Analysis of Secondary Attentional Defenses
Related to the Repetition of Trauma

In the aftermath of any significant trauma, there is a strong avoidance of situations with a close resemblance to the traumatic one. But what of the opposite of this avoidance—the actual repetition of the trauma? E did end up in a number of psychologically abusive relationships, where the exploitive aspects of her father's relationship to her and abuse of her, and her denial of it, were replayed. As we looked more closely at E's relationships it became clear that she avoided warm, loving ones where the person had a strong emotional investment in her. These made her very sad and, as was shown by what happened when she did persist in such a relationship, they threatened to bring to consciousness memories of her trauma. Ferenczi (1933) was well aware of the importance of the issue of contrast in such circumstances. He said that it was important that the traumatized patient come to deeply trust the analyst, and that the analyst behave in a completely open and warm manner, because then the contrast between the analytic relationship and the abusive one would help the patient to experience the trauma "not as an hallucinatory reproduction but as an objective memory" (p 160).

While the ability of contrasting situations to bring upsetting or traumatic realities to consciousness has been recognized, their importance has not. Feldman (1956) gives an excellent everyday example of this phenomenon in his paper on crying at the happy ending. While he notes other legitimate explanations of crying at happy endings, especially that there is a release of pent up tension, he highlights the issue of contrast. Adults know well enough that the true ending of life—loss, illness, and death—is not a happy one. A happy ending in a play, movie, or novel, if it is structured skillfully enough, evokes this knowledge by the contrast it presents to it, and thus also evokes the sadness associated with this knowledge of life's true ending. Feldman notes also that children do not cry at happy endings, since they do not truly believe in the inevitability of life's sad one.

All traumatized individuals avoid situations that contrast with that of their trauma. In fact they walk a very fine line between the dual dangers of anything that too closely resembles the trauma and threatens to evoke zero process memories of it, and anything that too sharply contrasts with aspects of the trauma and threatens to do the same thing. Hemmed in on both sides like this, the individual often enough veers off the line in one direction or another, thus evoking the primarily dissociated memories of the trauma. It is at this point that the person attempts to defend against the emergence of the memories by using such mechanisms as turning passive into active and identification with the aggressor. As an example when E's relationship with her quite warm, caring boyfriend who was careful not to force anything on her threatened, by its contrast to it, to evoke her trauma of sexual abuse by her father, she was shocked to find herself being quite cold and dismissive to him and was doubly shocked to associate this with the very similar behavior of her father towards her. In this sequence, once the avoidance of contrasting realities as a defense had failed, and the memories of the trauma were threatening to emerge, E identified with her brutal father, and treated her boyfriend as she had been treated. This kept the feeling of being brutalized and helpless at a distance, by pushing it onto her boyfriend.

I think that much of what passes for a repetition of trauma—for instance E's having relationships with abusive individuals—is actually partly a product of contrast defenses. The traumatized person cannot stray too far from the trauma without evoking it through contrast, so they end up in situations that look very similar to the traumatic one. If one looks more closely at these situations, however, one can also see that in these supposed repetitions the person tries very hard to not come too close to repeating the actual event of the trauma, as they walk their fine line. There are of course other processes that may cause repetitions, but I think that the particular one I am describing is a very common contributor to what is described as the compulsion to repeat a trauma.

What is the nature of contrast defenses? When E had met her new boyfriend she came to a number of sessions with various reasons why the whole thing was not right for her. Her arguments had the ring of rationalization to me, so I said that while I did not doubt the truth of what she said, I wondered about her motivation for stressing these things now. She admitted she was having trouble staying in the relationship. At this point I interpreted her contrast defense. I said that I thought she might be having trouble with the emotional investment and warmth of the relationship because it reminded her by contrast of the coldness and lack of caring of her mother. E began to cry, and to talk quite directly about how difficult it was. Her boyfriend had left a warm bathrobe in the washroom for her to wear after her shower. When she had seen it it had been almost unbearable. She was overcome by a feeling that she now recognized as extreme pain and sadness.

Our work on E's contrast defenses bore all the hallmarks of work on a denial defense. By pointing to its operation, I could relatively easily undo it and facilitate the emergence of the feelings that motivated it (pain and sadness). However, E would then talk about various tensions in, or negative aspects of, her relationship with her boyfriend and as she did this the sad feelings would recede. In this particular instance my interpretations were inaccurate, since they left out the defense against her father's exploitation of her, and against the memories of the sexual abuse. Despite this E's reactions demonstrate well enough the basic nature of a contrast defense—the use of attentional and intellectual ego functions to keep out of awareness certain extremely unpleasant realities.

An important dynamic underlying contrast reactions is that generalization is used as an intellectual defense against the full impact of the reality. For instance E might think to herself, at least preconsciously, that after all it's the norm, and perhaps even inevitable, that men will exploit her and not care deeply for her. This generalization hides the specificity of her father's attitude toward her, of his abuse of her, and the specificity of her feelings about it. If she fully acknowledges a reality that contrasts with this generalization, its usefulness as a defense would collapse and the unpleasant reality would then emerge.

The defense of repeating something close to a past denied reality in order not to remember it may strike the reader as an example of repeating as a defense against remembering, seen for instance in transference repetitions. This repetition is generally thought of as a compromise between wishes and past memories striving for expression and the forces of defense. So, have I really introduced a new idea with contrast defenses, or am I just redescribing in somewhat more convoluted terms a dynamic that we know very well already? For instance, could we see E's difficulty with her boyfriend as based on an oedipal inhibition? In other words this relationship brought together sexual feelings and fondness, which may have taken her back to repressed oedipal desires for her father. Her engaging instead in relationships where she was exploited could be a product of a regression to anal sadistic and masochistic wishes as a defense against these prohibited oedipal longings. The regression might be conditioned by E's frustrations and abuse at the hands of her mother (for instance the painful enemas) and her sexual abuse by her father. In other words these repetitions might be adequately explained by a complex combination of wishes and defenses against them. In fact if one were to take this idea a little further, one might say that my description of E's problems concentrates in an overly simplistic way on the external happenings in E's life, without an understanding or analysis of what she made of these happenings internally in relation to her drives and fantasies.

I will reserve a fuller discussion of the nature of contrast defenses for the chapter on masochism. I will say here, however, that the issue is not which interpretation is correct, one based on a denial defense (contrast defense) or one based on drives and a counterforce defense. The real issues are how do these defenses interconnect and how should we approach them technically? We have seen, and will see in later chapters, that a deeper understanding of denial defenses leads us to a more multifaceted understanding of the nature of the transference. Both in relation to the transference and elsewhere, an analysis of denial defenses to a certain depth is often necessary in order to usefully engage counterforce defenses. In the particular case of E the proof that a contrast defense was operative along with other defenses was that as this contrast was challenged the dissociated memories of the sexual abuse emerged, indicating that it was partly the working of this defense that usually kept them from consciousness.

While contrast defenses are not usually analyzed directly, they are often confronted indirectly in therapy by the therapist's behavior. Ferenczi (1933), in the passage quoted previously, essentially advises that the analyst assume a warm attitude so that, by its contrast with the abusive situation, this behavior will bring the memories of the abuse into consciousness. This advice of Ferenczi's has often been misconstrued to be that one should provide a corrective emotional experience to the traumatized patient. While he may have advised this as well, it is clear that in this passage he is advising the analyst to assume a certain stance because it will have an interpretive effect. In fact it is worthwhile considering whether some of what is usually classified as the therapeutic effect of the relationship and of corrective emotional experiences in therapy is actually the outcome of a confrontation of the patient's contrast defenses.

To give an example of this, one of the most powerful feelings related to trauma is a sense of aloneness and abandonment. Even in accidental traumas such as a car crash, the feeling of being abandoned by the superior powers of fate (the adult version of the child's protection by his or her parents) is overwhelming. In situations of abuse this feeling is much magnified. Although there are many factors involved, I think that an important cause of the difficulty with trust, and of feelings of distance and separation from others, of severely traumatized individuals is the operation of contrast defenses. In other words, the person avoids situations of warmth and human connection, and minimizes or denies their importance when they do occur, so as not to experience through contrast a revival of the intense feelings of being completely abandoned. The proof that this is actually the case is that direct interpretation of the contrast defense brings the painful feelings of aloneness to consciousness, and once these feelings are worked through the person is better able to engage in close relationships, and their feelings of separation from others lessens.

Most authors working with severely traumatized patients have emphasized the need to establish trust by behaving in an honest, warm, and open manner. Most often this is seen rather straightforwardly as related to the necessity for re-establishing a trust that has been broken. I think, however, that this underestimates the tremendous amount of active defensive work that such patients engage in so as not to feel trust or a connection to others. By analyzing the patient's difficulty remaining in therapy and by providing a deep sense of human connection, the therapist actually engages in a confrontation of this contrast defense. Many authors (e.g., Herman, 1992) have commented on how, when this trust is established, memories of the trauma begin to emerge. Again I would see the reason for this as being not only that the patient now feels safe to explore the trauma, but also that the patient's contrast defenses have been unwittingly confronted and partially undone.

Contrast defenses can also be seen to operate in other facets of the reaction to trauma. For instance the importance of establishing a sense of safety and reasonable self-care in the lives of abused patients is well known, but here too the active defensive use of lack of self-care in order to keep memories of the abuse at bay is usually underestimated. I presented an example of this in E's case, where taking care of herself was difficult because it brought up, by contrast, memories of neglect and abuse. As another example of the workings of contrast defenses, Terr (1984) notes the consistent finding of a foreshortening of the future in those who have suffered severe trauma. I think that for such patients to see a longer future would, by its contrast with it, evoke the feeling of certain death or of an unbearably bleak future that was part of the trauma.

There are other attentional defenses that protect against the emergence of traumatic memories. I will finish this chapter by discussing one other important class of these defenses. A member of this class is the defensive use of guilt. In this defense, the person clings to the feeling that the trauma was their fault. The hidden defensive reason for this is related to the fact that the subtext of guilt is responsibility. If one is guilty for the occurrence of something there must have been something one could have and should have done differently, and if there was, then of course one could not have been helpless. I will discuss the defensive use of guilt more extensively in chapter 7, in relation to masochism.

Defensive guilt can be understood as one member of a larger class of denial defenses used to keep at bay the utter helplessness that always lies at the heart of trauma. These defenses are usually established soon after the traumatic overwhelming and involve some sort of theory about why the trauma happened. The theories and guilt are like psychic Band-Aids that cover the gaping wound that trauma leaves behind. Words such as helplessness or despair cannot really capture the true nature of this wound. During the trauma there is a breakdown of the basic primal denials of death, vulnerability, lack of control, and aloneness—primal denials that protect each of us from overwhelming feelings. The various post-traumatic theories are attempts to restore order, meaning, and control to the situation, and to the person's life.

It may be tempting at times to take a more superficial view of post-traumatic theories (which includes the theory that one is guilty), seeing them as a product of misunderstanding due to mental confusion, young age, and the externalizations of abusers, who tell their victims that they are to blame. At a deeper level, one may analyze their connection with unconscious fantasies related to other issues that have become psychically entangled with the trauma. Each of these factors may play a part, but the analysis of the defensive use of theory, as a protection against the core traumatic experiences of loss of control and helplessness, is what is most helpful in allowing access to the zero process memories and the primal defenses that keep them from awareness. The thing to stress to the patient is how important it is to cling to these theories, given what emerges if one gives them up, and how understandable it is that these ideas would have formed as a protection against overwhelming passivity and helplessness. Once one has spotted these particular defenses, their analysis does not differ from that of other denial defenses—for instance the analysis of B's denial of her boyfriend's narcissism that was the first clinical example of this book. I have found that an active technique, bringing forward the defense and the helplessness defended against, will usually (if one is correct in spotting the dynamic, and correct in one's timing) lead to the evocation of some of the feelings. The patient will then resort to the same or a similar defense—for instance finding some other very good reason why they are guilty. This is the time to point out how as the patient thought of the guilt, or insisted on some other theory of the causation of the trauma, their more intense feelings of despair and helplessness disappeared. One will usually have to make these interpretations many, many times, from many different angles. As in the analysis of any other denial defense, it is important not to argue with the patient or to get frustrated, as if they are being willfully stubborn or dense in not understanding. This is not to say that one may not point out contradictions in what the patient is saying, or even looseness in their argument, but this should be done only with the larger aim in mind of making the patient aware of an unconscious defensive process.

There is much more that could be said about the analysis of trauma, but my aim has been only to describe some aspects of technique that come out of the new understanding of defenses that I have been developing.

Summary

In this chapter I have discussed trauma especially as it relates to the issue of defense. I delineated some characteristics of the traumatic process, demonstrating that it involves the breakdown of the ego's tendency to avoid pain (the unpleasure principle), which is the chief motivator for defense, as well as many ego functions, including the integrative and organizing functions. This leads to a breakdown of the ego's defensive structure as well as of the normal processing of perceptions and the normal laying down of integrated memory networks. Trauma does not serve as the motivator for defense, but is rather one of the few situations in life where the continuous working of defenses is put out of operation. Another important point about the traumatic process is that it is initiated partly by the sudden collapse of certain primal denials of our vulnerability and death. These defenses are part of a complex of processes that go under the general heading of the stimulus barrier, and it is a major breach of this barrier that initiates the traumatic process.

The unfolding of the traumatic process, with its lack of integration of elements, I referred to as primary dissociation. I argued that this was not a defensive process at all but a product of the breakdown of many ego functions during the traumatic process. I suggested secondary dissociation as a reasonable name for the active defensive process that uses aspects of the primary dissociation, especially the lack of integration, for defensive ends. The traumatic process leaves pockets of mental functioning that are not only separated off from the rest of the personality, but in which the nature of psychic functioning differs from both the primary and the secondary processes. I suggested the name "areas of primary dissociation" for these areas left over after the traumatic process has run its course.

The most important idea presented in this chapter is that there is a form of mental functioning that is a consequence of the traumatic process—a form that differs from both the primary process and the secondary process. I suggested the term zero process for this form of functioning. During trauma, the breakdown in the integrative function and other aspects of processing of perceptions leads to bits of perception that are generally uncoordinated with each other, except for some amount of sequencing in terms of time of occurrence. The laying down of memories of these perceptions is also interfered with and the consequence is a form of mental functioning in which there is precious little processing, with a much more frozen quality than either the primary or secondary processes. Zero process memories can be thought of as having characteristics of both perception and memory. They persist over time as does memory, and yet have the immediate, intrusive qualities of perception, as well as the tendency to unfold in a linear manner, as does actual perceptual experience. I suggested that one part of the strong tendency to repeat traumas is a product of the nature of the zero process, with its tendency to be evoked in a very concrete way by "triggers," and once evoked to play out parts of its contents as if they were present-day experiences.

I discussed a few aspects of the analysis of trauma. The nature of the zero process colors the nature of the transferences and countertransferences encountered when analyzing trauma. These tend to be evoked in a very concrete all or nothing manner and to replay the traumatic events with little symbolic processing. In analyzing the zero process, whether through transference/countertransference work or through work on symptoms, phobias, memory fragments, etc., I suggested an approach that combined activity in evoking aspects of the trauma, with slowing things down to help the patient modulate the intrusive manner in which the zero process emerges, along with a flexible moving back and forth from evoking the zero process reliving, allowing this to play itself out, and analyzing primal repressions and denials and secondary defenses that cut off the zero process and traumatic memories from the rest of the personality. An important aspect of the work in relation to the zero process could best be described as the construction of memories, in which one attempts to construct not just any set of memories, but something similar to the ones that would have formed if the whole process of perception, memory consolidation, connection to verbal and other symbols, and integration and interconnection with other memories had not been stopped dead in its tracks by the traumatic process. Along with this direct work on the zero process proto-memories, I also described two important attentional defenses that protect the core of a trauma: contrast defenses, and theories formed after the fact to "explain" the trauma, but which really act as Band-Aids, covering over the sense of absolute helplessness and meaninglessness that is present at the height of the trauma.

Terms

Area of Primary Dissociation: An area of zero process functioning that remains after the traumatic process has run its course.

Contrast Defenses: These are defenses in which the person attempts to avoid awareness of a very distressing reality by avoiding realities that contrast too sharply with it, because of the tendency of these contrasting realities to evoke the distressing one.

Primary Dissociation: The breakdown in many ego functions that is part of the traumatic process leads to a situation in which perceptions are not integrated one with the other, a situation that I have designated as primary dissociation. This is not a defense, but is rather the outcome of the traumatic process.

Secondary Dissociation: This is a defensive process in which the ego actively uses the lack of integration and changes in level of consciousness of primary dissociation for its own ends. Often secondary dissociation is used by victims of ongoing trauma to separate themselves from the trauma that they see is about to come, by going somewhere else in their fantasy or somewhere else in a more concrete manner, for instance somewhere else in the room or house in which they are being abused.

Zero Process: This is a basic form of mental processing. It is a consequence of trauma, and is to be contrasted with both the primary process and the secondary process. In the zero process there is, as the name implies, no symbolic processing of any sort, as well as a lack of integration and coordination between elements. The contents of the zero process have characteristics of both memory and perception. They have the persistence over time of memory, but have the immediacy, intrusiveness, and tendency to run in one time direction of perceptions. As with the primary and the secondary processes, so with the zero process, there is a core area where the particular characteristics of the zero process are displayed in pure culture—in the case of the zero process this corresponds to the core of the traumatic memories—while surrounding this are areas that are influenced by the nature of the zero process functioning but which blend this with characteristics of the primary or secondary processes to a greater or lesser degree.

Note

1. It is interesting, and important theoretically, that the sudden overwhelming of the counterforce defenses, as takes place for instance in pavor nocturnus (stage IV nightmare) and in the temper tantrums of the toddler age, do not lead to long-term sequelae (Yorke, 1986).

PART TWO

SPECIFIC CLINICAL PROBLEMS

In the chapters of this part, we will explore some aspects of specific problems faced by clinicians, in the light of the revised theory of defense presented in Part One.

To summarize the ideas of the first part in the most concise manner, I would say that there were two main themes. The first was the differentiation between two basic forms of defense: counterforce defenses and attentional defenses. These are distinguished by their basic mechanism. Counterforce defenses use partially neutralized aggressive drive energy to form a force that opposes the push towards awareness and action of drives and the memories and affects attached to them, while attentional defenses use the ego function of attention, supplemented by other ego processes, to keep from consciousness mental contents (usually remembered perceptions or judgments about inner or outer reality) that have less inherent push towards conscious awareness than the drives.

The second major theme of Part One was the disentangling of the defensive processes from the traumatic process. Freud had connected the two processes through his concept of traumatic anxiety as the motivator of primal repression. I argued that traumatic anxiety was a poorly chosen term since trauma, rather than leading to defensive operations, actually precludes the use of defenses. Disentangling the traumatic process from the defensive processes led to the concepts of pervasive affects as the motivators of a range of primal defenses, and to a clarification of the relationship between affects, primal defenses, after defenses, and secondary defenses (see glossary). This disentangling allowed not only a clearer and more coherent view of defensive processes, but of the traumatic process as well. This latter was seen as involving the breakdown in certain primal denials and as having as its consequence an area of functioning with qualities differing significantly from both the primary and the secondary processes. I proposed the term and concept "zero process" for this form of functioning.

In this second part I will describe a number of attentional, zero process, and counterforce defenses in relation to some specific clinical entities. In chapter 6, on narcissism, and chapter 7, on masochism, I will present ideas about specific forms of attentional defenses related to these two clinical problems. In chapter 8, on perversions, I will present some further ideas about the zero process, including the concepts of zero process defenses and zero process neuroses as well as specific examples of each of these.

CHAPTER SIX

~

Narcissism

As Pulver (1970) has noted, the term narcissism has been used to refer to quite a number of phenomena—a developmental stage, a sense of omnipotence, a type of object choice, a mode of object relating, self-esteem, and a form of perversion. Pulver distinguished these uses of the term from the metapsychological concept of narcissism, which refers to the investment of libido in the self. Freud (1914) had introduced the term narcissism in relation to the sexual perversion of erotic interest in oneself, but immediately went on to expand it by describing some neurotics and young children as having a strong narcissism. He said that "narcissism in this sense would not be a perversion but the libidinal complement to the egoism of the instinct of self-preservation" (1914, pp 73–74). Freud found evidence of an excess of this narcissism in the delusions of grandiosity of psychotics and in the self-centeredness of children. With the introduction of the dual drive theory— the death drive and the life drive (Freud, 1920)—the idea of ego instincts and ego interests were subsumed under the concept of libido and narcissism. The use of libido and its shifting investments as explanatory concepts had at this point reached its zenith.

A number of analysts (often referred to as ego psychologists) who followed Freud amended his theoretical ideas about narcissism. Hartmann (1950b) clarified that the counterpart of investment of libido in others is its investment not in the ego (which is a set of functions), but in the self (the whole person) or in the mental representation of the self. Hartmann also stated that we should look not only at the direction of drive investment but also at its degree of neutralization—its distance from raw sexuality (or aggression when this is invested in the self). Hartmann (1950b) and Jacobson (1964) also revived the idea of ego interests that are relatively independent of the drives. Hartmann noted that a broad definition of ego interests would include many non-narcissistic interests, such as an interest in judging reality correctly. However, an important subset of these ego interests involves what is commonly called self-interest or egoism. Jacobson (1964) noted that from early on the ego develops strivings towards its own enhancement and power that are relatively independent of the drives, even though they become secondarily suffused with aggression. While they do not fit under the narrower definition of narcissism as libidinal investment in the self, these self-interests of the ego would generally be called narcissistic by analysts and non-analysts alike.

Egoism, self-interest, and libidinal investment in the self are issues to be addressed in every analysis, since they occur in one form or another (including their negative form of too little of each of these things) in everyone. This leads to some difficulties in discussions of narcissistic disorders since this category can be narrowed to include patients with extreme grandiosity and psychopathic levels of self-interest (as Kernberg [1970] usually did) or expanded to include character difficulties closer to the neurotic range, as was done by Kohut (1977).

A full discussion of all aspects of narcissism is not the purpose of this chapter. Instead, I will look more closely at a specific defensive use of feelings of narcissistic enhancement, as seen in narcissistic character disorders, as well as other defenses engendered by a fixation on these feelings. While these dynamics involve drive and developmental issues, I see a subset as being at their core related to what Jacobson and Hartmann referred to as ego interests, although they are a very specific form of ego interest—a strong interest in recreating and not relinquishing certain pleasurable feeling states. A fixation on these pleasurable feelings leads to them being used to screen other, less pleasant realities. The nature and cause of this ego fixation on pleasurable feelings, and the screen defenses to which it gives rise, are the specific topics I will be addressing in this chapter.

It would be best to discuss these issues in relation to clinical material, which I will do by presenting further history from my patient D, who has already made a few appearances in this book.

Clinical Example: D

Some aspects of D's narcissistic fixation were touched on in the vignette used in chapter 4 to demonstrate externalization, a favorite defense of his. Those sessions also give something of the flavor of our interactions. I will proceed now with an outline of D's history and the course of his analysis, before giving more detailed descriptions of a few sessions from late in the analysis that demonstrate the nature of his narcissistic fixations and our work with them. I will then discuss this material in relation to narcissistic overgratifications, narcissistic defenses, and the analysis of these defenses. I should note that in order to give a good picture of D's history and dynamics, I have spent quite a bit of time on other aspects of his case, especially his sexual acting out. These descriptions will be used as examples of certain dynamics in the chapter of perversions (chapter 8). In the examples of two sessions presented below their connection with D's narcissistic issues is apparent.

D came for help with a number of forms of acting out that were playing havoc with his life. I found him personable and easy to relate to. He had been in therapy on and off from his mid-twenties till his present age in his late forties. As he told it, he often made friends with his therapists and he remembered in particular a recent one with whom he would spend the time discussing common interests such as books or movies. He had also talked a lot about his mother, a quite narcissistic woman, and his anger at her. He had a very early memory—from an age younger than two—of sitting on a toilet seat alone, abandoned, and afraid, with legs too short to reach the floor and get off the seat.

I had the feeling D had told me about his previous therapists so that I would not fall into the same trap. When we began to look at his difficulty facing unpleasant realities and adult responsibilities, and at his relationship to his father, D made good progress in putting his life together—he had been on the point of losing his management job at a large corporation. He said no one had looked at his relationship to his father—a close and warm one—or his strong reactions to his father's death. I felt very good about myself and the way I was conducting D's analysis, a feeling that I only fully understood in the later part of the analysis, although I sensed from the first that it had something to do with D's closeness with his father.

D's father had been away for the first year of his life for work reasons. D, the first born and much admired son, and his mother had lived with his maternal grandparents. He remembers both of them, with whom he was close until their death later in his life, as warm and loving. He described his mother as stunningly beautiful. I saw when he brought in a photograph of her that this description was not just a product of childhood idealization. She was also, as is common in people with extreme attractiveness, quite taken with herself and thrived on, and lived for, the admiration of herself by others.

When D had just turned one and his father was able to live with him and his mother, they moved into a modest house together. A sister, who clearly played second fiddle to D in the family, was born when he was two. According to his mother D was toilet trained at just over one year old, which coincided with the family's move out of the grandparent's home. D was intellectually precocious, doing extremely well in school. His father's intellectual ambitions had been stymied by the early death of his own father, after which he went to work to support his mother and siblings. He thus looked to D to fulfill these ambitions by proxy. Despite this use of D, his father's relationship to him was less narcissistic than that of his mother. As an example when D dropped out of a program in a private college designed as preparatory to the professional training that his father clearly yearned that he get, his father nevertheless wrote him a heartfelt letter saying that he should not be too distressed, and that he would always love him and support him in whatever he decided to do with his life. His mother, on the other hand, felt there was no further use spending extra money on this college, and said that D should come to live at home and go to a public institution. She was angry that she had been giving up her beauty treatments to fund this failed venture.

In the exchange used as an illustration of externalization in chapter 4 I gave some examples of the ways in which both of D's parents helped him to circumvent unpleasant realities. For instance, he was having terrible trouble completing a project at school so his father got a friend with expertise in the area to do the project for him. Another time his mother used her considerable charms to get a male teacher to give him a higher mark. D would hide the vegetables he did not want to eat under his plate at around age 7. His mother would clean up the table and never mention the stashed vegetables. D remembers thinking at the time that this was not the right thing for her to do. D was not, however, a completely spoiled and coddled child. There was reasonable discipline much of the time, as well as warmly remembered family dinners and outings. Perhaps it was the sporadic nature of the occurrences of being helped to circumvent reality that led to the mixed nature of D's relation to reality and responsibility—at times taking them quite seriously, at others circumventing them through lying and cheating. Much of the deleterious acting out that he came for help with involved denial and lying to others in an attempt to negate a more sober view of reality—for instance in relation to dubious get rich quick business schemes that cost him dearly.

Despite these obvious difficulties in facing reality D saw them as secondary to what he considered the cause of his problems—not being given enough love by his mother. He described many examples of this. For instance he remembered a solo piano recital as a young child where he froze, and then ran off the stage crying. His mother found him where he was hiding and proceeded to berate him for having so embarrassed her by his actions. He noted that even at present her conversations with him involved telling him how someone had told her how beautiful she was, while she had trouble being interested for very long in what he was saying about himself. If only he had been loved enough by his mother, or could be loved enough now by a woman, D felt that his self-esteem and confidence would be higher and that he would not have to resort to destructive actions to raise them.

Other than the lies and financial risk taking these actions included going to prostitutes for sex and to "massage parlors" where he would be masturbated. D had lived for many years in a long-term relationship (a common law marriage), and had since then had many girlfriends, living with some of them as well. Many of these women, including his former common law wife, had actually admired him, cared for him, and loved him, but through all these relationships he had continued various forms of acting out, including seeing prostitutes for sex or sexual massage. In fact the only times when D did not engage in these activities were not when his girlfriend was more loving, but when he was going out with a woman who seemed to him exotic or was in his mind for other reasons closely identified with a prostitute.

I pointed out to him that these reactions suggested that love itself would not cure him. I came early on in the analysis to feel also that his complaints about maltreatment by his mother were being used for defensive purposes (which is not the same thing as saying that they were not true or that the deficits in mothering had not actually been detrimental to his development). There was something very insistent about his complaints, which I interpreted as an avoidance of other things. What emerged was especially his close relationship with his father—which he had acted out rather than talked about in his previous therapies—and a strong need to be special. His complaints about maltreatment acted as a denial defense by shifting attention away from the intense pleasure he felt, and the fantasies related to his specialness that were aroused, when he got around unpleasant realities. These feelings were roused when he lied, or when he went to a massage parlor to get instant and intense satisfaction when his girlfriend had not done exactly as he wanted. In this early phase we also looked at D's insistent use of externalization to get rid of guilt or unwanted aspects of himself—an example from the analysis of which was presented in chapter 4.

By the second and third year of the analysis anal and oedipal wishes emerged in a workable form, both in the transference and outside of it. I gave a brief example of our analysis of positive oedipal wishes in chapter 2 when discussing primal repression. I also noted that the positive oedipal conflicts were partly used in a defensive way. Behind them lay D's sexual wishes towards his father, which were cast in anal terms. These popped up, for instance, when D noticed a carving of a rhinoceros I have in my office and then thought of me anally penetrating him from behind the couch. Such ideas came to D when I had made an interpretation D found unpleasant and not to his taste. These fantasies and wishes were far less available for analysis—except at a more intellectual level—than were D's heterosexual fantasies and conflicts. There was a certain amount of parallel in the way in which D used his feelings and wishes about his mother—whether sexual wishes or anger at being mistreated—to defend against certain other ones related to his father.

The sequence I have given of what material came up and what defend against what captures only the major movements of the analysis. Many issues, for instance sibling ones, also were part of the analysis. As well there was a layering of defenses, so that what was at one time used as a defense could switch roles with what was defended against. As an example, a number of times D's deep sadness and pain about his mother's narcissism emerged, and at these times he would use our work on his own narcissism defensively, saying that he was in fact the selfish one and he was just projecting this onto his mother. Analysis of this defense led to a painful, sobbing realization of what his mother was really like.

D worked well in analysis and in the third to fourth year we began to look in a more concerted way at adolescent issues, especially his strong resistance to the painful mourning of childhood's end. At the level of feeling childhood had never ended for D, and he fought hard to keep it that way. A very interesting dynamic also emerged, in which as a way of resolving his overwhelming oedipal conflicts, D had decided that it was really his father, who in reality so much admired and wanted success for him, who wanted D to marry his mother. This early fantasy using externalization was quite unconscious until we uncovered it.

As we analyzed dreams and associations that seemed to point to an early toileting trauma, intense fears of abandonment and death were experienced in the analysis. I had said at one point early on that he seemed to have less to talk about after going to a massage parlor, and that if he could hold off and put the feelings into words in the analysis we might get a better idea about what they were all about. As might be expected, D took this as an injunction not to go, and when he did he became intensely afraid that I would throw him out. The more adult, reality-related form of the fear was that I would get so frustrated with him going to massage parlors again and again, even as we analyzed its meaning from all angles, that I would declare him a hopeless case and send him on his way so that the time could be used by a patient in more need. In its more basic form, which popped up from time to time, D felt terrified of the abandonment, as if I would abruptly throw him out and he would float away into space, like an astronaut on a space walk whose lifeline had been cut.

These fears were at one level an expression of D's fear of me as his father who would punish him for masturbating while thinking of his mother and for having sexual contact with his mother, two unconscious meanings of the visits to the massage parlors. The castration fears were expressed in the sorts of abandonment fantasies typical of the oral stage because of D's oral/phallic fixations, which led to an easy regression back to oral passivity as a defense against unbearable oedipal conflicts. The fears had connections as well to his early toileting traumas. He had made a mess and would now be punished. It became clear that his memories of being left on the toilet, which had been put to good defensive use to screen his attachment to his father and the overgratifications of his childhood, also represented a real trauma. Flashbulb memories—for instance of the black and white tile pattern on the bathroom floor—and overwhelming feelings of desolation and death, emerged from behind what were at first relatively bland memories and ideas about being abandoned. A specific fear of falling into the toilet and being flushed away like a turd emerged with frightening intensity. D connected this to the fact that he had always had trouble walking to the edge of a precipice, no matter how secure the fencing, but that if there were a river or especially a waterfall at the edge, this difficulty would rise to phobic proportions. At these times nothing could get him anywhere near the edge. D's fear of putting his arm through the glass of my door in analysis and then bleeding to death as I watched because I was unable to help or because the psychoanalytic rules forbade me from interfering, were condensations of the messing/abandonment terrors from toileting with castration anxiety from somewhat later stages. Since D's castration anxiety was one of the main motive forces behind his primal repression of his positive and negative oedipal conflicts, this fact brings up again the question of the connection of the motives for active primal repression with the anxieties engendered by traumas.

The early traumas were found to be related to a splitting of the ego expressed in D's visits to prostitutes and massage parlors. This compartmentalization was used as a solution to many difficulties—D's wish to cling to childhood and yet be big like his father, for instance, and his oedipal anxieties and conflicts. In the sessions described below we get a view of the way in which this compartmentalization around the visits to the massage parlors was used to deal with feelings about his mother's lack of warmth and caring. A fuller

discussion of trauma and splitting of the ego, and trauma and repression, using D's case as an example, will be presented in chapter 8, on perversions.

I will now present details from some sessions. They contain quite a bit of
material related to D's traumas. I would ask the reader, however, to pay attention especially to D's narcissistic feeling of specialness, and how it is both
clung to and used for defensive purposes by him.

A Few Sessions

These sessions took place five years into our five times weekly analysis. D had
missed the Monday session because his back had been thrown out, and he was
in a great deal of pain. He had already cancelled Tuesday because of a meeting
at work. When I saw him Wednesday he wondered if he should pay for the
missed appointment. (He does not pay for sessions he attends, because the
services are covered by the provincial health insurance plan.) He knew that I
did not charge for missed appointments due to serious illness but he said that
he had gone to a work meeting, with a great deal of difficulty, for a few hours
in the late afternoon (our appointment had been in the morning). He felt on
this basis maybe he should just pay me, but I suggested that we instead talk
about it and see what came up, since it seemed entirely possible to me that his
back spasms had really been so severe in the morning that he could not come.
He pointed out that they still might have been psychologically caused. I said
that we could not just assume that, and in any case whatever their cause they
seemed to be quite debilitating. (I could see that D walked with a great deal
of pain and difficulty, and lay down and got up with even more.)

Over the remaining three days of the week D did not in fact discuss his
back or the missed appointment except to insist once more on paying, which
I held off. He did talk about going to massage parlors as a way of putting
pleasant feelings in place of unpleasant ones, so that he often formed the
intention to go after something had upset him. He thought of the idea of
telling his present girlfriend, with whom he had a very loving and in other
ways a quite open relationship, about his still going to massage parlous. He
had told her about a year earlier and she had been upset but also concerned
and understanding of his difficulties. He pictured telling her at the same
time that he had engaged in the sort of financial speculation that he had in
fact scrupulously avoided over the last few years. Why would he tell this lie
that would make him look even worse, he wondered? Maybe, he speculated,
his sense of guilt was so great that he had to make it worse for himself. I
suggested that perhaps the particular lie wasn't as important as clinging to

the idea that reality was a malleable thing. Perhaps since he had nailed it down in one area by telling his girlfriend the whole truth about what he had been doing, he had to demonstrate his power to change it in another way by telling the lie. D was very struck by this idea. He talked of how going to the massage parlors itself was like a fantasy come true. There was the lack of rejection, negativity, and complicated interpersonal issues, and there was the warm physical attention. Near the end of the session D's mood changed from an excited, almost euphoric interest in these ideas to something more irritable. "After all," he said, "lots of adults lie. Look at Donald Rumsfeld and all the people found guilty in the Iran Contra affair. Not only was their lying forgiven but they now hold positions of trust and power." D went on for a while getting more and more angry at these aspects of American politics. I said I couldn't disagree with him, but I wasn't sure how that negated what we were discussing about him. D saw quickly, because we had analyzed it so often, his attempt at externalization.

At the next session, which was Monday, D said he had had an interesting Friday. After our session he had felt a compulsion to go to a massage parlor, but had also been thinking of what we had said about his need to change reality. When he had gone for lunch he had seen a place he knew was a massage parlor across the street, but had not gone. A few hours later, on his way home, he had fished out a quarter but then didn't phone. He seemed, he said, to have more of a compulsion to think about what it all meant than to do it. He hadn't thought much about it since Friday, but was now thinking of it because he had a chiropractor's appointment scheduled today and thought maybe he'd go after it.

"I can't really remember if I went last week to the chiropractor. I must have gone, because of my back. But then I didn't come here. It's all getting very confused in my mind."

D fumbled for words and thoughts and then said, "I realize what it is now. I must have gone to the chiropractor's the same morning I didn't come here. That's why I couldn't get it straight."

"So you got all confused about the reality of what happened when."

"Yes. Its funny how on Friday I found it so easy *not* to go, which is the opposite of what it's like usually. I felt no compulsion. The idea would pass, then come back, but each time it was easy. Maybe it was that each time I knew I'd have an easy time if I didn't."

D then talked of going to see a herbalist. "His waiting room is very comfortable, with a couch too if you want to relax, compared to your waiting room." (I share a waiting area with a number of other therapists in what is really a large corridor in a large older house. It is equipped with some chairs that are certainly not the last word in comfort or style.) D said he now sits in the uncomfortable chair away from my wall because he's afraid he'd eavesdrop. He felt he would try to intrude if he sat in the other set of chairs. D described how it felt quite different sitting in the two sets of chairs, related to the physical geography of sharing a common wall. "I think it's been quite a while since I've sat on the other side," he said.

"Maybe there's something in the physical geography," I said, "that relates to mental geography or to us as people—our bodies—perhaps related to a wish and fear of merging, with the wall as the boundary between us."

"Well, maybe merging but merging seems inappropriate. I'd call it snooping, because before I would strain to hear the words. I couldn't actually make out the words, just a sort of rumble, but I wanted to snoop. I still want to do it in other ways, like looking at your books when I come in. It makes me think of you writing your book, at your desk. (I had asked D about a year previous to this for permission to use material from his analysis, to which he had agreed.) "I thought," he continued, "of how you might talk of my going to prostitutes and massage parlors. This might be a way for me to show it to Sherry" (his girlfriend). "I guess I'd be using you to clean up my mess."

I had the feeling, from the time D had mentioned suppressing having gone to the chiropractor's, that he had been chatting in a kind of upbeat tone that I had come to recognize he used when trying to stay away from an uncomfortable topic. I would find myself torn between continuing to listen to, and talk about, the seemingly relevant things D talked of, and a nagging feeling that kept surfacing that the really important thing was missing. This nagging feeling would usually get stronger and stronger until I blurted out something, usually something vague and poorly formulated, perhaps in keeping with the nature of the nagging feeling. So at this point I interrupted by saying, "I wonder about what you mentioned about the chiropractor and the missed session. I was thinking . . ."

"It's like by giving you permission for your book," D interrupted back, "I was hoping to be able to read about myself." He talked of his wish to have the expert opinion, the final word.

"As if if it's in print it will be more real," I added. D then talked of he and his girlfriend having an intense fight, and yet they could talk about it afterwards. He described a number of details, but seemed to be stressing just how angry they were and yet how it was O.K. It led to no permanent bad feelings. He had talked to his girlfriend about how he has had problems with these kinds of ambivalences, with getting angry with someone he loved.

"There's other things that bug me, that I get mad about—her taking control." D gave examples of this. I brought him back again to the chiropractor's and his whole conversation about the chairs in the waiting room, noting that perhaps he had wanted to foreclose on the whole thing by paying, but by leaving it open some interesting things had come to light.

"I can see how the issue isn't the hundred dollars, because I had wanted to settle it, but the principle of the thing."

"Maybe the principle is that reality is malleable and the lie is really secondary—really to serve to establish that principle."

"But you put that in the present. I can agree I was like that in the past. But I am really feeling more mature."

"Well I don't want to diminish the changes that have taken place, but analyzing it is an ongoing thing. Can you see what you've done? By putting this tendency in the past, you distance yourself from it. It's like expecting it to change with the snap of a finger."

D laughed. "No, I can see that very well. It really is like a wish for magic. Like I wanted you to solve this thing with Sherry by writing about me, and that also I'd have the final word once I had read your book."

"Well, we'll have to stop now," I said.

D got his coat and left, saying "thank you" and "see you tomorrow" a couple of times. His good-byes were more effusive and prolonged than most of my patients, creating a sense of a special relationship and a warm feeling in me.

Just before the next appointment D phoned to say he would be a few minutes late because of a delay in the subway. To my surprise, when I opened the door at the start of his appointment he was right there.

"Well," he said with a friendly laugh, "since I don't go to massage parlors any more, I can afford to take a cab." He then handed me a check for one hundred dollars as he lay down.

He described in detail a meeting at his work, where he and a number of senior people from his company had met with some consultants they had hired. He described how he had asked some very good questions, showing up these high priced consultants for the incompetents they were and getting the admiration of those present. At one point, in order to make his point to his fellow employees he had put himself in a bad light, as an example of someone whose qualifications on paper were an overestimation of his actual capabilities in certain areas. My feeling is that, given D's quickness of mind, especially in just these sorts of situations, and his skills at arguing a point, his description was not inaccurate, but probably skewed in his favor by emphasizing certain aspects of the meeting. At the time I found myself drawn emotionally into admiring D and sharing his glee at the exposure of the consultants.

"Maybe this is praise-for-me day," D continued. "I didn't even think of going to a massage parlor and my presentation at work went very well." (This presentation was a regular one he gave at work, not the meeting he had described earlier.) At that regular presentation he had gone off tangentially, talking of the homogenization of society and giving a number of personal experiences as examples. These were not really indiscrete but, in the context of the type of business meeting he was giving, were somewhat out of place. Still, he insisted, and given his engaging nature I was willing to believe him, people had responded well.

"I think," I said, "that from the beginning of this session you have been telling anecdotes. They're interesting and obviously they have significance for you, but I wonder that you are not free associating."

"Well, these things *are* on my mind." (pause) "Oh, but you mean they are connected stories I guess." I was struck by D's sudden difficulty understanding free association, since at other times in the analysis he did it quite well. "Well," D said, "I think of how good I'm feeling because of it—the massage parlors—being in the past. I think of Sherry, and of telling her about your book. I know maybe you think I need more work on all this. It'll be great to tell Sherry about the massage parlors, because they will be in the past."

I still got the feeling D was telling me a story to impress me. I said this, and wondered at his difficulty letting go, and seeing what came up.

"I think of smoking. That's a scary thought to think of something life threatening." (D had managed to quit smoking two years ago, although on very rare occasions—for instance when visiting his mother who was suffering from a debilitating illness—he had a cigarette.) "But really, it's just a little thought. It's funny how I keep using the word little," D laughed. "You used to point it out to me, but now I say what you would say. That little penis just follows me around. It worms its way into everything," D laughed again. "Even worm is like something sexual, worming into somewhere."

"If the worm is the little penis, it perhaps refers to your penis as a little boy, when you compared it to your dad's large penis."

"And if I'm the little boy then *you* decide if I'm cured and what exactly is wrong with me, by what you say in your book. You know it reminds me that a few days ago I had a fantasy of stopping, and what if you rejected me at the end. What if for the last session . . . Oh, Oh . . ." With this, D burst into sobs.

"If I reject you?"

"No, what I was going to say was . . . I'm almost going to cry again, it's funny—what if you don't love me. It's silly. I know you don't love me. It's a professional relationship. But you think about me—you have to think about me to write the book."

"I wonder though if you had a specific fantasy about the last session."

"I did. We get up at the end of the session and shake hands. That wouldn't be any problem. But I wondered then what would happen. Would I take it further as I often do with other men—with my male friends when we greet or say good-bye—of hugging you? My fantasies don't go any further than that—than wondering what would happen. The hug would be an acknowledgment of our equality. We had both worked on the therapy, to bring it to a conclusion."

"I wonder if this has something to do with your mother. What I mean is the connection with abandonment. I guess I was thinking of the toileting situation especially, and the emphasis on physical closeness and acceptance in fantasizing of our parting, as a contrast not just to your mother's absence but to the hardness and coldness you remember." (In our earlier work on this trauma, especially vivid fears of falling into the hard tile floor, and of how cold both he and the floor were, had emerged, along with intense feelings of aloneness and abandonment.)

"Well, it could be. I think that there was a lot of hardness there—the ceramic of the bathtub as well as the tiles. I'm thinking my mother did not hug me that much."

I got a feeling from the way D said this that he was minimizing, so I asked him, "Can you remember it at all? I know she could be quite caring when you were sick, bringing you soup and stuff, but I wonder if you can remember a hug."

"Well, there must have been a few of course, but I can't actually remember one. It's interesting. You can see it in the photos with me as a baby. She is always holding me out away from her, and she's preening for the camera. My father would have me close, with my face up against his. I remember the feel of his stubble, and the smell. But my mother . . ."

"She was more interested in admiration for her beauty," I said.

"Yes, she would get a lot of attention when she walked down the street." D went on to describe how his parents had made such a striking couple that people would comment. His dad would find it amusing, but his mother basked in the admiration. "I should bring in some photos of her," he said. "I don't really know what the rules are in here though."

"Well, you already brought some in."

"I did?"

"Yes."

"Oh yeah, I remember a little. But that was in psychotherapy. I don't know if it's allowed in analysis."

"I just had an idea! It's something I wondered about early on in the analysis: why you had an image of there being such rigid rules in analysis, almost as if there were a whole book of exact rules you had to follow. I wonder if it relates to your mother's coldness. Maybe the feeling's stronger now because you didn't go to the massage parlors, which neutralize that feeling with their warmth."

"Well, it makes sense. I'm trying to break the rules too. I'm thinking of my mother and of how she said I was toilet trained when I wasn't. I was too young. She just put me on the toilet till I went. How did I ever get a sense of accomplishment? I must have seen later that I could actually do things, but I never really felt I could, even when I did things as an adult. She must have just left me there till I plopped a few. I must have gotten more scared. Thought she'd never come back."

"So the actual situation of your mother, not you, accomplishing the toilet training stayed with you, even in situations where the accomplishment was yours. But I was also thinking of the structure of the analysis. You see it as hard, rigid—perhaps like it felt in your mother's arms. Maybe the hardness of the tiles condenses many experiences—maybe the thousands of experiences with your mother along with the actual experience on the toilet."

"I remember being cold. I even start to feel cold as I think about it. I think of the warmth in the massage parlor. I like that they keep them warm. And they clean you up with a warm cloth. And I usually take a warm shower before the massage."

"So the warmth is a kind of negation of the cold from these experiences. In fact, if we look at it, we could wonder if you try to keep the warm congenial relationship going in here to avoid the cold. It's like the feeling of me as your father protects you against the cold and terror of abandonment if I become your mother. So hugging me at the time of the final leaving re-establishes that I am your father with you on my shoulder, while if I reject your hug I am again your mother and you are overwhelmed by pain and anxiety."

"Wow. I guess for you as an analyst these sort of insights are a daily occurrence, but it leaves me amazed."

I felt a surge of self-admiration at this comment—a feeling with which I was very familiar in my interactions with D. "I'm glad the insight impresses you," I said, "but if you think of it even that comment re-establishes me as your admired father. You may have especially had to say it after my interpretation of the defense, to stop any bad feelings from arising."

"I agree completely. I see it very well, the way I use these good feelings. Even me standing up at the end, and us being equals. It's different than sitting on the toilet, not being able to get off of it."

With this comment the session ended. D continued to go to massage parlors, and our analysis of their meaning continued. As readers who are experienced analysts may already have surmised, by this point in the analysis D was in a state that would have been described, until this concept went out of fashion many years ago, as a full-blown transference neurosis. His going to massage parlors was much less than previously, if at all, related to events in his everyday life. Rather the actions, and D's reactions around hiding them from me lest I throw him out, had become enmeshed in a complex transference reaction with many layers. At the core of this intense transference were positive and negative oedipal conflicts and preoedipal trauma. More concretely, D unconsciously saw going to the massage parlors as masturbating to thoughts of his mother or as actually having some sexual contact with her, which he had to keep hidden from me as his father, by chatting to me and schmoozing. However, both the massage parlors and the analytic situation also had become powerfully connected to D's toilet training trauma both in ways that intertwined with the oedipal dynamics and in ways that were quite separate from them. These aspects of this case will be left to one side for now and taken up again, with additional clinical material, in the chapter on perversions. I chose these sessions not because the narcissistic dynamics were the only ones present but because the interchange demonstrates some of the aspects of narcissistic fixation and the dynamics of narcissistic defense that I wish to discuss. We now turn to this discussion.

Gratification, Deprivation, and Fixation to Feelings

At first sight D's case may seem a very good example of the common analytic view that maternal lack of empathy, neglect, and coldness are the prime cause of narcissistic character disturbances. However, one case cannot decide this issue. There are a great many cases of maternal neglect, rejection, and abuse—such as for instance the case of E, which I presented earlier and will describe further in the next chapter—that do not develop into narcissistic character disorders. There are many factors (including constitutional ones) interacting within a person throughout the course of their life, so that neither two cases, nor three or four for that matter, can decide the issue. However it is my impression that if one looks dispassionately at the whole range of clinical disorders, the level of maternal lack of empathy is not any higher in cases of narcissistic disorders than in many other forms of neurosis and character difficulties. In fact I think it is possible to find negative cases that would seem to disprove the connection of maternal neglect or lack of empathy with this disorder—cases in which the mothers were extremely solicitous and doting. Of course in such cases supporters of the maternal neglect theory generally point out that these mothers may have been giving the child what they wanted (e.g., adoration, quick satisfaction of many wishes) but not what they needed (e.g., reasonable limits, tolerable frustrations). This is seen as evidence—quite rightly—of the lack of true empathy for the child's actual situation—for instance for the anxiety caused by the lack of reasonable limits.

This last situation in some ways leads to the heart of the matter. I described how D would hide vegetables he did not like under his plate and how his mother would clean up the dishes but never mention the stashed food. D described the pleasure he felt at being able to get out of eating his vegetables but he also said he realized that it was wrong and that his mother should have confronted him (this, he saw, was what he needed). The series of incidents D described took place between ages 7 and 9, and his reaction shows that he had a reasonably well-functioning superego for his age, since he felt uncomfortable with his mother's behavior and knew it was wrong. However, the fact that his mother persisted in her way of handling the situation created (or rather, strengthened) a fixation on the pleasurable feeling of finding a sneaky, easy way out of facing unpleasant reality.

Looking at the issue of empathy, we can see that D's mother was empathic—overidentified, in fact—with his wish to have an easy way out from eating his vegetables. This empathy was most likely based on her own narcissistic tendencies, although many factors usually come into play in a situation such as this (for instance her treatment by her parents and her food issues) that are impossible to fully discern at a distance. At the same time D's mother showed a lack of empathy—again probably based on her own heightened narcissism—towards D's wish to follow the rules and be held accountable. She also showed a lack of understanding of the importance, in parenting a child, of helping them to deal straightforwardly with unpleasant tasks. My point is that the choice is not between whether D's mother was a good or bad parent or an empathic or unempathic one. Such distinctions do not help us in differentiating what leads to narcissistic fixations with a tendency to externalize problems from the causation of masochistic fixations with a tendency to overinternalize. To make this differentiation one needs to look from the inside out—that is, from the child's point of view. Repeated and sustained feelings of pleasure around a specific type of experience will lead—if not sufficiently counterbalanced by experiences of frustration and limitation—to a clinging to this feeling, to efforts to re-create the pleasurable situation, and to a use of the situation and feeling of pleasure as a defense against difficult conflicts and unpleasant feelings. Looked at from the inside, the sort of narcissistic fixation I am talking about is a stubborn unwillingness to give up a feeling of extreme pleasure that has been experienced over and over. If these fixations are numerous enough and strong enough, they will impede or even completely derail the decisive move into adulthood in adolescence.

Since the thesis of overgratification as a causative factor in narcissistic character disorder is both controversial and easily misunderstood, it may be worthwhile dwelling a bit more on our concrete example. Imagine D hiding his vegetables, just as he actually did, but imagine that instead of going along with this his mother had reacted differently. For instance what if she had mocked him for thinking a stupid ruse like hiding his vegetables would fool her? We could imagine her telling the story to his father, and perhaps even telling it to guests with a derisive laugh as D stood by in sullen, angry humiliation. Now, it is clear that this would have had a deleterious effect on D. He would probably have suppressed, perhaps internalized, his rage at his mother, while the humiliation would no doubt have affected such aspects of his narcissism as his self-esteem and self-image. It would not have led, however, to a narcissistic fixation, in the sense in which this term is being used here.

The idea that deprivation does not lead to narcissistic fixation cannot be proven once and for all as a generalization about deprivation and anything that causes unpleasant feelings, but I think this thesis holds up well if we look carefully at many individual cases. I will be presenting material to support this thesis in the next chapter. Even in the case of D, though, there were clearly areas of deprivation, especially related to his mother's narcissism. These were what he pushed forward when he first came to therapy. I think this was a denial defense that shifted attention from his need to re-create the intense pleasures of his childhood to the deprivations and traumas he had suffered. This defense is common—almost universal—in those with fixations to early overgratifications. It may be one factor that leads therapists who do not analyze it to stress the overriding importance of deprivations in the causation of narcissistic character disorders.

The analysis of this defense in the early part of D's therapy was very helpful in bringing to light his narcissistic fixations. The one that I have used as an example—his pleasure at his mother allowing him to get away with hiding his vegetables—was of course only one of innumerable gratifications of this sort. These began with his first year, growing up surrounded by the warmth and love of his adoring grandmother and grandfather. This is how he remembered both of them from later years, and certain reactions in the transference as well as entries in a diary his mother kept of his first year indicate that they were like this during his first year as well. Their attitudes no doubt mitigated the effects of D's mother's difficulties with being warm and empathic herself. When D's father returned and the family moved in together, D suffered both the partial loss of his grandparents (he still saw them at least weekly) and a traumatic early toilet training by his mother, who was unable to deal with the dirty diapers without the help of her own mother. However, there was the compensation of his adoring father, who was capable of much more physical and emotional warmth than was his mother and who saw in D the possibility of the fulfillment of all his frustrated hopes and ambitions.

This is not to say that D did not suffer from his mother's narcissism. He gave a graphic demonstration of how much and how painfully he did in the sessions I described above. But these sessions also demonstrate how D called up the pleasure and satisfactions he had experienced to serve as a defense against this pain. This basic dynamic is the essence of narcissistic character disorder. When the feelings and memories related to these experiences of gratification are revived preconsciously, the feeling of reality attached to the experiences colors the conscious experience of pleasure. Annie Reich (1954) also noted the importance of this observation—that such patients feel the narcissistic fantasy is not just a fantasy but a reality. This is the crucial difference between such cases and the defensive use of the ubiquitous fantasies of being admired, being successful, etc.

In the sessions described we witness D using the revival of major early gratifications defensively. He revived the close, warm, mutually admiring relationship with his father. The sessions demonstrated how his reliving this with me defended against the painful feelings related to his mother's self-centeredness, but the reliving also defended against the devastating narcissistic humiliations of the oedipal phase, for instance the humiliation of seeing his father's large penis and comparing it to his own quite small one. As well it was a powerful defense against his aggressive wishes to replace his father, although here it performed a function as a defense secondary to D's primal repression of these impulses. Later in his adulthood, when his father died, D also began to defend against this painful reality by reviving past gratifying experiences with him. This happened often within the analysis on the basis of a father transference, but the most striking instance I saw occurred on a trip back to his hometown. In the first session after the trip he described the people he had met, and how he had impressed them. He had been in complete "schmooze mode," he reported. Various acquaintances and friends had been very taken by him, and he by them as well. After he had taken up most of the session with his quite charming descriptions of these encounters,

I pointed out how one-sided his account was and wondered whether these glorious descriptions served to hide something. To my surprise, and his, D burst into tears. "My father's dead," he moaned. "My father's dead. I saw all those places and my father wasn't there."

"But it's as if you conjured him up in all your schmoozing."

"Well i'ts true. It's as if he was there. But it's funny you should say that. I had the feeling the whole time that I was somehow in a different space. Everything seemed and felt different, and really I'm just coming out of the glow of that."

"It's like a fantasy—the fantasy of being with your father—was conjured up to deny that really he wasn't there at all," I said, at which point D again burst into almost uncontrollable sobs. Here the defensive use of his close, warm relationship with his father was transparent.

The other major early gratification D used was that of being aided and abetted in getting around unpleasant realities. D's lying was also a way of keeping alive his belief that reality was malleable enough that the unpleasant parts could be hidden under a plate full of the things that he liked.

The form of fixation I have tried to illustrate in D has not gone unnoticed by other analysts. In fact the analytic literature on narcissism is full of cases demonstrating these fixations. Some authors (e.g., Reich, 1954; Spiegal, 1954; Greenson, 1958; Blos, 1962; A. Kris, 1979; Hanly, 1984; Coen, 1988; Tyson and Tyson, 1990; Shengold, 1991) have specifically cited narcissistic seductions and gratifications as causative of fixations in narcissistic character disorders, although the actual ways of conceptualizing the dynamics differ from author to author. Many others in their presentation of clinical material clearly demonstrate these sorts of gratifications and fixations. Kernberg (1970) said that all of his patients with narcissistic personality disorder had a special talent or beauty or were narcissistically used by a parent, for instance for display, or by being idealized and considered geniuses.

While with D I have looked at parental reactions, the comments by Kernberg show that the gratification can come in many forms. Jacobson (1959) noted the powerful fixation on being admired that a number of her female patients developed because of their exceptional beauty. D's mother's narcissistic tendencies were probably partly a result of such a fixation. The different things—situational, personal, and interpersonal—that can lead to such fixations are numerous. For instance a patient presented by Kestenberg and Brenner (1986) had tremendous difficulty abiding by rules and constraints, both outside of the analysis and within it, feeling instead that he should be treated as an exception and circumvent these rules. As a child this patient had been in hiding from the Nazis, and had been allowed to disregard all sorts of rules, and was given whatever he wanted, because otherwise his crying in frustration could have led to capture. Other examples are provided by first-borns who, quite apart from any admiration or special treatment they may get, enjoy a good deal of narcissistic satisfaction from being the first among siblings: the strongest, most knowledgeable, fastest, etc. A child who is a lot bigger and stronger than others of his age could get similar satisfactions. This is not to say that these situations necessarily lead to any major psychopathology. They may merely lead to character traits such as a sense of confidence or a tendency to be overbearing. Often other factors (such as constitutional factors, parental indulgence of acting out, trauma, and deprivation) are present in cases of marked psychopathology, which fixate the child on using the narcissistic feeling defensively. I have given some further examples of these sorts of situations, as well as discussing some of the relevant literature, in four papers (Fernando, 1997, 1998, 2000a, 2001).

There are a number of objections that may be brought against my formulation of the nature of D's narcissistic fixation. I would like just to mention two of them that might come from two very different quarters. Firstly, it may be objected that what I have described are merely superficial preconscious derivatives of certain drive fixations and conflicts from which D suffered. D for instance had negative oedipal sexual wishes towards his father, which were cast in anal terms. Was his clinging to closeness to his father largely a derivative of these wishes? And what about D's repressed castration fears, wishes to have a bigger penis than his father and in general replace his father—couldn't his intense need to convince himself that reality was malleable and would bend to his wishes be seen as derivative of these deeper drive-based issues? My answer to these questions would be that there was certainly an influence of one set of fixations on the other, but that the influence went both ways. For instance D's warm relations, to the point of blurred self/object boundaries, with his father, and his father's need for him to act as a proxy for his own thwarted ambitions, impeded the normal adolescent resolution of D's passive sexual inclinations towards his father. Similarly the way he was allowed, and even helped, to get around various unpleasant realities strengthened his use of splitting of the ego to deal with castration terrors. Thus these ego fixations on feelings and situations enter into conflicts and the causation of psychological problems, as well as into adaptations and achievements, as relatively independent factors.

If we look at D from a narrower classical viewpoint, we could say that he has strong oral and phallic/oedipal fixations, and could be classified as a hysteric. His narcissism may then be subsumed under his oral tendencies, as well as under his phallic narcissism. The analysis left no doubt about the importance of these drive fixations. However, D's narcissistic ego fixations that I have outlined cut across all developmental phases and drive positions. They are a different kind of fixation than drive fixations, by virtue of functioning according to the secondary process, yet in a less organized way than many other ego processes. They have many characteristics that differ from drive fixations. We have seen that one of these is that ego fixations are relatively superficial. They are defended against by denial defenses that may be quite stubborn but that are easier to undo than the primal repression behind which lie drive fixations. For this reason in a simplistically applied drive-defense model they may be seen as superficial derivatives of more important deeper issues. On the other hand as analysts saw more patients with significant ego fixations, many of them conceptualized these fixations in an either/or way. In other words, if these more "superficial" issues could be shown to be central to a patient's pathology, which they often were, then drive/defense conceptualizations would be proven to be of little or no consequence. A collapsing of all causation to causation from "below" (primary process and the drives) was replaced by a similar reductive collapsing to causation from "above" (realistic impingements and deprivations). I realize this description is itself simplistic regarding the more complex conceptualizations of many analysts, but a certain amount of theoretical reductionism of this sort has in fact often taken place.

A second objection to my view of D's narcissistic fixations might see the deficit in maternal empathy as primary. This would lead to a defect in the sense of self or self structure, and the use of narcissistically gratifying feelings—of being admired, for instance—would be attempts to cover up this primary defect. To use Kohut's (1977) language, we could see D's reenactment of his mutually idealizing relationship with his father in other aspects of his life as a compensatory structure, built up by D upon the mirroring and empathy offered by his father. This structure would stabilize D's self, compensating for the primary defect in maternal empathy. In some ways my formulation could be seen as a restatement of this in different language, but there are some differences. One is that Kohut saw these compensatory structures as basically healthy, rather than as defensive. Even here the disagreement could possibly be seen as a question of emphasis. I certainly think that D gained much that was valuable from his relationship with his father—things such as a warm, genuine responsiveness to others—that counterbalanced his mother's influence and that were not merely defensive. However, I would see the strength of D's fixations on certain overgratifications as having had a deleterious effect on his development. It is probably at this point that Kohut and I truly part company. Of all the analytic authors who have written on narcissistic disorders, Kohut (1977) was one of the most emphatic in insisting that overgratifications and spoiling are never in themselves harmful. He believed that it was always the lack of responsiveness to the needs of the child in the spoiling—for instance a boy's need for phallic assertiveness—that were the damaging factor. I, on the other hand, think fixations to feelings engendered by overgratifications are a common cause of psychological problems. Such fixations are of course ubiquitous, and I do not think they always lead to detrimental results, especially when mild. However when they do lead to problems, I think that our understanding and analysis of the person is greatly facilitated by a view that takes these fixations into account, rather than one that sees them as largely derivative or secondary to other issues.

If we consider D again, for instance, I think we can understand how his clinging to feelings of pleasure not only led to problems directly but also ensured that he did not struggle with and surmount early traumas and deprivations. When we find traumas and deprivations in someone's past we too often, I think, feel we have explained their continuing effect in the present. In fact many—perhaps most—traumas and deprivations do not lead to crippling psychopathology, although they often lead to minor neurotic tendencies or to various character traits and eccentricities. I would contend other factors are needed to explain how traumas and deprivations lead to more serious problems. These factors are varied, and interact with each other. They include constitutional vulnerabilities (e.g., a poor ability to neutralize aggression, specific cognitive deficits), the sheer magnitude of the trauma or total and sustained nature of the deprivation, and the timing of traumas which can lead them to be more strongly intertwined with phase specific developmental crises. Another common factor is the presence of significant narcissistic fixations, which lead the person to circumvent rather than engage and struggle with the difficult and painful feelings related to the traumas and deprivations that inevitably accompany development.

Narcissistic Defenses

In his early paper on narcissistic patients, Karl Abraham (1919) took as his starting point their various resistances to the analytic process. He pointed out that they tend to look for pleasure and success from the analysis, rather than cure of symptoms, and that they identify with the analyst rather than transferring aspects of past relationships onto him. These reactions indicate, thought Abraham, the basically childish nature of such patients. He was especially interested in the attitude of such patients to free association. He noted that while they seem to associate easily, it eventually becomes clear that they are not free associating at all, but rather controlling what they say for ulterior motives such as avoiding things and, especially, impressing the analyst and feeling superior to him. Abraham found these patients treated their associations like anal products: hiding them, and only letting them out when they wanted to. He saw this as demonstrating the fixation of such patients on anal narcissism.

It is striking how well Abraham's description fits D. That he looked for pleasure and admiration from the analysis and controlled his associations was demonstrated in the sessions presented. D also wanted very much to see us as similar in our political views, outlook on life, and in other ways. Many sessions not presented brought out the extent to which D saw his thoughts and associations as anal products, and how much pleasure he got from keeping them from me. This clearly demonstrated an anal narcissism, but it is an interesting question to ask why and how this differs from the anal fixation and control of associations seen in an obsessional patient. I think they look very different, and my short answer to the question would be that in patients such as D the anal narcissism is corralled into the service of grandiosity while in more obsessional patients the depth and strength of the anal drive fixations lead to such things as moral superiority and a feeling of being nicer and cleaner. In one the ego fixation on gratifications, superiority, and power come first; in the other id fixations on anality do.

Abraham's descriptions seems to be of cases where the denial defenses—avoidance of any unpleasure by control of associations—dominated the manifest picture, as compared to the more classical neuroses which were still relatively common in those early days. The distinction cannot be an either/or one, since both repressions and denial defenses occur in both types of disorders. It may be a question of the proportion of different defenses, but this is probably too simplistic. Many authors have commented on the change in the patients seen by analysts in the 20th century. Even by the middle of that century Greenson (1958) could see the shift from classic symptom neuroses to character disorders in between the World Wars, and then after the Second World War the rise of narcissistic disorders. In his very rich paper, Greenson (1958) presented some interesting ideas on the defenses of his narcissistic patients.

Greenson described the defenses of his patients as screen defenses, by analogy with the screen memories that both hide, and yet contain important aspects of, memories that have been repressed. He talked of a need—a hunger—of such patients for screen experiences, and of their use of these experiences, as well as other screens such as screen identity and screen affect, to hide unpleasant feelings and experiences. This describes very well what we saw with D, who used experiences of schmoozing and mutual idealization to screen various things, as well as using getting away with lies to cover over his distress at the limitations of reality. As was the case with D, Greenson found it was a fixation on specific gratifications that distinguished these patients from others, although they had of course suffered deprivations and traumas as well. This fixation seemed related to the hunger for screen experiences. An inquiry into why this might be so leads to the heart of this type of narcissistic defense.

Jacobson (1954) noted that experiences of overgratification "induce regressive experiences of reunion between self and object" (p 90), while frustrations throw the child back on his or her own resources, and stimulate secondary identifications and narcissistic endowment of the ego. Repeated overgratifications, which are usually in selective areas as was the case with D, leave behind pools of regressive functioning in the ego. Within these pools the usual processes that shore up primal repression—such as secondary identifications, after repressions, and suppressions—work poorly. The person is thrown back on forms of denial defenses. We can see this with D around the issue of lying and facing reality. He would quite regularly minimize things and change the topic, as well as externalize by getting quite indignant at the lack of honesty of various politicians, coworkers, and acquaintances. Not that these sorts of defenses are not common in all of us, but it is their strength and persistence in certain areas that mark these out as pools of regressive functioning.

But there is more. Not only is defensive functioning somewhat altered in these pools, but they can themselves be used as screens. These are the screen defenses Greenson described. To continue with the example from D, he lied and hid things as a way of counteracting the unpleasant feelings that came from realities he could not change. Grandiosity is another common form of screen defense. There is a heightened use of denial defenses within the sphere of the grandiosity, as well as the use of the grandiosity itself to screen feelings such as narcissistic mortification and failure.

Let us return to the original question though—what is the basic nature of narcissistic defenses? We have seen in the example of D's dynamics that strong narcissistic fixations lead to a number of consequences in terms of defenses. Firstly, in the areas of the fixations there is an increase in the use of denial defenses of various sorts: minimization, shifting of attention to other topics, and externalization. Second, the narcissistic ego fixations (areas of regressed functioning) are brought in as screens. If we were to define narcissistic defenses more strictly, it is probably the use of these narcissistic fixations (clinging to pleasurable feelings) as screens to which we should apply the term. In fact when we talk of narcissistic defenses clinically, it is usually these screen defenses to which we refer, even if we do not conceptualize them as such.

The basic nature of denial defenses was discussed in chapter 2. In attempting to understand screen defenses, it may be worthwhile to think back to the example I gave from Jacobson (1957) at the beginning of that chapter. Her example involved a psychotic man who gave direct expression to sexual wishes towards his mother. Jacobson pointed out that the breakdown of his repression barrier made this man especially terrified of succumbing to passive homosexual wishes that were flooding in, and he dealt with this by emphasizing and bringing to the fore another id fragment—also made available by the breakdown of his repression barrier—consisting of heterosexual incestuous wishes. I said in the chapter on denial that this was really an example of a denial defense, in that it used the attentional processes of the ego, in this case as a substitute for the primal repression that was not functioning too well. I think we can look at screen defenses in a similar way. In these cases primal repression is intact but after repression is not working too well in certain areas, and attentional processes which bring one thing to the fore to cover over another are called in to do the work of after repression. For instance D turned his attention to the fond, warm, admiring attitude his father had towards him as a defense against his aggression and death wishes towards his father, as well as using it as a defense against his own passive sexual wishes towards his father. These were wishes tied to strong drives, which were in D's case held back by primal repression, but the work of shoring up this primal repression was done by the screen defenses rather than after repression.

So far, however, I have dealt with screen defenses only in relation to shoring up repressive defenses. In the chapter on denial I made the case for a separate line of defenses that began with primal denial. At that time I suggested that just as after repression is patterned after, and works to stabilize, primal repression, so after denials do the same thing for primal denials. The actual situation cannot be so simple, as the various defenses interact in complex ways. To begin with, it might make it easier to discuss these issues if we again clarify our terminology and concepts. I have already defined primal defenses as those that are motivated by pervasive affect and are relatively stable, forming the template for after defenses, which use signals of affect such as anxiety and psychic pain. While I have followed Freud's terminology, I have expanded both the range of affects motivating primal defenses beyond anxiety and the forms of primal defenses beyond repression. There is one further difference, in that I do not think primal necessarily refers to "first." Many non-primal defenses precede the establishment of the relatively stable primal ones. These are best referred to simply by their name, such as denial or repression. Then there are the uses of non-primal defenses to shore up other defenses or primary dissociation. I have suggested the term secondary defenses for these. We saw an example of them when D used denials to shore up things once his primal repression was temporarily weakened. In a similar manner a classic hysteric who makes extensive use of repression will use this defense as a secondary defense to help in shoring up primal denials and primary dissociations left over from traumas.

In the case of patients such as D who use screen defenses extensively, these will come into play in various ways in relation to primal denial and trauma. I described how D used the idea of having been abandoned by his mother and not loved sufficiently by her—the idea but not the overwhelming feelings, and only the bare outlines of the dissociated traumatic memories—to screen his clinging to both the euphoric feeling when let off the hook by his parents, and the warm feelings from his mutually admiring relationship with his father. To compare this to our hypothetical hysterical patient who makes extensive use of after repression and secondary repression, and who had the same traumatic toileting and the same traumatic mother, I would expect this person to have the same primal denial of his mother's self-centeredness and the same primarily dissociated feelings and memories related to the toileting trauma. However, ideas or feelings that leaked through to consciousness despite these processes, as well as present-day events that made a connection to the past traumas and painful realities, would be dealt with quite differently. This patient would rely to a much greater extent on secondary repression to banish these feelings, ideas, and memories from consciousness, while D took up some of these derivatives of primal denial and used them for defensive purposes.[1]

Technically I think it would be a mistake to take these derivatives that are used as a defense at face value and use them as a starting point to analyze past deprivations and traumas without first—or actually at the same time as—analyzing their defensive function. It would also be a mistake, however, to see these aspects as unreal or unimportant because they were used in a screen defense. It is less likely these days that this would happen with D's complaints about his mother's lack of real caring, but it is very likely to be the attitude of many analysts toward D's toileting trauma. It would be seen as a screen trauma not only in its screening function just described but also in that his memory of it stood for innumerable instances of abandonment, especially emotional abandonment. While both the condensation and screening functions of these traumatic memories were important to analyze, the fact that a memory of an event is used in this manner does not by itself decide that it isn't—or is—an actual shock trauma that needs to be analyzed in its own right.

To return to the comparison of our hypothetical patient with D: we can see how the former would have blanks when attempting to free associate while D would go on and on in a very connected way about the particular thing being used at that moment as a screen. As Abraham (1919) noted, this only looks like free association, and is really carefully controlled. To look at it another way, however, all attempts at free association will be affected by defensive processes. The real question is not whether this is so, but what the nature of the effect is. The patient with the greater tendency to use secondary repression will stop talking, have their mind go blank, and then attempt to pick up the thread somewhere else, as compared to D's long rants and stories. The handling of this type of defense can be very difficult. Anton Kris (1983, 1990, 1994) has written quite perceptively and helpfully about these issues.

Having now given a basic outline of the nature of narcissistic defenses, it may be a good time to look at a number of these theoretical issues in relation to clinical psychotherapeutic practice.

Psychotherapeutic Technique

There was a lively debate in the 1970s and 1980s about how best to approach narcissistic disorders, with Kohut and Kernberg and their followers offering two quite distinct views. They were probably treating different populations of patients, with many of Kernberg's patients being in the borderline range while most of Kohut's seems more like neurotic level character disorders, although their presentation did not fit into any clear diagnosis of a symptom neurosis. I think this is because the narcissistic fixations interfere with development at many stages, so in these (non-borderline) cases, what you have is a certain level of developmental disorder[2] alongside more neurotic, conflict based problems. The question is, how to approach this type of disorder analytically?

Anton Kris (1994) has written a very interesting paper on Freud's treatment of a narcissistic patient as it emerges from a series of letters between Freud and Ernest Jones. Kris demonstrates that Freud knew that he had to be flexible—to hear out the patient's complaints and give her a reasonable amount of sympathy and admiration—in order to be able to draw her into the analysis. In this Freud was merely following his own advice, that the first task is to attach the patient to the treatment process and to the analyst. By contrast, during the 1960s and 1970s in the United States we witnessed the head on collision between an often extremely rigid technique (which had essentially vastly overgeneralized certain technical rules for the handling of displacement transferences) and a more narcissistic patient population that was particularly ill suited to this technique. From the wreckage arose a dissatisfaction with this technique, which spread to the basic theories of ego psychology to which it was believed to be connected—a dissatisfaction that led to the birth and subsequent popularity of a number of alternate theories and techniques.

These techniques, and psychoanalytic techniques in general at this time, lay great stress on the interplay of transference and countertransference and on the use of the analyst's reactions as a guide to what is going on within the patient. It is not my intent at this time to discuss this complex topic, but rather to just mention two ways in which these developments are connected with narcissistic disorders. Most obviously, the form of transference of defense and the resistance to internalization of such patients does indeed pull the analyst into subtle and not so subtle enactments where what the analyst is feeling is often a surprisingly reliable guide to either disavowed aspects of the patient or to an aspect of a former relationship of the patient's. However, this concentration on the intersubjective transference-countertransference exchange and on the analyst's feelings as a guide has become something of a standard technique in its own right, replacing the standard technique of the 1950s and 1960s. Just as with the former standard technique this one, if applied rigidly, narrows the field of inquiry to certain types of transferences, tending to leave other forms of transference and many other dynamics of patients more in the dark. I mentioned this in the chapter on repression, where I argued that some of these newer technical ideas impaired our ability to analyze repression.

The second connection between this technique and narcissistic disorders is that they both share certain characteristics: a tendency to blur self/object boundaries and to resist the imposition of objective reality. By saying this I do not mean to reductively invalidate these theoretical or clinical ideas. Any theory or therapeutic technique deserves to be judged on its own merits, in relation to the data of observation. The fact that a theory has connections with general sociocultural trends—as any theory will—does not invalidate it. Nor does it validate it, however. It is often said that these newer ideas are more in tune with, and more reflective of, trends in the wider culture, as opposed to classical analytic theory—and often enough the implication is that therefore these newer ideas are superior. I myself feel that the validity of theoretical and technical ideas is to be tested by observation, not their level of correspondence with cultural trends.

While I think that the clinical evidence is the best support for the view of the causation and dynamics of narcissistic disorders that I have put forward, one other piece of evidence for its validity is that it makes comprehensible the rise in narcissistic pathology through the latter half of the 20th century in a way that competing ideas—especially those related to maternal depriva-tion—do not. The general trend in Western industrialized nations towards more permissiveness and gratification in child rearing, and especially the growing sense of guilt and lack of authority felt by parents in imposing frus-trations on their children would lead, if the ideas presented in this chapter are valid, to a greater degree of narcissistic fixation in the population.

Analysis of Adolescent Issues
The resistance of narcissistic patients to internalization has an important effect on the psychic restructuring of adolescence, and especially on the formation of a mature system of narcissistic and moral ideals that usually occurs in late adolescence and early adulthood. I realize this may sound a little abstract. A discussion of this process is not made any easier by the dif-ferent terminology used by different authors. I prefer Jacobson's (1964) ter-minology, which distinguishes narcissistic ideals—structured as the wishful self-image—from moral ideals, conceptualized as the ego ideal that is part of the superego. This is a complex and at times confusing subject, but I would suggest that one reason for this is that the nature of these structures and their relationship changes over time.

To be more specific, with the acceptance and mourning of childhood's end and other limitations at the close of adolescence, the narcissistic ideals (wishful self-image for Jacobson, ego ideal or ideal ego for many others) be-come more realistic and comes into a closer relationship with the superego and its moral ideals. This is part of a more general process of integration and consolidation of character at the close of adolescence, a process that has been described in detail by Peter Blos (1979). He pointed out that at the close of adolescence, residual traumas are also absorbed into the adult character, by being reworked into enduring interests and attitudes. An example of this would be D's interest in teaching, and especially training those who were having trouble with the material because they did not have the background or abilities to master it. This interest was a reworking of D's overly early, harsh, and traumatic toilet training.

My reason for discussing these late adolescent processes is that the cling-ing to overgratifications of people such as D, if it is strong enough, derails the move towards maturation, internalization, and integration of the wishful self-image with the ego ideal. D clung to the mutually admiring relationship he had with his father, and repeated it in the analysis. At a point a few months after the sessions described earlier in this chapter, I interpreted the defensive

function of his compliments toward me and his holding up of his various accomplishments for me to admire. I said he was using a denial through action
to maintain the feeling that his father was not dead, just as he had used this
even before his death to defend against the realization that he was grown up.
These sorts of interpretations had been made many times before but something about the amount of analysis that had preceded this seemed to have
made him much more receptive and also allowed me to see this transference
of defense much more clearly. It became very clear to me that I had not pur-
sued the analysis of this issue vigorously because I did genuinely like D, and
because I did genuinely feel I was a good analyst. At this point I was much
more forceful in interpreting D's resistance, including his insistence on the
fact that I really was a likeable fellow who had helped him immensely.

"But you really *have* helped me a lot," he said, giving as an example his
ability to talk in public easily.

"But what about the things that haven't changed—like going to massage
parlors? Or not being able to change in front of other men?"

"But those are things I'm resisting doing. It's up to me to do them. You've
analyzed all sorts of connections."

"But if I'm not responsible for you not doing these things, why am I responsible for all the positive things you've done?"

Through interchanges such as this D became convinced of his need to
idealize me. In the session from which these quotes are taken, D began to
sing an old song and then said that, as he walked away from my office, he
often found himself singing this song from the time he was a little boy with
his father.

"Do you feel sad when you do this?" I asked him, since a few minutes
previously he had been sobbing about his father not being able to admire his
accomplishments.

"No, actually I feel lighter, as if I'm leaving the sadness behind me, in
your office."

These interchanges helped to move along our analysis of D's narcissistic
and sexual tie to his father. We saw through this how he resisted the weakening and mourning of these ties—resisted, in fact, the acceptance of the
frustration of his wishes which would come from decisively facing them with
reality. This is a process that would have led, and did lead belatedly in his
analysis, to the all-important structure formation of late adolescence (Blos,
1979). For instance we understood why, when his father had come to visit
and admire his new house when he was a young man, D had lied to him
about how much money he made. D knew very well that his father would
have been very impressed by his actual salary, but he had to increase it to

take it out of the realm of reality—out of the realm of an adult son impressing his father with his actual achievements—back to the fantasy achievements of his childhood.

Late adolescence is a decisive phase for the consolidation and coordination of the defensive processes as they take on their relatively fixed adult form. Blos (1979) maintained that it is in the crucible of this phase that the adult neurosis, the infantile neurosis as reconstructed in analysis, and the transference neurosis are formed. If this is true, we can understand why patients with narcissistic character disorder do not develop a transference neurosis until and unless their narcissistic defenses have been analyzed sufficiently. Their intense narcissistic fixations have impelled them to sidestep, rather than engage, the developmental struggles of late adolescence. Such patients present rather, as D did, a somewhat confusing and not very well coordinated set of reactions, defenses, and transferences. One more stable and powerful transference is a transference of defense—a transference of the screen defenses and narcissistic fixations of their childhood into the analysis. Because the decisive internalizations, especially of limits on childhood narcissism, have been sidestepped, there is also a much greater tendency to enact these narcissistic transferences, as D did. Of course D presented only one of a wide variety of possible forms of these transferences. Many are not so pleasantly seductive to the analyst as his was, but their basic structure is the same. For instance there may be an intense belittling and humiliation of the analyst—a transference of an attitude that acts as a screen against the patient's feeling small and belittled.

Analyzing Narcissistic Defenses and Transferences
I would now like to pull the threads of this discussion together into a more succinct set of statements regarding technique. To look first at the sorts of narcissistic defenses discussed in this chapter, we could divide them into two broad categories: the use of the feelings from a narcissistic fixation (for instance a feeling of specialness) for defensive purposes, and the use of various defenses to preserve and protect the narcissistic fixation itself. The most common of these latter defenses is a simple attentional one in which neglect, abuse, and trauma from the past are overstressed to cover the past overgratifications to which the patient still clings. I gave an example of this with D. I tried to present enough clinical detail and discussion to make it clear that the use of the complaints of neglect and maltreatment as a cover says nothing about the truth or falsity of these complaints. As a general rule there is some, if not quite a bit, of truth to them. Once one's conceptual understanding and clinical intuition are trained a bit, however, it is not that difficult to spot the

defensive use of these complaints. In a patient who externalizes, feels sorry for himself or herself quite a bit, assumes a superior attitude, or has other narcissistic traits, I would expect to find this defensive use of complaints to hide overgratifications. However, this particular dynamic is worth considering in many patients who are not so obviously narcissistic. My experience has been that this has been the key to unlocking many cases that have stopped progressing. In these instances there has been extensive work on very evident conflicts, deprivations, and traumas, but the hidden fixation to certain key overgratifications bars full progression into psychic adulthood and mature functioning. The traumas and deprivations are by this point largely clung to in order to hide the fixation and to feed the sense of self-pity. I have previously discussed these areas of focal narcissistic dynamics in non-narcissistic character structures in a paper on the psychological effects of physical defects (Fernando, 2001), and I would refer the interested reader there for detailed clinical material and a more extended discussion of this sort of situation.

This dynamic is not the only sign of a narcissistic fixation, but however we come to suspect its existence the real test, as well as the beginning of the analysis of this complex, is to put forward interpretations and to engage with the patient in exploration of their narcissistic defenses and fixations. There is nothing special in the analysis of these that would distinguish it from the analysis of other attentional defenses and the reconstruction of the past of other patients. Once one has mastered the basics of the analysis of attentional defenses, as outlined in chapter 2, they can be applied to the situation of narcissistic defenses as well. While some patients may become angry and display stronger resistances, many will acknowledge, as did D, the existence of these fixations, and even be quite interested in looking at these times of overgratification. They will usually, though, then shift back to how badly they were treated and the traumas in their past. This relatively easy initial undoing of the defense, but just as easy repetition of the attentional shift, is of course characteristic of denial defenses. The analyst has to be relatively forceful in actively speaking for the denied reality—in this case it would be the reality of the patient's overgratifications—and pointing out again and again the use of one thing—in this case deprivations and traumas—to shield another.

One way in which these issues can enter the transference is through a transference of defense, in which the patient tries to re-create certain feelings in the relationship with the analyst, such as D re-creating the warm, special relationship with his father in the relationship with me, as a screen that hides other feelings and realities. I went into some detail about this dynamic in D's case, which also demonstrated how this transference of defense becomes part of a transference that has multiple causes and serves multiple ends. In D's case there were object related transferences, both oedipal as well as pre-oedipal, intertwined with this transference of defense. If one is saddled with a unidimensional view of the transference, then one is less likely to spot these and other transferences of defense.

These narcissistic transferences come in many forms, but a common transference/countertransference situation to which they eventually lead is of the analyst becoming worried about hurting the patient with interpretations that he or she is "not ready to hear," or being torn between this attitude and feeling angry and resentful at being controlled by the patient. The patient induces these feelings by bringing forward their maltreatment and deprivations and accusing the analyst of retraumatizing them. Present-day analysts, just like present-day parents, are relatively susceptible to feeling guilty for wounding those in their care through frustrations and facing them with unpleasant realities. In the case of patients who have been overgratified by their parents in one area or another, the interaction between them and their analyst can come to resemble that between one or both parents and the patient. This is not to say that a strict or authoritarian attitude is the answer, since this plays into the patient's defenses as much as an overindulgent or overcautious one does, and in fact it is common for there to be swings from one of these attitudes to the other.

Where a transference/countertransference interaction has created a situation such as this, one may be tempted to see it simply as the transference of an object relationship (internal and/or past) into the analysis. This clearly happens in many cases such as D's. There is also a defensive, structural, and developmental aspect to these transferences, however. These all meet in the use of screen defenses (including the analytic situation) to avoid facing unpleasant realities, to avoid internalizing unwanted responsibilities, and to avoid the decisive move from adolescence into adulthood. Here too there are no specific or special techniques to be used in analyzing these dynamics. One will generally get pulled to some extent into the object related and defensive aspects of the transference, as I was with D when we developed a warm, friendly, joking relationship.

The key in this situation is not technique, but knowledge. Knowing that fixation to overgratifications are common sources of various narcissistic problems makes us open to spotting these fixations when they are present, and pursuing their analysis in relation to the transference. The aim is to analyze the various defenses in order to bring the fixation—the pleasure in special treatment, or other gratifications, into awareness. A good deal of working through of this is necessary, and even then it may not yield. Overgratifications lead to more powerful fixations than deprivations. They are of a different character, and do not contain the pain and suffering that acts as the main impetus to letting go of a clinging to the past. Of course the clinging to gratifications secondarily leads to suffering through blocking forward progression, maturing of the personality, and internalization, but the patient will always have varied denial defenses to keep the price they pay from coming to full awareness. These should also be analyzed so that the patient becomes upset and pained at the price they are paying for clinging to the childhood sense of specialness. This upset will hopefully provide some deeper motivation for change.

There is no guarantee at all that following these recommendations will lead to success with narcissistic patients. The fixation is surprisingly stubborn. Other factors also play a part: many patients can have what seems like a strong constitutional predilection to narcissism. Actual continuing narcissistic gratifications related for instance to wealth, attractiveness, or talent can also be a powerful force acting against relinquishment of the childhood sense of specialness. Work on this particular dynamic also takes place in the context of other issues and other dynamics, which will act in concert with narcissistic fixations. One should not overgeneralize the ideas related to narcissistic ego fixations. One should flexibly move between analyzing them and analyzing other dynamics and the various interactions between different dynamics. Narcissistic fixations are only part of the picture with any patient, but even in cases where they play a relatively smaller part than with patients such as D, these are things that, difficult as they are to analyze, we ignore at the peril of stagnation, stalemates, and interminable therapy.

Summary

Anna Freud (1965) suggested that the young infant first libidinally invests in the *feeling* of satisfaction before moving on to invest in the object (breast) or person that is connected with the satisfaction. This idea has fallen very much out of favour as many analysts insist that the human child is from the first object oriented. It is perhaps especially because of this trend that fixation to certain overwhelmingly pleasurable feelings has not received the attention that it deserves. These fixations, which can come from any stage in childhood or adulthood, and their connection to defenses, development, transference, and therapy have been the subject of this chapter.

I used the example of my patient D's clinging to the special feelings coming from the intense admiration he got in his childhood to illustrate fixation on overgratifications. These fixations come about because these overgratifications lead to pools of regressed functioning within the ego. I argued that deprivations, while they can certainly lead to problems, some of which will be discussed in the next chapter, do not lead to these sorts of narcissistic fixations. In these pools of regressed functioning, self/object boundaries are blurred and the functioning of secondary repression is compromised. This leads to a greater reliance on attentional defenses such as denial, external-ization, and screen defenses. These latter are a form of attentional defense in which these pools of regressed functioning themselves are called up—at the level of feeling and often through action as well—in order to cover over unpleasant realities and feelings.

The view of narcissistic disorders that I have presented here makes sense of a number of the seeming contradictions and theoretical confusions in this area. There is difficulty in classifying these disorders because such "primi-tive" features as a tendency to merger, archaic grandiosity, and structural immaturity exist alongside often excellent ego functioning in many areas and an ability to withstand the rigors of intensive analysis on the couch. The concept of areas of regressed functioning within the ego which lead to other defenses being substituted for secondary repression and which exist within a matrix of basically good ego functioning (i.e., no major constitu-tional or early-acquired deficits), explains these contradictions very well. From the point of view of defenses, the primal defenses are relatively intact, while secondary repression is replaced by denial defenses. This is in contrast to true borderline cases, where the primal repressions that form the repres-sion barrier are somewhat compromised. Since the regression brought on by intensive analysis on the couch is a sensitive gauge of the intactness of the repression barrier, by the stress it puts on it, we can explain why borderline patients often have trouble with this form of therapy but narcissistic charac-ter disorders without major borderline features do not.

I suggested that therapy with such patients does not involve any special techniques beyond those described in chapter 2 as necessary in the analysis of attentional defenses, but that a knowledge of the nature of narcissistic over-gratifications and their consequences defensively and developmentally are crucial in being able to perceive these dynamics and subject them to analysis. I described how, hidden within an object directed transference, there is usu-ally a transference of defense—specifically a transference of a screen defense. In this transference certain aspects of the relationship and certain feelings generated by the relationship are used to screen specific unpleasant realities, and more generally to screen the limitations that reality imposes. By screen-ing these, the patient attempts to avoid the painful mourning of childhood's end and the movement into adulthood. Because of this avoidance the nar-cissistic patient, no matter in what stage the original overgratifications and narcissistic fixations are located, always has a partial developmental arrest at the stage of adolescence, especially at late adolescence and early adulthood, which is when these issues come to a head. I discussed this developmental aspect of narcissism briefly, as well as its structural consequences: there is a resistance against internalizing limits, against objective realism, against the superego, and thus a persistence of externalizing defenses.

Terms

Narcissistic Ego Fixation: A clinging to the extremely pleasurable feelings of narcissistic enhancement and specialness that come from narcissistic overgratifications. Beyond this clinging, there are also three other important aspects to these fixations: the nature and extent of this clinging is kept from awareness by attentional defenses, the feeling that is clung to is itself used in screen defenses, and there are developmental and structural consequences to the clinging.

Screen Defense: A form of defense related to narcissistic ego fixations on feelings related to overgratification, in which the regressed functioning related to this fixation—at the level of feeling and action especially—is called up to screen more unpleasant realities and feelings.

Notes

1. This difference is essentially the difference between the patients that Freud describes in the *Studies in Hysteria* (Breur and Freud, 1893 –1896) and the patients described by Kohut (1971) in *The Analysis of the Self.* Changes in child-rearing practices and social and cultural influences affect secondary and after defenses to a much greater extent than they do primal defenses or primary dissociation. Thus the development of a detailed and theoretically and clinically sophisticated understanding of different primal and secondary defenses and their interaction, which is one of the aims of this book, will help us to understand both the change in psychological disorders over time, as well as the psychological aspects of both the causes and effects of historical processes in society.

2. By developmental disorder, what I mean is a disorder where there has been significant lack of progression past certain important developmental phases. As an example, D's clinging to childhood narcissism interfered with his progression from an oedipal stage into more reality and task oriented latency age attitudes, as well as interfering with progression from adolescence into adulthood. Many narcissistic character disorders have characteristics which would not seem so pathological if found at some point in adolescence.

CHAPTER SEVEN

~

Masochism

As was the case with the term narcissism, masochism was first used to designate a sexual perversion, and was then expanded to the point that now the most common use of the term in psychoanalysis is to refer to phenomena that are not explicitly sexual. Again as with narcissism the original point of connection between the two types of phenomena was provided by the libido theory. In his paper on "the economic problem of masochism" (1924) Freud asserted the primacy of erotogenic masochism—the feelings of sexual pleasure brought on by pain or humiliation—over the other forms. At the same time in this paper Freud for the first time used the term moral masochism to designate one of these other forms. Moral masochism had loosened its explicit connection with sexuality. The humiliation and setbacks suffered were in other spheres such as work or relationships. The term "moral" was used because it was assumed that this form of masochism involved interaction between a sadistic superego and a masochistic and guilty ego. Clinically, people who suffered from moral masochism felt an inordinate amount of unfounded guilt.

A lot has been learned about the dynamic and developmental aspects of masochism since Freud's initial studies. The aim of this chapter is to describe certain phenomena based on denial defenses that are still often lumped in with moral masochism even though their dynamics are quite different from those described by Freud and the classical analysts who followed him. To set the stage for our discussion of these phenomena, I will first briefly describe some of the classical ideas on masochism and then those of some early authors who first elucidated aspects of the denial dynamics that we will be discussing. I will then present clinical material that I will use as a point of departure for describing and discussing two basic dynamic configurations: the defensive use of guilt and defenses motivated by contrast feelings. While I will for the sake of completeness also mention other aspects of masochism, such as those related to drives and trauma, there will be no attempt to present an in-depth discussion of these aspects, which have been well described by other authors. The particular dynamics I will be concentrating on, on the other hand, have been relatively neglected, especially when one considers how important they are clinically. An important differentiation to keep in mind is that between *dynamic masochism*—in which there is an unconscious sexualized pleasure in pain and suffering that is expressed in symptoms and behavior, and *descriptive masochism*—in which other sorts of dynamics, not related to pleasure in pain, drive behaviors that on the surface (descriptively) appear to involve an attachment to pain and suffering. The particular attentional dynamics that I will be describing (contrast defenses and defensive guilt) are descriptively masochistic, although in many instances they lend strength to behaviors driven by other, dynamically masochistic aspects.

Classical Conceptions of Masochism

In Freud's 1919 paper on beating fantasies, he posited the specific oedipal stage fantasy of the father beating the child—a deeply repressed and regressively distorted expression of being sexually loved by the father—as the essence of masochism. It is through a fixation on this fantasy that the earlier connections between pleasure and pain were given a definitive and influential form. In his later paper on masochism Freud (1924) described not just the specific connection of oedipal stage sexual wishes with punishment and humiliation, but also more generally the way painful experiences, if they are sufficiently powerful, make a connection with the sexual instinct by virtue of their intensity itself. This is especially evident in the sexualization of traumatic experiences.

Later authors have explored some of the developmental antecedents of oedipal masochism. Galenson (1988) has described these early stages as protomasochism. She noted that by 6 months of age specific aggressive manifestations such as hitting appear. At 9 or 10 months there is a crisis, as aggression erupts forcefully as a response to maternal frustration. Normally the mother will help the child to channel and modulate this aggression, but some mothers take the child's aggression much more personally and react with counter-aggression. Faced with this response, the child usually becomes passive, inhibited, and regressed. Novick and Novick (1987) asserted that these sorts of painful interactions were a product of the mother's externalization of their own aggression onto the infant, a process we will see in the upcoming description of my patient E. They also noted that the defense of turning aggression against the self is first seen in the toddler stage, where the painful interactions with the mother escalate over toilet training, the child's own aggression, and separation. In the oedipal phase these painful experiences are libidinized and interwoven with the conflicts of that crucial stage.

In a paper that looked at both drive and ego aspects of the problem, Loewenstein (1957) noted that the phallic phase could be divided into an earlier passive phase, where the wish is to be touched and admired, and a later active phallic phase characterized by wishes to master the other and to penetrate. Masochism includes a fixation on passive wishes to be taken care of, although this fixation itself is not sufficient for masochism. One needs also an enjoyment of humiliation. From the ego side, Loewenstein described the dynamic of seduction of the aggressor, in which the weaker child plays at getting the stronger parent to attack or punish, but in a playful, libidinized way that is reassuring.

None of these dynamics by themselves explain why masochism develops in one person and not in another. Freud (1919) suggested a constitutional basis for this, but it has become increasingly clear that deprivation and painful and abusive interactions in early childhood are major causative factors. These interactions are conceptualized as being internalized in a sadistic superego or in other internal objects. However Hartmann (in Wallerstein, 1967) made the important observation that deprivation often leads not to a more severe superego but rather to an increase in certain ego defenses. This is the theme of this chapter.

Some Early Ideas on Masochism as a Defense

Beginning in the 1940s and 1950s a number of authors presented a view of masochism as a set of ego reactions to unloving, depriving, and often hateful early mothering. The most important of these early authors were Esther Menaker and Bernhard Berliner.

Berliner (1958) stated uncompromisingly that both sexual and moral masochism stemmed from disturbances in object relations and that all sexual masochists were moral masochists as well. He concisely summarized his view of masochism by saying that "masochism is the sadism of the love object fused with the libido of the subject" (1958, p 40). In other words, the only form of relationship offered the child was the parent's hatred of them and the child, having no other options and needing a bond with the parent for its very survival, accepted this hatred and formed a libidinal attachment to it. Berliner's most important contribution, in my opinion, was his elucidation of the particular denial defenses used by children who find themselves in such distressing situations. He stressed that the goal of these defenses was, despite appearances, not suffering but the avoidance of suffering.

Berliner was one of the first to describe the mechanism behind borrowed guilt: "The child's feeling of guilt, then, takes the place of what may be called the unconscious sense of the guilt of the parent. It is the defense against realizing the guilt of the parent for fear of losing him as a love object" (1947, p 467). Guilt is a powerful tool used to deny many unpleasant realities such as one's helplessness ("I could have or could still change things by behaving differently, since it's my fault") or the lack of caring of a parent ("if only I did things differently, she would have loved me"). I will discuss this defense in detail later. Berliner also made a start at describing what I have called contrast defenses: "When the child is given the opportunity at a later time to make comparisons, the need for being loved may prevent it from making criticisms and from differentiating between old conditions and possible new ones" (1940, p 326).

Esther Menaker (1953) described the dynamics of her masochistic patients in terms similar to Berliner. She saw the mothers of her patients as not aiding or as actively hindering the development of the ego functions of the young infant. The mother's lack of love is denied to maintain the relationship and is taken over by the child, so that frustration is experienced as coming from the worthless self. As with Berliner, Menaker stressed the fear of abandonment as the motive of this denial defense. While this is no doubt true early on, I think that later overwhelming psychical pain and sadness play an increasingly important part as motivators. In contrast to Berliner, Menaker stressed the importance of actual ego deficits and malformations caused by lack of response from the mother. Because of this stunting of ego growth she felt such patients lacked internal structures and did not develop a strong transference onto the analyst. She also felt that the lack of a critical faculty in such patients was in large part due to lack of development, not to active defensive measures.

Both Berliner and Menaker stressed the importance of a warm, accepting attitude on the part of the analyst. Menaker saw this as part of an education of the patient, and as a way of giving them what they had not received as children, although she also said that the interpretation of the patient's denial of the lack of love was crucial. Berliner saw the warm relationship as a means to an end—the end of facilitating the breakdown of the patient's denial of the nature of his or her actual treatment as a child. He stated that a stern or distant attitude on the part of the analyst would lead to an impasse, partly because such an attitude is actually a potent form of gratification for the masochistic patient. On the other hand a warm and unrestrained attitude can be a deprivation. While this is certainly a simplification, it does point out that neutrality and abstinence on the analyst's part cannot be defined without reference to the specific wishes and transferences of the patient. In other words they are relative concepts.

These views expressed by Berliner and Menaker were criticized for being one-sided and leaving out oedipal and other drive aspects of masochism. However the criticism, and even comments by those in support of their views, often missed the key aspect of their observations: they were describing complex and powerful denial defenses motivated by an extremely distressing reality. For example Brenman (1952), in an often-quoted paper, argued for a multidimensional view of masochism that considered contributions from the drives, reality, and the ego. However, it is clear from her discussion that on the ego side Brenman was referring to defenses against the drives. She did not consider the defenses described by Berliner and Menaker. Later work, such as the developmental study of masochism by Novick and Novick (1987), gave reality factors a lot of weight, but the contribution of specific denial defenses was not brought into focus. Many modern authors from ego psychological, self psychological, and other schools have taken up and expanded on the idea of ego deficits stemming from deprivation. In the work of these authors as well, denial defenses related to the deprivation and maltreatment are often downplayed.

It could be argued that the denial defenses I am talking of cannot strictly speaking be considered masochistic since, as Berliner himself said, their aim is not suffering but the avoidance of suffering. Thus the pain and suffering brought on by these defenses is a secondary, unintended byproduct of attempts to avoid even worse suffering. We could say that these dynamics are descriptively masochistic—they lead to suffering—but are not masochistic in the true dynamic sense of pain and humiliation being connected with pleasure. While all this is true, a deeper understanding of these dynamics is still important both because of their frequency and because they are often confused with, and analyzed as, more narrowly masochistic dynamics, or are analyzed in terms of deficits. I will now present some clinical material to aid in the discussion of these issues.

Clinical Example: E

I described E's primal denial of her mother's lack of love and caring in chapter 3, and some aspects of her traumatic sexual abuse at the hands of her father in chapter 5. As can be seen even from these short excerpts from her analysis, her childhood was an extraordinarily difficult one, filled with much trauma and deprivation. E had come for help with severe depression, serious suicidal impulses, and a lifelong tendency to end up with uncaring or at times emotionally abusive lovers and friends. E could also be quite cruel to herself—denigrating successes, minimizing opportunities for pleasure or enjoyment, and at times having images of sadistic and bizarre tortures being imposed on her.

Both of E's parents were quite disturbed, but in very different ways. Her mother functioned on a borderline level in terms of her ability to control her impulses and to relate to others. Her father's psychopathy emerged later in the analysis. I have already given details of both of these realities and of E's attempts to deny them. In fact it became clear that much of E's masochism, in the descriptive sense of the term, was a product of the specific denial defenses that she used to deal with the very distressing realities of her upbringing.

We reconstructed the extent of E's mother's physical and emotional neglect of her from infancy on. She had not held her or cuddled with her, had fed her erratically, and most probably tried to force feed her. She had not interacted with her in a warm or joyful way. Essentially her mother could not react to E as a person with separate needs, and was far too narcissistic and aggressive to interact lovingly or warmly with her. I gave a brief example of how we came to reconstruct these realities in discussing E's primal denial of her mother's lack of love for her. At that time we analyzed E's lifelong yearning for direct physical warmth and yet her difficulty giving it to herself. She described, for example, how as an adult she had taken a hot water bottle to bed with her one night and slept wonderfully. The next night she had looked rather disdainfully at the bottle, as if the whole episode were somehow silly, and had not used it again. It was especially through a careful and repeated analysis of emotional and physical reactions such as this, both inside and outside of the analysis, that we came to reconstruct this very early period in E's childhood.

These reconstructions became at first more complicated but eventually clearer once we realized the reactions from this time were intertwined with dissociated and repressed memories of E's sexual abuse by her father. This had occurred around ages 7 to 9, when he had come into her bedroom after being out late drinking, and had forced her to take his penis into her mouth, and had ejaculated into her mouth. A whole range of avoidances around food and eating situations (she could not sit down to eat in her apartment, for instance, but did it standing up), as well as E's avoidance of performing oral sex with men, could be traced to these incidents of abuse. As more and more memories emerged of the abuse, we became aware of a back and forth movement in which every time E got too close to memories and feelings about it, she would start to talk of her mother's abuse and neglect of her and feel relief. When the feelings about abuse and neglect by her mother became too intense, she would talk of her father's abuse of her. The most overwhelming feelings came when she could see the abuse by both of her parents, and that she really had nowhere to turn most of the time. The only true love and warmth had come from her paternal grandmother and from friends and parents of friends with whom she tried to spend as much time as possible.

A series of specific point traumas that we reconstructed were that on many occasions in early toddlerhood E's mother had left her strapped to her high chair for hours on end—probably especially after her sister's birth in her second year. E's mother, who was not that functional at the best of times, was left to cope by herself with these two young children along with a somewhat older brother, and she was certainly not up to the task. The physical restraint at a time when there is a strong developmental push to channel aggression into walking, running, and other muscular activities played a part, I believe, in the causation of E's turning of aggression against herself. E's depression and suicidal impulses clearly showed the extent of this vicissitude of aggression, although she did not cut herself or in other ways harm herself physically, which I think demonstrates despite everything that there was some developmental progression on the lines of libidinal investment in the body and mentalization of aggression.[1]

The traumatic feelings from the instances of being tied down were powerfully entwined with the oral sexual abuse, where E had felt frozen in disbelief and horror at what was happening. Her frequent impulses to get up and run from the room in therapy, which could mushroom into an overwhelming feeling that the analysis was "relentless" and impossible to bear, derived from a reliving of both these traumas condensed together.

It was not just specific point traumas that fuelled E's turning of aggression against herself. E's mother was also relentless in her externalization of aggression onto her, implying that E had all sorts of wishes that really were her mother's. This led to ongoing confusion about whose anger, hate, and aggression was whose, and thus greatly impeded E's tolerance, neutralization, and channeling of her own aggressive drives. E's mother also attacked her verbally and at times physically. What E called her "inner mother," who would tell her off or lead her to picture vicious physical attacks on herself, was probably an early introject formed on the model of her actual attacking mother, fuelled by E's own unmastered aggression. This introject had remained quite primitive and sadistic. This lack of maturation suggested a strong link between it and the unmetabolized early experiences of deprivation, abuse, and severe trauma.

These dynamics—early deprivation, abuse, and actual hate of the parent for the child leading to turning of aggression against the self, a sexualization of pain and abuse, and the development of severe and abusive introjects—have already been well explored by classical and object relations psychoanalysts. It is not on these aspects of E's case, therefore, that I would like to concentrate, but rather on the various defenses against the reality of her situation to which she resorted. These were quite varied. For instance E reacted to her episodes of being strapped into her chair by her mother by developing a constant need to be on the move physically and making sure she never stayed in a repetitive, monotonous situation, such as a job where similar duties were repeated at the same time day after day. Not only did the physical movement give E an outlet for her energy and aggression, but also it and the constant change in routine were a form of denial through action. It all meant "I am not and never have been strapped down, unable to move, and monotonously waiting out the hours." This sort of reaction demonstrates Hartmann's point (Wallerstein, 1967) that frustration can lead not just to a turning of aggression against the self but also to a marked increase in defensive activity. I will now present some material from E's analysis demonstrating an internalizing defense—defensive and borrowed guilt—as well as further describing E's use of contrast defenses. From a clinical point of view analysis of these defenses is often crucial in moving cases of masochism such as E's forward.

About six and a half years into her therapy, which at that time was being conducted face to face three times a week, E was experiencing quite powerful feelings and memories related to her father's sexual abuse of her. She felt sick to her stomach and then very nasally congested for a week, just as she had at the time of the abuse in latency. She also was flooded by intense feelings of loneliness and sadness. She was even more overwhelmed as she thought of also having been sexually stimulated by her mother—probably at a very young age. Repression of these memories was clearly breaking down, and in one session E got furious at me and then had the thought of taking her skin off, like clothing, and throwing it on the ground and saying, "Don't do it to me." She then had the image of crawling under her chair and disappearing. At the next session, after the weekend break, she said, "I've been sleeping a lot, and dreaming. I can really feel I want to run away." (For the first five years of the therapy these wishes to run away were powerful and at times felt like they were on the verge of being acted on. By the point reached in this vignette there had been a very noticeable shift, where neither she nor I felt this would actually happen. She also missed very few sessions, while previously she would often miss sessions through sleeping in or feeling too overwhelmed to come.)

"I had two dreams last night," E said. "My family had come home, but they were strange. My mother is there, and my father looked strange. He has something to do with water. It seems he's part of some kind of arrangement, with other people, but he steps out of it and takes me somewhere bad where adults take children. Then I was lying beside him and something like a squashed mushroom was in his mouth. Then I had another dream. I was running down the street with my dog. A rhythm to it and then I came to a scene of horrible devastation. Of a rotting horse, bones of dead animals."

E talked of the clear connections of some of the images to sexual abuse—such as the rhythmic running and the place where bad things happen to children.

"And I wonder about the mushroom in your father's mouth," I said.

"Yes, I didn't think of that. It's very much like a penis with the head. But the dream has another meaning too. It's about devastation in general. I've been feeling very hopeless about humanity, very depressed. We're all capable of these things. People do such awful things."

"I wonder if you're generalizing here because of how awful the particulars are."

"But I really do feel it's not just my dad. It's all of humanity who is capable of these sorts of things. It must be all of us, really."

"Is it, really? Could you do the things your father did?" I asked, and then went on a rather long discourse on how many soldiers in armies would not shoot the enemy, even though they had the blessing of their nation. I went on in a rather intellectual way about this. It is interesting to see in retrospect how even as I pointed out E's intellectual generalizations, I also mirrored this defense. I realized what I was doing enough to go back to E, pointing out how it seemed to me that she would not really be capable of what her father had done. "I know we all have sadistic wishes, but picture yourself in a situation with children as your father was. Could you see yourself doing it?" I asked.

"No," E said quietly and sadly. "No, I couldn't do it."

"So you see how you tried to generalize it and then turn it on yourself?"

"Yes, you're right," E said, but then I had the impression that she quickly moved off this topic, talking of how lonely she had been feeling lately.

"I wonder if you moved off to other things so the idea that you bear no responsibility couldn't really sink in."

"Just as you said that I had the thought, 'He can't help it, he was a psychopath.'" E laughed at this, but then said more seriously that after all it was true. In a sense it wasn't his fault that he was a psychopath.

I pointed out how she was quite capable of holding herself and all of humanity responsible for the possibility of committing these crimes, but could not hold her father responsible for actually committing them. "I get the feeling," I said, "that you want to cling to your responsibility."

E began to cry. She talked of someone else who recently had treated her badly. "I don't want to be a victim," she said. She went on to describe how this person was victimizing her, but then began wondering how she might be able to talk to him and work things out.

"But what about just getting mad at him?" I asked.

"Can I do that?" E asked back in a naive, little girl's voice.

"Well, can you?"

"Maybe it's too much like giving over control, if I just get mad at him. Maybe that's why I keep it all inside."

"And you make yourself the bad one. That's something you can then control."

We talked about this particular dynamic a bit, and E talked again of being similar to her father. I was tempted again to interpret this internalizing defense, which protected her from her sadness, but I found myself struck by another idea, which I shared with E. I said that perhaps she perpetuated the blurring of boundaries between her and her father, and her and her mother, because it served so well the purpose of taking over certain of their characteristics that were just too painful to perceive. E thought about this. She said that by talking about it she felt much more firmed up. In fact my clue about this particular aspect of E's internalizing defense was a feeling during the session that E's fragility at that point was playing into her need to be close to her parents by being as disturbed as them. It was only as I thought of this further that I realized that the blurring of boundaries also helped E to take on her father's lack of caring and empathy, in order to defend against fully seeing just how strong these traits were in her father.

This aspect of E's defensive use of guilt demonstrates the complex interplay of causation that is the norm—a complexity that is actually impossible to fully capture in any verbal description. The early years with her mother, whose mothering was as far as could be imagined from helping her through warm love, attunement, and acting as an auxiliary ego, certainly left E with a fragile sense of self and insecure self/other boundaries. Ongoing shock traumas at many stages led to numerous areas of primary dissociation within her personality—areas where the boundaries of the self were weak or nonexistent. E also identified with her mother's own borderline functioning, even though she did not have the same level of global deficits in ego functions (insecure repressions, weakness in the synthetic function, and unstable libidinal investments) as her mother. Along with these causes, constant use of confusion between herself and her parents for defensive purposes strengthened and perpetuated the lack of firm boundaries. In situations such as this, analysis of any of the contributing factors will help to some extent, but it is usually only the analysis of all the major factors deeply enough so that reconstruction of their interlocking causation becomes emotionally real that leads to deeper, lasting changes.

The excerpt just given from E's analysis was just one example of ongoing analysis of her internalizing defenses from many angles. Another theme in E's therapy was the analysis of contrast defenses. I gave an example of this in the material presented about E in the chapter on trauma. There I described how E resisted accepting genuine caring from a boyfriend, and in fact resisted caring for herself too deeply or warmly, because this would have contrasted with the cold and uncaring attitude of her mother. The example I gave a bit earlier of E sleeping with a hot water bottle and feeling well rested, but then looking rather disdainfully at the bottle the next night and seeing it as silly, is another example of defenses motivated by contrast. If she had continued to give herself the warmth she craved, and got the feelings of peace and inner relaxation that this brought, it would have contrasted too starkly with the coldness of her mother, especially the coldness in physical handling of her in very early childhood. This contrast would have powerfully evoked the feelings from the earlier time, and thus evoked also the pain and sadness and longing brought about by her mother's coldness. The proof of this is that analysis of this difficulty giving herself warmth did lead to these feelings, and we could see the denial defense in action as E then talked of the coldness of others, re-establishing the contrast defense and not feeling sad any more.

In the earlier example of our exploration of E's contrast defenses we were connecting them especially to her early treatment by her mother. It was only later in the analysis as we more fully explored the areas of primary dissociation related to E's sexual abuse by her father, that we became aware of just how psychopathic her father was, and how she in part clung to and repeated her mother's externalizing abuse of her because this had a level of relatedness, however primitive and narcissistic, that simply was not present with her father. E's insistence that after all we are all capable of the sorts of things her father did was a generalization that was part of her contrast defense in relation to her father's psychopathy. Her difficulty accepting the warmth and caring of her boyfriend, described in chapter 5, which I at that time related to her mother, had an important causation as a contrast defense in relation to her father. To fully accept this man's warmth would be too great a contrast with her father's emotional attitude, and would have triggered her feelings about the latter. Later in the analysis in relation to other instances, including my being empathic with her, we looked at how she avoided accepting these contrasting realities, and at the horror, anger, and sadness she felt about her father's relating to people essentially as things, not as human beings.

With the analysis of E's primal denial of her father's psychopathy, achieved especially through analysis of contrast defenses and her use of guilt as a defense, E experienced a revitalizing surge of energy, just as she had when we had analyzed her primal denial of her mother's narcissism and psychological disturbance.

Borrowed Guilt and the Defensive Use of Guilt

That guilt is a common accompaniment—even one of the main components—of masochism is easy enough to observe. In his paper "A Child Is Being Beaten," Freud (1919) traced the guilt accompanying the beating fantasy to the guilt of the oedipus complex. With the introduction of the concept of the superego and the understanding of guilt as representing a tension between the superego and the ego, one could talk of guilt as related to the sadism of the superego and the masochism of the ego.

In E's case there were sadomasochistic superego-ego interactions. There was depression and attacks on herself—for instance picturing awful things being done to her. E also ended up in relationships where she was psychologically abused, and stayed in them, making excuses for the other person. One reason for this related back to her traumas of sexual and physical abuse, as well as their quite intricate interweaving with her oedipal wishes and disappointments. At the same time E took on the guilt and badness that was externalized by her mother, as well as using feelings of guilt for defensive purposes, to deny both the guilt of her parents and the hopelessness of her situation as a child.

These two dynamics are very common, and have been often described in the analytic literature. The work of Sperling (1950) and Brody (1965) are early examples of very perceptive descriptions of the uncanny way children will take on the role assigned to them by parents, often because of the parent's own externalization. The motive given for the child's acceptance of the assigned role was the terror of abandonment and the fear of loss of love, along with simple conditioned learning through reward and punishment. The Kleinian literature is full of presentations of the dynamics of how one person tries to project aspects of themselves into another, and the methods used to induce the other to accept what is projected. Introjection and projective identification are the main concepts used in these descriptions.

I have previously discussed the dynamics of externalization along with the acceptance of this maneuver by the other party, using the idea of a borrowed sense of guilt (Fernando, 2000b). I emphasized the use of the borrowed guilt as a defense, especially against seeing the narcissism and lack of caring of the externalizing parent. Berliner (1947, 1958), who I think saw the dynamics most clearly because he did not link them to either drive/defense or internal object conceptualizations, outlined the two motives for the child accepting the parent's externalization and substituting their own guilt for their parent's guilt. These motives were a fear of losing the love of the parent, and that taking on the guilt was a way of denying the badness of the parent. Fairbairn (1952) described what he called the "moral defense" as having two steps. True to his object relations view, he asserted that "to say that the child takes upon himself the burden of badness which appears to reside in his objects is, of course, the same thing as to say that he internalizes these bad objects and cannot part with them because of his dependence on his parents" (p 65). After this internalization Fairbairn saw the second step as the child using this inner badness to deny the parent's badness.

One of the characteristics of this early work that has been carried forward into later explorations of this dynamic is that fear of loss of love and of abandonment have been stressed as the main motivators for the defensive use of guilt. While these fears play a key part in very early reactions, where the child takes on the part assigned to them by the parent for these motives, I have been much more impressed by the importance of painful longing, intense sadness, and feelings of hopelessness as motivators for the later defensive use of guilt. We can see this very well with E in the sessions described. As I pointed out how she was talking of her own badness in order to shift attention away from her father's, E became intensely sad.

At this point it may clarify matters to distinguish two processes and describe their relation to each other. The first involves the taking on of a role and feeling about the self assigned—usually externalized—by the parent. The motive for this is often fear of abandonment and loss of love. It is thus closely tied to early attachment and libidinal processes, and is reinforced by later developments of the libido, especially oedipal wishes. Much self-destructive and maladaptive behavior is a consequence of this process of continuing in the behavior and feelings assigned in childhood. The core of this is an attachment to the painful feelings (Valenstein, 1973) that were the only form of relating offered by a caregiver. E was seen as nasty, grasping, and mean by her mother, and while E resisted acting out these traits, she certainly tortured herself as if she had done so. Various traits can be accepted, and acted on to a greater or lesser extent, including stupidity, being a failure at undertakings, nastiness, laziness, and many others. While the dynamics of this process can come to involve attentional defenses in important ways, it is anchored in libidinal attachments and the fear of loss of the object or of its love.

Riding on the back of this or existing independently we can find another process—the defensive use of guilt. This has all the characteristics of an attentional defense. It has, of course, the shifting of attention. The shift is relatively easily undone but just as easily reinstates itself, and it is used against the perception of a reality the full appreciation of which would produce intensely unpleasant feelings. These unpleasant feelings are the motive for the defense. They disappear with the operation of the attentional shift and appear when it is undone. In the example with E we saw how as she began to fully perceive her father's psychopathy, she shifted attention to her own supposed badness. I have referred to this particular shift as defensive internalization (chapter 4). It is the exact mirror image of the defensive externalization D used to avoid the unpleasant feelings that came from seeing aspects of himself. When I undid E's shift by pointing it out to her she became very sad and then did it again, and her sadness went. (It may seem to be an obvious point, but it is easy to forget, that the entire process, except for the feelings of sadness, was unconscious.)

This defensive internalization of guilt by E was largely independent of externalization by her father. Like all abusers he tried to shift the responsibility for the abuse onto E by saying such things as, "I didn't hurt you, did I?" and minimizing what had happened. However, E's defensive use of guilt related to her father's lack of caring, coldness, and psychopathy—his sadistic pleasure in exercising power over others. He had never tried to externalize these aspects of himself onto E. What this demonstrates is that the defensive use of guilt does not need the attempt to forcefully externalize and get the other to accept guilt. I have found it useful to reserve the term borrowed guilt for the interaction where externalization processes of another person meet the internalization processes of the borrower half way, and to see this borrowed guilt as a special case of the larger category of the defensive use of guilt, which could more simply be called defensive guilt. E's use of guilt to defend against awareness of her father's psychopathy is an example of defensive guilt that was not borrowed guilt. E's feeling that she rather than her mother was nasty and mean is an example of borrowed guilt.

Just as borrowed guilt is a special case of defensive guilt, so is defensive guilt just one example of the myriad forms of defensive internalizations people resort to—all of which are forms of attentional defenses against seeing unpalatable realities. E had a defensive internalization like this in relation to her mother's serious mental disturbance. E thought that she herself was also quite disturbed or crazy, thus shifting attention from the disturbing and scary reality of her mother's craziness. Among these various internalizing defenses, however, defensive guilt has a special place. It is the most common and seems often to anchor other internalizations. I think there are a number of reasons for this. To begin with, while more disturbed parents will form fixed externalizations onto their children of various aspects of themselves—such as their lack of competence for instance—in order to stabilize their weak psychic structure, guilt and responsibility are some of the most frequently externalized aspects of a person, whatever their level of disturbance. Thus these externalizing parents both fixate the child on the guilt because this is the one way they will relate to them, and also show the child a very efficient way of denying the parent's lack of caring.

Another reason that defensive guilt is so often used relates to certain characteristics of guilt itself. As one of my patients who had been severely traumatized pointed out, guilt has a past-present-future orientation while the moment of trauma felt all too present—there was no way out and no hope. With guilt comes hope. The implicit message of guilt is "it is or was within my power to change the situation if I so chose, and that is what makes me responsible for, and guilty about, what happened." Thus the guilt which invariably follows trauma, even when the trauma does not involve an abuser who is attempting to make the victim guilty, has an origin as a defensive guilt, along with causation by regression, liberation of raw aggression, and the primitive defense of turning this aggression against the self. The guilt that follows trauma can be seen to have a causation from "below," related to the movements of the aggressive drive, and one from "above" in the form of defensive guilt. Defensive guilt acts like a bandage over the scar of helpless feelings left after a trauma, and its use to protect against the emergence of these feelings explains why traumatized individuals cling to it so tenaciously. This has important clinical implications. Analysis of this defense can be very helpful in bringing forward dissociated traumatic feelings that can then be worked through.

The characteristic of guilt that it implies hope is also the reason that it is so often used to defend against sadness and painful feelings caused by characteristics of someone that one cannot change, such as a lack of caring or a serious psychological disturbance. With guilt comes not only hope but also a call to action and thus a feeling of activity. One of the most difficult aspects of trauma is the passive helplessness, and sadness in the face of parental failure also comes with an unbearable feeling of passive helplessness. Guilt impels one to make plans in order to better the situation. E, for instance, constantly tried to change herself or her actions so the relationship with her mother or with other abusive people would work. The resistance against re-experiencing the profound passivity of trauma or severe parental failure is very strong. Defensive guilt, anger, and the constant action physically or in thought that they impel one toward, are powerful weapons against this passivity.

Clinically it is relatively easy, once one gets the hang of it, to distinguish defensive guilt from realistic guilt. Realistic guilt—the product of tension between the superego and the ego if the person transgresses a moral ideal (ego ideal)—is an extremely uncomfortable state that the person quickly tries to escape, either by a defense such as repression or externalization, or by definite actions such as apologizing or making amends. Defensive guilt, on the other hand, is clung to, and the person takes a pleasure and satisfaction in it that one does not see in realistic guilt. It is a much trickier thing to distinguish defensive guilt from neurotic guilt—that is, guilt related to unconscious conflict and repressed aggression. One reason for this is that the determinants of both these forms of guilt are unconscious, and they are not easily distinguishable by superficial examination. Also, these two forms of guilt are not actually separate. The ego takes the neurotic guilt feelings that exist in each individual and uses these for defensive ends. This defensive use of neurotic guilt is a powerful force holding it in place and working against its analytic resolution. In my experience analyzing defensive guilt to a reasonable extent allows a deeper and more effective analysis of neurotic guilt such as that over oedipal stage death wishes.

An interesting aspect of defensive guilt is that a form of it seems to exist in all of us as part of our universal primal denial of our weakness, fragility, and eventual death, and of the lack of caring of fate and nature for us. I discussed this primal denial in chapter 3. I noted then that it had its origins in our denial of our helplessness as young children, and of the only limited amount of love, caring, and protection even a well-loved child gets. Defensive guilt is an important part of this primal denial. A little reflection makes it obvious why this should be so, since guilt provides the perfect antidote for the feelings of hopelessness, helplessness, and psychic pain that come from a realization of our fragility and eventual death. If we are guilty then we are responsible, active, and have some control. Perhaps we have the power to change these unpleasant realities. (I am not suggesting that this reasoning makes any sense, but it does not have to. The defense is in the end at the level of feeling, not thought.) One line of evidence that defensive guilt plays an important part in the universal primal denial is that when this denial partially breaks down—when a person comes to accept their immanent death or when aging leads to a partial emotional acceptance of death—then people often report a lowering in a feeling of guilt that has been nagging them their whole lives. Only when it is significantly reduced do we notice that we have been living with this guilt all along. It is probably this universal primal defensive guilt that is referred to as existential guilt—a guilt that comes by virtue of becoming aware of oneself as a lone agent with no higher authority to rely on in deciding one's actions, or for protection. (Existential guilt no doubt has an oedipal dimension as well, in connection with the killing off of God or other higher powers.)

I do not want to diminish the importance of oedipal and other drive-based guilt, which of course also dogs us all of our lives. One could think of there being a universal guilt from "below" and from "above." What is especially fascinating to consider is how the universal oedipal primal repressions interact with the universal primal denials, in all their forms. As we explore it in more detail, it becomes evident that the universal primal denial is a quite complex structure, with many effects on the personality.

Contrast Defenses

I will continue here the discussion of contrast defenses that I began in the chapter on trauma. To avoid misunderstanding I should emphasize that in this case, I am actually defining a set of defenses by their motivation. The more accurate, but more cumbersome, term would be "defenses motivated by contrasting realities." In fact even this is not quite accurate, since the defenses are actually motivated by the unpleasurable feelings connected to the original reality, which are evoked by experiencing the contrasting reality. One can see how a fully descriptive name would be impractical, so I have fallen back on "contrast defenses," which should be understood to mean that such defenses are motivated by contrast.

In general I do not think it is a good idea to classify defenses based on their motivation. While there are some links between types of motivation and types of defenses—for instance intense anxiety and repression—it makes more sense to classify defenses based on their mode of operation, rather than their motivation or what they defend against. However, contrast defenses do have a common mode of operation—they are various forms of attentional defenses—and from a clinical point of view they are most easily recognized by, and interpreted in terms of, their motivation.

The setting up of a contrast defense begins with either a trauma or some other unpleasant reality. Having briefly dealt with contrast defenses in relation to trauma in chapter 5, let us now consider a very common cause of contrast defenses that leads to the appearance of masochistic behavior—an unloving parent. The lack of caring and love leads to a powerful yearning for these things and a wish that the parent would change. Through early childhood these longings become caught up in sexual longing for the parent—in the case of E her oedipal longings for her father—which are then swept into the unconscious by the oedipal primal repressions.

The child's denial of the parent's lack of love has to be strengthened as their appreciation of reality increases—especially with the rapid increase in the ability to objectively judge reality that begins at about age 7. From this point on if someone is loving or invested in the child, the suppressed longing for the parent's love threatens to emerge, as does the awareness of the parent's lack of love as shown so clearly by the contrasting example presented to the child. The sadness and pain are then on the point of breaking through. The easiest way to avoid this is to avoid such people, something that is a common occurrence in unloved children. Often various compromises are forged. For instance a certain number of relationships with kinder and more loving friends, teachers, relatives, etc., will be maintained, but will remain on the emotional periphery, with much greater investment of time and interest given to those who are unkind and narcissistically self-involved. The relationships with those who are more loving may also be seen by the person as more superficial. Perhaps the other person is just humoring them, they will say to themselves, and does not really care that much. All this to avoid the feeling of sadness that comes from the contrast.

During adolescence, with its attendant increased ability to think abstractly, the person forms various theories about humankind—for instance that no one really cares for other people. These theories help the person not to feel the contrast when they are the recipient of love. These theories may not be overtly expressed and the person may not be a cynic. Certainly E was not, but she used such generalizations, along with avoidance and attempts to derail loving relationships, to not feel the contrast. I described in chapter 5 the trouble E had accepting love and caring in a relationship.

Contrast reactions are quite common and have been described by others. The Kleinians talk of them as involving attacks on good objects and envy of goodness. The clinical descriptions are often compelling, but I think the conceptualization suffers from attempting to understand a defense against reality in terms of defenses against the drives. Krystal (1978b) pointed out that not being able to care for oneself involves complex dynamics, not merely a lack of parental care that has been carried forward through learning. He said that "when exposed to a potential good object, such patients panic and may have to ward off their yearning for love and acceptance" (p 212). Despite some explicit conceptualizations such as such Krystal's, the dynamics of contrast defenses have not been explicated by analysts to the same extent as defensive guilt, nor has their importance generally been appreciated. In my reading of the literature I have often found good clinical descriptions of contrast reactions, for instance of sadness when being loved and appreciated, but the explanation given is usually that the person is unused to love or does not really know what love is, given their past. This is often the explanation given for the avoidance of loving relationships as well. I myself have never found this to be the case. In every patient I have seen with these reactions and avoidances, I have found significant attentional defenses protecting the person from contrast reactions. Certainly at least some of my patients, for instance E, can claim to come from an extremely unloving family. Yet E had many contrast defenses and it was our analysis of them that allowed her to move toward (or actually to not move away from) kind and loving friends and relationships.

This is not to say that just because contrast defenses are not recognized, they are not analyzed. Even looking at them using quite different conceptualizations often helps patients to work through the feelings. Also, the most important working through of contrast reactions comes through the therapeutic relationship, in which the patient comes to accept the analyst's interest in and caring for them, and works through the distressing feelings that this brings up. It is often said that for many such patients the analytic relationship is the first reliable, trustworthy one they have had in their lives and the first time that someone has taken such a deep interest in them. I think it is often not appreciated to what extent these patients have turned away from such relationships in the past because of contrast effects, nor to what extent this seeming cure through the relationship involves the implicit confronting and working through of a powerful and complex defensive structure.

Despite the fact that one can analyze contrast defenses without recognizing them as such, I think there is a great therapeutic advantage to analyzing them directly as well. This speeds up the analytic work and allows one to work through more fully the painful, sad, and hopeless feelings from the past, leading to deeper and more lasting changes. After termination a good awareness of contrast defenses will expand the patient's self-analytic abilities and allow better protection against future difficulties. I have also found direct analysis of contrast defenses, as well as defensive guilt, to be very helpful with once or twice weekly psychotherapy cases. The structure of these treatments does not usually allow primal repressions to be fully analyzed, but the analysis of these other defenses can be of great benefit and also frees up the defensive structures enough to allow some access to, and reworking of, more deeply repressed conflicts and traumas.

As with defensive guilt, contrast defenses are present in all of us, and play an important part in structuring our lives. They also are part of the complex of attentional defenses that make up each of our universal primal denials around fragility and death. While our deep unconscious guilt that stems from aggression and death wishes also plays a part, contrast defenses act in concert with this guilt in making us move away from too much contentment and happiness even when it is practically achievable. Such happiness would contrast not only with the sad trials and tribulations of our past but also with the sadness and tragedy we know is to come, so we generally lace our contentment with enough discontent and trouble to keep these sad feelings at bay.

Psychotherapeutic Technique

A proper understanding and analysis of defensive guilt and contrast reactions is, in my experience, helpful with a broad range of patients. The analysis of these defensive dynamics presents no special difficulties, once one has mastered the general technique needed for attentional defenses. It is necessary to explain something of the nature of these dynamics to the patient. These sorts of explanations may worry analysts as possibly playing into intellectualizing defenses of some patients but it cannot be helped, and any defensive use of the explanations should be analyzed. One needs to be relatively active in bringing to the patient's awareness the realities that the defensive guilt and contrast defenses are keeping at bay. I gave examples of this in the chapter on denial in analyzing E's primal denial of her mother's inability to love or care for her, and earlier in this chapter in the excerpt from our analysis of her defensive use of guilt. In both cases my active bringing forward of these realities evoked the particular attentional defenses that were being used to keep them from awareness, and these could then be analyzed in more depth.

This more straightforward aspect of the analysis of these attentional defenses is the part that is also easiest to demonstrate with brief examples. But not every feeling of guilt is defensive guilt, and not every reaction to situations that differ from the past is a contrast reaction, so, as always, there are judgments to be made based on intuition, knowledge, empathy, and countertransference feelings, about what the surface manifestation is actually a manifestation of. Even when these dynamics are present so are many others, as they were in E's case, and part of the art of therapy is knowing what avenue to pursue when, and when to pursue none and let more material emerge.

Defensive Guilt
In the case of defensive guilt there are certain characteristics that I have mentioned earlier that help to distinguish it from realistic guilt. In general any situation involving trauma, and any situation that is not traumatic in the narrow sense but involves prolonged exposure to a feeling of helplessness in the face of a distressing reality such as parental disturbance, will engender defensive guilt. In these situations no amount of demonstration to the patient that their sense of guilt is ill founded, based on a misunderstanding of the past situation, will lessen the guilt. It may lead to its being suppressed and buried under more "rational" self-assertion, but this only adds an extra layer of defense. Similarly, this sort of guilt will not give way to attempts to analyze its roots in aggression turned inwards and/or the internalization of sadistic external objects. (In E's case, for instance, these dynamics existed in relation to her mother's attacks on her, but analysis of these did not succeed in truly loosening up the guilt feelings.) Only interpretation of the sense of helplessness and/or psychic pain motivating the defensive guilt, and the realities that lead to these feelings, will get the ball rolling, and only the long and difficult working through of these realities and feelings will truly lessen this guilt.

Contrast Defenses
The complex of generalization, intellectual rationalization, avoidances, and enactments that are combined into a contrast defense is one of the main factors leading to repetition both outside of the therapeutic situation and within it. In many situations, contrast reactions and contrast defenses are the major contributors from the side of the organized ego and the secondary process to repetition of the past. Classical psychoanalysis has largely concerned itself with repetition whose source was the push towards expression of primary process wishes, and with the repetitions related to traumas that have their own source in the nature of the zero process. In these two cases the ego plays its part in forming the repetition but it does so as part of a compromise, with contributions from the primary or zero processes, while in contrast defenses the entire process takes place within the ego under the laws of the secondary process.

Many other ideas about repetition have been advanced by different theoretical schools within psychoanalysis. While these ideas, such as internalized object relations and the importance of implicit memories, do not explicitly acknowledge contrast defenses, I believe that some of the phenomena they seek to explain are the product of these defenses. However one could ask the obvious question: if this cause of repetition is so important, why has it not featured prominently in anyone else's ideas about repetition? My answer is that in a disguised way it has, but because it was not conceptualized clearly, those seeing the existence of these phenomena have proposed various enactive measures to deal with these dynamics, and have often overgeneralized their findings to cover all forms of repetition, leading then rather unsurprisingly to a backlash and a dismissal of these ideas by other analysts. I will begin with two of the best known early investigators of these phenomena.

Sandor Ferenczi and Franz Alexander

Sandor Ferenczi's (1921) first experiments with what he called "active technique" involved prohibiting certain actions on the patient's part, or requiring that the patient do certain things, in order to deny conflicts an outlet and thus to force them into the analytic conversation. Ferenczi saw this as an extension, or perhaps merely an application, of the technique of abstinence and frustration of the patient's wishes, a technique that denied substitute satisfactions and forced the conflict into the open. In his later development of active technique it is clear that Ferenczi (1925) was dealing not only with drive/defense conflicts, but with conflicts related to reality. He talked of not giving the patient what they are used to and want—for instance giving them privation if they are used to love and affection. In 1929 Ferenczi stated, "We see then that while the similarity of the analytic situation to the infantile situation impels the patient to repetition, the contrast between the two encourages recollection" (p 109). In the last years of his life Ferenczi was concerned with the clinical problems of treating the effects of reality impingements, especially traumas of abuse and deprivation, and he made many observations and clinical and conceptual innovations in following this line of inquiry, including his description of contrast effects.

Franz Alexander (1950) explicitly connected his active technique to Ferenczi's ideas, but took Ferenczi's recommendations regarding activity to something of an extreme. He noted that the analyst's acting differently than the patient's parents acted towards them brings forward the suppressed feelings from these past deleterious relationships. This led to what Alexander called a corrective emotional experience. He held a very one-sided view of neurosis as a product of parental mistreatment or spoiling of the child carried forward into the present, so that the person expects similar situations. This left out many factors related to internal wishes, variable reactions to the actual childhood situation, fantasy transformations, and much else, but even at the level of the reality impingements themselves what were left out were the complex defensive maneuvers to which the child resorted. Despite this Alexander, similarly to Ferenczi, was observing and attempting to analyze contrast reactions, although he did not understand their depth (i.e., the various unconscious attentional defenses working to keep the past reality out of awareness, and the relation of these defenses to the avoidance of contrasting situations). The activity recommended by both Ferenczi and Alexander differs from what I have called the activity needed to analyze attentional defenses. This later activity involves the therapist bringing denied realities into the conversation rather than waiting for them to appear in the patient's associations, and doing this not just as an occasional maneuver, but in a consistent and persistent manner. The activity of Ferenczi and Alexander involved different sorts of actions on the part of the therapist: prohibitions, actively playing a part in the interpersonal drama with the patient, and other maneuvers such as changing the frequency of sessions. There are many problems with this kind of activity. It interferes with a rational working alliance and trust in the therapist, it assumes more knowledge on the therapist's part about the particular dynamics causing the patient's difficulties than the therapist usually has, it cuts off further discoveries of differing dynamics, and perhaps its biggest failing is that it assumes that we can know how the patient will react to various maneuvers on our part. More often than not our interventions will trigger reactions from many levels related to different dynamics, and it is only by an open and flexible attitude and technique, as well as good therapeutic and working alliances, that we can turn this unpredictability of the patient's responses to advantage.

It may be objected that the activity that I have been proposing shares some of the disadvantages that I have listed as pertaining to those of Ferenczi and Alexander. This objection would not be completely without merit. The analysis of attentional defenses, I have argued, requires some level of activity and what I have attempted to fashion in relation to these defenses is a technique that balances this need with enough flexibility and protection of trust and the alliance that other aspects of each patient's dynamics, including those needing different and contradictory techniques, can also be analyzed. In relation to the topic of attentional defenses generally and contrast defenses more specifically, I think that the examples of Ferenczi's and Alexander's technical innovations demonstrate an awareness on their part of the need for some sort of activity in analyzing these new sorts of dynamics of which they, and especially Ferenczi near the end of his life, were gaining a dawning awareness.

Weiss and Sampson

Once one's eyes have been opened to the dynamics of contrast defenses one can see them in many clinical descriptions by various authors, and in their theoretical conceptualizations as well. This is not to say that these clinical cases or theoretical ideas can, or should, be reduced to contrast defenses, any more than those of Ferenczi and Alexander should be. Rather, contrast defenses and their effects are one piece of the puzzle.

As an example, Weiss and Sampson (1986) present a theory of neurosis and of therapeutic change based on the idea that the patient suffers from unconscious pathogenic beliefs acquired in the deleterious circumstances of their childhood. They feel that the patient is constantly trying to disconfirm, rather than merely repeat, these beliefs in other situations but the circumstances, including not feeling safe and trusting enough, do not allow this. They contrast this idea of an active ego process, including the patient's plan to move towards cure in analysis through testing out their unconscious pathogenic beliefs, with what they characterize as Freud's automatic functioning hypothesis, in which the ego gives a signal of anxiety to set defensive processes in motion. These processes then move forward in an automatic manner, regulated by the pleasure principle.

Of course Freud did not have only an automatic functioning hypothesis, and Weiss and Sampson acknowledge this, but argue that an automatic functioning theory and one based on meaning, planning, and beliefs are incompatible. While the issue is somewhat tangential to the main line of argument and discussion at this point, it is central to theories of defense and to psychoanalytic theory in general. Weiss and Sampson's view of the incompatibility of these two types of theories, a view which is shared by many analysts, puts aside what I consider to be two key aspects of psychoanalytic theory: the multiple determinants of any phenomenon, and emergence. The idea of multiple determination needs no explanation, being a key organizing idea in psychoanalysis from the beginning. Emergence refers to the origin, at different levels of investigation and reality, of properties that are neither completely based upon, nor predictable from, properties of the interacting phenomena that through their interaction give rise to these properties. For instance one may conceptualize not only brain physiology, but many aspect of mental functioning as automatic—the manner in which perceptions and memories are organized at one level, or the interplay of forces at one level of the defensive processes, as examples, while at the same time having meaning and intention emerge from these automatic processes at another level. I would not suggest that emergence is an easy or uncontroversial idea, but without an appreciation of it there is often the tendency to collapse all explanation either downward towards mechanism or upward towards meaning. Freud did not do this. He instead moved back and forth between different levels of explanation. His intuitive understanding of the importance of these multiple levels of explanation and of the phenomenon of emergence is to my mind one of his great strengths as a thinker, although others have seen his movement between these different levels of explanation as a sign of inconsistency, and a product of his clinging to 19th-century mechanistic ideas even as he developed a science of meaning. I will continue this discussion in chapter 9, in considering basic theoretical issues.

To return now to the main thread of our discussion: Weiss and Sampson argue for one level of explanation—the level of intention, meaning, and planning. They suggest that pathogenic beliefs are at the core of neurosis, that the patient is motivated to disconfirm their pathogenic beliefs, and that he or she has a plan in analysis to do just this when it is safe to do so. Much of their detailed and extensive clinical material clearly relates to various attentional defenses, including the defensive use of guilt.

Contrast defenses are also much in evidence. Weiss and Sampson give details from a patient, Mrs. P, who had a history of childhood neglect and did not feel she deserved very much. Because of these very powerful feelings of lack of self worth she felt she could not stay in analysis. That her difficulty staying was related to her lack of entitlement was interpreted and this seemed to convince her to stay. Mrs. P then remembered, with strong feelings of sadness, a scene of her mother not protecting her as a child (1986, p 170–171). In considering this sequence, the authors argue that this incident was repressed not just because of the bad feelings but because at that point the patient did not believe that she deserved any better. Can a belief by itself lead to a defense? Or does one need also a lower level force—a mechanistic explanation—added to the higher level one? Weiss argues that, from the fact that this memory emerged without much anxiety, one can infer that Mrs. P had already changed her unconscious pathogenic belief and that this was the decisive shift. This argument neglects another possibility—that it was pervasive painful, sad feelings that motivated the defense or defenses, which may have consisted of complex combinations of attentional and repressive defenses. It is possible, for instance, that this pervasive psychic pain held in place (motivated) certain primal attentional defenses, and that some of the memories associated with the incident were defended against by secondary repression, which helped to buttress her primal denials.[2]

It would seem likely, from the description of what happened, that one of these attentional defenses was a contrast defense. Mrs. P was having trouble staying in the treatment as it deepened. It is possible, given her background of neglect, that the fact that she had her therapist's attention and was listened to with respect threatened to evoke, by contrast, the pain and sadness related to her childhood neglect. This possibility is raised to the level of near certainty by Mrs. P's reaction to interpretations about her difficulty with entitlement that led to her being convinced to stay in treatment. She not only remembered the scene of her mother not intervening, but felt the pain and sadness of her situation then, pain and sadness that had for a long time been held at bay.

It is worth reemphasizing that this contrast effect comes about partly because accepting the contrasting reality contradicts and therefore weakens certain generalization defenses that work to deny the original painful reality. We can picture Mrs. P as a child coming up with such generalizations as "no one will care for me," and "people aren't really interested in me or in what happens to me." These generalizations would help to mask the very specific memories and specific incidents of lack of caring on her mother's part. These general ideas could be referred to by Weiss and Sampson as unconscious pathogenic beliefs, but what is added here is the dynamic dimension. This is present to some extent in Weiss and Sampson's theory but it is not developed. What the theory of contrast defenses asserts in these sorts of situations is that below the manifest layer is a set of attentional defenses, such as the very common one of generalization, motivated by intense affect such as psychic pain. The attentional defenses work against full awareness of the dreadful reality that would give rise to these feelings. In Mrs. P's case, these generalizations and other defenses, such as minimization and defensive internalization ("I'm not caring enough of my parents"), would work in combination with other dynamics (for instance her actual anger and aggression at her parents could be used to "prove" the reality of her badness as part of the internalizing defense, even as part of it came from oedipal conflicts). Mrs. P would also have to avoid, or at least limit, her exposure to situations (such as a good analysis, or a caring friend), which would rouse her longing for care and love, threaten her generalization defenses (what Weiss and Sampson call her pathogenic beliefs), and thus threaten to evoke the feelings and memories associated with her neglect.

My reason for going into detail about this, including repeating what I have already said about contrast defenses, is that I think that there is an important point to be made here, and one that has a much wider application than just the ideas of Weiss and Sampson. I chose Weiss and Sampson's work because they give quite detailed clinical material in their book, including verbatim transcripts of many sessions in another, longer case, that displays the same contrast defenses that Mrs. P had, so the reader can themselves decide based on this extensive material if the alternative explanation that I am putting forward seems reasonable. My point is essentially that many authors from many different theoretical orientations conceptualize phenomena that are the outcome of contrast defenses in an overly superficial, largely non-dynamic, manner—for instance saying that a patient such as Mrs. P has developed a theory, from her years of neglect, that guides her present behavior, or that she did not know real love and caring in her formative years and so now does not know how to let it in, and tends to move naturally to situations similar to the ones she came to see as normal in her childhood. Despite the fact that deeper dynamics are largely ignored or at best hinted at in these conceptualizations, the contrast defenses are partially confronted and analyzed, without being made explicit, by the patient's having experiences in the analysis or therapy that challenge their generalizations and evoke the pain of their past. This pain is experienced and partially worked through, but its full working through is impeded by the fact that there is not a proper reconstruction of the sequence of how the patient dealt with their painful childhood realities.

Different authors understand the change that is brought about by this implicit confrontation of contrast defenses in different ways. Weiss and Sampson present the idea of the patient changing their unconscious pathogenic beliefs by testing them in the analysis when they feel it is safe enough to do so. Their theory of change includes an intellectual and a dynamic element (making the unconscious beliefs conscious) plus a relational one—the trust and positive relationship that allows the pathogenic beliefs to be tested. Other authors also generally see dynamic along with non-dynamic factors as driving the repetition and some combination of interpretative and relational factors as the cause of the clinical change. This was the case with Ferenczi and Alexander, both of whom stressed the therapeutic relationship as a major agent of change. Ferenczi had a much more sophisticated understanding of how this may come about, and often seems to me to be half way towards explicating the dynamics behind contrast defenses, while Alexander's conceptualizations were more simplistic. Alexander was also more "modern" than Ferenczi in stating that recovery of memories was usually a byproduct of other, deeper changes, rather than being intrinsic to the change, a view that Weiss and Sampson also endorse.

Even if my point that the therapeutic change attributed to relational factors is partly a product of the implicit analysis and working through of contrast defenses has some validity, does it make any clinical difference? Are these defenses perhaps just as well (perhaps better?) analyzed implicitly instead of through explicit defense interpretation? My experience has been otherwise. I have found that many analyses have been greatly helped once

I have spotted a contrast issue and have pointed out the various defensive maneuvers to the patient. This is not to say that even when this is done some—perhaps quite a bit—of implicit analysis of the contrast and other attentional defenses does not also take place, but my experience has been that this is greatly aided, deepened, and consolidated by concurrent explicit analysis.

Other Theorists
In recent years theorists from various perspectives (self-psychological, relational, infant researchers and other developmental theorists, attachment theorists) have emphasized relational factors as agents of psychotherapeutic change. Some authors take the view that these are one factor among many, while others (as an example Stern and his coworkers—Stern et. al., 1998; Boston Change Process Study Group, 2007) take a more radical stand, asserting that these relational factors are the major or only ones leading to change. I would be merely repeating myself if I took examples from these various authors and teased out aspects that I believe are explainable using the idea of contrast defenses. Rather than repeat what I have already said regarding Weiss and Sampson's clinical case, I will merely repeat my conclusions: that many of the effects and changes attributed to the analytic relationship by various theorists are actually caused by the implicit, partial confrontation and analysis of contrast defenses, and that in this process the analyst's actions serve as agents of change through the hidden interpretive effect that they possess.

In making this argument regarding the hidden interpretive effect of the therapeutic relationship, I am *not* making the further claim that all or most seeming relational effects are actually related to the confrontation of contrast defenses. The situation is more complex and multilayered than this. Many explicitly interpretive interventions may have a portion or even most of their effect through implicit, unacknowledged relational factors. It is easy enough to imagine how this happened in E's analysis, for instance, where availability in the analysis of a stable emotional environment and a non-judgmental and reciprocal relationship were important, and had a positive effect partly through the provision of a new object relationship. This relational effect not only works alongside the interpretive, uncovering one, but the two also reinforce each other. The new object relationship is the basis for the real relationship and an important part of the therapeutic and working alliances, which are all necessary for effective interpretive work. This is easy enough to see in the case of E, who had been so abused and traumatized in her past, had trouble with deeper closeness and trust because of this, and entered therapy seriously depressed and suicidal. On the other hand analysis of traumatic memories and defenses allows patients to make use of opportunities for new object relationships within and outside of therapy. This also was evident in E's case where analysis of her traumas, oedipal guilt, defensive guilt, and contrast defenses, among other dynamics, made her more and more able to make use of the new relationship opportunities in her analysis and in the rest of her life. This general point is not a new one, but what I hope to have added to it is a description of a specific layer of attentional defenses whose existence, and whose analysis, is often hidden within what is thought of as the non-interpretive, relational aspects of therapy.

Transference of Defense

As with the screen defenses described in the last chapter, defensive guilt and contrast defenses often enter the analysis in the form of a transference of defense. I have already given the example of a deepening of the therapeutic relationship threatening to bring up contrast reactions, and leading to contrast defenses. In the case of defensive guilt I have observed on a number of occasions that as the work and the transference deepen, there occur quite marked instances of defensive internalization and defensive guilt, as a response to a mistake or series of mistakes that the therapist makes, such as not being very attentive for a while, and thus not hearing some key things the patient had said. The patient will turn this around and see it as their fault in various ways, and cling to this defensive guilt so as not to feel painful disappointment in the therapist. When these responses are more pronounced than the regular use of them that the patient makes in other situations, then there is an opportunity for a deeper analysis—for instance the reconstruction of some of the overwhelming realities that led to the original formation of the primal versions of these attentional defenses.

In this and the previous chapter I have been discussing specific attentional defenses and describing their entry into the analysis as a transference of defense. Is it only attentional defenses that manifest as a transference of defense? I would answer, no. There are two other broad categories of transferences of defense. One of these I have already discussed in the chapter on repression—the manner in which the counterforce of primal repression is transmuted into the transference resistance. This is actually a special case, in that only in repression is the core mechanism or inner working of the defense melted down and reformed in the crucible of the therapeutic relationship into the resistive aspects of the transference. This is possible because the core of repression is formed from partially neutralized aggressive drive energy, and the malleability and displaceability of drive energy allows these sorts of transformations. In the transferences of defense based upon attentional defenses, the mechanism uses secondary process ego energy, and thus this transference is largely an intensification of the defense, repeated within the analysis, rather than a complete transformation that allows the defensive process to enter the therapeutic relationship much more radically, as it does in the case of repression. A third type of defense, to be put alongside counterforce and attentional defenses, are forms of defense based upon characteristics of the zero process (zero process defenses). These will be described in chapter 9, as part of a discussion of perversions. At that time I will also describe the transference of defense based upon these forms of defense.

I have suggested that transference is a multidimensional phenomenon. Most analysts see it as multidimensional in terms of its content (a positive transference, a father transference, a sibling transference, a transference from early infancy, a transference from the oedipal phase), but the multidimensionality I am suggesting relates to the mechanism or process whereby the transference is established and maintains itself. This is not a new idea. Many authors have differentiated displacement from externalizing transferences, for instance. The view presented here of various forms of transference of defense is one way of conceptualizing the different dimensions of transference.

At the most straightforward level these ideas can make the clinician more aware of certain aspects of the transference—it might be more appropriate to refer to them as separate transferences—that are intertwined with and hidden behind the aspects of which we are usually more aware. To give a brief example of this, I have previously described D's father transference, and how it involved oedipal elements of competition, and the wish to denigrate and destroy me, as well as sexual love for me (the analyst/father). I have also described how D used a warm, chummy relationship with me to both cover over the competition and express in muted form the love. This chummy relationship was also an important part of the transference resistance, as D fell back on it again and again to avoid deeper work, through chatting and telling stories. The chumminess had other meanings, however: it was a screen defense as well as a denial in action. By acting as if I were his father, and by evoking the same warm and loving feelings he had had in his father's presence, D was telling himself, "It's not true that my father is dead. Look, he's right here and we are having a fine old time." D did not say this explicitly or consciously, but it was rather contained in his feelings and actions within the analysis. There were many other actions, for instance not visiting his father's grave, that were part of D's denial. I bring up this example to illustrate the point that awareness of, and sensitivity to, this other form of transference (transference of an attentional defense) opens up important areas for analysis.

Another way in which the conceptualization of these different forms of transference of defense can be helpful is that we can come to consider other aspects of therapy connected with the transference from this angle. As an example, I will end this chapter with a few comments on countertransference in relation to transferences of defense.

Because attentional transferences are processes that remain, to a much larger extent than displacement transferences, within the secondary process, the deeper reverberations with the analyst's own repressed conflicts does not take place to the same extent. This is not to say that the therapist does not have responses to these transferences, but these responses are not to the same extent a product of unconscious communication. For instance a patient who transfers their defensive guilt and internalizing tendencies, as E actually did in her analysis, might make the analyst feel overly comfortable, and lessen his or her sense of realistic self criticism, as he or she realizes that the patient is covering for their mistakes. These responses can be of use in discovering and exploring the patient's transference of defense. In a case such as E's, if one ferrets out a particular failure on the analyst's part that the patient has used defensive guilt to hide, one has a good opportunity to use transference interpretations to demonstrate to the patient this dynamic in a very immediate way. Recognizing these sorts of counter-reactions on the part of the analyst to the patient's transference of attentional defenses, and differentiating them from other forms of countertransference, can help in understanding and analyzing these transferences.

I presented E's use of defensive guilt as an example of transference of an attentional defense, but it should be emphasized that many different attentional defenses can be transferred and their effect on the analyst, in terms of the counter-reactions that they elicit, will vary quite a bit based on both the form of defense that is transferred and on the analyst's own issues and personality. Among the other defenses that can be transferred, I have already given examples of screen defenses and denial in action with D, as well as contrast defenses. As an example of how the analyst's personality can come into play, we could imagine how an analyst with important narcissistic fixations would especially be drawn into the comfort offered by a patient who protects them through minimization of their mistakes and by defensive guilt. The patient's tendency to use guilt defensively to deny the responsibility and flaws of the other fits perfectly in such a situation with the therapist's tendency to externalize. I have seen evidence of more than one such situation leading to quite detrimental acting out on the part of the analyst.

There is one particular attentional defense whose role in forming transfer-ences has been discussed quite a lot—externalization. The use of this defense is usually subsumed under the heading of projection of internal objects or of projective identification, and in the conceptualizations of Kleinians and some other object relations theorists, *all* transference is reduced to this dynamic. There can be little doubt of the importance of this defense in its transferred form, but I think this can be, and should be, distinguished from both classic displacement transferences based on repression and from transferences of other attentional defenses, as well as from zero process transferences.

I discussed defensive externalization in chapter 4, describing it as a denial defense that involved the shifting of attention from an internal reality to an external one. In the example I presented in that chapter D shifted his atten-tion from his guilt to mine. Strictly speaking this type of externalization is a transference of an attentional defense. However, as I described in the case of D, this strictly attentional defense shades over into a form of interpersonal counterforce defense, where a drive derivative and the powerful affects based on it are externalized to, and evoked in, the analyst, and an aggressive coun-terforce is used to distance the patient from the externalized drive element, now felt as belonging to the therapist. This is projective identification more narrowly defined. It leads to quite striking and powerful counter-reactions on the part of the therapist. Not all countertransferences are based on this dynamic, however.

I have in this and the last chapter elucidated a number of specific at-tentional defenses and used these specific examples to discuss certain more general aspects of attentional defenses, such as how they interact with other dynamics and the manner in which they enter the transference. In the next chapter we will consider in detail specific defenses based on trauma and the zero process.

Summary

The specific dynamics I have discussed at length in this chapter—defensive guilt and contrast defenses—are only masochistic in the descriptive sense, in that they lead to behavior that is self defeating and self injurious. They are not dynamically masochistic. They do not involve actual pleasure in self-injury, as does erotogenic masochism. Each person's self-destructive behavior is a unique mix of erotogenic masochism, attentional defenses, turning of aggression against the self, and other causes such as identification with a masochistic parent. E for instance had a good deal of what might be called aggressive masochism (turning of aggression against the self) along with her defensive masochism. A fuller explication of masochism would involve tracing in detail the interaction (or lack of interaction) of these various processes in specific patients. This project is beyond the scope of this chapter, which has attempted to describe the details of some very common defensive processes that have, I believe, not been generally well understood or given their due in analysis up to this time. These defenses were defensive guilt and contrast defenses.

From a clinical standpoint I noted how these defenses need to be analyzed actively. One cannot usually wait for the denied realities to emerge but must pursue them. I also noted how contrast defenses are often analyzed without either analyst or patient being explicitly aware that this is going on and how this process, and the emergence of strong feelings and memories, is ascribed to other therapeutic factors such as the positive effect of the relation between therapist and patient. I argued for the usefulness of the explicit analysis of both defensive guilt and contrast defenses. I also discussed the more general concept of transference of defense. I pointed out that the manner of action, including the effect on the analyst, of transferences of attentional defenses is different from other forms of transference.

Terms

Defensive Guilt: An attentional defense in which a sense of guilt is emphasized in order to hide something else that is more distressing. The thing screened by the guilt usually belongs to one of two categories: either the guilt of someone else, most often a narcissistic parent or sibling, or feelings of helplessness and passivity, either from a trauma or some other situation. Guilt serves as a very good defense against these latter feelings because guilt has the subtext of "you could have done something and therefore you were responsible and guilty, but not helpless." Guilt is invariably used as a defense against the helplessness of trauma. It is also invariably a product of growing up with a seriously narcissistic parent, where it does double duty, defending against both the lack of guilt of the parent (borrowed guilt) and the feelings of despair and helplessness when the child realizes that the parent is incapable of caring.

Notes

1. Many patients with far less trauma, deprivation, and specific developmental impingements, such as E's mother tying her up, have a much less secure libidinal investment in their bodies than E, and engage in serious cutting and other forms of self

242 ~ Chapter Seven

harm. I think that this points to the important contribution of constitutional factors in the ability to form stable libidinal investments in self and others.

2. I present this only as a crude outline of possible dynamics, different from the one Weiss dismisses (repression motivated by anxiety) and from the one that he proposes (repression of the memory and avoidance of closeness based on an unconscious pathogenic belief that she deserved nothing). Given the ubiquitous layering and intertwining of primal and secondary defenses we would expect that Mrs. P would also have primal repressions, for instance primal oedipal repressions, which secondary denial defenses would interact with, including secondary denial defenses derived from the primal denial of her mother's lack of care. For a discussion of these sorts of interactions, see the section "Interaction of Denial and Repression" in chapter 3, on denial.

CHAPTER EIGHT

~

Perversions

The theoretical understanding of sexual perversions has been an important part of psychoanalysis—always as a reflection of the current state of psychoanalytic theory, and at times as a source of new and challenging ideas. For this reason analysts have been reluctant to relinquish the term perversion, even as it has fallen into disfavor elsewhere because of its pejorative connotations. In this chapter I will first very briefly summarize the ideas of a few key authors on perversions, then present some clinical material, and finally use this material and the ideas presented earlier in this book to develop certain theoretical ideas about the nature of the dynamics in the perversions. Perversions provide an opportunity to discuss trauma and the zero process again. We will explore the interaction of the zero process with other factors, the forms of neurosis in which the zero process predominates (zero process neuroses), and defenses that are specifically built upon the characteristics of the zero process (zero process defenses).

Psychoanalytic Theories of the Perversions

In 1905 Freud said, in "The Three Essays on the Theory of Sexuality," that "Neuroses are, so to say, the negative of the perversions" (p 175). In other words, neuroses were the result of defense against the perverse sexual impulse. For instance repression of an oral sexual wish to suck on a penis may lead to the neurotic symptom of anorexia, which both expresses the oral wish and its rejection. Perversions, on the other hand, were seen as the relatively direct expression of one or more sexual wishes from childhood, which had survived unchanged into adulthood. These included, for instance, masochistic impulses and voyeuristic ones. After 1905 Freud discovered a number of specific psychosexual stages—the oral, anal, and phallic—each of which had its corresponding perverse wishes, the repression of which led in each case to different forms of neurosis—for instance the regression to, and repression of, anal wishes led to obsessional neurosis.

In his paper "A Child Is Being Beaten" (1919) Freud traced a perverse masturbatory fantasy that a child was being beaten through a series of transformations in childhood. One of Freud's key findings was that the fantasy in its final form was a regressively distorted substitute for a deeply repressed passive sexual impulse towards the father. In other words the perverse fantasy was itself a product of regression and repression, and was a distorted expression of a deeper sexual impulse, in much the same way as a neurotic symptom was. This new view of perversions, as the endpoint of a complex development and as involving various defensive processes, was the beginning of the modern psychoanalytic conceptualization of perversions.

In an early paper Hans Sachs (1986, [1923]) noted that in the perversions one piece of infantile sexuality was held onto throughout development, and this piece carried the pleasure charge of all that was repressed. It was held in the lower (i.e., closer to the id) portion of the ego and aided in the repression of other portions of childhood sexuality, especially the oedipus complex. Gillespie (1956) also talked of one part of infantile sexuality entering into the service of repression, and added that which part will be so used was determined by parental attitudes, often covertly communicated to the child, as well as by what was found acceptable to the child's superego. Fenichel (1945) said that experiences of sexual satisfaction which simultaneously gave feelings of security allowed a denial of overwhelming fears, and were therefore held onto and overemphasized. He compared this process to very similar ones involved in the formation of screen memories.

In fact the particular dynamic described by these authors is reminiscent of the screen defenses discussed in the chapter on narcissism, and we could wonder if the overgratifications that I had suggested lead to this form of defense also play a part in the causation of screen defenses that use sexuality and lead to perversions. Fenichel and Gillespie both suggest this. Janine Chasseguet-Smirgel (1974, 1981) described the process in more detail. She felt that the mother of the future male pervert seduced the child narcissistically, so that the child believed that he had won the oedipal struggle. He did not project his ego ideal in front of him, but felt rather that he was already at one with it. He did not need to strive because he had already arrived. She said that the fetish stands for the anal phallus, the only sort of phallus the child can have that is equal to his father's. By emphasizing the anal phallus and anality in general, the child banished the father's penis from the oedipal scenario, and attempted to negate the differences between the sexes and the generations, differences that he found so narcissistically wounding. Chasseguet-Smirgel's ideas involved an interesting blend of ego determinants (narcissistic fixations) and id ones, with less emphasis on trauma and structural considerations.

To return now to the chronology of Freud's work: he approached the topic of perversions from a fresh angle in the last phase of his theorizing. In his 1927 paper on fetishism he asserted that the fetish stood for a woman's penis, and more specifically for the penis of the mother, the lack of which enormously increased the boy's fear for the safety of his own penis. Freud went further, however, by suggesting specific dynamic processes that led to the fetish. He felt that the affect aroused by the sight of the female genital was repressed, but that the idea—the memory of the perception and the idea of what this meant—was disavowed. By this he meant that a double attitude was taken toward the perception—that castration existed and that it did not. This double attitude was the beginning of a split in the ego.

In this same paper Freud traced some of the particular objects used as fetishes to the moment just before the perception of the female genitals took place—for instance a shoe, stocking, or undergarment seen as the boy looked up towards the woman's genitals. Freud noted that this was reminiscent of the stopping of memory just before the moment of impact of a trauma. He reiterated this connection in his paper on the splitting of the ego by saying that this splitting "occurs under the influence of a psychical trauma" (1938b, p 275). He also noted that this sort of splitting of the ego could take place in relation to distressing realities other than the sight of the female genital. He mentioned as an example the combined acceptance and denial of the death of his father by a patient in his childhood.

While Freud traced splitting of the ego to trauma, his explication of the actual process of this splitting invoked phenomena other than trauma. He on the one hand linked splitting to the wish to disavow an unpleasant reality. In the "Outline of Psychoanalysis" he said that "the disavowal is always supplemented by an acknowledgment; two contrary and independent attitudes always arise and result in the situation of there being a split in the ego" (1938a, p 204).[1] On the other hand Freud linked splitting of the ego to the drives, noting that the process involved two sides, one of which takes account of reality "and another which under the influence of the instincts detaches the ego from reality" (1938a, p 202). Here he attempted to understand both splitting and disavowal in terms related to repression and reaction formation, as a battle between the ego and the drives. In neither of these two attempts to explain the actual process of splitting of the ego did Freud refer to psychical trauma.

The majority of psychoanalysts writing on perversions after Freud have linked it explicitly to trauma (Loewenstein, 1957; Greenacre, 1968; Stoller, 1975; Hopkins, 1984; Arlow, 1987; Massie and Szajnberg, 1992; Bass, 2000; Brenner, 2001; Oliner, 2000, to name just a few of them). Of these Greenacre and Stoller have explored this link in the most detail. Before discussing their ideas and developing some fresh ones about the defensive processes at work in the perversions, I will present clinical material from a familiar patient, D, to serve as the basis for the discussions that follow.

D: Clinical Material

Material from D's analysis has been presented in chapters 2 (Repression), 4 (Externalizing and Internalizing Defenses), and 6 (Narcissism). To summarize briefly: D came for help with financial risk taking behavior that had led to his ruin, as well as for the more general problem of having difficulty in facing reality. D had been in therapy (but never in analysis) with a number of different people on and off since his mid-twenties. The main problem he remembered working on was the lack of love shown him by his mother, although a number of the therapists had commented on his difficulties with responsibility.

D was quite desperate for help when he first came, but over the year of twice weekly therapy that we engaged in, before beginning five times a week psychoanalysis on the couch, he put his life back in reasonable order personally and professionally. In chapters 4 and 6 I detailed the ways in which D's parents had helped him to avoid unpleasant realities, and how his fixation on this, and on his special position in the family as the first born son and proxy for his father's thwarted success, led to certain difficulties. He clung to the feeling and the fantasy of being the special one, which interfered with his development, especially the mourning of childhood's end in adolescence that would have allowed him to move emotionally into his adult life. He also clung to the feeling that reality was malleable and that he was not completely subject to the dictates of either outer reality or the inner reality of his conscience.

While my discussion of D in the chapter on narcissism concentrated on his ego fixations and externalizing and screen defenses, the clinical material presented dealt also with D's early toileting trauma, the effects of his mother's narcissism and lack of empathy, and his long-standing habit of visiting massage parlors. It is these behaviors, which D engaged in quite compulsively even when in a sexual relationship, which we will look at in this chapter. Dividing up a patient such as D into different parts—his "repressions," his "externalizations," his "narcissism," and now his "perversion"—as illustrations of certain theoretical ideas is a somewhat artificial enterprise. To a certain extent, however, this dividing up of D (and of my other main case E) is undone both in the clinical material and in the theoretical discussion, as the intrinsic connections between different aspects of each person assert themselves. Thus the clinical material on D in the chapter on narcissism involved quite a bit about his visits to massage parlors, including their connection to his early toileting trauma.

D had begun these visits after the birth of his second child, which recreated his family of origin, with himself in the position of his father. I wondered if this attainment of a position similar to his father's roused his castration anxiety and oedipal guilt, and whether the sexual acting out served to protect against these overwhelming feelings. In the chapter on repression I described how D had had a feeling of triumph, which had led him to have a sexual dream about his mother and then act out his sexual wishes towards her with a prostitute. He tried to hide all this from me and when he did tell me about it, D for a few seconds felt an intense physical fear of me. Associations showed that this was a fear of me as his castrating father, but also that these castration fears were inextricably interwoven with equally intense fears of abandonment and of body disintegration.

We linked his visits to the sexual massage parlors to a toileting trauma from very early on, when his mother had trained him by putting him on the toilet when she could see he was straining. Entries his mother had made in a baby book dated these incidents to between his eighth and tenth month. D had no connected memories for these events, but he did have flashes of memory—for instance of the tile color and pattern on the bathroom floor. He also had physical reactions, feelings, dreams, and various symptoms (a phobia of getting too close to water falling over a waterfall, for instance) that helped in the reconstruction of the traumas. Clearly some of these reactions and ideas about what may have happened also condensed into the traumatic memories the cold, hard handling of him by his self-centered mother during infancy and early childhood. For an example of how we analyzed this connection, I would refer readers to the clinical material in chapter 6, under the heading "D" and "A Few Sessions." Some analysts may be tempted to interpret this toileting trauma as nothing more than a screen trauma, clung to by D because it gave concrete expression to the extended and very painful ongoing trauma of his mother's lack of empathy for him. I myself do not think it was only a screen, although it served a number of screen functions.

In our reconstruction it seemed that D's mother had left him on the toilet (not a potty) with an insert so he would not fall in, and when he did not defecate right away had on one or more occasions left the bathroom. D had become more and more frantic as he could not get down from the toilet, and eventually experienced overwhelming abandonment panic. These are the elements that I am reasonably sure were part of the original trauma or traumas. Many other elements were reported as memories or came up as associations, which seemed to be later additions or to be amalgams of other feelings, fantasies, or experiences with flashes of zero process memory from the trauma. In these sorts of situations one often cannot be sure of the exact parceling out of what comes from what period. An example of one of these amalgams was a fear that D had of falling off the toilet and hitting his head on the hard tiles. It is quite possible that this fear came from the actual trauma, while also condensing the lack of secure holding, at both the emotional and physical level, that D had experienced at the hands of his mother. However the fear would often go further, involving D being cut by the sharp edge of one of the tiles and bleeding to death, something that seemed to be a product of his phallic oedipal stage and its castration terror. D's intrusive thoughts of putting his arm through the glass of my French doors and his fantasy that he would then be lying there bleeding to death while I looked on because the rules of analysis would not let me help, was the transference version of this fear, which condensed the abandonment and death fears of the trauma with the castration fears of later periods.

This trauma and its later elaborations had many connections with D's perversions, the most obvious being that the actions in the massage parlor reversed the worst parts of the trauma. D was warm, not alone but in fact tended to by a woman who lovingly (he would feel at the time) coaxed a "mess" out of his penis and then cleaned it up. The massage that preceded the masturbation reversed the situation of his cold handling by his mother and seemed to allay anxieties about the integrity, safety, and lovability of his body. The ability of what happened at the massage parlors to negate anxieties of many types—castration, abandonment, body disintegration—as well as to soothe painful feelings related to deprivation, goes a long way towards explaining the hold the visits to these places had on D. This reversal of what had happened in the trauma was not simply imagined in fantasy, but was also based on actual situations where D had experienced repeated gratification. Two of these have been mentioned already: his physically and emotionally warm relationship with his father and the way his mother let him get away with lies and distortions of reality. Another that was especially relevant to D's perversion was the loving physical care he received from his grandmother—including changing his diapers and cleaning him—during the first year of his life. This use of recalled actual feelings of gratification from the past to screen unpleasant ones is shared by perversions and narcissistic disorders. I would like now to present some details of a session from about a year before termination, which give some idea of how the material related to abandonment, D's mother's early handling of him, and trauma and its elaborations presented themselves.

This session was the second last before a planned two and one half week break that I was taking. D came in and began by recounting a dream from the night before. "I had this dream that sort of analyzes itself," he said. "It started with an accolade I didn't deserve. Then I panicked and was running on very narrow piers onto water that was brown—like shit brown. I felt vertigo because the piers were so narrow. I felt I would fall down. Something was chasing me. I felt I had no escape. There was no way for me to get back to land. The piers were narrow but they were also floating. [His girlfriend] was there trying to comfort me. If she wasn't there I would have fallen into the water. The dream was quite scary. It makes me think of getting undeserved praise, and how it has led to such bad reactions. I think with the water of my fear of falling into the toilet bowl. Maybe [his girlfriend] was a bit like my mother being there."

"There seems to be a strong fear in the dream," I said.

"Maybe of death?" D responded. "I don't know. It's a kind of dread. I think of the piers as wafers. It was like a jigsaw puzzle. It reminds me of a log rolling because I had to keep running to keep my balance. When I stopped I got vertigo, and then I began running again. I was almost dragging [his girlfriend] behind me. Maybe that's like having some kind of human contact. Maybe I felt there were no humans around. Maybe that's what it was like with my mother and the toilet: hard and cold, except it wasn't [in the dream]. It was a warm clime—like shitting and then being warmed by the radiator." (This referred to an incident from his childhood.)

"I wonder again what you think of the piers," I asked.

"They were thin, not supported by anything. I'm really thinking of other things. In a way I think the dream is obvious."

"Is it the associations that you want to get away from?"

"No, it's just that before you asked me about the piers I was thinking about the world situation." D began to talk very loudly. "There's just people plunging the world into a terrible conflict." D talked of a number of worrying things in the world and then about how scared he was of the fundamentalist

Christians, "like John Ashcroft. They don't care if there's a nuclear Armageddon. They're just waiting for the afterlife anyway. You know I'm very depressed about all of this."

"It's hard to disagree with anything you've said, but you went to this from your own personal fears."

"I can see it really. It's my own panic."

"I wonder if you were beginning to be overwhelmed by feelings from your past."

"As I was talking of the world situation, I was feeling especially bad for children. I pictured little children, around two."

"So this allows you to feel it but distance yourself from what has been coming up the last few sessions."

"Yes, I can see that. It's like a fear of a fear. It's too scary to really go into it."

"And you didn't master it the first time. Maybe you're afraid you won't this time as well."

"It's a fear of disappearing—in the end a fear of death, of being gone, not having any connections. Like the connection to you, or to [his girlfriend], or to my father." At this point D burst into tears and moaned, "Oh god, he's not alive, he's dead." D cried a bit more but calmed down quickly, saying, "What does that mean, 'he's dead?' What can that mean since I know it?" D became quite calm as he went on in an intellectual way like this for a while.

"You seem to know it intellectually," I commented, "but I wonder if you still basically think of him as alive."

"I'm thinking of the shit brown water: like I would drown, would die, would disappear into it. There was something seductive about it though—the calm. I'm sick of you prodding me about these things! I want to forget it!" D said, raising his voice. "I'm angry it's not Friday. I want to move on to music, to spring."

"I wonder if it's a kind of merger experience, with the water," I suggested.

"I think more of my mom and of how she took care of me so well when I was sick. The water was like a siren calling but I knew to stay away. I used to make chocolate pudding with my mother. [D had talked a number of times about pleasant occasions spent cooking with his mother.] I had to make it nice and smooth. I didn't like any lumps. I haven't thought of that in a long time. It's one of the few nice experiences with my mother."

"I wonder about the brown water—whether it also refers to me. [I'm brown skinned.] It's nice, seducing, but scary."

"I guess it could. What I thought of was—well it's actually a bit insulting, but why should it be? I thought that you're my chocolate pudding doctor." D laughed, seemed light hearted, but then let out a loud moan, and then another, and then fell silent.

"Is nothing coming up?" I asked.

"Well it is, but I didn't want to say it. I want to take you to [the city where he grew up, which he would be visiting on the weekend]. It seems too silly." D went on to talk a bit about his home city, but seemed to be talking around something.

"Is it hard to approach something?" I asked.

"It's that I love you. But how can I know that? I don't even really know you." D went on for a bit in an intellectual vein about the nature of love.

"Earlier you got angry at me for prodding you. I wonder if the love has homosexual connotations."

"I'm sure it's not that. It's more like a warm feeling, a closeness."

"Why then do you think you suppressed it and had such a hard time bringing it up?"

"I know it's because it wouldn't be reciprocated, that why. I can't see it at all. I think it will displease you or make you angry."

"Why would I be angry about love?"

"Because we'll leave. It'll end so I can't fall in love. I won't be able to call you up for a coffee. We can't have this love because it will be broken."

"Earlier you cried about your father being dead; now you think of our relationship being broken. Was it just his death? Or the movement from childhood, where he said you would not kiss any more?"

"At a certain point he said we should only shake hands, because I was a man now."

"As with the fantasy you had of us shaking hands or hugging at the end of the analysis. O.K., let's stop here."

In the next session D said he would miss the analysis when I went on vacation. He thought of the good sessions and cried, saying he would miss me, and then worried that something might happen to me during the vacation. We ended up discussing the ending, and D said that he never wanted to end, even though he knew he had to. Couldn't he be the exception? The special one? The one who never ends?

This material relates in many ways to the narcissism and deprivation I described in chapter 6. I present it here because it shows the intimate relation of the toileting trauma and the abandonment anxiety experienced then to the more ongoing deprivations D suffered at his mother's hands. The dream clearly relates to the anxieties of the trauma, including that of falling into the toilet and being flushed away like a turd, but it relates this anxiety both to the transference (the brown water) and to phallic fears. At another time we interpreted the floating piers as phallic symbols, and the thing chasing him as his father, about to castrate him. D hangs onto his girlfriend, and the chocolate water reminds him of warm times spent with his mother and grandmother and relates to the transference, serving both as a protection against the castrating father and as reassurance against abandonment. The seductive but dangerous brown water also had another meaning—a dynamic which emerged more powerfully closer to termination—of a homosexual, passive anal surrender to his father and to myself as his stand-in.

In the sessions after I came back from the vacation, the connection of all this to the visits to the massage parlors came to the fore, as D struggled between wanting to go and thus neutralize all of the anxieties that were coming up, versus experiencing these feelings, which were at times quite overwhelming. A consistent aspect of our analysis of these fears was that D would hold off the experience of these feelings in various ways, including by going to a massage parlor, but at a certain point would be flooded by feelings and strong body experiences. Among the latter were a terrible coldness and shivering and retching that was quite severe, even though he did not actually vomit out anything. These experiences would also disappear as quickly as they had intruded, although with the overwhelming physical reactions D would be left somewhat shaken. The sudden appearance and disappearance of these feelings and reactions had the flavor of zero process functioning.

There were many more subtle physical actions as well. For instance in the second session after the break, D was talking of abandonment. I interpreted a connection to the toileting. He bent his legs one after the other as he lay on the couch and undid and retied his shoelaces. I pointed out that this might relate to what we were talking of—specifically that tying his shoelaces reassured him about being able to get off the toilet. He was at first unconvinced but then it struck me that a breakdown he had had a number of years before beginning analysis had begun when he bent down to tie his shoes and became confused, not remembering how to do it. I pointed this out to D and wondered whether during the breakdown there had been a regression back to the toileting trauma, where he could not get down from the toilet. D then said that in fact he had remained stuck in the bent-over position trying to tie his shoelaces and had become terrified that he would never be able to sit up from the position again.[2] In fact as we both watched more closely from this point on we realized that D's reaching down to tie his shoelaces was a reliable sign that anxiety that was in some way linked to his toileting trauma was beginning to emerge.

There were many similarities between the behavior of material related to the trauma and that related to D's perversion that point, I think, to their deeper connections and to the structural and dynamic similarities between the two. The shoelace tying was repetitive action performed for reassurance, and one that had a concrete tie to the trauma. This was also true of the perversion. Once some of the meanings of the tying became clear, D a number of times caught himself about to do it and mentioned it, but even with my urging he found it almost impossible not to perform the action once the urge was upon him—again very similarly to the visits to the massage parlors. The feelings, memories, and thoughts related to the trauma often popped up quite suddenly and powerfully, triggered by something we were talking of, and would then subside and disappear almost as quickly as they appeared. Similarly D would often be triggered to think about and then visit the massage parlors by certain circumstances, such as seeing an advertisement or getting angry with his girlfriend, although there were other determinants as well. He would be compelled to go, but immediately after he had gone the actual visit would seem quite vague and feel as if it had happened a long time ago. At the time, however, the experience was more intense and immediate than normal experience. This compartmentalization of the visits displays certain characteristics of the zero process.

About four or five months after the sessions described, after having talked about termination on and off for six months, we set a date seven months ahead. One of the first things to come to D's mind after we had set the date was an incident that had occurred when he was 10 or 11. The usual babysitter had not been available and a young girl of 15 had been employed for the evening to look after the two children while D's parents went out for the evening. This babysitter had come in while D was in the washroom, pulled down his pants, and begun to fondle his penis. She had opened up the buttons of her blouse to show him her breasts at the same time. She did not ask him to fondle her, and he thought she had stopped after a few minutes.

D had vaguely and in passing mentioned this incident a couple of times previously. This time he went into a bit more detail, but then tried to dismiss it as unimportant. I was struck by the similarity of this incident to what happened in the massage parlors and pointed this out to D. He seemed to see this too, but never himself went back to the incident. I had to ask him very direct questions in order to get the details of what had happened. I asked D about how he was feeling when the babysitter fondled him. He said he was perhaps curious. I interpreted that perhaps he had experienced what the babysitter had done as a humiliation. He insisted this was not the case. If anything he thought he had gotten some pleasure from it. I pointed out that if we looked at it from the angle of pleasure we could see that it quite neatly reversed a number of unpleasant aspects of the toileting trauma. A woman was present, giving him pleasure and taking an interest in him and his body, reversing the abandonment of himself and the rejection of his stool that he had experienced in his early toilet training. It was like the other screen defenses we had looked at, where he had screened unpleasant realities and feelings with pleasant ones. He agreed with my ideas but did not use them to explore the incident with the babysitter any further. In fact I always had to be the one to bring it up, and each time I did D would laugh as if to say, "Oh, that little thing—you're still harping on it?" I pointed out—with little effect but I think there was some truth in it—that perhaps because he acted it out with the women at the massage parlors, the memory of the fondling had little emotional charge.

A number of traumas were contained in the visits to the massage parlors. A splitting of D's experience was taking place, which allowed him to keep what happened in the massage parlors separate from, and untouched by, what happened in other areas of his life, and vice versa. D never thought about his girlfriend or other parts of his life when he entered the massage parlor. In fact he experienced a kind of threshold phenomenon in which after passing through the door to go inside he felt relaxed and almost like a different person. Similarly he became anxious as he stepped back outside after the sexual massage, but then quickly forgot what had taken place. This was not the sort of forgetting produced by repression, since on questioning he could talk about what had happened, but D simply did not think of it.

During a quite productive termination phase the visits to the massage parlors and the details of what went on in them acquired an even stronger transference meaning than previously. Beyond me as D's father prohibiting the visits as transgressions, it became evident that I was also the woman who would give the sexual massage. He said a number of times that he would not give up going to the massage parlors because of the intense pleasure he got there. Slowly I discovered the various schemes D was hatching to also not terminate the analysis, or to come back later under false pretenses. Ending had the meaning of traumatic abandonment and of castration and, as he had done in his oedipal phase and in adolescence, rather than grappling with these anxieties, and with the sadness of the passing of time and of childhood's end, D tried to sneak around them by various stratagems.

Material that emerged especially during the last part of the analysis linked to D's sister threw some further light on these issues. D had talked very little about his sister when discussing his childhood. Feelings (brought to light in the face of considerable resistances) about patients who would be replacing him after he finished were linked to early reactions to his sister's birth and her continued presence in the house. Murderous impulses were remembered. D was especially jealous of the attention and interest shown by his father in his sister. His father, who was the one warm and emotionally reliable parent that D had, did not ignore D after his sister's birth, but was clearly very fond of his new daughter. D was incensed also that his sister got to dirty her diaper with impunity, given the strict demands made upon him. He formed a strong wish to be taken care of passively like his sister by his father—in effect to replace his sister in her relationship with his father. In the phallic phase this wish acquired an overtly sexual form—to be touched and fondled on his penis by his father. Anal wishes, which came out in the form of anger that I was prodding him from behind, seemed to be a regressive expression of the passive phallic wishes as well as a defense against, and punishment for, his active phallic oedipal wishes towards his mother.

The impulses related to his father were very forcefully repressed because they came to involve a wish to be a girl and to lose his penis. This was connected both to the toileting trauma and to being put to sleep for his tonsillectomy when he was in his oedipal stage. Being passively helpless, dying, and having his self and body fall apart or dissolve, all experiences and fears emanating from these traumas, became entwined with, and regressively used to express, D's castration anxiety from the oedipal phase, but also his passive sexual wishes towards his father. When the babysitter fondled D it brought forth these passive phallic wishes and showed him the way to use this pleasant experience to cover over the trauma in the toilet and his mother's cold handling of him. D connected the babysitter experience to a situation in the washroom, but in this case one that involved pleasure, although there was an aspect of humiliation and overstimulation as well. (In fact an important aspect of the visits to the massage parlors was that they compartmentalized and sexualized a huge amount of aggression against women: against his mother, his sister, the babysitter, and his girlfriends. I have not gone into this aspect in detail for reasons of space, not because of its lack of importance.)

D did not develop the perversion he had at the start of the therapy until later adulthood. The birth of his second child brought up both castration anxiety in relation to now fully replacing his father, and his fury at women— at his wife/mother for neglecting him and his daughter/sister for taking his place as the special one. D began to see prostitutes as a way to split off and bind his aggression and protect against his castration anxiety. This behavior also meant that he was not a big man but still an adolescent or a child. D was especially intent to see that the prostitutes did not react badly to his penis—which they never did. He reasoned that being experienced and having seen all sizes of penises if they did not reject his it meant it was acceptable. Already in this the incident with the babysitter—where a more experienced female showed an interest in his penis—was being re-experienced unconsciously, and used to cover over both his oedipal disappointment (when his penis did not measure up to his father's and was not big enough for his mother), and the traumas and deprivations of his childhood, when he often did not interest his mother sufficiently, and was abandoned because he could not produce a turd (the penis he produced for the prostitutes was his turd).

It was only a number of years later that D settled into the perversion related to the massage parlors. This involved a further regression to passivity and harked back to the one time when his mother was quite solicitous and caring—whenever he was lying in bed sick. But the regression went further—to a time during his first year of life when he and his mother lived with his maternal grandmother and grandfather. His grandmother was physically warm and loving with him and also was the one to change his dirty diapers, since his mother had such an aversion to it. His father only came to live with them at the end of his first year, when he could get a job there, and D and his parents then moved to their own apartment. This was when his early toilet training and the toileting trauma took place, because his mother had such a hard time with his dirty diapers and feces. The perverse actions took D back to a time before the traumas, before his sister's birth, and before his oedipal conflicts—to a time when he was lovingly diapered by his grandmother. Here again there is the use of a pleasant experience to screen unpleasant and traumatic ones. The visits to the massage parlors also bound tremendous rage at women and turned many terrible things—his mother's disgust at his anal productions, for instance—into pleasurable experiences—the woman helping him to create a mess with his ejaculate, and lovingly (he felt) cleaning it up. He was on the changing table like his sister, and like her he was loved and adored by his father. The most deeply repressed meaning of all this was that the actions in the massage parlor meant to be passively loved sexually by his father, taking the place of his sister and his mother. This meaning only became apparent as we approached termination and the end of the analysis came to mean losing his father—as we saw in some of the clinical material presented. The deepest denial contained in his perversion was a denial of the constraints of reality and the passage of time: the book that told of the past was not yet finalized, and it could be rewritten over and over again.

The Causation of Perversions

From what I have said about the development of D's perversion in his adulthood it is evident that he differed from the more classic cases, where the perverse scenario or fetish object is formed in latency. To some extent this difference is not as great as it may appear at first, since even these classic perversions go through changes in adolescence and adulthood, changes that often involve a process of regression, return of the repressed, and return of the denied, just as in D's case. There must be differences, however, and no doubt there are limits to the generalizability of the findings in D's case. But these limits go both ways, so that a case such as D's may be a better place to look for insights into the sorts of perversions more similar to his—which are more common than the classical ones.

In any case my interest is not in the general theory of perversions but in certain defensive and structural aspects of these disorders, and for this D's case serves reasonably well. However, since these aspects cannot be discussed in isolation from other factors, I will present a brief overview of some possible causal factors in the case of D, using especially the multifaceted view of perversions to be found in the work of Phyllis Greenacre, since her conceptions cover so many aspects. In her early paper on fetishism and faulty development of the body image Greenacre (1953) described a continuous lack of warmth, cuddling, and surface stimulation for the infant and young toddler leading to an inadequately defined body surface. In D's case his mother most definitely had trouble with cuddling and physical warmth. He noted that all the photos taken by his father showed her holding him at a distance. She also had powerful aversive reactions to feces and diaper changing, as evidenced both through reconstructions and through her extreme reactions to her grandchildren's soiled diapers. Greenacre (1953) talks of the child being treated as a contaminated object by the mother, and this seems to have been true for D at least in the limited sense that he was treated this way when he had soiled his diaper or had dirtied himself in other ways. The warm physical and emotional relationship with his maternal grandparents in his first year, his having the same with his father after this, and the fact that his mother was capable of emotional closeness at times, all probably protected D from a more severe perversion.

The move away from the grandparents led D's mother to attempt very early toilet training, which she carried out in a way that severely traumatized him. Greenacre (1955) emphasized the presence in those suffering from perversions of these sorts of very early stresses such as mutilating attacks, operations, and accidents at the time of the transition from the dominance of the primary process to the secondary process, in the second year of life. This led to a melding of drive and affect discharge channels and to a huge increase in aggression. Stoller (1975) also stressed the importance of severe trauma and the massive aggression that this brings up.

The presence of D's need for warmth, body surface stimulation, and a reassurance against abandonment in his visits to the massage parlors are obvious enough. In the analysis the visits were very concretely linked to the emergence of feelings from early neglect and traumatization, and were analyzed as attempts to reassure himself. Here we can see the operation of the sort of screen defenses discussed in the chapter on narcissism, which were favorites of D's. The screen experiences involved especially the cuddling and physical and emotional warmth shown him by his grandmother and father and the experience with the babysitter in his preteen years, all of which were recalled unconsciously in the perversion. This screen aspect of perverse behavior was pointed out early on by Sachs (1986 [1923]) and Fenichel (1945). We may be tempted at this point to advance a tentative dynamic formulation, saying that perversions are a form of screen defense in which actual experiences from the past of physical pleasure and of sexual excitement are used as a screen against early traumatic experiences. Such a formulation clearly has some validity, but it is incomplete because it leaves out splitting of the ego. This splitting can be inferred from the clinical material, for instance from the way in which the visits to the massage parlors would feel like so long ago soon after they had happened. I will deal with splitting of the ego in the next section.

We could wonder at this point, however, about what leads to the sexual screen defense being adopted. The factors of neglectful mothering and early trauma are relatively nonspecific, and can by themselves lead to a number of other disturbances instead of a perversion. Following the ideas presented in the chapter on narcissism, we would expect that repeated experiences of sexual satisfaction and bodily gratifications would lead to a fixation and the use of these experiences for screening purposes. This is evident in D's experience with the babysitter, although his general narcissistic overstimulation and tendency to use screen defenses probably made him more likely to use this particular experience as a screen. Other factors were the timing (in early adolescence as certain passive wishes and sexual feelings from childhood were being strongly revived) and the fact that the incident occurred in a washroom just as had the earlier traumas. Even taking these other factors into account, however, our earlier considerations regarding screen defenses should warn us not to underestimate the importance of overgratification, which I have already said in D's case involved not just the babysitter incident, but also his father's intense investment in him and warm physical and emotional love of him, his grandparents with whom he lived in his first year of life and who loved him so dearly, his grandmother's physical warmth, and even his mother who, when he was ill with minor illnesses, was extremely solicitous and coddling.

What was said about early neglect and trauma, however, could also be asserted regarding overgratifications: they are not particularly specific to the perversions. Even bodily overgratifications do not have any simple causative link to the perversions, although they obviously play a part. It would seem that the ego fixations that result from overgratifications are a fertile soil for the growth of perversions, but that there has to be a confluence of a number of factors for a perverse outcome. Greenacre (1955) suggested that the specific factors in the perversions are phallic phase traumas such as for instance seeing a bleeding miscarriage. Stoller (1975) also emphasizes a trauma specifically directed against the masculinity or femininity of the young child. He said that the perversion is a reliving of an actual historical trauma aimed at the child's sexuality. "How better to prove his triumph than to be potent in the face of the original trauma?" he asks (p 79). For Greenacre (1955) it was a combination of early trauma and disturbances in early care, followed by these later phallic phase traumas, that were the specific causative factors in the perversions. Roiphe and Galenson (1973), based partly on their observational studies, also emphasized that it was the interweaving of intense abandonment and body disintegration anxieties with the fears from the phallic-oedipal phase that lead to perversions, and they contrast this to the more focal anxieties about the genitals seen in other situations.

If we examine D's case in relation to these ideas, we can observe that he had a phallic phase trauma in the form of the tonsillectomy, which he certainly fantasized as an attack on his genitals. However it lacked the character of some phallic phase traumas that much more specifically target the genitals. To give an example: a patient of mine with a severe perversion that developed in latency experienced an incident at age 4 where an older cousin, an aggressive and bullying type, coerced a mutual female cousin, also 4, to pull down her panties and expose herself. My patient had tagged along with the older kids and his young female cousin, not really knowing what was planned. He felt scared and excited, and as his young female cousin pulled down her panties he was shocked, thinking immediately that "what she had between her legs looked like a penis pulled out by its roots." He was "in a daze" and felt "numb." His use of these words to describe the experience clearly marked it out as a trauma. He had become terrified that he would be asked to expose himself next, and that the older boy would rip off his penis. At its deepest level this represented both a fear and a wish.

Such an incident would not be traumatic to every young boy who experienced it. My patient was vulnerable. He had been raised by a cold, rigid mother in a very restrained family, where open displays of feeling were taboo. He had no sisters and his mother was very careful with undressing, so that the incident was probably my patient's first sight of a female genital. There had also not been any discussion of male/female differences by the parents. Thus the sight of his cousin's genitals was truly a shock, especially given the circumstances (a bullying older boy made her do it) and my patient's being in his phallic phase with its intense interest in his penis.

In fact this patient provides an interesting contrast to D on a number of points. On the one hand, the lack of emotional and physical warmth in his early (and later) childhood was much more pronounced than was the case with D, who had the warm love and interest of both of his grandparents and of his father. The relationships with their fathers of these two patients provide the greatest contrast. I have already described the love, emotional availability, and warmth of D's father. My other patient's father was very shy, quiet, and almost nonexistent in his emotional reaction to the patient, except for the very occasional mocking remarks. This emotionally absent father is what is described most frequently in the history of males with perversions. That this situation makes a boy's sense of his own masculinity more fragile, and his castration anxiety stronger, is obvious enough.

Stoller's (1975) ideas about core gender identity allow us to be more specific about what the problem is, as well as bringing out one reason for the higher prevalence of perversions in males versus females. Stoller maintained that the first identification of both male and female infants is with their mother. This is a very powerful primary identification, and in order to establish a secure masculine core gender identity[3] a male child needs an involved father or father figure whom they can use to pull themselves out of this first primary identification. (Greenson [1966, 1968] gives a very clear description and example of this process.) In the absence of such a figure, or if the mother interferes with this process, or both, then the young boy is left with a dread of being engulfed by the mother, which is to a great extent a dread of giving in to their own powerful primary identification with their mother. The perversion helps shore up the person's core gender identity. This is especially true of the fetishistic aspects of the perversion where the valued fetish is unconsciously both the penis of the mother and, through the fetishist's merger with the woman, becomes a hard, indestructible phallus for the male as well (Greenacre, 1955, 1968). (These ideas of Stoller and Greenson have not gone unchallenged. Diamond [2004] summarized the criticisms of others as well as presenting his own. A full discussion of this issue is beyond the scope of this chapter, but I will say that I think these newer ideas relate to secondary identifications—for instance Diamond mentions the boy's identification with his mother's idea of masculinity as being a part of his gender identity—and do not really contradict those of Stoller, which relate to the primary identification that takes place before the establishment of secure self/object boundaries.)

My patient with the absent father developed a fantasy of a young girl sitting on his chest with her panties on, as he stared at her crotch. This was his first masturbation fantasy. It caught the moment just before he saw his cousin's genitals. There were of course many determinants of this fantasy and its later elaborations in adult perverse actions, but one central one was that the panties covering the crotch and later derivatives of this such as the thick pubic hair of women he would have sit on him, had the fetishistic meaning of a symbol for the female phallus. (Another important determinant was the patient's sight of his mother in her underwear as she dressed.) In a case such as this the insecure male core gender identity is one of the factors, maybe the main factor, making the phallic phase happenings so traumatic. While there were hints of similar issues in the case of D (as there would be with any man, since male core gender identity is generally not as secure as female core gender identity), they were not nearly so dominant. His perversion certainly represented his feminine wishes to be loved sexually by his father, but his terror of giving way to this wish was nowhere near that of my other patient, and thus his perversion proved more amenable to analysis.

As can be seen from the clinical material presented in the last section, for D the narcissistic issues of changing unpleasant realities, clinging to childhood pleasures, and being able to reverse time and never put a final stamp of reality on occurrences he did not like dominated his perverse actions, as they did so many areas of his life. Janine Chasseguet-Smirgel (1974) has especially stressed this aspect of perversions. My other patient also had powerful denials that were expressed in his sexual practices, but these were to a much greater extent focused on sexual differences and the woman's lack of a penis. However, each patient had this more narrowly focused denial, as well as the more broad denial of unpleasant realities such as the passage of time, contained in their perversion. It was only the relative weighing of the factors that differed. Both patients had body disintegration anxieties, which were inextricably interwoven with their castration anxiety. Both had early deficits in mothering, but also areas of overgratification (my other patient had a skin condition on his penis that his mother tended to for many years) to which they clung unconsciously as a screen for the pain of the deficient mothering. Both had early, pre-phallic shock traumas (I have only described D's) and both had phallic phase traumas. These were all factors observed by Greenacre to be key determinants of perversion. However, there were crucial contrasts, most importantly in their father's relation to them, which led to some important differences in the dynamics of these two patients. The other major difference was in the nature of the phallic phase trauma, which was a more direct threat to the genitals in my other patient than in D.

It would seem that it is the confluence of numerous factors that leads to the final outcome of structured adult perversions, and that these perversions can differ quite a bit in their structure and meanings depending on the presence and relative weight of these various factors. None of what I have said so far about perversions is original, although I have stressed the importance of overgratification and screen defenses, not because this aspect is more important than others but because it is sometimes neglected. Where we can break new ground is in the application to perversions of some of the ideas developed in earlier chapters with regard to trauma.

Splitting of the Ego

I think that what Freud (1938a, 1938b) called splitting of the ego is a compound defense, combining primary and secondary dissociation with denial. As Freud described it, in splitting of the ego the person takes two opposite attitudes toward a distressing external reality. In the example he used most often a young boy, when faced with the female genital combined with earlier threats from adults that his penis would be cut off if he touched it, takes two opposite attitudes to the experience. He is convinced that the girl's or woman's genitals are the product of castration, in which her penis was cut off, and becomes terrified that the same will be done to his. On the other hand he denies what he has seen, insisting that the girl has a penis and thus that he is not in danger. Freud said that these two attitudes existed side by side, without influencing each other or leading to some kind of compromise, as is more normal in neuroses.

The patient whom I described briefly in the last section, who was traumatically exposed to his young cousin's genitals at the age of 4, is a good example of this sort of split. In his analysis many fantasies relating to women having a hidden penis of some sort either within the vagina or in the pubic hair emerged. These were actually toned down versions of the core belief, that his cousin had had a penis when he had looked at her. This idea existed alongside the knowledge of the true nature of male and female genitals, and alongside the memory, actually one encoded into zero-functioning during trauma, of what he actually had seen that fateful day when his cousin pulled down her underwear. What especially marked this as a splitting of the ego was the fact that the fantasies about the female genital were quite accessible to consciousness if the patient turned his attention to them—which is characteristic of denial defenses. In the more normal situation such fantasies from early childhood are energetically repressed, along with the childhood sexual desires and experiences with which they are connected. This patient, when he was describing these ideas, could get to the point of talking of them with full conviction, in an almost trance-like state. He could then snap out of this in an instant and seem quite realistic in his assessment of the nature of male-female differences. There were connections from each of these attitudes toward reality that led back to the traumatic incident with his cousin.

We can see from this patient's reaction in analysis the melding of the attentional aspects of a denial defense with the split that comes from primary dissociation. We can infer this tight linking of the different defenses in such a compound defense from their behavior during analysis, where it is found to be impossible to analyze one part (for instance in this case the denial or the dissociation) separately. This is in contrast to other situations, for instance examples of D using various attentional defenses to avoid facing what he did at massage parlors, where the attentional defenses could be analyzed quite separately from the dissociation. I gave examples in the clinical material of D using various maneuvers to supplement his dissociation of his early traumas, which were separate from the dissociation and not part of a compound defense. In the chapter on repression I presented examples of using denial defenses to buttress a weakening primal repression, while in the chapter on denial I described (in the section titled "transference") how E's primal denial of her mother's lack of love was helped by a secondary repression. In these and other situations of defenses acting in concert or sequentially, the resistance to which each defense gives rise can be analyzed separately. This is not the case with compound defenses. A compound defense is composed of two or more basic defensive processes, such as a denial and dissociation, which act in concert and are quite tightly bound together. In the case of defenses acting together that are not compounded, one can generally analyze each part separately, but the inability to do this indicates that the defenses are more tightly bound in a compound defense. (I will describe other forms of compound defenses later in this chapter.)

Unfortunately Freud, and many analysts after him, took findings regarding splitting of the ego—a specific compound defense involving primary and secondary dissociation and denial—and generalized them in two directions: with regard to trauma and dissociation, and with regard to denial. To deal with the generalization related to denial first: Freud suggested that all denials involved a split in the ego, an idea that inhibited the study of denial as a separate defense. This is not to say that nothing valuable has come out of this way of looking at things. Some authors have usefully conceptualized the avoidance of unpleasant realities as involving the use of splitting of the ego. Arlow (1971) described "character perversion," where the ability to see but also not see unpleasant reality was used quite pervasively. Arlow traced this form of character back to the denial of genital differences through splitting of the ego. His view was that this was a specific defense, which these men used more generally than when it is seen in a circumscribed perversion. Grossman (1992, 1996) has also written about the perverse attitude toward reality. He described patients looking away from, looking without experiencing, not focusing on, and not registering distressing realities. His examples clearly involve the defense of splitting of the ego.

D is an excellent example of the sort of patient Grossman and Arlow described. He used the opportunity offered by his original splits to deal with all sorts of unpleasant realities. They would end up compartmentalized—not repressed, but simply not thought about because they were in another room in his mind. As Grossman described it, D saw certain realities, such as his father's death for instance, but did not focus on them or fully register them. Or actually he *did* register them, but in a compartment of his mind that also contained his split off traumas. He both saw and did not see, knew and did not know; and the part of his mind that saw and knew contained traumatic memories and functioned in a different manner than the normal secondary process, but different also from the primary process of the id. This zero process mode of functioning led to these denied realities being dealt with in quite characteristic ways, especially involving concrete actions.

One thing I would point out about D, however, is that not all of his denials were as closely tied to his ego splits as was his denial of his father's death. D's fondness for denial had a number of sources: his many overgratifications discussed in the chapter on narcissism, an identification with the example offered by his mother, as well as the early traumas that led to the use of splitting of the ego. But looking at D's major denials at least, we could wonder if Freud was right all along to connect all denials to splitting of the ego. D's experience of his mother's narcissism and lack of love was tied to the major shock trauma of the early toileting as well as, no doubt, other traumas of varying intensity related to emotional abandonment. Perhaps denials, even if based on other factors as well, need the splitting seen in trauma to anchor them, strengthen them, and give them persistence over time. Is it also possible that the splitting left over from trauma provides the structure that is needed for the knowing but not knowing of denial to be produced?

My answer to the last question is that while the split provides such a structure in the particular defense of splitting of the ego, this structure is not a necessary prerequisite for someone to use the defense of denial, even if it is a strong denial with great persistence through time. I have already put forward (in chapters 2 and 3 especially) the idea that pervasive negative affect can lead to the setting up of primal defenses. Pervasive affect is too strong for normal working over (physical, psychical, and verbal expression) to handle, but it does not lead to the shutting down of many ego functions seen in trauma (that is to say, it does not massively breach the stimulus barrier). Rather, defenses such as repression and forms of denial are brought into play to deal with the cause (e.g., a drive, a distressing reality) of the pervasive affect. These are the defenses I have suggested should be designated as primal defenses (e.g., primal externalization, primal reaction formation). They serve as the templates for many later (after) defenses.

What is the proof of this? Let's take for instance D's denial of his mother's coldness and lack of deep caring for him. I presented a little bit of our analysis of this defense in the chapter on narcissism. After interpreting various denials such as minimizations and defensive internalizations, D came face to face with the shallowness of his mother's love for him and felt intense sadness. His last line of defense—a common one that I think reflected a primal denial—was to forcefully say, "It isn't true. It can't be true. I don't want it, and I won't think it. I won't." The point I am trying to make is that one can get to primal denials such as this and uncover the pervasive affect that motivates them, without finding signs of trauma such as primary dissociation or zero process functioning. Similarly one can get to the core of certain primal repressions, which condition later after repressions, and find only pervasive anxiety and a strong counterforce motivated by it, not the signs of trauma. This was the case with D's repression of his death wishes towards his father and sexual wishes towards his mother. When we approached the core of these defenses in the analysis (see chapter 2) there was intense anxiety but again no real sign of trauma. However, I shall describe shortly how D's oedipal wishes did get entangled with his early traumas, something that probably happens to some extent for everyone.

In reiterating, in relation to Freud's concept of splitting of the ego, the basic idea that denial defenses, even in their primal form, are not necessarily a product of trauma, I am anxious not to throw out the baby with the bath-water. Freud's mistake in relation to splitting of the ego was not one of obser-vation or necessarily even of conceptualization, only of overgeneralization. He was clearly correct in seeing that his patients had suffered from traumas and that the defense he was observing was a product of trauma. I have de-scribed his overgeneralization with regard to this defense being the basis for all denials. Freud to some extent, but also other analysts who followed him, overgeneralized in another direction. They often saw splitting of the ego as the basic traumatic defense, while in reality it is only one of many possible defensive constellations that can be produced to deal with trauma. In fact in the early days of psychoanalysis Breuer and Freud (1893) described patients who employed another of these—a compound defense that melded dissocia-tion and repression. This defense plays an important role in the spectrum of dissociative identity disorders (formerly called multiple personality).

An important point to remember is that primary dissociation is not a defense—that is, it is not an ego function or the outcome of an ego activity. In fact one could say it is exactly the opposite: the outcome of a lack of ego activity. To be more specific, it is the structural outcome of trauma, a product of the breakdown of ego functions that occurs when the stimulus barrier is overwhelmed. This breakdown in functioning leads to the laying down of the "frozen" memories that occupy areas of primary dissociation. These are the classic traumatic memories. It is only as the ego resumes some level of normal functioning after the trauma that defenses such as denial begin to operate against these memories. It could be argued that these defenses, for instance denial combined with primary dissociation, are not strictly speak-ing compound defenses. They involve the combination of a defense and the structural outcome of a trauma, which distinguishes them from, for instance, compound obsessive defenses, where two active defensive processes, a coun-terforce one and an attentional one, are combined (see "conclusion" to this chapter, below). On the other hand examples of splitting of the ego where denial is combined with secondary dissociation do involve the melding of two defensive processes.

Defenses become associated with the primary structural split of trauma in various ways that are not, strictly speaking, compound defenses. They can operate against one aspect or another of the split. For instance the frozen traumatic memories can be repressed. These memories can also be denied in various ways—as an example D used a screen defense against the abandon-ment and coldness of the toileting trauma, by having experiences of warm physical contact in the massage parlors. Denial can also use the split for its own purposes. Areas of primary dissociation provide a ready-made compartment in the mind, into which unpleasant realities can be thrown and the psychic door closed. E did this with her oedipal fantasies and wishes. These were associated with the split off memories of her father's abuse of her and denied along with it. A split attitude toward reality can be laid on top of the original split from the trauma. For instance D both accepted the reality of his smallness and weakness, and his small penis compared to his father, and denied it, feeling he was the big man in the house, and had won the oedipal competition for his mother. The reality of his smallness and helplessness became associated with the split off memories from the toileting trauma, while the denial of this smallness was associated with the other side of the traumatic split, where the situation of utter helplessness had not occurred. D's castration anxiety was regressively represented by his fear of falling into the toilet and being flushed away as his turd had been.

This intertwining of oedipal issues with trauma is one of the hallmarks of perversions. In D's case this solution—actually an attempt to avoid a resolution—of his oedipal complex was not consolidated until his adolescent and early adult years. In other cases, such as the other patient I presented earlier with a fixed perversion, the oedipal resolution at latency already clearly was based on the compound defenses of trauma, especially splitting of the ego. It is not a question of either/or, however, since in these cases also adolescent and adult reworking of the latency resolution takes place. But the difference on where the accent falls is important. In D's case it was my impression that causation from "above"—especially the narcissistic ego fixations that I described in the chapter on narcissism—was the more important factor. D was determined in adolescence and young adulthood that he would not fully accept the limitations of reality and morality. This especially involved not resolving his negative oedipus complex, the resolution of which leads to a more fully internalized superego and wished for self-image. D defended against this resolution in many ways. One of them was to push the issues back into his early childhood, and use the intertwining of his oedipal conflicts and earlier trauma to good effect. By continuing to frame his oedipal conflicts in terms of the toilet training trauma, D became the victim, and his mother the aggressor. He was too young to know right from wrong or to have any responsibility for what happened to him. He could feel sorry for himself as a victim, and use this feeling as a powerful tool to avoid feeling guilt and facing responsibility. In other cases, such as my other patient with a perversion, the accent falls more strongly on the severe early traumas and deficits in parental involvement. Splitting of the ego is, according to the conception I have presented, a compound of dissociation and denial. In terms of their defenses D's splitting of the ego was driven more by the denial (attentional)

268 ~ Chapter Eight

aspects of this compound defense, while the splitting of the ego of my other patient was weighted more towards his primary and secondary dissociations.

Trauma and Anxiety

I should at this point address a seeming contradiction between what I have just said regarding D and what I have asserted previously. In the chapter on repression I presented a few sessions from D's analysis, using this data as part of my argument that the motive force for repression is not traumatic anxiety—an overwhelming of the ego—but is better conceptualized as pervasive anxiety—an unpleasant affect that cannot be worked over through normal channels. I have just said, however, that D's castration anxiety was regressively represented by a fear that had reached unbearable heights during his toileting trauma: the fear that he would fall into the toilet and be flushed away like a turd. Castration and body dissolution anxieties thus were intertwined, with D's body, turd, and penis all being connected symbolically. One way to resolve this contradiction would be to say that the initial repression of D's oedipal wishes took place in the way suggested earlier (motivated by pervasive anxiety) and that the repressed contents became secondarily connected with the traumatic memories. This was certainly true, and in fact these secondary connections were made at various times in his life. For instance when D began having sex in later adolescence, he became quite frightened by the woman's loss of control as she reached orgasm. He would often lose his erection at these points. He explained this as being a consequence of his fear of engulfment by the woman, or that the loss of control scared him because he did not know what she would do. These fears seemed clearly related to being castrated by the woman, and to the more regressive fear of losing his identity and being merged with the woman. What was interesting was that when we delved more deeply into D's actual fear we came to a fantasy of being sucked—first his penis and then his whole body—into the woman's vagina as she lost control. This was shown by D's associations to be a version of his traumatic fear of being sucked down into the toilet when his mother left him there at too young an age. The woman's moaning and the rhythmic contractions of her vagina were quite concretely connected in his mind with the whooshing sound of the flushing water and its being pulled down out of the toilet bowl.

This example is a good illustration of the way in which traumatic memories that are under the sway of the zero process, especially those from the height of the traumatic fears, provide the concrete content of the basic childhood fears. The intense genital anxieties of the oedipal period and earlier body disintegration and abandonment anxieties seem especially to become linked to concrete traumatic memories. This is an aspect of what Freud was getting at by referring to traumatic anxieties as the motive for repression.

It is also true, however, that these traumatic memories can only provide a motive for the working of repression or any other defense after the true trauma has passed and ego functioning has been restored. In the more severe, "classic" perversions, such as the other patient I presented with the perversion starting in latency, the core sexual anxieties are related to trauma right when functioning is restored—in fact they reach their height during this phase, and thus we see the predominance of splitting defenses. In D's case the connections were to a greater extent drawn secondarily, although the trauma of the tonsillectomy during the phallic phase was closer to a primary connection. To say that perversion depends on trauma being too intimately connected to a person's sexual conflicts and anxieties is really to repeat what has been said by others, such as Stoller and Greenacre, but I have tried to delve more deeply into the defensive aspect of this connection.

It is clear that looking at this aspect of perversions cannot answer all the questions about these disorders. However I think the conceptualization of different defenses based on primary and secondary dissociation is helpful not only in deepening our understanding of certain aspects of perversions, but also of many other disorders. I have already mentioned dissociative identity disorder, but others also come to mind. For instance in phobias there is also an intimate connection between core developmental anxieties and zero process traumatic memories, but the compound defenses are different from the perversions. At the same time each perversion is built around a core phobia of certain sexual situations and acts, for which the perverse actions substitute.

To go much further into the connections of the perversions and trauma would completely break the boundaries of our investigation into the processes of defense. I hope to undertake a book length investigation of trauma and the zero process in the future, which will include not only the issues already mentioned, but which will also attempt to look at topics such as developmental aspects of the zero process, the zero process and dreams, neurophysiological and evolutionary aspects, zero process symptoms and neuroses, and a number of other topics. However, to do this will require a much deeper investigation of the zero process itself. It will also necessitate a differentiation of the splitting caused by trauma from the more general and widespread splits seen in borderline disorders, which I believe have a different causation. I feel that this sort of investigation has the possibility of revolutionizing a certain aspect of both the theory and practice of psychoanalysis, and of our conception of the functioning of the mind more generally. To give an idea of what I mean by this, I will very briefly touch on a few topics that relate to perversions, but which also give a glimpse of these more general ideas, and of the wider vistas that can be opened up by investigations of the zero process. These topics are zero process symptoms, zero process neuroses, and zero process defenses.

Zero Process Symptoms and Zero Process Neuroses

As is evident from the examples and discussion so far, many characteristics of the perversions are best explained as products of zero process functioning. This is not to say that the perversions are a pure expression of the zero process, any more than dreams are a pure expression of the primary process. Rather, as is the case with dreams and the primary process, in perversions we can see many of the unique characteristics of the zero process, even if clothed in dynamics related to the primary and secondary processes. I have already mentioned the "triggering" of the actions by concrete realities, and the tendency for the perverse symptom to repeat, in a disguised but rigid manner, aspects of the trauma. In D's case, once it was triggered, the pull towards action was powerful. The actions themselves in the massage parlors followed a sequence that felt compelling and was relatively invariant, both characteristic ways in which the zero process expresses itself.

While we can see quite clearly the connection of D's perverse enactments with the zero process, his entire neurosis was not dominated by these dynamics. I think it is reasonable to refer to these enactments as *zero process symptoms*: that is, the symptom was at its core under the domination of the zero process. The other perverse patient I described briefly, with the phallic phase trauma of seeing his cousin's genitals in an aggressively charged atmosphere, provides a more "classic" example of a perversion. His personality and his life were to a much greater extent under the spell of his trauma. I would designate this patient's disorder, and those like it, as a *zero process neurosis*. By this term I mean that the zero process and zero process defenses (see below) are at the core of the key symptoms and dominate the character of patients suffering from these neuroses. This is not to say that in such circumstances there is not a large admixture of libidinal and aggressive fixations and fantasies—for instance in this patient's case, oedipal fantasies and castration anxieties were intermixed with the contents of areas of zero process functioning. As well, reality issues—for instance in this patient's case his quite cold and rigid mother—and their distorting effects on development and the attentional defenses used against them, were important, but were also largely refracted through zero process functioning. I would call these zero process neuroses not because of the absence or small importance of these sorts of drive and reality fixations, conflicts, and defenses, but because they are to a great extent absorbed into, and expressed through, aspects of the zero process. There is no doubt a continuum here. At one end would be patients with at least some zero process symptoms (if we look closely enough we all fall at least into this category), while as these increase in importance and scope, we move into the area of zero process neuroses. I think it can be shown that phobias, conversion symptoms, and perversions are zero process symptoms, and can be conceptualized as zero process neuroses if these symptoms dominate the patient's dynamics.

Along with triggering effects and a characteristic rigid form of post-traumatic repetition, the perverse symptoms of D and my other patient display a number of the other characteristics of the zero process. These include the lack of integration of aspects of memory with each other and with other parts of the person's mental functioning, as well as the frozen yet quasi-perceptual nature of what appears in the symptoms. The latter aspect I discussed in the chapter on trauma in relation to episodic, perceptual memories. There I noted that these zero process memories have characteristics of both perception and memory: they had the retentive quality of memory, but otherwise behaved as a present perception that unfolded outside of the subject's ability to stop it or scan it back and forth, as he or she could do with a regular memory.

This characteristic of the zero process extends beyond episodic memories, however. Within an area of zero process functioning affects, drives, wishes, actions, bodily sensations, semantic (knowledge) memories, and implicit (emotional and procedural) memories all have the retentive quality of memory, but in other ways when triggered impinge immediately as a present, lived experience. Given that the height of trauma involves a lack of processing of affects, a numb feeling, and a frozen state in many other ways such as action and drive, it may seem unlikely that affects, for instance, could be part of the zero process. However, I believe they are. Much of the zero process exists as potential experience. Affects and actions, as examples, involve the potential affects and actions that were brought to a halt by the traumatic process, but can come into present experience when triggered. This "potential" nature of the zero process demonstrates the limits to the frozen nature of its contents: they are not processed in most of the usual ways—for instance there is no abstraction, categorization, or retranscription of memories, nor abreaction of affects—but there is triggering and reliving of what De M'Uzan (2003) called repetition of the identical. Similarly, while the contents of the zero process are not integrated in most of the usual ways, with each other or with the

rest of the person's psyche they can, when triggered, "repeat the identical"—
i.e., the bits and pieces of the zero process memory are strung together in
sequence to give an "instant replay" of parts of the trauma.

The material already detailed regarding D and his perversions shows these
aspects of the zero process at work. Other zero process neurotic symptoms,
such as phobias, share the hyper-real quality and the immediacy of an intense
reliving that were also present in D's perverse symptoms. Of course the differences between these different types of symptoms suggest a different way in
which these areas of zero process functioning are dealt with and expressed.
Every trauma leads to phobias. D, as I described, had intense fears of water-
falls and of women's orgasms, both of which were linked to his early toileting
trauma.

In relation to both perversions and phobias, conceptualizing the zero
process characteristics of the symptoms allows us to understand the seeming
contradiction of often excellent ego functioning in areas outside of the symptom and the almost psychotic, quasi-delusional qualities of the symptoms,
in terms of the intensity of the affects and the disregard for many aspects
of reality. These qualities have led some to consider perversions as half way
between the neuroses and psychoses, but I think this is a mistake. It puts perversions on a continuum with other disorders with regard to characteristics
of the primary process (level of drive regression) and secondary process (level
of ego impairment), when really these "psychotic" qualities of the perversions have to do not with the primary or the secondary processes, but with
a different world of phenomena. These zero process phenomena cannot be
arranged on a continuum with primary and secondary process manifestations.
The seemingly contradictory and confusing nature of perversions comes from
trying to comprehend these manifestations using ideas developed in order to
understand other types of mental functioning.

Zero Process Defenses

In general, the basic mechanism of a defense is an ego maneuver, in which
the ego either uses one or more of its own functional abilities (attention,
thought, etc.), or actively uses an aspect of the primary or zero processes.
In repression the ego makes use of the aggressive drive as well as its own
ability both to neutralize aggression and to deploy this partially neutralized aggression for various purposes. Common instances of the ego's use
of primary process characteristics for its own purposes are displacement
transferences, both within and outside of therapy. In these the ego makes
use of the primary process tendency towards displacement along lines of

superficial similarity, as well as condensation and archaic symbolization, for defensive purposes.

There is also a quite large class of defenses in which the ego makes use of certain characteristics of the zero process for defensive purposes. I would suggest that these defenses could be referred to as *zero process defenses*. We have already looked at two of these defenses—secondary dissociation and splitting of the ego.

There are other defenses that make use of the lack of integration of areas of zero process functioning with the rest of psyche. Splitting of a person's identity is a major one. This defense dominates the clinical picture in dissociative identity disorder (formerly called multiple personality disorder—see Brenner, 2001, 2004). Using the terminology I just introduced, dissociative identity disorder can be conceptualized as a zero process neurosis. The particular defense of splitting of identity also exists in people without the full-blown zero process neurosis of dissociative identity disorder. In these cases it is often undetected. I described a bit of this with E in the chapter on trauma, but at the time of her analysis my understanding of this defense had not progressed as far as it has at this point. Many, perhaps all, people who suffer ongoing trauma develop a splitting of their identity. This is often kept relatively hidden, for instance in separate trains of thought, or during times of silence when other identities may be more active. I realize this is a controversial area for many analysts, who may see these separate identities as fantasies or as some kind of play acting of various fantasy structures, perhaps aided and abetted by naïve therapists who treat these identities or personalities as real and separate entities.

I am not able to go into the controversies about multiple personality at this point. I myself think that these separate, often hidden personalities are "real" in the sense that they are intrapsychic structures that go beyond merely a fantasy. They are real in the same sense as introjects, for example, or the superego. Splitting of the identity is another defense that uses the split off aspect of the zero process. The clue as to what the mechanism of this defense is, is that there is always a good deal of mutual animosity between the separate identities. This animosity can in some instances be hidden, but if one analyzes the relationship between the identities it is always there and as it is uncovered its strength is often quite arresting. As we were analyzing the attitude towards each other of the two identities of one of my patients who had suffered serious sexual abuse, I suggested that these two identities disliked each other. "They *loath* each other," she said quietly and emphatically. I believe that this mutual animosity is a version of a counterforce defense, using aggression that is quite a bit less neutralized than it is in repression.

When analyzed as a defense—that is, when I have interpreted that the mutual denigration of the two identities is a way of protecting the patient from memories and powerful feelings—there is usually the emergence of certain unpleasant affects that seem to motivate the defense. As the mutual animosity between the identities is re-established, these intensely unpleasurable feelings disappear. Looking at this particular defense from the point of view of the basic components of a defensive process (motive, mechanism, object), I would say the motive can be quite a number of affects (psychic pain and anxiety being the most common); the mechanism involves aggression added to an original split caused by trauma, in order to keep two psychic conglomerates separate; and the object of this defense—what it defends against—are especially drives and strong affects. The wishes and affects contained in the separate identities are kept apart by mutual aggression. This is not to say that the identities do not contain and keep apart certain memories and pieces of knowledge as well, but I think this is analogous to the way in which various memories and pieces of knowledge are repressed, along with drives, into the primary process. These are caught up in the larger defensive process because of their connection with the drives and affects, and are not the main object of the defensive mechanism.

I realize all of this may sound a little strange, especially when the ideas are presented without illustrative clinical material. In fact the way in which the areas of the mind and defenses operate when under the influence of the zero process *is* quite strange. At the same time much of this area is quite fascinating. In relation to the use of the zero process splits (primary dissociation) for defensive purposes, we can distinguish two basic forms of defense: an attentional one (splitting of the ego) that combines denial with the split, and is used especially to deal with unwelcome realities; and a counterforce one (splitting of the identity), in which aggressive drive energy is combined with zero process splits to defend against drive wishes and strong affects. These defenses have similarities to denial and repressive defenses that do not use aspects of the zero process, as well as some important differences. One similarity is that when it comes to defending directly against powerful drive wishes and associated affects, some form of aggressive drive energy is usually used, while shifts of attention and other more purely secondary process based maneuvers are used to defend against aspects of reality. A key difference is that repression and denial work to keep certain feelings, wishes, and realities from conscious knowledge, while zero process splitting defenses do allow some access for these defended against elements into consciousness, and work partly by splitting consciousness itself. This access of both sides of the split to conscious awareness challenges our ideas about what the aims of a defense are, and about how a defense mechanism achieves its aims.

Lack of integration is only one characteristic of the zero process, and there are defenses in which the ego makes use of other characteristics of zero process functioning. An important, varied, but largely unrecognized class of these defenses uses the "in-between" nature of the zero process: its contents have not yet been processed to form a past experience but are rather, from a psychical perspective, still an about-to-happen, potential experience. One way to describe this class of defenses is to say that they attempt to change the past. At a psychic level, traumatic experiences under zero process functioning have not yet happened, and these defenses make use of this to rewind the tape and avoid the upset that would come after the occurrence of the trauma. "No need to worry," the defenses would say, if they could speak. "We haven't yet written the final chapter of that book, so we really don't know how it will turn out. Everyone may end up living happily ever after." Originally these defenses are used to keep at bay the overwhelming affects related to the trauma itself but, as with zero process splitting defenses, they are subsequently called in to deal with various conflicts and upsets—for instance oedipal conflicts, and the painful relinquishment of childhood during adolescence and early adulthood. Many painful things can be kept in the future by being tied to the core zero process memories. This was an important defense for D, who remained in the position of a child who had not yet had to face the disappointments of childhood—or adulthood for that matter. The loss of his special place in the family, of his childhood when he was coddled by his father and grandparents, and the loss of his father through death—all these things were placed, through the magic of the zero process, in D's future. They had not happened yet, and there was no reason to mourn or otherwise come to terms with these losses.

Many of the fantasies and enactments in perversions are a product of these sorts of zero process defenses. For D the toileting trauma and what happened with his babysitter in later childhood had not yet happened. He could enter the psychic space where they were about to happen, as he visited a massage parlor, and there he could enact a different outcome. Of course the past cannot really be changed, but through the magic of the zero process its arrival can be held in abeyance. *In the realm of the zero process the past is something that is always and forever about to happen.* In both perverse enactments and phobias, the dreaded arrival of the past is continually put off as something that will happen in the future. When, through our work in the analysis, D got to the point of preventing himself from going to a massage parlor, he began to feel anxious, and then felt a growing and terrifying sense of aloneness and coldness. His perverse enactments had served to keep these feelings at bay. In this way they seemed to behave as any other defense might. But these particular feelings of coldness, aloneness, and terror were zero process memories of his trauma, and the defenses kept these memories in their about-to-happen state. These defenses involved sexualization and various attentional maneuvers.

There is another process, which could be considered a defense but is also part of normal development, that partakes of the experiential quality of the zero process—introjection. An introject stands apart from the self, and behaves as a present experience of an interaction with another person. E's "inner mother" is an example of such an introject, and in this case the connection of her introject's attacks on E with traumatic attacks suffered at the hands of her mother was evident. The connection of zero process characteristics with aspects of internal object relations, especially with introjects, holds the promise of clarifying many aspects of the nature of these objects: their immediate experiential quality, the repetitive nature of the self-object interactions, and the way in which aspects of these interactions exist quite separate from, and untouched by, other aspects of the person's life. I am not suggesting that introjects, or other aspects of internal object relations, are merely zero process phenomena. But I do think that our understanding of the nature of introjects and of introject-self interactions will be greatly clarified once we elucidate the part that the zero process plays in forming them and in their ongoing functioning.

I hope these brief comments on zero process neuroses and zero process defenses have given the reader at least an inkling of the exciting theoretical and clinical vistas that open up once we conceptualize trauma and post-traumatic functioning on their own terms, rather than confusing them with other processes, such as the early development of the ego, the primary process, or early mother/infant interactions.

Psychotherapeutic Technique

In relation to the perversions I should at least mention the particular transferences formed in these disorders, which have characteristics that seem to derive from the zero process. Etchegoyen (1978) described transference perversion, while Renik (1992) talked of the use of the analyst as a fetish, and Reed (1997) of the analyst's interpretation being used as a fetish. In other disorders as well the analysis often gets caught up in the patient's symptoms, and in some ways what these authors describe is not much different from the way in which the "ritual" of analysis—coming to sessions at the appointed time, laying down, etc.—often replaces an obsessional patient's other symptomatic rituals. However, the patient's use of the analyst as a fetish, or the whole analytic interaction as a perverse act, occurs without any slow build-up, as happens for instance in the obsessional. This displays the triggering aspect of the zero process. The analyst also becomes caught up in the disguised enactment of the perversion in a way that usually does not occur in such situations as an obsessional making the analysis into an obsession. In the perverse transference we meet the uncanny inducement of feeling and action in another, which I would suggest is one of the ways in which the zero process expresses itself, at least in some circumstances when it is combined with other dynamics. One of these circumstances is probably related to narcissism and narcissistic fixations, which seem related to a resistance to internalization and to the use of defensive externalization. Forms of narcissistic fixation, especially related to sexual and bodily overgratifications as well as narcissistic ones, are also usually present in the perversions, and their combination with the zero process probably goes some way towards explaining the type of transference seen in these patients.

Many authors (e.g., Renik, 1992; Reed, 1997) have stressed the need to be more active than usual in the case of perverse patients, because otherwise their dynamics simply will never be brought forward. One reason for this need relates to the nature of denial defenses and the sorts of things—perceptions of inner and outer reality—against which they usually defend. These perceptions do not push for expression in the same way that drives and strong feelings do, and so one has to be more active in speaking for these disavowed aspects of reality, which then brings the defensive dynamics into play and allows them to be analyzed. However, another reason for the need for active intervention, especially in relation to the perverse symptoms, is the way in which the zero process functions. Given that the contents of this form of functioning are triggered in an on/off manner by similar experiences, they are even less likely to come to light than other memories of perceptions and judgments about reality. Furthermore, these triggering experiences are generally avoided or covered over using defenses related to the perverse structure. I have given some examples of these defenses from D's analysis. Often neither D's acting out at the massage parlors nor the traumas which lay behind them came to light of their own accord, even with the interpretation of defenses and avoidances connected with them. I had to be more active in asking D about both his acting out and the details of the traumas, at times encouraging him to remember and feel them, and helping him along by talking of the memories and feelings that he had described at other times. This talk on my part helped, I think, because it acted as a trigger for certain things held within zero process functioning. This can be seen in the details I presented of my active questioning, not only with regard to D's perversions, but also when we were led to analyze his traumas. While helpful, this sort of activity should be used judiciously. At other times, analysis of various zero process defenses, rather than merely questioning, is called for.

While the methods of analyzing splitting of the ego has received some attention in the literature, those needed in analyzing other zero process defenses, such as split identities kept apart by mutual aggression, still need to be worked out. Similarly, while there has been some preliminary descriptions of zero process transferences, under the heading of perverse transferences as well as in discussions of the treatment of trauma, a fuller description of various transferences and countertransferences related to the characteristics of the zero process and to zero process defenses is work that still remains to be done.

While the classic analytic techniques of free association, evenly hovering attention, and analysis of transference and defense are essential in analyzing trauma, there are some quite different techniques that are especially important in penetrating to the heart of a trauma and zero process memories. I have already mentioned questioning and other forms of activity designed to "trigger" the traumatic memories. Freud's (1937) advice regarding technique in the case of phobias, that one needs at the appropriate moment to use one's influence to push the patient to confront the phobic situation concretely, falls into this category of triggering techniques. Phobias rank alongside perversions as the most common zero process symptoms. Freud noted that unless the patient is forced to face the phobic situation, core dynamics and affects will remain sequestered within the avoided phobic object or situation. This makes perfect sense if we consider the important part zero process functioning plays in the phobias. Essentially Freud was suggesting a technique for dealing with the lack of integration of the zero process, although of course he did not conceptualize things in this way. Perversions always have a phobic component (e.g., D's fear of a woman having an orgasm while his penis was inside her) as well as a sexualized screen defense. Both the phobic aspect and the pleasurable screen have to be confronted in much the same way that Freud suggested for phobias. For instance I suggested that D refrain from going to massage parlors for as long as he could manage. When he did, important material regarding his traumas emerged in a much more immediate and workable form. Of course there was also the inevitable transference reaction based on my suggestion, in which I became the prohibiting oedipal father, and this had to be dealt with. This can get complicated, but I do not think there is any way around these complications.

The specific techniques necessary in analyzing splitting of identity, such as talking of the two identities as separate even as one analyzes the defensive forces (mutual aggression) that keep them structured this way, would strike many analysts not only as strange, but also perhaps as non-analytic. These especially, but also other techniques I have mentioned, would only make sense in the context of a fuller discussion of zero process symptoms and defenses, so I will stop the discussion at this point.

Summary

In this chapter, specific aspects of the perversions have been discussed. A review of some psychoanalytic ideas about the causation and dynamics of the perversions, followed by the presentation of clinical material, led us to especially emphasize the idea of a sexual screen defense, where an overgratifying physical experience is held onto, and acted out in disguised form, as a defense against the re-emergence of traumatic memories and feelings. Most authors have stressed the importance of trauma in the causation of the perversions, and with this I certainly have agreed. I have applied some of the concepts developed earlier in this book to the dynamics of the perversions, conceptualizing the splitting of the ego described by many authors as important in these disorders as a compound defense, consisting of primary and secondary dissociation combined with forms of denial. These defenses, combined in the characteristic compound form we refer to as splitting of the ego, are present in every structured perversion. (Of course there can be descriptively perverse actions without this structure—for instance as a product of the regressive dissolution of sexual repressions in the psychosis.)

In the later part of this chapter, I used the specific example of the perversions combined with the idea of the zero process as a springboard to introduce some concepts with more general applicability. I described zero process symptoms, zero process neuroses, and zero process defenses (all defined below), as well as presenting the idea that some internal objects and internal object-self relationships (particularly introjects) are based on the characteristics of the zero process. I was only able to discuss these topics, and the techniques needed to analyze zero process symptoms, up to a certain point. To go any further would have required a deeper exploration of trauma and the zero process, which I will pursue in a future publication.

Conclusion

Having completed our survey of basic defensive processes and then having described a few variations of these defenses in specific clinical disorders, it is time to take stock. A number of defenses are missing from the descriptions.

To some extent this is a product of limitation in space, so that only some examples of each great class of defenses could be described. The largest omission in this category are the obsessional defenses.

Obsessional defenses are a form of defense that I have not had the space to delineate. In fact, obsessional defenses complete our list of basic compound defenses: they involve a drive counterforce combined with ego processes such as attention and thinking. It is the counterforce component that makes a defense such as obsessional intellectualization, for instance, so much harder to analyze than more straightforward intellectualization as a pure attentional defense. To take another example, the very characteristic obsessional defense of reaction formation involves the attentional movement to the opposite of what is being defended against, for instance friendly feelings versus anger, to which is melded a drive-based counterforce. It is this counterforce that gives reaction formation its stability and makes it so difficult to undo. Simply pointing out that the person is stressing the opposite, and that they are perhaps angry at the individual they are being so friendly with, will not bring the defended against affect to awareness, as it often does in the case of pure attentional defenses.

If we add obsessional defenses to the list, we have three basic compound defenses: splitting of the ego (attentional defense plus dissociation), splitting of the identity (counterforce defense plus dissociation), and obsessional defenses (attentional defense plus counterforce defense). These three are the three possible combinations of the three basic forms of defense: attentional, counterforce, and zero process.

My main aim in this book has been to conceptualize these three basic forms of defense in enough detail and depth so that we can move forward both clinically and theoretically on a number of fronts. Much of the recent work on defenses has approached things from the other side, looking at complex defenses such as projective identification used in complex situations such as borderline disorders, in order to gain deeper insight into the nature of defenses and of mental dynamics more generally. While the descriptions of these clinical situations are often insightful, I think that the conceptual tools that are used to understand the dynamics involved need to be improved. This is where approaching defenses by investigating and conceptualizing in depth the basic defensive processes, before going on to more complex situations, can be of help.

Armed with the conceptual tools developed in this work, I think we are in a position to approach these more complex situations. I have mentioned the idea of projective identification as an interpersonal counterforce defense. I think what is needed to develop this further is a more in-depth exploration of the different forms of splitting. I have begun this here, with the description of the zero process and zero process defenses, and have talked of a future work that would explore these phenomena further. In this work I hope to compare post-traumatic splitting with the more general weakness in synthesis seen in borderline disorders, in order to gain a deeper understanding of post-traumatic disorders, severe neuroses, and borderline disorders.

Terms

Compound Defense: A compound defense is composed of two or more basic defensive processes, such as a denial and counterforce, which act in concert and are quite tightly bound together. In the case of defenses acting together which are not compounded, one can generally analyze each part separately. The inability to do this indicates that the defenses are more tightly bound into a compound defense.

Introjection: A form of internalization in which aspects of one person are set up internally in another person's mind, as separate from the person's self. Introjects partake of many of the characteristics of the zero process, especially the immediate, experiential nature of its contents.

Splitting of the Ego: In relation to the concepts introduced in this book, splitting of the ego can be described as a compound zero process defense in which denial is combined with primary and secondary dissociation. It is used especially to defend against unpleasant aspects of reality, beginning first with certain realities of the trauma that led to the primary dissociation. Splitting of the ego is the zero process version of an attentional defense.

Splitting of Identity: In this compound zero process defense, aggression is combined with primary and secondary dissociation, to create two or more identities within a person. The identities are kept apart by mutual aggression—dislike, disparagement, loathing—of each identity for the other. Each identity holds strong drives and affects, and splitting of identity is used especially to defend against these drives and affects, which belong both to the original trauma and to other conflicts. Splitting of identity is the zero process version of a counterforce defense.

Zero Process Defense: A defense in which the ego uses certain characteristics of the zero process for defensive purposes. This can involve using actively a characteristic of the zero process, such as lack of integration or quasi-experiential qualities. Additionally, the ego can combine other defensive maneuvers it has at its disposal, such as attentional and counterforce defenses, with these zero process characteristics, and with secondary dissociation. Splitting of the ego and splitting of identity are examples of that later type of zero process defense.

Zero Process Neurosis: A neurosis in which zero process symptoms and dynamics centered on zero process functioning dominate the clinical picture. Perversions and phobic neuroses are examples. Further study will probably demonstrate that other neuroses fall into this category.

Zero Process Symptom: A symptom in which the dynamic picture is dominated by characteristics of the zero process. Perverse, phobic, and conversion symptoms are all zero process symptoms.

Notes

1. Note that Freud not only linked splitting to disavowal, but he also said that disavowal inevitably leads to splitting, an influential opinion that has hampered a deeper investigation of both different forms of splitting and the various forms of disavowal (which I have called denial) ever since.

2. This breakdown was short-lived but severe and was misdiagnosed as a manic or perhaps catatonic psychosis. Brief psychoses, often severe, are well known to psychiatrists. Unlike the more slowly developing loss of reality connection, these appear quite suddenly with severe symptoms, but typically resolve completely and quickly. I would suggest that perhaps this diagnostic entity actually involves a flooding of the ego by the zero process memories of one or more traumas—a zero process psychosis, to give it a name.

3. Core gender identity should be distinguished from choice of partner and from secondary identifications. For instance most male homosexuals have a male core gender identity, even though they choose other males as sexual partners and may have certain feminine mannerisms or traits based on secondary, selective identifications with their mother, sisters, or other women.

PART THREE

THEORY

CHAPTER NINE

~

A General Psychoanalytic Theory

Psychoanalysis has changed a lot in the last few decades. Freud's metapsychology, and even more so its development by ego psychologists such as Heinz Hartmann, and within this development especially energic concepts, have been rejected by more and more analysts. The whole focus on the inner workings of one person's mind has come under attack from various schools. Ideas about the importance of reconstruction, of what really happened in the past, and even of our ability to know anything at all about reality, have been rejected as antiquated by a number of modern analysts.

In relation to these trends, the approach taken in this book, or at least some aspects of it, may be seen as old-fashioned or regressive. Obviously this is not my opinion, but rather than engage in general theoretical arguments on these issues I have chosen up till this point largely to concentrate on applying the concepts of Freud, Hartmann, Anna Freud, and others to the elucidation of various forms of defenses, and to some clinical entities related to these defenses. This application has, I hope, demonstrated the fruitfulness of these ideas. It has also led to formulations which can be concretely tested against clinical data. This follows what Hartmann has said about more general concepts such as libido and neutralization: "That these constructs, which are introduced because of their explanatory value, cannot be directly defined in terms of observational data, but that inferences from the constructs can be tested by observation, has long been known in psychoanalysis" (1959, p 344). More than a few readers may be driven to object that after all even if they find ideas such as, for instance, contrast defenses and the defensive use of guilt to be useful and supported by observation, that would not necessarily lead to the acceptance of concepts such as libido and neutralization. I would agree with this, but this line of thought brings up the whole issue of the relationship between the various ideas presented in this book to each other and to other psychoanalytic ideas. In other words, it brings up more general theoretical considerations.

In this chapter I will first briefly look at some very general scientific issues: the nature of reality and what is real, experience-near versus experience-distant ideas, what's real in the mind, and ideas about different types of scientific theories and methodologies. These general issues are connected to the specific ideas developed in this work in a number of ways. The topics of defenses against reality, of the importance of reconstruction with both denial and repressive defenses, and the importance of analyzing what actually happened in a trauma all depend on a realist philosophical position. The general psychoanalytic theory that I am using and developing itself depends on a realist position, but also on certain ideas about the nature of evidence and the structure of theories in a field such as psychoanalysis. Following the discussion of more general issues, I will pursue some ideas about the nature of psychoanalytic theory, arguing for the validity and usefulness of a coherent general theory, and presenting the basic psychoanalytic model with which I work, and that has been the basis for my thinking on defenses.

Reality

A frequent comment heard at psychoanalytic meetings these days is that "after all, you can't really know what's real," or that "of course we can never know what really happened in the patient's past." Many in the audience will nod in agreement with such statements, perhaps because they seem self-evident, at least in the present postmodernist context. Analysts may think that they have even more reason than others for supporting such ideas, given what we know about the remodeling of memory and of perception by emotional factors, a phenomena that has been described and investigated since the early days of psychoanalysis (Freud, 1899).

However, if we take a moment to consider such statements as "after all, you can't really know what's real," we can see that they contain a contradiction. They make a quite definite declaration about the nature of reality (it is unknowable), which is also a statement about the reality of our ability to have knowledge about reality. If the reality of things is so unknowable, how can such definite statements be made about it? Supporters of such views may argue that after all, what is being asserted is merely that knowledge of reality can never be certain. This is an idea most people could agree with. Even ideas about reality that seem quite certain can be overturned by new evidence or new ways of looking at things. This attitude of critical realism (Hanly and Fitzpatrick-Hanly, 2001)[1] is that adopted by the vast majority of scientists, even in these postmodern times. The problem, however, is that many people slide from this easily defensible position of critical realism to more radically subjectivist ones, such as a belief that all points of view on reality are equally valid, or the view that as long as a theory has internal consistency (coherence) it is as valid as any other. This sliding can also happen when these views are criticized. All but the most staunch supporters of a radically subjectivist position will, in my experience, slide back the other way, saying that there is undeniably a reality which constrains beliefs to some extent, but that our view of reality is also constrained or distorted by subjective factors.

It may be thought that this kind of sliding is a product of loose thinking on the part of some individuals or, alternately, that it may be a positive sign of trying to take a middle position between two extremes. My own view, however, is that it is a product of the contradictions contained in the radical subjectivist position. To begin with, no matter how staunchly a person adheres to this position, they cannot live their day-to-day life by it, nor can they conduct an analysis based upon it. To drive a car, to play a game of tennis and keep score, and to discuss with a patient what could be the meaning of something they said or did requires an attitude of realism. (I am using the term in the philosophical sense of a conception that the objects of our perception and thought exist independently of our perception and of our ideas about them.) Thus, since at the level of our most basic attitude toward reality most non-psychotics operate during most of their waking life as realists, defense of the subjectivist view requires that one actually move back and forth between these two views. Usually what this amounts to is confusing two levels of conceptualization: psychological subjectivism and the more self-contradictory position of epistemological subjectivism (Hanly and Fitzpatrick-Hanly, 2001).

As a concrete example of this, we can consider a statement by Zachrisson and Zachrisson (2005) in an article that attempts an even handed comparison of coherence (subjectivist) theories and correspondence theories (realist ones, based on the idea that what makes a statement valid is the degree of correspondence between the idea and external reality). Zachrisson and Zachrisson note that one problem with the correspondence theory is that perceptions at their inception are molded by theory and emotion. Now, how could we actually know such a thing? The statement that perceptions are molded by theory and emotion, just like the statement that memories are remodeled through development, only makes sense within the correspondence (realist) framework. Underlying these statements and any research—whether neuroscientific or psychoanalytic—supporting them, is a conceptualization of a real world which is represented in our minds, however imperfectly. Findings related to the influence of emotions and other factors may lead us to a more critical, sophisticated realism, as opposed to a naïve one, but if we completely abandon realism, how can we make statements such as that everyday emotions affect our perceptions at their inception—since this is at base a statement about reality? Beyond this, the idea of a distortion of perceptions and memories itself rests on the idea that there was an original, less distorted version, which surely rests on a conception of an independent external reality.

Zachrisson and Zachrisson's finding of a "problem" with the correspondence position makes sense only if we look the other way as they use a realist position to develop an idea that they then use against this position. One reason we might not even notice this contradiction is that we take the realist position so much for granted—after all, we all use it every day to navigate our way in the world—that we do not notice that we are using it in developing this criticism.

This basic realist position was conceptualized by Freud (1911b) as the reality principle, supported by the ego function of reality testing. Some within analysis have tried to subsume this principle under the theme of the acceptance of parental authority or the "law of the father," but I would agree with Hartmann (1956) that the reality principle is far broader than this, and involves a number of primary autonomous ego functions. The establishment of an oedipal conflict or a battle over accepting authority already assumes a more basic position of realism, as well as the various ego functions that support reality testing, such as perception and the various forms of memory. The partial resolution of the oedipal conflict has more to do with acceptance of the reality principle and a partial relinquishment of narcissistic fantasies than with the establishment of reality testing as such. Of course these distinctions should not be maintained too strictly and this partial relinquishment of narcissistic and omnipotent hopes helps pave the way for the leap to a more objective view of reality, which comes around age 7—although this leap is certainly also due to the maturation of a number of autonomous ego abilities at this time.

Actual testing of reality does not form the whole support for the reality principle. As Hartmann (1956) pointed out, there is also an important social aspect to the reality principle. There is a conventional reality that we learn about and take over from those around us and from society at large. It may be thought that this conventional reality is inferior to reality that we have tested for ourselves, but in fact none of us can do without a good deal of it. The need to test every aspect of reality for oneself is more likely to be a sign of excessive oppositionalism or some other issue with authority rather than a sign of a well-functioning reality orientation, and in fact this do-it-all-by-yourself approach is not feasible. A well-functioning reality orientation requires a well-developed organizing function of the ego, which decides on a hierarchy of methods for assessing and dealing with reality, including assessing the reliability of conventional knowledge by methods other than testing each piece of it. This applies in a somewhat modified way to workers in any science, where one has to make a considered judgment about many pieces of knowledge that one cannot test in any detail.

Objective knowledge and reality testing lead to the need for the sorts of attentional defenses the study of which has occupied us for a good part of this book. I have also described how inner reality is often defended against, for instance by defensive externalization. I hypothesized in the chapter on denial that awareness of defenses, which are also an aspect of inner reality, is blocked by attentional defenses.

But are defenses something that we could become conscious of in any case? Are they perhaps not unconscious but non-conscious: that is, processes in the mind of which we are simply not capable of becoming aware? And what about their reality? Are defenses real in the sense that a feeling, a perception, or a memory is a real aspect of the mind? Or are they only abstract concepts or ideas which help us to organize more concrete data? This second set of questions about the reality of defenses may seem separate from our ability to become aware of them, but many people do connect these issues. It is this aspect of theory—what is considered real in the mind—to which we now turn.

What's Real in the Mind?

As the fracturing of psychoanalysis into many competing theories gathered momentum in the 1980s, Robert Wallerstein (1988, 1990) proposed an influential idea. He stated that general psychoanalytic theories (metapsychologies) were not formulated in ways that allowed empirical testing and were thus really scientific metaphors, with only a loose association to clinical reality. Thus this empirical, clinical reality could not be used to decide among them. On the other hand psychoanalysts shared the common ground of "experience near" clinical theory, a set of ideas that could be directly tested against experience, as compared to the "experienced distant" abstract theories. This basic point of view had been argued forcefully and influentially by a number of psychoanalysts in the 1970s (Klein, 1969/1970; Holt, 1975). Wallerstein's clear exposition of this dichotomy, and probably the timing of his papers as well, led to the adoption of his ideas by many psychoanalysts as almost self-evident truths.

These ideas were not new, however, as metapsychology had been under attack ever since its inception. In arguing against these attacks Hartmann, Kris, and Loewenstein (1953) noted that clinical observation did not take precedence over theory, but in fact that it was formed in part by theory. Brenner (1980a) echoed these ideas, pointing out that even the simplest observations in a science involved the most abstract ideas. For instance the clinical theory that Wallerstein talked of can only be formulated using such general ideas as the unconscious and psychic determinism, among many others. Wallerstein could only talk of a "common ground" with respect to psychoanalytic clinical theory by assuming that those in agreement shared these basic general theoretical ideas.

Let us look at defenses in relation to these ideas. It would seem that the most "experienced near" aspect of a defense is the resistance one meets within the analytic situation. However, even to see this requires some conception of the mind as an entity with dynamic forces working within it, including some that are outside of awareness. These ideas did not begin with psychoanalysis, and before its inception people were capable of thinking that someone was avoiding something or protesting too much—but even then, there had to be a dynamic conception of the mind, even if it remained unarticulated. But where do these general ideas come from? Do we discover them in what we see? Or does starting with these general conceptions help us to perceive and conceive of resistance? It would seem that it's a little bit of both—or actually a whole lot of both, as there is a movement back and forth between the general conceptions helping us to see things and what we see having an impact on, and shaping the evolution of, our general conceptions.

Do these general conceptions refer to real things, or are they merely ideas that aid us in our investigations—that is, are they only of heuristic value? The trend within analysis is not only to see the most general ideas as heuristic, but also to expand the category of heuristic ideas so as to include within it a great many psychoanalytic concepts. For instance Fulgenicio (2005) argues that all metapsychological concepts, such as drive, energy, and topography are merely organizing ideas. "It is possible to say," he asserts, "that for Freud drives are not facts but conventions, abstract ideas which organize the facts" (2005, p 114).

But what about resistance? This is surely a concrete thing, not merely a convention. However, even at this "experience near" level of conceptualization, one is using various ideas to organize data, and creating reality to some extent. This is so in every science, and the fact that an idea is "experience near" does not make it more immune from error than an "experience distant" one. At each step of the chain of inference leading to experience distant ideas, even at the first link in the chain—the so-called experience near concept—one is creating reality in this way, although one is not creating it out of nothing. As one moves from resistance to defense to the inner workings of the defense such as a counterforce, I do not believe that one is moving from the concrete to the abstract, but rather along a chain of inference beginning with what is more readily observable. Each of these concepts refers to a real thing; it is just that some of these things we can observe, while others we cannot. This is not to say that there are not heuristic and abstract concepts in psychoanalytic theorizing, but not every experience distant concept is an abstract one.

Interestingly, in other sciences we are usually willing to see experience distant concepts as referring to real things. For instance the conceptualization of atoms and molecules as making up matter is certainly distant from direct experience, and has been arrived at through long chains of inference from observed data. Yet many people—both scientists who work with these models and laypeople—will say that the table in front of them, for instance, is "really" made up of atoms, and that what looks like solid matter is "really" largely empty space. Here the experience distant idea is treated as more real than the experience near one. This particular experience distant idea can in turn be seen as an approximation to reality, but as less "real" than a more sophisticated quantum mechanical description of the atom using probability concepts and complex mathematical equations. This tendency is to be found not only in physics. Many people would say that the little twinkling spots of light we see in the night sky are "really" either unimaginably large balls of fire generated by fusion reactions turning matter into energy, or huge collections of these balls which are so far away that they look like little twinkles of light. Or we might say that a piece of rock with some marks on it is "really" the fossilized remains of a sea creature that lived hundreds of millions of years ago.

I can imagine many objections to equating these sorts of scientifically discovered realities with metapsychological ideas such as drive or energy, or even defense. It may be argued, for instance, that these non-analytic scientific ideas about reality are better substantiated than the analytic ideas. It certainly cannot be an issue of experimental methodology, however, since the existence of faraway galaxies or the history of life on Earth was not discovered or validated by controlled experimentation. In any case, what I am discussing here is not the truth or falsity of these analytic concepts but whether they could *possibly* refer to real things, or whether they are by their very nature only abstract, heuristic concepts.

It is clear that my examples and many other ideas from other sciences are much more easily accepted as real than many analytic ones, even by analysts. Why is this? Part of the explanation is probably the influence of conventional knowledge. Many ideas of the physical sciences—such as atoms for instance—have entered the realm of conventional knowledge for many educated people, and they have thus acquired that added feeling of being real that seems to only come with conventional knowledge. Even within a science and among scientists an important part is played by conventional scientific knowledge, which should not be underestimated. For instance in the middle of the 20th century the structural theory and the oedipus complex would have been conventional knowledge for young analysts in the United States, while in many areas of South America dominated by Kleinian thinking, conventional knowledge would have been somewhat different. In the beginning of the 21st century ideas about the overriding importance of the early mother-child relationship, and of projective mechanisms and the countertransference in psychoanalytic therapy, are conventional knowledge for many analysts. Of course this sketches things very crudely and in reality conventional knowledge varies subtly across different local psychoanalytic cultures. Whatever the conventional knowledge is, it carries the danger of being overgeneralized, because it has that extra dose of reality feeling as compared to other knowledge. Other ideas, which may be as well supported by evidence, are not felt to be as real as those that have entered the realm of conventional knowledge.

Another factor working against our acceptance of psychological concepts as referring to real things is that our perceptual functions are largely oriented towards the outside world, or at least the world outside our mind, which includes body feelings. These perceptual functions are not well suited to giving us information about many aspects of our minds. Generally the aspects of our minds that are accessible to consciousness are those connected to perceptions of external reality, or to bodily sensations. These include memories, fantasies, and the bodily sensations connected with affects. Even thinking, which we generally see as a mental function accessible to consciousness, is at first unconscious, as Freud (1923) long ago asserted. It only becomes capable of being conscious when connected to perceptual aspects—either visual images or verbal residues. We can become conscious of certain states of mental tension and of mental pleasure and unpleasure beyond bodily sensations, but these are meager compared to the range of our external perceptual abilities. We often do not pay too much attention to this limitation of our perceptual abilities since there are quite a lot of things that we actually can perceive in the mind because of their connection with the external perceptions: feelings, fantasies, and memories, as well as various combinations of these such as internal objects (structured memory/fantasy complexes) and wishes.

However, there are many aspects of mental functioning as conceived in classical psychoanalytic theory that are not capable, or are only partially capable, of becoming an object of conscious awareness. These include the drives, changes in drive energy quantitatively and qualitatively, many structural aspects of the ego and superego, ego functions, and various processes such as regression. Do defenses belong on this list? They have some perceptual referents, for instance feelings of tension and the unpleasant feelings that motivate them, and fantasies connected with them, but aspects of their inner nature—what is often called their mechanism—are inaccessible to direct experience. Even when we interpret this aspect of a defense to a patient and they become aware of it, they are to some extent being asked to take a number of inferential steps. This is one aspect of "making a defense conscious," and it can have a positive therapeutic effect. Along with the unpleasant feelings that motivate them, other aspects connected with a defensive process, such as a wish or a judgment about reality, have a number of perceptual qualities, and making these conscious is usually an important part of the analysis of a defense.

As we move up the ladder of inference, for instance to the nature of the energy used in a defense, or structural aspects of a defense, we are certainly less likely to interpret the ideas directly to a patient. This series, moving inferentially from experience near ideas to ideas more distant from immediate experience, has often been conceptualized as a movement from the concrete to the abstract, in other words as relating to levels of abstraction. I have argued that such a series refers rather to levels of inference than to levels of abstraction. These two things have often been conflated in psychoanalytic theorizing. Starting with this conflation many inferred, experience distant concepts have been rejected as abstract, speculative theorizing with no evidential foundation and they have been replaced with more experience near, supposedly less speculative concepts. Thus the conflation of inference with abstraction is compounded by the equation of abstract with speculative and concrete with well founded, another false equation (Brenner, 1980a).

An idea such as "counterforce defenses" can without argument be classified as an abstract or general concept, as can the division of defenses into the two categories of counterforce and attentional ones. However, the idea of a specific counterforce defense, such as the conception of a specific repression in an individual, while it involves certain inferential steps, would refer to a concretely real aspect of the mind, according to the argument I have been developing. If we move a few levels of inference further we arrive at the specific nature of the counterforce, as involving partially neutralized aggression. The inferential steps are from various data—for instance from the negative transference and aggressive outbursts that come from the weakening of repression, from a comparison of reactions to the undoing of repression versus the undoing of denial, and from the weak repressions in psychotics, who seem at the same time to suffer from a deficit in the ability to neutralize aggression. Of course these data themselves are not a given, but are collected through a combination of observation guided by various conceptualizations, along with already a certain amount of inference. I have tried to demonstrate some of this process in the parts of this book dealing with these issues.

Is the concept of neutralized aggression forming the core of defensive counterforce an abstract concept? It can be a general one, if we speak about repressions in the general sense, but it is in the first instance discovered (inferred) in a specific form. For instance, the neutralized aggression my patient D used in the repression of his oedipal wishes in the example presented in chapter 2 is as concrete and specific as the wishes that he repressed, as well as being as real. Of course when I say that neutralized aggression or an oedipal fantasy is real, it is a shorthand way of saying that the concepts that the words represent refer or point to real things. Many have warned about the dangers of reification—taking our concepts or terms themselves to be real things—but the opposite danger, of taking concepts to refer to purely abstract or constructed hypothetical entities, is also present and also leads to confusion and poor theory construction. To my mind concepts, whether verbally or mathematically expressed, are tools that allow us to model reality, including those aspects of reality, which are actually the much larger part, of which we have no direct perceptual awareness.

The complex interconnected web of observation, use of general organizing ideas, and inference, that leads to the concept of neutralized aggression as a counterforce in the mind may contain errors which would necessitate revising, refining, or abandoning the concept for a better one, so that when I say that the concept refers to a real thing, I do not mean to imply that it is absolutely true. I merely mean that it can have the same reality as mental phenomena we can more directly observe—such as memories—and as physical realities that we take for granted as real but the knowledge of which also involves these complex inferences—such as black holes or electrons.

Whether they agree with them or not, I can imagine some analysts may find that these considerations are themselves overly abstract and not related to their central concerns. However, ideas which equate inferred concepts that have no direct perceptual referents (concepts such as drive or ego mechanism) with abstraction, speculation, and a lack of proof or connection to observation have become widely accepted. This growing acceptance has had an enormous impact on the development of psychoanalytic theory, and on psychoanalytic practice as well. Theories which replace inferred concepts with fewer direct perceptual referents—such as ego processes—with ideas closer to perception have largely superseded the older theories.

Not only defenses but many other structural and functional concepts developed by Freud and others have been replaced by ideas about inner object relations, which picture self and object and the interactions between them along with the accompanying affects, all of which are of course closer to perception than ego mechanisms. This concentration on inner object relations and their external enactment has led to many new and valuable findings and ideas. More recently the intersubjectivists have taken the concentration on what can be perceived to a new level, as they reduce many intrapsychic concepts—for instance defense—to interpersonal interactions and their subjectively perceived effects. This abandonment by many analysts of structural, energic, and some dynamic concepts has been a serious loss in my estimation. It has impaired our ability to investigate and conceptualize many aspects of mental functioning. I make this point now in the abstract, but at one level this whole book has been an attempt to demonstrate in a concrete manner, in relation to defenses especially, that these experience distant, inferred concepts and realities are of value in psychoanalytic investigation and theorizing, as well as in clinical practice.

This is not to say that these concepts themselves should be taken as immutable givens. I have myself in this book looked to revise, for instance, Freud's ideas of traumatic anxiety and of basic categories of mental functioning, in the latter case by adding the idea of zero process to the more familiar primary and secondary processes. However, I hope I have demonstrated the usefulness of both the old ego concepts and some new ones, in their ability to help us make sense of complex and multifaceted phenomena such as defense. The simple distinction between attentional and counterforce defenses, for instance, helps us not only to organize and comprehend many aspects of defensive processes, but also helps us to ask many further questions, leading to a deeper understanding of these processes.

Having discussed, however briefly and inadequately, the issue of the reality of such things as ego processes from the theoretical angle, in terms of their position as real processes inferred from observations, we are still left open to what many would consider the far more serious charge that even the observations from which they are inferred are of dubious value. This charge has in the past come mainly from non-analysts. These days many analysts as well feel analytic observations made in the clinical setting are not fully scientific. What kind of a science is psychoanalysis? Or is it perhaps not a science at all? And how can we relate our discipline and its methods and findings to those of sciences such as physics or biology?

The Mathematical and the Conceptual Sciences

Freud saw psychoanalysis rather straightforwardly as a science like any other, with a set of discoveries and theoretical ideas based on observations, most of which were derived from the psychoanalytic situation. I myself share this view, but many do not. Some think that because of its unique subject matter psychoanalysis is not a science like any other—or not a science at all. Perhaps it is a science of meaning, or of intersubjectivity. Others wish psychoanalysis could be a science, but feel the psychoanalytic situation lacks the appropriate control of variables, and experimental reproducibility for the data derived from it, which are necessary in a science. Many within psychoanalysis have met these concerns by developing sophisticated methodologies to study the psychoanalytic situation itself. At the same time the theoretical discussion within psychoanalysis as to what should be considered a scientific methodology has also become much more sophisticated (e.g., see Kächele et al. [2006] for a discussion of different methodologies applied to a specific case, and Kernberg [2006a, 2006b] and Perron [2006] for a general discussion of theoretical and methodological issues).

Perhaps we could begin by going back to the basic questions and asking, "What is science?" The most general definition of the *word* science is a body of knowledge, but in the discussion about psychoanalysis and science the word is really a short form for "natural science," which could be defined as a body of knowledge about reality or the physical world. More narrowly, it is a body of theories and laws about this world, which many think of as having been obtained through controlled experimentation. Most of us are first exposed to these ideas in school when we are taught about the "scientific method." This is said to consist of a hypothesis, which is tested through experimentation which either confirms or disconfirms the hypothesis. At the same time we are taught many scientific facts and theories that are not primarily derived from this method: facts about astronomy, the theory of evolution, and the reconstruction of the story of life on earth, to name just a few.

It may be objected that these simplifications and contradictions from our school days have little relevance for a more sophisticated understanding of what science is. I bring them up here, however, because they capture something of the contradictions that I think are often present in these more sophisticated discussions as well. Scientific findings and theories are arrived at through a wide variety of methodologies and theoretical strategies, often combined in complex ways. More general discussions of science, however, often present a simpler picture, or at least posit a simpler ideal, regarding both methodology and theory construction. It is often felt that sciences should at least strive towards this ideal, which includes an experimental methodology where variables can be quantified and controlled. Other methodologies such as qualitative research are certainly described, but often are seen as ways of adapting the ideal method to recalcitrant subject matter.

Within psychoanalysis there are quite a wide range of views on this issue, and the point of view I am arguing against is certainly not the only one. Quite a number of authors take the view, as I do, that there are many possible methodologies for research, including clinical ones, each with its own strengths and weaknesses. For instance, Leuzinger-Bohleber and Fishman (2006) divide these into clinical and extra-clinical forms of research, with the extra-clinical divided into empirical, conceptual, and interdisciplinary. Their discussion is quite detailed and balanced. In their scheme, what I have done in this book would be considered largely conceptual research, although I think (and they make this point as well) that conceptual research is closely tied to clinical investigation and testing of the ideas that are developed. I will address this point a bit later, but want first to look more generally at the nature of science.

To my mind science is simply the attempt to study reality systematically. More detailed definitions, at least when they attempt to be prescriptive of what science should be, do not, I think, take account of the truly remarkable variety of methodological and theoretical strategies scientists have invented to probe nature. In dealing with the limitations—and possibilities—of the particular aspect of reality they are trying to investigate scientists have often shown themselves resourceful and creative. Thankfully, many have not felt bound by various limitations that have been pronounced from on high by philosophers of science or by scientists from other fields.

As an example Darwin used intense naturalistic observations and an ability to detect patterns within this data to construct a complex and comprehensive theory of evolution. The theoretical structure he constructed was quite different in nature from that constructed in other sciences—for instance by Newton in physics. In the first half of the 20th century a number of other evolutionary biologists modified and added to this theory, and brought modern genetics into the theory, which at that point came to be called the "modern synthesis." Here too, naturalistic observation and the observation of "experiments of nature" played a large part, and the nature of the theory remained quite distinctive. As Ernst Mayr, one of the architects of the modern evolutionary synthesis, noted, "There was no room in the scientific method of the mechanist's for the reconstruction of historical sequences, as occurred in the evolution of life, nor for the pluralism of answers and causation that make prediction of the future in the biological sciences impossible. When evolutionary biology was examined for its 'scientificness' according to the criteria of mechanics, it flunked the test" (Mayr, 1997, p 28).

Mayr pointed out that Karl Popper, based on his ideas of falsifiability, declared in 1974 that Darwinism was not a testable scientific theory (although he later recanted). Mayr went on to note that "the occurrence of exceptions to a probabilistic theory does not necessarily constitute falsification. And in fields such as evolutionary biology, in which historical narratives must be constructed to explain certain observations, it is often very difficult, if not impossible, to decisively falsify an invalid theory" (Mayr, 1997, p 49).

The ideas of Popper and others regarding falsifiability and decisive experiments which would prove or disprove a theory still have considerable sway among scientists and the general public. Evolutionary theory, especially when one comes to understand it in depth, can be seen to not fit very neatly into many people's conception of what a scientific theory is,[2] and to have a number of similarities to psychoanalytic theory. Of course there are also differences. Psychoanalysis has its own methodology and forms of theory construction, as does every science. It is interesting, however, to look at different sciences not prescriptively, in order to decide which are "scientific" enough, but descriptively, to see the commonalities and differences between different types of science. Any such attempt cannot help but be a simplification, given the enormous complexity and variation, even within one branch of science, of method and theory construction. With this caveat, I will present one such attempt at a description.

Sciences are often divided into the "exact" or "hard" sciences (mainly physics, chemistry, and some areas of biology) and the "soft" sciences (all of the rest). The "hard" sciences are those where the phenomena are amenable to quantification and controlled experimentation. Often workers in an area of "soft" science try very hard to emulate the quantification and experimentation of the "hard" sciences—for instance in psychology and sociology—with mixed results. Many of the reasons for the difficulties are well known, including the complex historical nature of the phenomena under study, the tight coupling of many variables, which make it impossible to vary them independently, and the very large number of variables, many of which are impossible to control at all. Beyond these, there is another fundamental reason for the differences between these two types of sciences.

In the exact sciences the principle of identity applies to the phenomena under study (Mayr, 1982). For instance every electron is, except for a few characteristics such as its spin, identical to every other electron. Similarly gravitational attraction, or electromagnetic waves, or many other physical phenomena, are assumed to be identical with other instances of the same phenomena, and this assumption stands the test of observation quite well. This fact allows for the full quantification of the phenomena under study, and the mathematical manipulation of these quantities (since the principle of identity, such as $1 = 1$, applies also in mathematics), as well as the derivation of laws that are, at least until limiting cases are discovered, universally valid.

The reliance on quantification and mathematics runs into difficulties when considering historical phenomena and phenomena which are individually unique in other ways. The study of living organisms is one field that brings us up against the limits of the exact or the mathematical sciences. There is a large gray area, for instance in molecular biology and physiology, where the assumption of the principle of identity can be fruitful, controlled experimentation can yield important results, and the formulation of universally applicable laws is often possible. Even in this area of overlap between the mathematical and other sciences, a different way of doing science appears. This type of science is distinguished by a greater reliance on description and especially by its main intellectual tool, which shifts from mathematics to concepts. (Mayr [2004] also makes this point.) I would distinguish these two areas of science, with the understanding that there is no sharp boundary between them, as the mathematical and the conceptual sciences. One of the reasons for the many striking similarities and analogies between evolutionary biology and psychoanalysis is that both deal with phenomena that, because of their uniqueness and individuality, require a similar treatment using a complex, multileveled conceptual theoretical structure.

In the conceptual sciences such as psychoanalysis, it is not true that our methodology and theory construction leave something to be desired because of the lack of controlled studies, quantification, and experimental reproducibility. Rather, our particular manner of doing science is suited to the data with which we deal. In processes in which the principle of identity cannot be applied because each instance or individual is unique, it is concepts that are the main intellectual tool of the scientist, and the use of mathematics plays a subsidiary role. By contrast, in the mathematical sciences such as physics, it is mathematical equations that are the primary intellectual tools of the scientist and the most accurate statement of a theory, and concepts play a secondary role.

The issue of the theoretical tools of a science is intimately bound up with the issue of methods of data gathering. A deeper discussion of these topics would have to trace the concrete connections between these two aspects of science. It is clear that they are intimately related in complex ways. Each branch of science, in attempting to study its particular area of reality as objectively and systematically as possible, develops its own methodological and theoretical tools. The ones that Freud developed (the psychoanalytic situation, free association and interpretation, transference/countertransference, as well as the unique theoretical idea of a number of different conceptual points of view on each phenomena) have proved enormously powerful. The methodology has produced many more clinically and theoretically fruitful ideas than other methodologies. In saying this I am not advocating for methodological purity in psychoanalysis, as some have, who insist that only data gained in the analytic situation, and perhaps even more narrowly within the transference/countertransference, is "true" psychoanalytic data. I consider this type of purity as being as misplaced as the "purity" that insists on controlled experimentation as an ideal in all sciences.

I do believe, however, that clinical psychoanalytic investigation is as fully fledged a scientific method as any other. Of course in relation to certain prescriptive criteria it could be seen as flawed in a number of ways, for instance in terms of reproducibility and the presence of control groups. If we take a specific example such as resistance and defense, however, we can see that other methods have their own limitations and flaws. Pooled data from a number of subjects cannot possibly give us a detailed view of the inner workings of a defense, as can careful clinical work with single patients, whose data are then compared and contrasted. This has been the approach taken in this book and I hope the results show that the potential of this method has been far from exhausted. This method also allows us to see how different defenses interact, what motivates them, what they are directed against, and many other aspects which are difficult, and in some cases impossible, to investigate in such depth with other methods.

My point is not to pit one methodology against another. Non-clinical methodologies can throw light on certain aspects which are more difficult to access clinically. Charles Fisher's studies on subliminal perception, dream imagery, and the primary process (e.g., 1954, 1956) were an early and very good example of this, as is Howard Shevrin's extensive further work along these lines. Observational studies of infants and children have for a long time been important sources of data for psychoanalysis. Studies of grouped data and trials, whether of therapeutic outcome or other aspects of analysis, have become much more inventive and sophisticated not only methodologically but also conceptually. These often give us information that would be hard or impossible to obtain clinically. At the same time there are aspects of, for instance, the mental life of infants or of psychoanalytic outcome, which are better accessed through clinical methodology. My point, as I have said, is not to argue for one methodology over another but to argue against the privileging of one as an ideal, with others seen as secondary, less scientific, or even unscientific. Fortunately, this more comprehensive view of methodology is gaining ground within psychoanalysis (Leuzinger-Bohleber and Fishman, 2006).

Whatever methodology is used psychoanalysis is, at the theoretical level, a conceptual science. I would like now to turn to this theoretical aspect of psychoanalysis.

Psychoanalytic Theory

Freud developed a general psychoanalytic theory that he called metapsychology, in which each phenomenon was looked at from a number of points of view: the dynamic (conflict), the economic (movements and transformations of energy), and the topographic (positioning in the spatial model of the mind) (Freud, 1915c). Rapaport and Gill (1959) added to this list the genetic (genesis in the person's past), structural, and adaptive points of view. They viewed metapsychology as the most general set of assumptions that were necessary and sufficient for psychoanalytic theory. I think this is an overly deductive view of metapsychology and psychoanalytic theory in general, in which psychoanalytic theory is seen as deducible from a number of general propositions. I would lean towards Brenner's (1980a) view that metapsychology is merely psychoanalytic theory.

One of the most important aspects of Freud's innovation of taking a number of separate theoretical points of view on each phenomenon is that it works against one of the biggest difficulties in the conceptual sciences—the tendency towards theoretical reductionism. Reductionism is often used as a synonym for oversimplification, but reductionism in the sense of the reduction of a massive amount of data to a few inferred underlying processes or realities is a necessary part of every scientific—in fact every intellectual— endeavor. A different form of reductionism has been called explanatory and theoretical reductionism by Mayr (1982) and been referred to as theories by reduction by Hartmann (1950a). In this form of reductionism a complex, multilayered theory (developed in order to comprehend an equally complex reality) is reduced to one or a few of its parts. Analysis has been prone to theoretical reductionism since its early days.

Theoretical reductionism seems to be a part of every conceptual science. Mayr (1982) pointed to examples of it in evolutionary biology—as an example the reduction of the complex theory of evolution to population genetics (the effect of natural selection on gene frequencies in succeeding generations). This is an important aspect of the modern theory of evolution, and in fact many non-biologists—and a few biologists as well—think it *is* the modern theory of evolution. This example demonstrates a characteristic of most theoretical reductions. The outcome is not an untrue theory—in fact it is often a theory that is well supported by the data. The difficulty in theoretical reduction is not what has been kept in but what is left out.

The tendency towards the formation of partial theories has often been commented on in psychoanalysis. Leo Rangell has argued passionately throughout his long analytic career, for instance in his psychoanalytic autobiography (2004), for what he has called total composite theory. Shevrin (2003) has echoed this call for a guiding general theory that could make room for new findings noting that, sadly, analysts have generally abandoned the task of formulating and refining such a theory. The partial theories proposed are myriad. One of the most popular is the attribution of the genesis and causation of many disorders to failures in early mothering—in its containing function, in helping the child to mentalize, or in some other important functions. Object relations theories that see much of intrapsychic functioning as involving the interplay of internalized object relations, and interpersonal interaction as involving the externalization of these object relations, to my mind can, in the hands of some theorists, involve a theoretical reduction. Of course theoretical reduction is not the preserve of one theoretical orientation. The work of Charles Brenner, which has been enormously influential among modern-day American Freudians, is an excellent example of this form of reductionism. In following Brenner's work from the 1960s right to the 21st century one can observe the progressive reduction of more and more of the conceptual tools of psychoanalysis to the idea of compromise formation.

Each of these partial theories—the pervasive influence of very early mothering, internal object relations, and compromise formation—is abundantly supported by psychoanalytic data, and in fact one could find evidence for each of these in almost any fragment of an analytic case. This is what convinces adherents of the validity of these ideas, and of course they are valid, but their overextension to engulf and supersede other aspects of psychoanalytic theory is not only invalid but extremely detrimental to the development of psychoanalysis. Many analysts have tried to make up for the deficiencies of partial theories by taking an eclectic approach and using different partial theories at different times when they seem to fit or be relevant, or even looking at the same phenomena from the point of view of a number of different partial theories.

This latter manner of dealing with the oversimplifications of partial theories could perhaps be seen as a reasonable way to take advantage of the strengths and explanatory power of each theory. However, the concepts of the different theories are not coordinated with each other. While this form of eclecticism can be superior to a strict adherence to a partial theory this lack of coordination leads, I think, to a kind of static hodgepodge, with little dynamic potential for conceptual and theoretical development. This development is so important because through it new questions can be asked and new discoveries made.

To look at an example of this: most of the findings I presented related to trauma have of course been discussed previously in the analytic literature. However, by looking carefully at how these were related to the theory of defense, we were able to correct Freud's misleading terminology and conceptualization of traumatic anxiety as leading to primal repression. We could see that true trauma—the massive overwhelming of the stimulus barrier—leads to a shutting down of many ego functions, including the ability to mount a defense. Keeping the big picture of a general theory in mind allowed us to ask on the one hand, if trauma did not motivate primal repression, what did?—which led to the idea of pervasive affect motivating different primal defenses—and on the other hand we could look at the outcome of trauma and inquire into its actual relation to defenses. None of this was new. I pointed out that Yorke, Wiseberg, and Freeman (1989), among others, had articulated ideas about the true motivation of primal defenses, while of course innumerable investigators within and outside of analysis have elucidated aspects of trauma such as dissociation and the very different type of memory that is formed during trauma.

It is clear that a total composite theory or a general theory was not necessary for these discoveries to be made. However, in a general theory concepts are connected one with the other, with such things as levels of inference and levels of abstraction of different concepts having been at least partially worked out. This allows discoveries to be contained and not overgeneralized, but this very restraint put upon discoveries leads to a greater potential for their further development. For instance in this case a number of authors have proposed that the dissociation or lack of symbolic processing related to trauma is the basic starting point for all other defenses. A general theory protects against such a theoretical reduction. The theory is really a collection and coordination, through more general and abstract ideas, of a large number of observations and inferences and the concepts built upon them. If one wishes to extend the reach of new ideas one should look carefully at the evidence for the old ideas—in this case the whole range of repressive and denial defenses. If we do this we can find many cases of defenses not based on trauma in the narrower sense.

To my mind the larger total theory does not in any way prescribe what can or cannot be true about reality. For instance it is possible that upon looking closely at the findings about, and conceptual understanding of, various defenses it would turn out that they actually are all based on trauma and its sequelae. In this case working with the larger theory would allow us to see the further ramifications of such findings, and to develop them in many directions, while of course at each step the new findings may turn out to have to be limited by other findings and ideas. I do not think in this case that the idea of trauma can be extended in this direction (that is, as the basis of all defenses), but on the other hand in looking at dissociation we saw that it had a primary, passively suffered, form and an active secondary one, and that these could be combined with denial to form the compound defense of splitting of the ego. Aspects of the total theory, for instance an understanding of ego regression and the nature of defenses, can help us further elucidate the nature of this compound defense, while at the same time other aspects of the theory, such as an understanding of the weakness of the synthetic function in splitting in borderline disorders and of the nature of the defense of isolation in obsessionals, prevents us from performing the theoretical reduction of claiming that all splitting is splitting of the ego, or perhaps to go even further and claim that all defenses are based on splitting of some sort. As the theory limits the scope of new findings, it also leads us to ask further questions and develop the findings in other ways, such as for instance wondering if there are compound defenses involving dissociation and other defenses, for example dissociation and repression.

In this case a deeper understanding of the nature of the zero process and the development of some clinical ideas regarding the activity necessary to analyze zero process phenomena, led me to probe more deeply with a number of patients whom I was treating who had suffered severe ongoing sexual and/or physical abuse. I was already aware of the ideas of various analysts and others working with trauma about split identity, but as I analyzed more deeply at the clinical level I was surprised to discover for myself the ubiquity of split identity. This clinical research took place a number of years into the work on this book, so that I was already in the habit of not reducing findings around trauma to other dynamics, such as those related to the drives. I was starting to appreciate the extent to which trauma and its aftermath, especially areas of zero process functioning, constituted a world of phenomena with quite different characteristics to that of the primary and secondary processes. As I analyzed split identity in a number of my patients this knowledge, as well as my readings of other authors, led me to be much bolder than previously in talking of the two identities not just as aspects of the person, but as separate people. I realized this was true at the level of psychic reality within the area of zero process functioning, and over many years of working with severely traumatized individuals I had become more adept at both spotting these areas of split identity and at working with them in the active and concrete manner that is necessary when analyzing the zero process and zero process defenses. I remembered that I had in my reading come across the idea of mutual antagonism of different identities serving defensive purposes, and it was obvious enough that they held different aspects of the trauma. It then suddenly struck me that perhaps this antagonism might be a form of counterforce defense—a kind of zero process version of repression—and I proceeded to try out this line of interpretation. I said such things as, "I wonder if the dislike and even hatred that the two parts have for each other is a way of keeping things separate" and interpreted that both identities actually had a common goal of keeping up the mutual aggression and avoiding reconciliation. This line of interpretation led eventually to a better understanding of the economic and dynamic aspects of splitting of the identity. This seems to me to be only the beginning of a deeper investigation. I have described this beginning in order to provide a concrete example of how a larger general theory can put newer ideas into context. While this may limit their generalization (for instance I realized there were other forms of splitting defenses and splits related to lack of synthesis, not all reducible to split identity), it at the same time allows a deeper and more profound development of the new ideas.

Thus this example demonstrates concretely how the very restraints put on the overgeneralization of discoveries and conceptual innovations by a general theory actually aids in the further development and deepening of the new insights. By preventing an overly quick but superficial broadening of the insight, a general theory can lead to the asking of productive questions which guide one into developing the idea more fruitfully and linking it to various other aspects of the theory. Any of the major ideas developed in this book can be looked upon as examples of this: for instance the concepts of the zero process, of attentional defenses, and of contrast defenses.

Critics of ego psychology, metapsychology, and an overarching general theory of psychoanalysis have said exactly the opposite of what I am asserting here. They have argued that these theories exercised in the past a stultifying effect on innovation through a hegemonic control of which ideas were considered acceptable and which were not. It is certainly true that the theory was used in this way by some, while others were able to themselves use the theory productively: for instance Erik Erickson in studying society and the individual, Peter Blos in studying adolescence, and Margaret Mahler and Edith Jacobson in investigating the early development of the self and object relations. Each of these authors brought findings and ideas into the main body of psychoanalytic ego psychological theory and the theory both prevented the findings from being overgeneralized as well as giving these authors the tools to further develop their ideas.

The misuse of psychoanalytic ego psychology to stifle debate or exclude innovative ideas is to my mind not at all argument against its validity or usefulness. Narrow mindedness and intellectual totalitarianism are not confined to a particular historical period or to a particular theory. These tendencies will use whatever is at hand for their purposes.

I would not at all deny that a general theory can stultify innovation, as supporters of such a theory take its ideas—or at least some of them—as fundamental and not to be questioned. In relation to this, I should clarify what I have said about a larger theory guarding against overgeneralization and the resulting theoretical reduction by limiting the scope of new discoveries. I do not mean by this that there are certain immutable givens to the general theory that *a priori* limit a new finding or idea—that is to say, that the new finding or idea should not be allowed to transgress against these *a priori* givens. I believe that *any* aspect of a general theory, even its most basic and general principles and its seemingly most secure and important findings and ideas, should be seen as open to revision or complete rejection. I feel that a larger general theory putting limits on the range of applicability of an idea is not to be equated with its putting limits on freedom of thought or inquiry. Rather, by having a well-conceptualized theory in which the differentiation and integration between different ideas is worked out in some depth, one can get a sense of where a new idea or set of ideas, and new data, fit in. However, it is important, when we use a general theory in this manner, that we have a deep enough knowledge of the interconnecting web of evidence (clinical and extra-clinical) and inference that have been used to build the conceptual structure of the theory, as well as understanding the interconnection and various levels—of abstraction and of inference—of these concepts. If one has new concepts and/or data, they could quite legitimately replace or rework older ones, but only once they come up against this "deep" aspect of the theory. For instance in this book, my reworking of ideas about repression and denial were strengthened by going through this process. In doing this some aspects of the original theory, for instance ideas about the relation between denial and splitting of the ego, and ideas about denial as a more primitive defense that is over time superseded by repression, were seen to be confusing, not well worked out, and often contradicted by clinical evidence. In this situation, there is no reason not to rework a concept such as denial, or even to completely overthrow one, as I did by replacing the idea of traumatic anxiety with pervasive anxiety, thus delinking trauma and repression. But in order to jettison aspects of the theory, one should know the full extent of what one is throwing out—this is what I mean by a "deep" understanding of the theory—and one should be certain that the new ideas can contain and explain all the findings that led to the original theory.

Of course this description does not accurately portray the messy way in which we intuit new ideas, play with them in our mind in all sorts of ways, and test them against various forms of evidence. During these early phases of creativity a general theory should not weigh too heavily—in fact at times it's best if it is hardly considered at all—as one plays with all sorts of seemingly outlandish ideas, and tries them on for size. If a general theory does weigh too heavily at this phase, it may either crush the creative spark, or one may be tempted to simply jettison the whole theory because it is such a burden and a hindrance to free thought and investigation. However, as one tests and more seriously develops ideas, they should in the end be considered in relation to a deep understanding of the general theory. One danger of not doing this is that new ideas, or retreads of old ones, can run like a wildfire through psychoanalytic theory, destroying many valuable aspects of it without good reason, and without offering a reasonable replacement set of ideas to explain the findings that led to the original theory (Shevrin, 2003).

A recent example of this process is the overextension of ideas about implicit memory. Findings and ideas regarding implicit memories (procedural and emotional) are used now by authors from many analytic theoretical orientations to explain phenomena related to repression and trauma. I have gone into some detail earlier about this topic, and will not repeat the specifics of my arguments at this time. I only bring it up here as a good example of overgeneralization and theoretical reduction that is ongoing at present. The authors who extend the idea of implicit memory to cover repression and traumatic memories do not, in my opinion, address in detail the findings that have led to older analytic theories. For instance in the case of repression these include the transference resistance and the recovery of whole areas of declarative memory, as detailed for instance in the work of Ernst Kris (1956b, 1956c). In fact in these classic studies of repression Kris noted that the massive childhood repression that swept away so much of the autobiographical (declarative and semantic) memories of childhood spared procedural memories. Children during the ages of 5 and 6, when these major repressions are instituted, do not show a decline in the physical or mental skills supported by procedural memory, unless these become caught up symbolically in repressed conflicts. Kris demonstrated, through detailed clinical examples, the importance, and continued influence, of repressed autobiographical memories, as well as the changes in symptom and character that came through the recovery of these repressed explicit memories.[3]

I am not suggesting that these formulations of Kris, or my own regarding repression presented in earlier chapters, should in any way be taken as final statements about the nature of repression. I merely mention them to point out how ideas that attempt to explain many of the phenomena related to repression using the concept of implicit memory do not engage earlier findings and ideas about repression in any depth. Similarly, ideas about implicit memories have been proposed as an explanation for various post-traumatic phenomena. Here too the connection of these newer ideas with a century of findings with regard to trauma, including many that I have conceptualized using the idea of the zero process, is often not explored in any depth. If it were, the importance of declarative memories in post-traumatic phenomena would have to be recognized and the explanatory reach of the idea of implicit memories would have to be limited.

The question is not whether the idea of implicit memories is valid or not. Clearly implicit memories play a part in post-traumatic phenomena and in repression, but the question is what their role is and how it fits in with, and interacts with, the better understood dynamics related to declarative and semantic memories. My own comments on implicit memories in this work have been largely negative, in that I have been trying to argue against their overgeneralization and the consequent theoretical reductions, which has led to a number of well-established ideas and findings being thrown out the window without full consideration of why this had been done. This demonstrates again the fact that in theoretical reductions, what is proposed as an explanation has validity and usefulness, but this very validity of the new ideas can blind people to their destructive power when they are overextended. In the long run my negative commentary would need to be supplemented by positive attempts to find the true part played by implicit memories in repression, trauma, and other dynamics. For instance implicit emotional memory seems to play an important part in the hyperarousal and the automatic "triggering" responses following trauma, while procedural and implicit emotional memory are involved in the automatization of defenses over time, which makes them so stable, and so hard to reverse in therapy. Implicit emotional memory may play a part in what I have called pervasive anxiety. Part of the working through process, so long and so arduous, but often so fruitful, that follows on insight, no doubt also relates to the persistence of implicit memories. It may seem that limiting the reach of this concept weakens it, but in the long run it does the opposite. By finding the proper scope and reach of a concept, we actually promote a deeper exploration of what it can explain rather than a superficial, but often ephemeral, attempt to use it to explain everything.

I would not suggest that these considerations regarding overextension of concepts can by themselves decide such issues as the proper place of implicit memories within psychoanalytic theory. Even the ideas of overgeneralization and theoretical reduction can be overextended beyond their proper sphere of usefulness. I have merely gone into a bit of detail with regard to a few issues in order to illustrate concretely what I mean by the useful guidance that a larger general theory can give, and how this guidance, and constraint, can actually strengthen and deepen new ideas and findings.

I would like now to describe a few aspects of the specific larger theory with which I work, and which has guided me in developing the ideas presented in this work.

Aspects of a General Theory

The basic theoretical postulates I have used, and at times revised, have come from Freudian metapsychology and the additions to it from ego psychologists, especially Heinz Hartmann. I work with the idea of two basic drives—the aggressive and the sexual. This is not to say that there are not other imperative needs—for human contact, or for food, for instance—but the two first mentioned drives differ from these in important ways. The idea of an aggressive drive seems to be especially problematic for many people. It is often maintained that aggression is either a response to frustration or a response that can be mobilized to provide the driving force for achieving other goals. Many instances of aggression fall into these categories but others—for instance clearly pleasurable scratching, hair pulling, and pinching which appear near the end of the first year of life—do not. I think there is a good deal of this sort of observational as well as psychoanalytic evidence for an aggressive drive. Of course there are many transformations and uses of aggression so that, as with so much else in psychoanalysis, there is no simple or single piece of evidence for or against the conceptualization of aggression as a drive.

I have described one transformation of aggression, in its use as a defensive counterforce, but there are many others, including its use for motility, separation from the object both physically and mentally, and assertiveness, to name just a few. In fact it is this plasticity through displaceability and neutralization which distinguishes the two drives of sexuality and aggression from other drives such as hunger, thirst, or attachment. These two basic drives are, unlike the many others we possess, quite distanced from reality, and Freud discovered a whole unconscious fantasy life based upon them.

Hartmann (1948) presented a basic idea about the evolutionary development of these two drives that I think helps us make sense of a number of aspects of human psychology. He noted that the instincts (including the sexual and aggressive instincts) of most "lower" animals (such as insects for example) include both the drive (i.e., propulsive) aspect and the connection to specific external perceptual releasers and specific behaviors. In certain evolutionary lines of development, including mammals, the reality adaptation and the propulsive force aspect have become to some extent separated. Hartmann stated that "the freeing of many abilities from close connection with one definite instinctual tendency, we could described analytically as the emergence of the ego as a definable psychic system" (1948, p 81). With this development, which certainly did not begin with Homo Sapiens,[4] many functions that help in reality orientation such as perception, memory, and attention become to a variable extent independent of the drives. This of course allows a greater flexibility and adaptability in reactions to reality.

The other side of this coin is that the sexual and aggressive drives become more estranged from reality. This does not mean that they have no contact with reality. Such so-called ego functions as perception and memory are clearly available to the id. (It is hard to conceive of how an id wish [drive derivative] could exist without these functions.) However the id is estranged from reality in the sense that it does not take an adaptive stance towards it. Thus such processes as attention, judgment, and inhibition are not part of id functioning. The ego and the id interact in complex ways to bring about the adaptation to reality achieved in lower animals by their instincts. The displacement and neutralization of the drives provides much of the energy that powers various functions such as motility, various ego interests, and other ego functions. At the same time these drives, through an inner fantasy life, live a life partly separate from, and often in opposition to, reality adaptation. This is the aspect of mental functioning that Freud devoted most of his life to studying.

When investigating the interaction of the ego and the id Freud looked especially at defenses: ways in which the ego opposed the direct expression of these drives that were now so estranged from reality. This was the first meaning of defense, but it was obvious enough to Freud that defenses also often worked against a full knowledge of reality. Freud studied these defenses against the awareness of reality especially near the end of his life, using the concepts of disavowal and splitting of the ego. I have in this book expanded on these ideas and revised them, as well as attempting to demonstrate that these defenses against reality are equal in their importance for normal functioning and for neurosis to the better known defenses against drives and affects.

In terms of the evolutionary development from unitary instincts to a partial separation of their drive and reality-oriented components, we can understand the development of defenses against the drives as one way that the ego came to gain some mastery over these now unruly drive components of the original instinct.[5] They were one function, among others such as neutralization and sublimation, that the ego substituted for the former constitutionally given tight coupling between drive and reality adaptation.[6] But why would defenses against reality develop (i.e., be favored by natural selection)? In fact if one thinks of the gradual emancipation, in some lines of evolution, of many functions related to reality orientation and adaptation (perception, memory, attention, motility) from a close tie to largely pre-programmed instincts, one can see that this development opens up great possibilities for flexibility and adaptation, but also presents certain problems. Just as there is a lessening of the preset coordination between the processes of adaptation to reality and the drives, so is there a lessening of this preset coordination between the ego and reality. This is replaced to a great extent (but not completely) by learning, which greatly increases adaptability but also presents its own complications. One consequence of this lack of pre-programmed coordination between the ego and reality is the propensity of mammalian species, even ones relatively far removed from humans such as dogs and cats, towards psychic traumatization when their stimulus barrier is overwhelmed. While the nature of this traumatic response varies between species there are clearly also similarities, such as traumatization occurring especially with surprise, the triggering of memories of the trauma by perceptions similar to the original, and the development of phobias based on these.

With the further development of judgment and thinking freed from a tight coupling with instinct, a perception of unpleasant realities (i.e., ones that cause unpleasant affects) leads to the development of the various defenses against reality as ways of protecting the ego from being overwhelmed by these affects. Here too, as with the drives, the ego's greater autonomy and the diminishing of the area where preset responses reign leads to greater flexibility, but also leaves the ego vulnerable. In this case there is a vulnerability to the perception of extremely distressing realities. Somewhat distressing realities are not a problem, since the affects are not overwhelming and since the perception of these realities and the ensuing affective reactions are important in leading the ego to plan adaptive responses. Even at this level, attentional defenses and suppression can prove useful in keeping upsetting feelings at bay till the reality can be dealt with. Extremely distressing realities, about which the person is helpless to do anything, are another matter, and can lead to the pervasive affect which I have suggested as the motivation for primal denials. The reality of death is a good example—the prototype in some ways—of the sort of reality that leads to these primal denials.

I am convinced that forms of these defenses exist in other mammalian species, but the questions of what these forms consist of, and of how their evolutionary development may have taken place, will have to be left to another time. An investigation of these questions, as well as similar ones related to defenses against the drives, would require a careful working out of the true connections between the concepts of evolutionary biology, such as populations, species, speciation, and genetic programs, and those of psychoanalysis. Attempts at working out some of the connections between these two fields began with Freud (1913) and have continued since, for instance in the work of Max Shur in the 1960s and more recently by Slavin and Kriegman (1992). Recent advances in our knowledge of the evolution of hominids open up intriguing possibilities in this direction, as do advances in general evolutionary theory and in genetics. A whole new field—evolutionary developmental biology—has emerged recently from these advances (Carroll, 2005). This field involves the study of the changes in developmental programs that take place in evolution, and that in fact mediate between genetic variations and evolutionary change. It may be quite fruitful to attempt a coordination between our own psychoanalytic insights into development and the ideas in this rapidly advancing field. I have hopes that the ideas developed in this book may help with this coordination, as well as with a more general coordination between evolutionary biology and psychoanalysis, but this is a task for another day. I intend to devote a later work to this topic.

To return now to psychoanalytic theorizing: we might ask whether there are characteristics that apply generally to defenses, beyond their function of protecting the ego on the two fronts of reality and the drives. I think that the short answer is no. The ego uses whatever tools are at hand for the job. Some defensive processes, such as turning against the self and reversal, involve the use of characteristics of the primary process by the ego, while others such as attentional defenses use basic ego functions that are used at other times to comprehend reality accurately, and still others such as repression use neutralized drives in a process quite unique to the defense. Characteristics of the zero process are also taken up by the ego and used in various forms of defense.

The fact that we use the same word to designate these different processes should not lead us to attempt a falsely unified theory of defenses. The thing that is the most different about different defenses is their inner natures—the processes by which they accomplish their task. The things that are most the same are the function of defenses (to keep certain things from awareness and action) and their motive (always an unpleasant affect).

It may be worthwhile at this point to think about how affects fit into the basic psychoanalytic theory I have presented so far. Kernberg (2001) has argued that affects are the building blocks of drives. He described peak affect states combining with unconscious meaning to produce the sexual and aggressive drives. Shevrin (1997) argued conversely that the modern neuroscientific understanding of the brain supports the idea of drives as independent entities, not as derivatives of affects.

Affects are ego processes that, unlike some others such as defense or neutralization, are easy to observe in oneself. I noted earlier in this chapter that there is much in the mind that is only partially or not at all amenable to this direct perceptual knowledge, and that these things have to be inferred. As many psychoanalysts have moved away from using these inferred realities in their explanations, affects have assumed a central place. This is not to say that affects would not have an important place in any psychoanalytic theory, but in some newer theories a theoretical reduction is affected in which aspects of drive theory are collapsed into the theory of affects. To my mind affects can have two major instigators: perceptions or judgments about reality, and the drives. (Jacobson [1971b] has presented a detailed and subtle explanation of this basic view of affects.) It is certain affects that arise in relation to reality perceptions that are the motivators of defenses. Any unpleasant affect can act in this way.

But of what use are affects, and why would their development and proliferation have been favored during the evolutionary development of the ego and the id out of the original unitary instincts of lower animals? There is no doubt more than one answer to these questions. Affects help to communicate to others our state as well as informing us of various aspects of our inner and outer reality, and affects can help with inhibition of action by allowing some amount of discharge of drive or ego tendencies that impel us to action. It is especially the informative aspects of affects that are relevant to the study of defenses. At the same time affects seem to have the power to set defenses in motion because there is something about them—probably partly related to the bodily processes that occur—that gives them a very compelling quality.

Affects may originally have arisen from the delay of discharge and action, as Darwin (1872) has suggested, but they have come to serve many useful functions. As an example, as many ego functions became partially freed from instinct, rudimentary forms of thought and judgment would have developed in many animals. But, as I have noted previously with humans, the perceptual apparatus of these animals would not have been well suited to perceiving these processes of thought. Affects were one major way in which the outcome of these thought processes could be brought to perception in these animals, just as affects perform this function in humans.

I described one example of this use of affect in the "gut feelings" that we get when we first meet someone. We may, for instance, feel anxious, or relaxed, or confused. These feelings may be partly a product of picking up on the affect of the other person, for instance their anxiety, as well as being a product of unconscious communication from the other person. However they are also the product of, or the expression of the end point of, a process of thought and judgment about the person. While some people make good use of these gut feelings, many others do not trust them, partly because they come without any knowledge of how the conclusions were arrived at. This is a general characteristic of this sort of affect—they inform one of the outcome of a process of thought, but not of the steps along the way. Before the development of language certain memories of perceptual experiences could be evoked by thought and give some indication of its content and progress, but many aspects of thought could not be well represented in this fashion and often, as the example of gut feelings shows, there is no representation at all of the processes of thought, only of their conclusions.

I think this aspect of affects was of central importance to the functioning of thinking and judgment as the ego developed evolutionarily. Early on in their development these reactions were closer to the pre-programmed reaction patterns of lower animals, but out of these developed the connection of affects to more complex thought. These simpler reactions were never lost, and even at present exist alongside the later developed ones, just as these later developed ones exist alongside symbolic, verbal thought.

As the ego developed, through evolution, its partial autonomy from the drives and from reality, it developed various tools from aspects of the mind that already existed in order to both protect this autonomy and to regulate its interactions with the drives and with reality. A certain class of these tools we designate as defenses, because they block certain mental contents from awareness and from direct translation into action. The signals that set defenses into motion were unpleasant affects, which were the outcome of a process of thought and evaluation. Before thoughts themselves could significantly come into awareness (that is, before the development of symbolic language), affects were the source of knowledge about the outcome of thought processes, and along with influencing action they also formed part of a phylogenetically early regulation by the ego, involving defenses, of mental functioning. The unpleasant affect (anxiety, psychic pain) linked evaluation of a situation and the judgment of a bad outcome (danger) with the internal action of one or more defenses.

In arguing for this point of view one would have to deal with those philosophers and psychoanalysts who equate thought with language. I think it is quite evident that higher animals and young humans before the acquisition of language are capable of thought and judgment. Of course the representation of thought by symbolic language allows an enormous expansion of the capabilities of thought. One becomes conscious of the acoustic or visual aspects of language and can thus become conscious of thought. We could say that at this point the thought has become preconscious: it can now be made the object of consciousness if attention is turned towards it. Since in philosophy one thinks about thinking or thinks about other topics, such as the nature of reality, in an abstract and self reflective way, one can see why philosophers so often conceptualize thinking as requiring language. One cannot think about thinking without language, but one can certainly think without it.

Thus the thinking that notices, judges, and connects various clues, both with each other and with previous experiences, in order to come to the conclusion that a person (despite their smile) is not to be trusted and in fact is dangerous, does not need language. Of course to express the conclusion of this piece of thinking as I have just done requires language, but one might just as well become aware of it through a feeling. For instance one's hair might stand up a bit on the back of one's neck, and one may get a feeling of fear. If this person is one's parent, one might also feel the pain of longing that cannot be fulfilled. If intense enough, these feelings may become the motivation for a primal denial. (This was what happened in E's case in relation to her psychopathic father—see chapters 3, 5, and 7.) To further consider these thoughts at a distance requires language, but the setting up of this primal denial precludes the later reworking of one's awareness and of what one's reactions should be, at the level of language. Rather, the primal denial sets up a fixed pattern, becoming more and more automatic during development, that is the basis for other, secondary and after, defenses.

The analysis of defense consists essentially in the raising of these automatic processes to the level of awareness and of symbolic thought. When this is attempted one meets resistances to the awareness of the defense. I have argued in the chapter on denial that these defenses are attentional ones— directed against the awareness of an inner reality. Since this inner reality (a defense) is already difficult to bring to conscious awareness because of its lack of perceptual qualities and because of its increasing automaticity, it is my impression that these defenses against the awareness of defenses do not have to be particularly strong until we attempt to pull the defense into consciousness. This is one area where the concept of forms of implicit memory is needed to understand the processes involved. It is most likely that forms of priming and procedural memory are involved in the automatic processes that keep defenses in place, and only with the challenge to this automatic regulation brought about by psychoanalytic work are these overcome enough that we see the attentional defenses against the awareness of defenses, and can bring it to conscious awareness.

When we do manage to make the original defense conscious, it slowly loses its force in the working through process and we gain access to what is defended against (in the example given it would be the knowledge of the lack of caring and connection and the lack of conscience of the parent). At this point the whole complex of thought, judgment, and defense can be raised to the level of symbolic language.

The importance of symbolic thought in the analysis of defenses should not lead to a denigration of the importance of the sequence of non-symbolic thought, affect, and defense in normal, adaptive functioning. Even after the analysis of her primal denial of her father's psychopathy, in the example just given above, a patient such as E will still be left with the basic primal denials around helplessness and death, as well as dealing with the issues around her father through a combination of symbolic language processing, suppression, compartmentalization, and some amount of remaining denial. The best resolution of the problem of a fixed, automatic defense that was adaptive at one time but has become much less so is not a replacement of all such defenses by higher language-based thought and judgment, but rather a better organization and ordering of the different methods of regulation (Hartmann, 1950b), so that each can perform the tasks to which it is best suited at the present point in the person's development. Even as, through the course of life, more tasks can be taken over by language-based thinking, there still remain many tasks of importance that are best handled by other means, of which defensive processes are one. In fact the movement during development is as much, or even more so, to move many processes to the level of automatic functioning so that higher order conscious and symbolic thought can be left free to pursue other aims. This is more obvious with certain physical skills. For instance as one gains experience driving a car, and as more and more aspects of the act of driving becomes automatic, not needing conscious attention except in unusual circumstances, one becomes a better driver, as there is more attention left for important tasks such as looking ahead for possible problems, thinking about where one might have to turn, etc. This same movement towards automatization is an important part of development in the mental sphere as well, as more and more lower order processing is done automatically. The fact that we try to reverse this automatization in analysis, which we do with a specific goal in mind, should not mislead us into thinking of automatization as maladaptive. It is in fact vitally necessary for adaptive mental functioning.

This topic—the automatization of defensive processes—is one that has not been addressed in any depth in this work. To do so would require further work in developing a better understanding of how implicit and explicit memory processes interact, and how they and other processes, such as drive neutralization and the ego's integrative function, lead to the development of automatization. Hartmann (1939) made a beginning in conceptualizing these phenomena, but did not go much beyond describing them.

There are quite a number of topics and areas of conceptualization in relation to defenses that I have not dealt with in this book. I do not see this as a deficiency, since what I set out to do was not to write a textbook on the topic, but rather to present original ideas and new integrations of older ideas. The whole feeling I hoped to convey was not of a completely formulated, closed conceptual system, but rather a feeling of the opening up of new vistas, most of which remain to be explored. In presenting my ideas, of course I advocated for them. But the best ideas in psychoanalysis, as I have stated in arguing for a general theory, are those that do not destroy all other ideas in their path, but rather allow us to see a new facet of the complex, multifaceted phenomena that a truly general psychology seeks to explore.

Summary

I argued in this chapter for a realist position in relation to the science of psychoanalysis. That is, I argued that the currently popular idea that the data of psychoanalysis are completely subjectively or intersubjectively determined is not tenable from a logical point of view. From this more general argument, I looked at the nature of psychoanalytic conceptualizations, arguing that we have trouble thinking of many mental contents and functions as "real" both because of their lack of perceptual referents and because ideas about them have not become part of conventional knowledge. As a consequence of this difficulty, many psychoanalytic ideas are seen as abstract, when in fact they are not at a high level of abstraction, but rather at a high level of inference, as are many other scientific ideas such as an atom or a dinosaur, which we more readily understand to refer to real things.

In looking at the main intellectual tools of psychoanalysis, I noted that they are concepts. I discussed why the use of concepts makes sense in our kind of science, and made a differentiation between the conceptual and the mathematical sciences, based on their main theoretical tool. I also discussed a general problem in science, which is also an issue in psychoanalysis. This is theoretical reductionism, which occurs when a concept is overextended in its explanatory reach, so that other independent ideas are subsumed under it or are completely done away with and replaced by the overextended concept or set of concepts. One of the best defenses against theoretical reduction is a well worked out general theory in which different concepts are coordinated one with the other in terms of their proper sphere of explanatory power, levels of abstraction, and levels of inference. I argued for the superiority of such a theory over a pluralistic use of many partial theories. While the dangers of a larger general theory in stifling debate and innovation are certainly real enough, such a theory is indispensible in coordinating various concepts and findings. It is this coordination that leads to further questions, that leads us to spot inconsistencies and false deductions and inferences, and that allows us to place a new discovery in its proper context, in relation to other findings and ideas. The fact that a general theory can be misused is no reason to dispense with it, as many psychoanalysts have done. The strongest argument for the fruitfulness of having a general theory, and for the usefulness of a particular general theory, are concrete instances of its use. I would suggest that the theoretical and clinical explorations in this book can all be looked at from this particular angle, as demonstrating the dynamic potential of a well-coordinated theory, and specifically of the theories of ego psychology that see mental functioning as a product of a number of independent factors: ego functions, the drives and the primary process, and the zero process and its particular contents and mode of functioning.

I ended the chapter with a brief description of the specific general theory with which I work. This theory sees the human mind as a product of a long evolutionary development in which the instincts of animals with simpler nervous systems changed in certain ways. These instincts involve a tight coupling of the "drive" or motivational component with specific perceptions that trigger largely pre-programmed responses. In certain evolutionary lines, including mammals, this pre-programmed coupling was loosened. The "drive" portion of some instincts became to a certain extent separated from preset environmental triggers and behavioral responses. Thus the evaluation of the environment and control of behavior was partially freed from an instinctual tie, and from this developed various ego functions such as attention and various forms of thought. The relative independence of the ego from the drive portion of what was a unitary instinct led to much more flexibility and opened up enormous adaptive possibilities. I suggested that the nature and functions of the various defenses we find in humans can be understood as one of a number of methods of interaction between the now partially autonomous ego and the drives and reality which it now confronts without as many preset responses.

Term

Theoretical Reduction: The replacement of a number of concepts in a complex, multilayered theory by a single set of ideas, when these ideas do not have the proper explanatory reach of the concepts they replace. Another way of putting it is to say that a portion of a complex theory is overgeneralized to become the sole explanation for various phenomena. In such a situation the overgeneralized part is usually a useful and powerful set of ideas, so that it is not in itself wrong. What is wrong, and often very detrimental to the further development of a theory, is that many other important findings and concepts are replaced, left out, and thrown out by the overextension of a useful set of ideas.

Notes

1. I would refer readers to this article and its references, as well as others in the analytic literature, for an in-depth discussion of the philosophical aspects of this issue. My own discussion is of necessity brief and focused on a few points.

2. For a detailed account of the quite complex nature of the theory of evolution, see Mayr's book *The Growth of Biological Thought* (1982). Gould's (2002) comprehensive book on the theory of evolution takes issue with aspects of the evolutionary synthesis, and also provides a good demonstration of the complex conceptual structure of the theory, with its many levels of inference and abstraction, the phenomena of emergence, as well as the myriad methodologies which are used to collect the data used in the construction of the theory.

3. It is probably worth repeating that confusion can arise if the words "explicit" and "implicit," used to designate specific forms of memory, are equated with "conscious" and "unconscious." There are two forms of explicit memory—declarative (perceptual) and semantic (knowledge), both of which can be repressed into the unconscious. The word "implicit" suggests something deeper and more hidden than

"explicit" memories, but again, the word really just refers to the fact that these forms of memory normally function unconsciously, while explicit memories are at times brought into conscious awareness (when they aren't repressed or otherwise defended against). Even this distinction is not absolute: one can become aware of the functioning of implicit memory to some extent, while undefended explicit memories quite regularly guide our thoughts and actions without our being aware of them (i.e., they are processed preconsciously).

4. Freud (1938a) felt that higher animals, along with humans, had the structural separation into an ego and an id.

5. It is important to keep in mind that many behaviors remain, even in humans, more pre-programmed than others, and even the two malleable drives are not without some amount of pre-programming and reality orientation. The discussion about the ego and the drives and their evolutionary development in this section has been much simplified.

6. To say it this way implies that the ego was deciding the course of evolution, which of course was not the case. I am just using a verbal shortcut for describing evolutionary change through natural selection.

Conclusion

What probably stands out most about this work, at least on first inspection, are the various conceptual distinctions that I have made and the new concepts that I have introduced. I have distinguished between attentional defenses, counterforce defenses, and zero process defenses. Each of these three great classes of defense corresponds to one of the three great forms of mental functioning: attentional defenses to the secondary process, counterforce defenses to the primary process, and zero process defenses to the zero process. I do not mean that these defenses are each only a product of a particular mode of functioning. All defenses are active, intentional measures taken by the organized part of the personality—the ego—and thus in this sense are all intimately related to the secondary process. However the ego takes over, and uses for its own purposes, characteristics of the other modes of functioning. In this sense different groups of defenses can be said to be related to, and share some of the characteristics of, different modes of mental functioning. Another connection between the classes of defenses and modes of mental functioning can be seen in the usual object of each class of defense. Attentional defenses usually act against judgments about reality and other contents that reside within the ego and under the sway of the secondary process, and these defenses protect the ego against being overwhelmed by reality. Counterforce defenses usually act against derivatives of powerful drives pushing up from the id under the influence of the primary process, and they set up a boundary and a barrier between the primary and the secondary processes (the repression barrier). Zero process defenses usually defend against the upsurge

321

of memories and affects related to trauma that are under the sway of the zero process, and these forms of defense set up and maintain a boundary between the ego and areas of zero process functioning.

What I have described is the basic lay of the land in terms of the conceptual distinctions that I have made in developing a new theory about defenses. Looked at from another angle, however, the theoretical ideas that I have presented not only make distinctions but also show us new connections and integrations. For instance not only repression, but many other defenses as well, were seen to have a primal form, each motivated by pervasive affects. Another example of a new connection is that a number of symptoms and disorders—perversions, phobias, splitting of the identity, and conversion symptoms—were conceptualized as being expressions of characteristics of zero process functioning. Four very important, but seemingly quite different, defenses—repression, obsessional defenses, splitting of the identity, and projective identification—were proposed as all having at their core a counterforce formed from aggressive drive energy. In each of these defenses except repression the counterforce is combined with other defensive processes.

While I have often stated my findings and ideas in a categorical form, perhaps giving the impression of a fully formulated theoretical system, I would not want to end this book before asking the reader not to be fooled by this appearance of completeness. To begin with, it is clear that a number of the ideas introduced were not developed past a very crude first formulation. Examples include the idea of zero process neuroses, and of splitting of the identity and projective identification as counterforce defenses. I find it quite exciting to consider where a more detailed investigation of these ideas, and the phenomena to which they refer, may lead us. Beyond this, every idea that I have introduced, even ones that were more extensively worked over, could easily lead to many questions that would in turn lead to deeper investigation and perhaps a reformulation of parts of the theory. To pick a question that comes to my mind as I write this: I have defined primal defenses by their motive— pervasive affect. I have also asserted that the motive for a defense is the most variable aspect of the process, and that defenses are best defined in terms of their mechanism, not their motive or their object. Given this, does the term "primal defense" perhaps suggest more of a commonality in these defenses than is really present? Are they just stronger versions of secondary defenses? Or are there other unique characteristics of primal defenses? Are primal defenses a special case, where the nature of the motive affects quite profoundly the nature of the defensive process? Or perhaps is there not so much commonality between different primal defenses, so that some of these questions would have to be answered differently for different primal defenses?

This issue of defining a defense by its motive brings to my mind contrast defenses. I have found this idea extremely helpful clinically, but here too I defined the defense by its motive—an unpleasant feeling that was part of a contrast reaction. I noted that most contrast defenses involved denial (attentional) mechanisms. Do they always? Could we define contrast defenses as only attentional defenses that are motivated by contrast reactions? Perhaps there are repressive or zero process defenses with this motivation—that is, counterforce and zero process contrast defenses. Are these also important defenses that, as with attentional contrast defenses, have gone unrecognized because we have not had the conceptual tools to help us see them and think about them?

My point in asking these questions is not to answer them but rather to demonstrate how, even though the new concepts that I have put forward may have been presented in a manner suggesting a closed theory, one can open things up quite quickly with the proper questions. The questions that I presented were generated at the theoretical level, but of course clinical work could also lead to questions about the theory. I chose the examples, of primal and contrast defenses, to ask questions about because they were the first that came to mind. I think any of the ideas that I have developed in this work can be approached in this manner, with questions that crack open the seemingly solid theoretical structure. I do not think that this is a weakness of the theory that I have put forward, but rather a strength. It demonstrates a point that I championed in the last chapter: that a well worked out theory, with concepts that connect and integrate with each other at many levels of abstraction and inference, is a theory that has the potential to be more dynamic and fruitful in opening up new lines of inquiry and areas to explore.

All of this is another way of saying that this—that is, this conclusion to this particular work—is not only an ending but also a beginning. I have already mentioned two directions in which I intend to further the theoretical and clinical explorations begun here: an exploration of these ideas in relation to human evolution, and a deeper and broader investigation of trauma, the zero process, and splitting. There are many other topics that have been opened up that would repay further work.

It has been said that the brain is the most complex object in the universe. The mind, an expression of the workings of the brain, has a depth and complexity to rival that of the brain. It also has the paradoxical quality of being both everywhere and ever-present—it is our whole and only experience—and yet strangely elusive, like the air we breath. Freud showed us how little we know of the workings of the mind, and through his ideas of defense, drives, the primary process, and the dynamic unconscious, opened up a whole world of phenomena that analysts have been exploring now for over a century. It is sometimes said that Freud discovered the unconscious, but this is not true, as the idea had been around for a long time in one form or another. His original, and monumental, discoveries were of a different form of mental functioning that was usually unconscious—the primary process—as well as the discovery of childhood sexuality, including the oedipus complex and the phases of libidinal development. Freud's discoveries expanded not only our knowledge of the mind, but our very conception of its nature, extent, and reach. While Freud's early work concerned especially the deeper unconscious, the new knowledge about the drives, the developmental aspects of sexuality and aggression, and the primary process led to a quite different view of those parts of the mind—the ego and the secondary process—that were more familiar. In fact, these more familiar aspects can look strange and alien when seen from this new vantage point, with new knowledge.

This book has been about some of these familiar things—people's defensiveness and avoidance of what causes pain and distress—made strange and unfamiliar in interesting ways, by being looked at from the vantage point of the psychoanalytic method and psychoanalytic theory. The consciously perceived aspect of defense—the avoidance of, and resistance against thinking and feeling, certain things—has been shown to be a small piece of a large and intricate web of interwoven dynamics. I have tried to expand and deepen our knowledge of aspects of this web. I hope that I have in the process expanded the conception of the nature, extent, and reach of defenses, as a contribution to the larger project of exploration and expansion begun by Freud well over a century ago. But one thing leads to another in psychoanalysis and, to paraphrase the quote from Freud in the epigraph to this book, I set out to study defenses, but found myself developing ideas that went to the very heart, not only of the processes of defense, but of the workings of the mind more generally. I believe these ideas point the way to further insights into the developmental and evolutionary origins of the human mind, and in this sense they go to the very heart of how human nature has developed, and of what it means to be human.

~

Glossary

Active Primal Repression: See *primal repression.*

After Defense: After defenses are milder versions of a primal defense that build upon the primal defense and buttress it. They are motivated by milder versions of the pervasive affect that motivates the original primal defense. These milder versions are referred to as signal affect. As an example, after repression helps by repressing drive derivatives (for instance derivatives of a murderous impulse) that manage to get by a primal repression, and is motivated by a signal of anxiety that the ego puts out as it senses the danger associated with these derivatives.

Area of Primary Dissociation: An area of zero process functioning that remains after the traumatic process has run its course.

Attentional (Denial) Defense: A form of defense, usually directed against unpleasant realities (internal or external), which uses a shifting of the ego's attention as its basic mechanism.

Broad View of Technique: A view that sees the technical aspects of the analytic relationship, and the technical aspects of patient/analyst interactions, as applying to the totality of these interactions and of the relationship.

Compound Defense: A compound defense is composed of two or more basic defensive processes, such as a denial and counterforce, which act in concert and are quite tightly bound together. In the case of defenses acting together which are not compounded, one can generally analyze each part separately. The inability to do this indicates that the defenses are more tightly bound into a compound defense.

Contrast Defenses: These are defenses in which the person attempts to avoid awareness of a very distressing reality by avoiding realities that contrast too sharply with it, because of the tendency of these contrasting realities to evoke the distressing one.

Counterforce (Repressive) Defense: A form of defense, usually directed against a drive derivative or strong affect, which uses a strong counterforce to push its objects out of awareness and to keep them unconscious. The counterforce is formed from partially neutralized aggressive drive energy.

Defense: A psychical reaction or process that attempts to keep some mental content—a wish, feeling, judgment, etc.—from conscious awareness and/or behavioral expression. The usual, narrow definition sees a defense as the mental process or mental mechanism—as an example a shifting of attention—that accomplishes this end. Looked at more broadly a defensive process involves a *motive* that sets in motion the mechanism that acts against a mental content (the *object* of the defense) to keep it from awareness.

Defensive Externalization: An attentional defense in which, in order to avoid awareness of an unpleasant internal reality, such as an aspect of the self or a moral failing, the person shifts their attention to some similar aspect of external reality.

Defensive Guilt: An attentional defense in which a sense of guilt is emphasized in order to hide something else that is more distressing. The thing screened by the guilt usually belongs to one of two categories: either the guilt of someone else, most often a narcissistic parent or sibling, or feelings of helplessness and passivity, either from a trauma or some other situation. Guilt serves as a very good defense against these latter feelings because guilt has the subtext of "you could have done something and therefore you were responsible and guilty, but not helpless." Guilt is invariably used as a defense against the helplessness of trauma. It is also invariably a product of growing up with a seriously narcissistic parent, where it does double duty, defending against both the lack of guilt of the parent (borrowed guilt) and the feelings of despair and helplessness when the child realizes that the parent is incapable of caring.

Defensive Internalization: An attentional defense in which, in order to avoid awareness of a distressing external reality, such as the lack of caring of a parent, the person shifts their attention to an aspect of themselves.

Identification: A process in which a person shapes an aspect of themselves on the model of someone else. Identifications can be more global, or involve partial characteristics of the person identified with.

Internalization: A general term that covers many processes in which some aspect of external reality or external relationship shapes an internal process or structure of a person's mind. Identification, introjection, and defensive internalization are all types of internalization.

Introjection: A form of internalization in which aspects of one person are set up internally in another person's mind, as separate from the person's self. Introjects partake of many of the characteristics of the zero process, especially the immediate, experiential nature of its contents.

Motive for defense: The motive for defense is what sets the defensive process in motion. The motive seems always to be an unpleasant affect (conscious or unconscious), such as anxiety or psychic pain.

Narcissistic Ego Fixation: A clinging to the extremely pleasurable feelings of narcissistic enhancement and specialness that come from narcissistic overgratifications. Beyond this clinging, there are also three other important aspects to these fixations: the nature and extent of this clinging is kept from awareness by attentional defenses, the feeling that is clung to is itself used in screen defenses, and there are developmental and structural consequences to the clinging.

Narrow View of Technique: A view that sees the technical aspects of the analytic relationship as only one aspect of the interaction, existing within a matrix of the reality aspects of the situation and the real relationship.

Neutralization: In neutralization of a drive, the energy of the drive is left largely intact but its aims and nature are distanced from their original state. As an example, partially neutralized aggressive drive energy is used to form the counterforce of selective repression. In this defense the raw destructive aims of the drive are tamed and put to use to push other drives and strong feelings into the unconscious, and hold them there through a continuous application of force. This counterforce has some of the aims of the drive, but tamed and stabilized. A very similar partially neutralized aggressive drive energy is used in erecting and maintaining stable boundaries between the self and others.

Object of a defense: The thing (a mental content) against which a defense is directed, in order to keep the object from conscious awareness and/or behavioral expression. Wishes that are derived from basic drives, and judgments about reality are examples of objects of defenses. Not only mental contents but also mental functions such as specific cognitive functions or the integrative function can also become objects of a defense.

Passive Primal Repression: An outcome of development in which, as the mind matures and language and symbolic processing is acquired, some of the mind's contents (affects, memories) are not taken up into the more mature, secondary process functioning, and remain behind in the id, subject to the primary process. This was Freud's original idea of primal repression, which he later abandoned.

Pervasive Affect: An affect of such strength and intensity that the ego's usual methods of dealing with affect (including expression in bodily processes, action, and words, containment by symbolic processing, and suppression) are not sufficient, and powerful defensive processes called primal defenses are used to manage the affect. They often do not manage the affect directly—for instance primal repression does not usually repress pervasive anxiety, or at least that is not all it does. Rather the cause of the affect— for instance sexual wishes that lead to the pervasive castration anxiety—is attacked by the defense.

Primal Denial: A process whereby a powerful and very stable attentional defense is used to defend against an unpleasant reality that evokes a pervasive affect. The pervasive affects that motivate primal denials include pervasive anxiety, pervasive psychic pain, and pervasive sadness.

Primal Repression: A defense in which partially neutralized aggressive drive energy is used in forming a powerful counterforce that bars drive derivatives (wishes) and the affects and explicit (declarative and semantic) memories associated with them from conscious awareness. These are the objects of primal repression. The motive for this defense is usually pervasive anxiety.

Primary Dissociation: The breakdown in many ego functions that is part of the traumatic process leads to a situation in which perceptions are not integrated one with the other, a situation that I have designated as primary dissociation. This is not a defense, but is rather the outcome of the traumatic process.

Primary Process: A form of mental functioning, closely related to the drives, in which energies are easily displaceable, along lines of superficial similarity, and in which one element can come to stand for many (condensation). The primary process is geared towards immediate gratification and discharge of drive energies. There is a disregard for logical consistency. Contradictory ideas and impulses coexist side by side without conflict. There is no time sense nor are elements of the primary process affected by the passage of time.

Screen Defense: A form of defense related to narcissistic ego fixations on feelings related to overgratification, in which the regressed functioning related to this fixation—at the level of feeling and action especially—is called up to screen more unpleasant realities and feelings.

Secondary Defense: A secondary defense is any defense, other than an after defense, that helps to buttress a primal defense. These may be any sort of defense that the ego finds at hand and finds useful in secondarily defending against contents that escape the original primal defense. For instance it is common for various forms of denial to be used against some of the derivatives that escape primal repression.

Secondary Dissociation: This is a defensive process in which the ego actively uses the lack of integration and changes in level of consciousness of primary dissociation for its own ends. Often secondary dissociation is used by victims of ongoing trauma to separate themselves from the trauma that they see is about to come, by going somewhere else in their fantasy or somewhere else in a more concrete manner, for instance somewhere else in the room or house in which they are being abused.

Secondary Process: A basic form of mental functioning, the secondary process works with tightly bound, stable energies. It uses verbal symbols and logical, rational thought. It is ruled by the reality principle, compared to the primary process, which is ruled by the pleasure principle.

Splitting of the Ego: In relation to the concepts introduced in this book, splitting of the ego can be described as a compound zero process defense in which denial is combined with primary and secondary dissociation. It is used especially to defend against unpleasant aspects of reality, beginning first with certain realities of the trauma that led to the primary dissociation. Splitting of the ego is the zero process version of an attentional defense.

Splitting of Identity: In this compound zero process defense, aggression is combined with primary and secondary dissociation, to create two or more identities within a person. The identities are kept apart by mutual aggression—dislike, disparagement, loathing—of each identity for the other. Each identity holds strong drives and affects, and splitting of identity is used especially to defend against these drives and affects, which belong both to the original trauma and to other conflicts. Splitting of identity is the zero process version of a counterforce defense.

Theoretical Reduction: The replacement of a number of concepts in a complex, multilayered theory by a single set of ideas, when these ideas do not have the proper explanatory reach of the concepts they replace. Another way of putting it is to say that a portion of a complex theory is overgeneralized to become the sole explanation for various phenomena. In such a situation the overgeneralized part is usually a useful and powerful set of ideas, so that it is not in itself wrong. What is wrong, and often very detrimental to the further development of a theory, is that many other important findings and concepts are replaced, left out, and thrown out, by the overextension of a useful set of ideas.

Therapeutic Alliance: The mutual adjustment and attunement of the analyst and patient to each other, most of which takes place unconsciously, based on preverbal and non-verbal aspects of the relationship. This was the original definition of the term when Elizabeth Zetzel introduced it, but at present therapeutic alliance is often used to refer to both the working and the therapeutic alliances together, while the term working alliance is less used. I have kept the distinction between these two terms in this book, because it helps us to think of these different aspects of the mutual work in analysis.

Traumatic Anxiety: Freud gave this name to the overwhelming anxiety that motivates primal repression. It is a misleading term, however, and I have suggested that it should be dropped in favor of the term pervasive anxiety. In true trauma many ego functions, including processing of affects and the defensive processes, are temporarily put out of commission. This does not lead directly to repression.

Universal Primal Denials: These are primal denials that we all share because the realities that they defend against, such as the reality that we will cease to exist one day, are a part of the human condition and give rise in each of us to pervasive affects that necessitate these defenses. Universal primal denials are complex structures that usually include defensive guilt and contrast defenses, along with other defenses.

Working Alliance: A more rational alliance between patient and analyst, with contributions from both the positive transference and countertransference, the real relationship, and the patient's selective identification with aspects of the analyst's analyzing function.

Zero Process: This is a basic form of mental processing. It is a consequence of trauma, and is to be contrasted with both the primary process and the secondary process. In the zero process there is, as the name implies, no symbolic processing of any sort, as well as a lack of integration and coordination between elements. The contents of the zero process have characteristics of both memory and perception. They have the persistence over time of memory, but have the immediacy, intrusiveness, and tendency to run in one time direction of perceptions. As with the primary and the secondary processes, so with the zero process, there is a core area where the particular characteristics of the zero process are displayed in pure culture—in the case of the zero process this corresponds to the core of the traumatic memories—while surrounding this are areas that are influenced by the nature of the zero process functioning but which blend this with characteristics of the primary or secondary processes to a greater or lesser degree.

Zero Process Defense: A defense in which the ego uses certain characteristics of the zero process for defensive purposes. This can involve using actively a characteristic of the zero process, such as lack of integration or quasi-experiential qualities. Additionally, the ego can combine other defensive maneuvers it has at its disposal, such as attentional and counterforce defenses, with these zero process characteristics, and with secondary dissociation. Splitting of the ego and splitting of identity are examples of this later type of zero process defense.

Zero Process Neurosis: A neurosis in which zero process symptoms and dynamics centered on zero process functioning dominate the clinical picture. Perversions and phobic neuroses are examples. Further study will probably demonstrate that other neuroses fall into this category.

Zero Process Symptom: A symptom in which the dynamic picture is dominated by characteristics of the zero process. Perverse, phobic, and conversion symptoms are all zero process symptoms.

~

References

The abbreviation "S. E." refers to *Standard Edition of the Complete Psychological Works of Sigmund Freud*. Under the General Editorship of James Strachey. London: The Hogarth Press.

Abend, S. (1981). Psychic conflict and the concept of defense. *Psychoanalytic Quarterly* 50: 67–76.

———. (1986). Sibling loss. In Rothstein (1986), pp 95–104.

Abraham, K. (1919). A particular form of neurotic resistance against the psychoanalytic method. In Abraham (1988), pp 303–311.

———. (1988). *Selected Papers on Psychoanalysis*. London: Maresfield Library.

Alexander, F. (1950). Analysis of the therapeutic factors in psychoanalytic therapy. *Psychoanalytic Quarterly* 19: 482–500.

Altshul, S. (1968). Denial and ego arrest. *Journal of the American Psychoanalytic Association* 16: 301–318.

Arlow, J. A. (1971). Character Perversion. In *Currents in Psychoanalysis*, ed. I. M. Marcus. New York: International Universities Press, pp 317–336.

———. (1987). Trauma, play and perversion. *Psychoanalytic Study of the Child* 42: 31–44.

Basch, M. F. (1983). The perception of reality and the disavowal of meaning. *The Annual of Psychoanalysis* 11: 125–153.

Bass, A. (2000). *Difference and Disavowal: The Trauma of Eros*. Stanford: Stanford University Press.

Berliner, B. (1940). Libido and reality in masochism. *Psychoanalytic Quarterly* 9: 322–333.

———. (1947). On some psychodynamics of masochism. *Psychoanalytic Quarterly* 16: 459–471.

———. (1958). The role of object relations in moral masochism. *Psychoanalytic Quarterly* 27: 38–56.

Bion, W. R. (1962). *Learning From Experience*. New York: Basic Books.

Blos, P. (1962). *On Adolescence: A Psychoanalytic Interpretation*. New York: The Free Press.

———. (1979). *The Adolescent Passage*. New York: International Universities Press.

Blum, H. P. (Ed.) (1980). *Psychoanalytic Explorations of Technique: Discourse on the Theory of Therapy*. New York: International Universities Press.

———. (1983). Forward: defense and resistance. *Journal of the American Psychoanalytic Association* 31, Supplement: 5–18.

———. (1994). *Reconstruction in Psychoanalysis: Childhood Revisited and Recreated*. Madison, CT: International Universities Press.

———. (2003). Response to Peter Fonagy. *International Journal of Psychoanalysis* 84: 509–513.

———. (2005). Psychoanalytic reconstruction and reintegration. *Psychoanalytic Study of the Child* 60: 295–311.

Bohleber, W. (2007). Remembrance, trauma and collective memory: the battle for memory in psychoanalysis. *International Journal of Psychoanalysis* 88: 329–352.

Boston Change Process Study Group (2007). The foundational level of psychodynamic meaning: implicit process in relation to conflict, defense and the dynamic unconscious. *International Journal of Psychoanalysis* 88: 843–860.

Brenman, M. (1952). On teasing and being teased: the problem of moral masochism. *Psychoanalytic Study of the Child* 7: 264–285.

Brenner, C. (1966). The mechanism of repression. In Loewenstein et al. (1966), pp 390–399.

———. (1980a). Metapsychology and psychoanalytic theory. *Psychoanalytic Quarterly* 49: 189–214.

———. (1980b). Working alliance, therapeutic alliance, and transference. In Blum (1980), pp 137–157.

———. (1982). *The Mind in Conflict*. New York: International Universities Press.

———. (1986). Discussion of the various contributions. In Rothstein (1986), pp 195–203.

Brenner, I. (2001). *Dissociation of Trauma: Theory, Phenomenology, and Technique*. Madison, CT: International Universities Press.

———. (2004). *Psychic Trauma: Dynamics, Symptoms and Treatment*. Lanham, MD: Jason Aronson.

Breuer, E., and Freud, S. (1893). On the psychical mechanism of hysterical phenomena: preliminary communication. *S. E.* 2: 1–17.

———. (1893–1896). *Studies in Hysteria*. *S. E.* 2

Brody, W. (1965). On the dynamics of narcissism: 1. Externalization and early ego development. *Psychoanalytic Study of the Child* 20: 165–193.

Carroll, S. B. (2005). *Endless Forms Most Beautiful: The New Science of Evo Devo and the Making of the Animal Kingdom*. New York: Norton.

Chasseguet-Smirgel, J. (1974). Perversion, idealization and sublimation. *International Journal of Psychoanalysis* 55: 349–358.

———. (1981). Loss of reality in perversions—with special reference to fetishism. *Journal of the American Psychoanalytic Association* 29: 511–534.

Coen, S. J. (1988). Superego aspects of entitlement (in rigid characters). *Journal of the American Psychoanalytic Association* 36: 409–427.

Cooper, S. H. (1989). Recent contributions to the theory of defense mechanisms: a comparative view. *Journal of the American Psychoanalytic Association* 37: 867–891.

Darwin, C. (1872). *The Expression of the Emotions in Man and Animals*, ed. Francis Darwin. London: John Murray.

De M'Uzan, M. (2003). (Originally published in French in 1984). Slaves of quantity. *Psychoanalytic Quarterly* 72: 711–725.

De Wind, E. (1968). Contribution to symposium on psychic traumatization through social catastrophe: the confrontation with death. *International Journal of Psychoanalysis* 49: 302–305.

Diamond, M. J. (2004). The shaping of masculinity: revising boy's turning away from their mother's to construct male gender identity. *International Journal of Psychoanalysis* 85: 359–380.

Dowling, S. (1986). Discussion of the various contributors. In Rothstein (1986), pp 205–217.

Eissler, K. R. (1966). A note on trauma, dream, anxiety, and schizophrenia. *Psychoanalytic Study of the Child* 21: 17–50.

Etchegoyen, R. J. (1978). Some thoughts on transference perversion. *International Journal of Psychoanalysis* 59: 45–54.

Fairbairn, W. R. D. (1952). *Psychoanalytic Studies of the Personality*. London and Boston: Routledge and Kegan Paul Ltd.

Feinsilver, D. B. (1998). The therapist as a person facing death: the hardest of external realities and therapeutic action. *International Journal of Psychoanalysis* 79: 1131–1150.

Feldman, S. S. (1956). Crying at the happy ending. *Journal of the American Psychoanalytic Association* 4: 477–485.

Fenichel, O. (1941). *Problems of Psychoanalytic Technique*. New York: The Psychoanalytic Quarterly, Inc.

———. (1945). *The Psychoanalytic Theory of the Neuroses*. New York: W. W. Norton and Co.

Ferenczi, S. (1921). The further development of an active therapy in psycho-analysis. In Ferenczi (1980a), pp 198–217.

———. (1925). Contra-indications to the "active" psycho-analytic technique. In Ferenczi (1980a), pp 217–230.

———. (1929). The principle of relaxation and neocatharsis. In Ferenczi (1980b), pp 108–125.

———. (1933). Confusion of tongues between adults and the child. In Ferenczi (1980b), pp 156–167.

———. (1980a). *Further Contributions to the Theory and Technique of Psycho-analysis*, ed. M. Balint. New York: Bruner Mazel.

———. (1980b). *Final Contributions to the Problems and Methods of Psycho-analysis*, ed. M. Balint. New York: Bruner Mazel.

Fernando, J. (1997). The exceptions: structural and dynamic aspects. *Psychoanalytic Study of the Child* 52: 017–028.

———. (1998). The etiology of narcissistic personality disorder. *Psychoanalytic Study of the Child* 53: 141–158.

———. (2000a). Superego analysis in narcissistic patients with superego pathology. *Canadian Journal of Psychoanalysis* 8: 99–117.

———. (2000b). The borrowed sense of guilt. *International Journal of Psychoanalysis* 81: 499–512.

———. (2001). On the connection between physical defects and the character type of the "exception." *Psychoanalytic Quarterly* 70: 549–578.

Fine, B. D., Joseph, R. D., and Waldhorn, H. F. (1969). *The Mechanism of Denial. Monograph 3, Kris Study Group of the New York Psychoanalytic Institute.*

Fisher, C. (1954). Dreams and perceptions—the role of preconscious and primary modes of perception in dream formation. *Journal of the American Psychoanalytic Association* 2: 389–445.

———. (1956). Dreams, images, and perception—a study of unconscious-preconscious relationships. *Journal of the American Psychoanalytic Association* 4: 5–48.

Fonagy, P. (1999). Memory and Therapeutic Action. *International Journal of Psychoanalysis* 80: 215–223.

Frank, A. (1969). The unrememberable and the unforgettable: passive primal repression. *Psychoanalytic Study of the Child* 24: 48–77.

Frank, A., and Muslin, H. (1967). The development of Freud's concept of primal repression. *Psychoanalytic Study of the Child* 22: 55–76.

Freeman, T. (1978). *A Psychoanalytic Study of the Psychoses*. New York: International Universities Press.

———. (1988). *The Psychoanalyst in Psychiatry*. London: Karnac Books.

Freud, A. (1936). *The Ego and the Mechanisms of Defense*. New York: International Universities Press.

———. (1954). The widening scope of indications for psychoanalysis: discussion. *Journal of the American Psychoanalytic Association* 2: 607–620.

———. (1965). *Normality and Pathology in Childhood: Assessments of Development*. New York: International Universities Press.

Freud, S. (1894). The neuro-psychoses of defense. *S. E.* 3: 41–48.

———. (1895). Project for a scientific psychology. *S. E.* 1: 281–397.

———. (1896). Further remarks on the neuropsychoses of defense. *S. E.* 3: 57–185.

———. (1898). The psychical mechanism of forgetfulness. *S. E.* 3: 287–297.

———. (1899). Screen memories. *S. E.* 3: 299–322.

———. (1900). *The Interpretation of Dreams*. S. E. 4–5.

———. (1901). *The Psychopathology of Everyday Life*. S. E. 6.

———. (1905). Three essays on the theory of sexuality. S. E. 7: 123–245.

———. (1909a). Family Romances. S. E. 9: 235–241.

———. (1909b). Analysis of a phobia in a five-year-old boy. S. E. 10: 1–149.

———. (1909c). Notes upon a case of obsessional neurosis. S. E. 10: 151–320.

———. (1911a). Psychoanalytic notes on an autobiographical account of a case of paranoia (dementia paranoides). S. E. 12: 1–82.

———. (1911b). Formulations on the two principles of mental functioning. S. E. 12: 213–226.

———. (1913). *Totem and Taboo*. S. E. 13: 1–61.

———. (1914). On narcissism: an introduction. S. E. 14: 67–102.

———. (1915a). Instincts and their vicissitudes. S. E. 14: 109–140.

———. (1915b). Repression. S. E. 14: 141–158.

———. (1915c). The unconscious. S. E. 14: 159–215.

———. (1917). Mourning and melancholia. S. E. 14: 237–258.

———. (1916–1917). Introductory lectures on psychoanalysis. S. E. 15–16.

———. (1918). From the history of an infantile neurosis. S. E. 17: 1–123.

———. (1919). A child is being beaten: a contribution to the study of the origin of sexual perversions. S. E. 17: 175–204.

———. (1920). Beyond the pleasure principle. S. E. 18: 1–64.

———. (1921). *Group Psychology and the Analysis of the Ego*. S. E. 18: 65–143.

———. (1923). *The Ego and the Id*. S. E. 19: 1–66.

———. (1924). The economic problem of masochism. S. E. 19: 155–170.

———. (1926). Inhibitions, symptoms and anxiety. S. E. 20: 75–175.

———. (1927). Fetishism. S. E. 21: 147–157.

———. (1937). Constructions in analysis. S. E. 23: 255–269.

———. (1938a). An outline of psychoanalysis. S. E. 23: 139–207.

———. (1938b). Splitting of the ego in the process of defense. S. E. 23: 271–278

———. (1954). *The Origins of Psychoanalysis: Letters to Wilhelm Fliess*, ed. Marie Bonapart, Anna Freud, and Ernest Kris. New York: Basic Books.

Fulgenicio, L. (2005). Freud's metapsychological speculations. *International Journal of Psychoanalysis* 86: 99–123.

Furman, E. (1986). On trauma: when is the death of a parent traumatic? *Psychoanalytic Study of the Child* 41: 191–208.

Furst, S. S. (1978). The stimulus barrier and the pathogenicity of trauma. *International Journal of Psychoanalysis* 59: 345–352.

Gaensbauer, T. J. (1994). Therapeutic work with a traumatized toddler. *Psychoanalytic Study of the Child* 49: 412–433.

Galenson, E. (1988). The precursors of masochism: protomasochism. In Glick and Meyers (1988), pp 189–204.

Geelard, E. (1965). Two kinds of denial: neurotic denial and denial in the service of the need to survive. In Shur (1965), pp 118–127.

Gill, M. M. (1963). *Topography and Systems in Psychoanalytic Theory.* New York: International Universities Press.

——. (Ed.) (1967). *The Collected Papers of David Rapaport.* Northvale, New Jersey and London: Jason Aronson.

Gillespie, W. H. (1956). The general theory of sexual perversions. *International Journal of Psychoanalysis* 37: 396–403.

Glick, R. A., and Meyers, D. I. (1988). *Masochism: Psychoanalytic Perspectives.* Hillsdale, NJ: The Analytic Press.

Good, M. I. (1994). The reconstruction of early childhood trauma: fantasy, reality and verification. *Journal of the American Psychoanalytic Association* 42: 79–101.

Gould, S. J. (2002). *The Structure of Evolutionary Theory.* Cambridge and London: The Belknap Press of Harvard University Press.

Gray, P. (1994). *The Ego and the Analysis of Defense.* Northvale, NJ: Jason Aronson.

Greenacre, P. (1953). Certain relationships between fetishism and faulty development of the body image. *Psychoanalytic Study of the Child* 8: 79–98.

——. (1955). Further considerations regarding fetishism. *Psychoanalytic Study of the Child* 10: 187–194.

——. (1968). Perversions: general considerations regarding their genetic and dynamic background. *Psychoanalytic Study of the Child* 23: 47–62.

Greenson, R. R. (1958). On screen defenses, screen hunger and screen identity. *Journal of the American Psychoanalytic Association* 6: 242–262.

——. (1966). A transsexual boy and a hypothesis. In Greenson (1978), pp 289–304.

——. (1967). *The Technique and Practice of Psychoanalysis.* Madison, CT: International Universities Press.

——. (1968). Disidentifying with the mother: its special importance for the boy. In Greenson (1978), pp 305–312.

——. (1969). The nontransference relationship in the psychoanalytic situation. In Greenson (1978), pp 359–386.

——. (1978). *Explorations in Psychoanalysis.* New York: International Universities Press.

Grossman, L. (1992). An example of character perversion in a woman. *Psychoanalytic Quarterly* 61: 581–589.

——. (1996). Psychic reality and reality testing in the analysis of the perverse defense. *International Journal of Psychoanalysis* 77: 509–517.

Hanly, C. (1984). Ego ideal and ideal ego. *International Journal of Psychoanalysis* 65: 253–261.

——. (1992). On narcissistic defenses. *Psychoanalytic Study of the Child* 47: 139–158.

Hanly, C., and Fitzpatrick-Hanly, M. A. (2001). Critical realism: distinguishing the psychological subjectivity of the analyst from epistemological subjectivism. *Journal of the American Psychoanalytic Association* 49: 515–533.

Hartmann, H. (1939). *Ego Psychology and the Problem of Adaptation.* Translated by D. Rappaport (1958 edition). New York: International Universities Press.

———. (1948). Comments on the psychoanalytic theory of the instinctual drives. In Hartmann (1964), pp 69–89.

———. (1950a). Psychoanalysis and developmental psychology. In Hartmann (1964), pp 99–112.

———. (1950b). Comments on the psychoanalytic theory of the ego. In Hartmann (1964), pp 113–141.

———. (1953). Contributions to the metapsychology of schizophrenia. In Hartmann (1964), pp 182–206.

———. (1956). Notes on the reality principle. In Hartmann (1964), pp 241–267.

———. (1959). Psychoanalysis as a scientific theory. In Hartmann (1964), pp 318–350.

———. (1964). *Essays on Ego Psychology*. New York: International Universities Press.

Hartmann, H., Kris, E., and Loewenstein, R. M. (1947). Comments on the formation of psychic structure. *Psychoanalytic Study of the Child* 2: 11–38.

———. (1953). The function of theory in psychoanalysis. In Loewenstein (1953), pp 13–37.

Hausner, R. S. (2000). The therapeutic and working alliances. *Journal of the American Psychoanalytic Association* 48: 155–187.

Herman, J. (1992). *Trauma and Recovery. The Aftermath of Violence—From Domestic Abuse to Political Terror*. New York: Basic Books.

Herman, J., and Van der Kolk, B. A. (1987). Traumatic antecedents of borderline personality disorder. In Van der Kolk (1987), pp 11–126.

Hoffer, W. (1968). Notes on the theory of defense. *Psychoanalytic Study of the Child* 23: 178–188.

Holt, R. R. (1975). The past and future of ego psychology. *Psychoanalytic Quarterly* 44: 550–576.

Hopkins, J. (1984). The probable role of trauma in a case of foot and shoe fetishism: aspects of the psychotherapy of a 6-year-old girl. *International Review of Psychoanalysis* 11: 79–92.

Inderbitzin, L. B., and Levy, S. J. (1994). On grist for the mill: external reality as a defense. *Journal of the American Psychoanalytic Association* 42: 763–788.

Jacobson, E. (1954). The self and the object world. *Psychoanalytic Study of the Child* 9: 75–127.

———. (1957). Denial and repression. *Journal of the American Psychoanalytic Association* 5: 61– 92.

———. (1959). The "exceptions," an elaboration of Freud's character study. *Psychoanalytic Study of the Child* 14: 135–154.

———. (1964). *The Self and the Object World*. New York: International Universities Press.

———. (1971a). *Depression: Comparative Studies of Normal, Neurotic, and Psychotic Conditions*. New York: International Universities Press.

———. (1971b). On the psychoanalytic theory of affects. In Jacobson (1971a).

Juni, S. (1979). Theoretical foundations of projection as a defense mechanism. *International Review of Psychoanalysis* 6: 115–130.

Kächele, H., Albani, C., Buchheim, A., Hölzer, M., Hohage, R., Mergenthaler, E., Jiménez, J. P., Leuzinger-Bohleber, M., Neudert-Dreyer, L., Pokorny, D., and Thomä, H. (2006). The German specimen case, Amalia X: empirical studies. *International Journal of Psychoanalysis* 87: 809–826.

Kernberg, O. (1970). Factors in the psychoanalytic treatment of narcissistic personalities. *Journal of the American Psychoanalytic Association* 18: 51–85.

———. (2001). Object relations, affects, and drives: toward a new synthesis. *Psychoanalytic Inquiry* 21: 604–619.

———. (2006a). The pressing need to increase research in and on psychoanalysis. *International Journal of Psychoanalysis* 87: 919–926.

———. (2006b). Research anxiety: a response to Roger Perron's comments. *International Journal of Psychoanalysis* 87: 933–937.

Kestenberg, J., and Brenner, I. (1986). Children who survived the holocaust: the role of rules and routines in the development of the superego. *International Journal of Psychoanalysis* 67: 309–316.

Klein, G. S. (1969/1970). The emergence of ego psychology and the ego in psychoanalysis: a concept in search of an identity. *Psychoanalytic Review* 56D: 511–525.

Kohut, H. (1971). *The Analysis of the Self*. New York: International Universities Press.

———. (1977). *The Restoration of the Self*. New York: International Universities Press.

Kris, A. O. (1979). Persistence of denial in fantasy. *Psychoanalytic Study of the Child* 34: 145–154.

———. (1983). Determinants of free association in narcissistic phenomena. *Psychoanalytic Study of the Child* 38: 439–458.

———. (1990). Helping patients by analyzing self-criticism. *Journal of the American Psychoanalytic Association* 38: 605–636.

———. (1994). Freud's treatment of a narcissistic patient. *International Journal of Psychoanalysis* 75: 649–664.

Kris, E. (1956a). On some vicissitudes of insight in psychoanalysis. In Kris (1975), pp 252–271.

———. (1956b). The personal myth: a problem in psychoanalytic technique. In Kris (1975), pp 272–300.

———. (1956c). The recovery of childhood memories in psychoanalysis. In Kris (1975), pp 301–340.

———. (1975). *The Selected Papers of Ernst Kris*. New Haven and London: Yale University Press.

Krystal, H. (1978a). Trauma and affects. *Psychoanalytic Study of the Child* 33: 81–116.

———. (1978b). Self representation and the capacity for self care. *Annual of Psychoanalysis* 6: 209–243.

LeDoux, J. (1996). *The Emotional Brain*. New York: Simon and Schuster.

Leuzinger-Bohleber, M., and Fishman, T. (2006). What is conceptual research in psychoanalysis? *International Journal of Psychoanalysis* 87: 1355–1386.

Lewin, B. D. (1950). *The Psychoanalysis of Elation*. New York: The Psychoanalytic Quarterly Inc.

Linn, L. (1953). The role of perception in the mechanism of denial. *Journal of the American Psychoanalytic Association* 1: 690–705.

Lipton, S. D. (1977). The advantages of Freud's technique as shown in his analysis of the Rat Man. *International Journal of Psychoanalysis* 58: 255–273.

Loewald, H. W. (1957). On the therapeutic action of psychoanalysis. In Loewald (1980), pp 221–256.

———. (1980). *Papers in Psychoanalysis*. New Haven and London: Yale University Press.

Loewenstein, R. M. (1953). *Drives, Affects, Behavior*. New York: International Universities Press.

———. (1957). A contribution to the psychoanalytic theory of masochism. *Journal of the American Psychoanalytic Association* 5: 197–234.

Loewenstein, R. M., Newman, L. M., Schur, M., and Solnit, A. J. (Eds.) (1966). *Psychoanalysis—a General Psychology. Essays in Honor of Heinz Hartmann*. New York: International Universities Press.

Lustman, S. L. (1969). Introduction to panel on the use of the economic viewpoint in psychoanalysis: the economic point of view and defense. *International Journal of Psychoanalysis* 50: 95–102.

Massie, H., and Szajnberg, N. (1992). The ontogeny of a sexual fetish from birth to age 30 and memory process: a research case report from a prospective longitudinal study. *International Journal of Psychoanalysis* 73: 755–771.

Matthis, I., and Deutsch, J. (2005). International Society of Neuro-Psychoanalysis, Toronto Group. *Neuro-Psychoanalysis* 7: 228–229.

Mayr, E. (1982). *The Growth of Biological Thought*. Cambridge, MA: The Belknap Press of Harvard University Press.

———. (1997). *This Is Biology*. Cambridge, MA: The Belknap Press of Harvard University Press.

———. (2004). *What Makes Biology Unique: Considerations on the Autonomy of a Scientific Discipline*. Cambridge: Cambridge University Press.

Meltzer, D. (1966). The relationship of anal masturbation to projective identification. *International Journal of Psychoanalysis* 47: 335–342.

Menaker, E. (1953). Masochism—a defense reaction of the ego. *Psychoanalytic Quarterly* 22: 205–220.

Novick, J., and Novick, K. K. (1970). Projection and externalization. *Psychoanalytic Study of the Child* 25: 69–95.

Novick, K. K., and Novick, J. (1987). The essence of masochism. *Psychoanalytic Study of the Child* 42: 353–384.

Oliner, M. M. (2000). The unsolved puzzle of trauma. *Psychoanalytic Quarterly* 69: 41–61.

Perron, R. (2006). How to do research? reply to Otto Kernberg. *International Journal of Psychoanalysis* 87: 927–932.

Person, E. S., and Klar, H. (1994). Establishing trauma: the difficulty distinguishing between memories and fantasies. *Journal of the American Psychoanalytic Association* 42: 1055–1081.

Phillips, S. H. (1991). Trauma and war: a fragment of an analysis with a Vietnam veteran. *Psychoanalytic Study of the Child* 46: 147–180.

Pulver, S. (1970). Narcissism: the term and the concept. *Journal of the American Psychoanalytic Association* 18: 319–341.

Racker, H. (1957). The meanings and uses of countertransference. *Psychoanalytic Quarterly* 26: 303–357.

Rangell, L. (2004). *My Life in Theory*. New York: Other Press.

Rapaport, D., and Gill, M. M. (1959). The points of view and assumptions of metapsychology. In Gill (1967), pp 795–811.

Reed, G. S. (1993). On the value of explicit reconstruction. *Psychoanalytic Quarterly* 62: 52–73.

———. (1994). *Transference Neurosis and Psychoanalytic Experience: Perspectives on Contemporary Clinical Practice*. New Haven and London: Yale University Press.

———. (1997). The analyst's interpretation as a fetish. *Journal of the American Psychoanalytic Association* 45: 1153–1181.

Reich, A. (1954). Early identifications as archaic elements in the superego. *Journal of American Psychoanalytic Association* 2: 218–238.

Renik, O. (1992). Use of the analyst as a fetish. *Psychoanalytic Quarterly* 61: 542–563.

Roiphe, H., and Galenson, E. (1973). The infantile fetish. *Psychoanalytic Study of the Child* 28: 147–168.

Rothstein, A. (Ed.) (1986). *The Reconstruction of Trauma: Its Significance in Clinical Work*. Madison, CT: International Universities Press.

Sachs, H. (1986 [1923]). On the genesis of perversions. *Psychoanalytic Quarterly* 55: 477–488.

Sandler, J. (1976). Countertransference and role-responsiveness. *International Review of Psychoanalysis* 3: 43–47.

———. (Ed.) (1987). *Projection, Identification, Projective Identification*. Madison, CT: International Universities Press.

Sandler, J., and Freud, A. (1985). *The Analysis of Defense: The Ego and the Mechanisms of Defense Revisited*. New York: International Universities Press.

Sandler, J., and Sandler, A. M. (1998). *Internal Objects Revisited*. Madison, CT: International Universities Press.

Shengold, L. (1991). A variety of narcissistic pathology stemming from parental weakness. *Psychoanalytic Quarterly* 60: 86–92.

Shevrin, H. (1997). Psychoanalysis as the patient: high on feeling, low on energy. *Journal of the American Psychoanalytic Association* 45: 841–864.

———. (2002). A psychoanalytic view of memory in the light of recent cognitive and neuroscience research. *Neuro-Psychoanalysis* 4: 131–139.

———. (2003). The consequences of abandoning a comprehensive psychoanalytic theory: revisiting Rapaport's systematizing attempt. *Journal of the American Psychoanalytic Association* 51: 1005–1020.

Shur, M. (Ed.) (1965). *Drives, Affects, Behavior Volume 2*. New York: International Universities Press.

———. (1966). *The Id and the Regulatory Principles of Mental Functioning*. New York: International Universities Press.

Simon, B. (1992). "Incest—see under oedipus complex": the history of an error in psychoanalysis. *Journal of the American Psychoanalytic Association* 40: 955–988.

Simpson, R. B. (2003). Introduction to Michel De M'Uzan's "Slaves of Quantity." *Psychoanalytic Quarterly* 72: 699–709.

Slavin, M. O., and Kriegman, D. (1992). *The Adaptive Design of the Human Psyche*. New York and London: The Guilford Press.

Sperling, M. (1950). Children's interpretation and reaction to the unconscious of their mothers. *International Journal of Psychoanalysis* 31: 36–41.

Spiegel, L. A. (1954). Acting out and defensive instinctual gratification. *Journal of the American Psychoanalytic Association* 2: 107–119.

Stein, M. H. (1981). The unobjectionable part of the transference. *Journal of the American Psychoanalytic Association* 29: 869–892.

Stern, D., Sander, L. W., Nahum, J. P., Harrison, A. M., Lyons-Ruth, K., Morgan, A. C., Bruschweilerstern, N., and Tronick, E. Z. (1998). Non-interpretive mechanisms in psychoanalytic therapy: the "something more" than interpretation. *International Journal of Psychoanalysis* 79: 903–921.

Stewart, W. A. (1970). The split in the ego and the mechanism of disavowal. *Psychoanalytic Quarterly* 39: 1–16.

Stoller, R. J. (1975). *Perversion: The Erotic Form of Hatred*. London: Karnac Books (1986 reprint).

Sugarman, A. (2006). Mentalization, insightfulness, and therapeutic action: the importance of mental organization. *International Journal of Psychoanalysis* 87: 965–987.

Terr, L. C. (1984). Time and trauma. *Psychoanalytic Study of the Child* 39: 633–665.

Tyson, P., and Tyson, R. L. (1990). *Psychoanalytic Theories of Development: An Integration*. Yale and London: Yale University Press.

Valenstein, A. (1973). On attachment to painful feelings and the negative therapeutic reaction. *Psychoanalytic Study of the Child* 28: 365–392.

Van der Hart, O., Nijenhuis, E., and Steele, K. (2006). *The Haunted Self: Structural Dissociation and the Treatment of Chronic Traumatization*. New York and London: W. W. Norton & Co.

Van der Kolk, B. A. (Ed.) (1987). *Psychological Trauma*. Washington, DC: American Psychiatric Press.

———. (1996). Trauma and memory. In Van der Kolk et al. (1996), pp 279–302.

Van der Kolk, B. A., McFarlane, A. C., and Weissreth, L. (1996). *Traumatic Stress: The Effects of Overwhelming Experience on Mind, Body and Society.* New York: The Guilford Press.

Van der Kolk, B. A., Van der Hart, O., and Marmar, C. R. (1996). Dissociation and information processing in post-traumatic stress disorder. In Van der Kolk et al. (1996), pp 303–327.

Wallerstein, R. (reporter) (1967). Panel: development and metapsychology of the defense organization of the ego. *Journal of the American Psychoanalytic Association* 15: 130–149.

———. (1988). One psychoanalysis or many? *International Journal of Psychoanalysis* 69: 5–21.

———. (1990). Psychoanalysis: the common ground. *International Journal of Psychoanalysis* 71: 3–20.

Weiss, J., and Sampson, H. (1986). *The Psychoanalytic Process: Theory, Clinical Observations and Empirical Research.* New York and London: The Guilford Press.

Wurmser, L. (2000). *The Power of the Inner Judge. Psychodynamic Treatment of the Severe Neuroses.* Northvale, NJ: Jason Aronson Inc.

Yorke, C. (1986). Reflections on the problem of psychic trauma. *Psychoanalytic Study of the Child* 41: 221–238.

Yorke, C., and Wiseberg, S. (1976). A developmental view of anxiety: some clinical and theoretical considerations. *Psychoanalytic Study of the Child* 31: 107–135.

Yorke, C., Wiseberg, S., and Freeman (1989). *Development and Psychopathology.* New Haven and London: Yale University Press.

Young-Bruehl, E. (1988). *Anna Freud: A Biography.* New York: Summit Books.

Zachrisson, A., and Zachrisson, H. D. (2005). Validation of psychoanalytic theories: toward a conceptualization of references. *International Journal of Psychoanalysis* 86: 1353–1371.

Zetzel, E. (1965). The theory of therapy in relation to a developmental model of the psychic apparatus. *International Journal of Psychoanalysis* 46: 39–52.

Index

repetition, 154–58, 229–30; analysis of, 162–67

repression, 1–2, 27–69; clinical examples of, 29–32, 34–38; and denial, 28–29, 73, 76–78, 93–98; development of, 32; and dissociation, 266; mechanism of, interpreting, 60–65; nature of, 28–29; selective, 51–52

resistance, 291

Roiphe, H., 259

Sachs, Hans, 244, 258

Sampson, H., 232–36

Sandler, Joseph, 111–12, 118

science: development of, 50; and experience distant concepts, 291; psychoanalysis as, 296–301

screen defenses, 195–98; definition of, 208

screen memories, 52–54

secondary defenses, 40–42, 198; analysis of, 162–67; definition of, 68–69

secondary dissociation, 143, 145, 151, 155–56; definition of, 170

secondary process, 32–33, 121, 146; definition of, 69

selective repression, 51–52

semantic memory, 157

sexual drive, 46–50, 309–10

Shantz, William, 148

Shevrin, Howard, 157, 300–302, 313

Shur, Max, 149, 312

signal anxiety, 39, 129

silence, and neutrality, 21

Slavin, M. O., 312

Sperling, M., 220

splitting of ego, 2, 274; definition of, 281; and denial, 94–95; and perversions, 245, 258, 262–68

splitting of identity, 273–74, 304–5; analysis of, 278–79; definition of, 281. See also dissociation

Steele, K., 158

Stein, M. H., 20

Stern, Daniel, 55, 236

stimulus barrier, 127–29

Stoller, R. J., 258–60

sublimation, 49

Sugarman, A., 57

superego, 50–51

suppression, 15

technical and therapeutic implications: and defenses, 15–23; and denial, 95–104; and externalization and internalization, 119–22; limits of, 17–23; and masochism, 212–13, 228–40; and narcissism, 199–206; and perversions, 276–79; and repression, 56–65; and trauma, 152–67. See also broad view; narrow view

Terr, L. C., 166

theoretical concepts, overextension of: critique of, 307–9; and hostile response, 64; and recovered memory, 58

theoretical reductionism, 301–2; definition of, 319

theory, 14, 285–320; importance of, 301–9

therapeutic alliance, 19; definition of, 25; versus identification, 118

thinking, 292–93; and language, 315

total composite theory, 302

transference: broad view of technique and, 59–60; of defense, 203–5, 237–40; and denial, 102–4; displacement, 120; and externalization and internalization, 119–22; and narcissism, 200, 203–6; and narrow view of technique, 18; and perversions, 276–79; and trauma, 153–54; zero process, 154

~

About the Author

Dr. Joseph Fernando is past president of the Toronto Psychoanalytic Society and a training and supervising analyst at the Canadian Institute of Psychoanalysis. He received his medical training at McGill University. He trained in psychoanalysis at the Toronto Institute of Psychoanalysis, where he has taught for over ten years. Dr. Fernando has had a full time practice in psychoanalysis and psychoanalytic psychotherapy for over twenty years. He is on the editorial board of the Canadian Journal of Psychoanalysis and has published papers in leading psychoanalytic journals on guilt, symbolism, narcissism, and the sense of entitlement.

Breinigsville, PA USA
09 March 2010

233845BV00002B/2/P